Praise for *IT Security Metrics*

"I think that one reason security metrics is so hard is because there is no single recipe for success. It is not just about the math. It is about understanding what knowledge you seek and how quantitative analysis can help. To create a successful and sustainable metrics program, you must start with a well-reasoned framework. Lance's book begins by presenting one. He then enriches the theory with practical case studies that illustrate how you can incorporate the framework into your own context. This treatment has something new to say to security measurement veterans and beginners alike."

—Elizabeth A. Nichols, Ph.D., PlexLogic, LLC

"The author provides a timely and practical overview of information security management that speaks directly to people charged with performing the tasks. It takes you from overview to application in clear, readable chapters that emphasize real-world application over technical details. This book will give you the insights and confidence to apply the metrics that matter for your organization."

—Andrew Dillon, Dean and Yule Regents
Professor of Information Science,
School of Information, University of Texas

"Security practitioners everywhere are making a concerted effort to measure what we do so that we can be more productive, more efficient, and can demonstrate the security we deliver. This book is rich in real-world experiences and offers the kinds of practical approaches we all need to apply to security metrics."

—Dr. Mike Lloyd, Chief Scientist,
RedSeal Systems, Inc.

"Today's security practice is about efficacy and that requires a sound measurement process and metrics reporting. This is no longer about cobbling together best practices, following groupthink, or continuing a practice simply because we have always done it that way. Effective security practice is about setting a strategy, implementing it, and proving it works. *IT Security Metrics* by Lance Hayden codifies the differences between measurement and metrics, reminds us all that you get what you measure so be mindful before starting, and seeks not only to demystify but to augment our industry's current practice, which too often is to add more to—instead of getting more from—what you already have."

—John N. Stewart, Cisco Vice President
and Chief Security Officer

IT Security Metrics

A Practical Framework
for Measuring Security
& Protecting Data

LANCE **HAYDEN**

New York   Chicago   San Francisco
Lisbon   London   Madrid   Mexico City   Milan
New Delhi   San Juan   Seoul   Singapore   Sydney   Toronto

The *McGraw·Hill* Companies

Cataloging-in-Publication Data is on file with the Library of Congress

IT Security Metrics: A Practical Framework for Measuring Security & Protecting Data

1234567890 DOC/DOC 109876543210

ISBN   978-0-07-171340-5
MHID   0-07-171340-9

Sponsoring Editors
Jane Brownlow
Megg Morin

Editorial Supervisor
Jody McKenzie

Project Manager
Vastavikta Sharma,
Glyph International

Acquisitions Coordinator
Joya Anthony

Technical Editor
Caroline Wong

Copy Editor
Lisa Theobald

Proofreader
Claire Splan

Indexer
Claire Splan

Production Supervisor
George Anderson

Composition
Glyph International

Illustration
Glyph International

Art Director, Cover
Jeff Weeks

Cover Designer
Ty Nowicki

To Jayne, my partner and friend in all the risks
and rewards. And to Wyatt, you are
literally too cool for school.

About the Author

Lance Hayden is a Solutions Architect and Information Scientist with Cisco System's World Wide Security Practice. Lance's insights into security measurement and operations grow out of a unique 20-year professional experience that spans the public, private, and academic sectors. He began his career as a HUMINT officer with the Central Intelligence Agency (CIA) before successfully transitioning from government to the private sector as an information security expert. For more than a decade, Lance has helped Cisco's customers make more informed decisions about their security operations, reducing risk and uncertainty through consulting and empirical assessment of threats and controls. He has spoken at a variety of security industry events and has written articles for security trade magazines. He holds CISSP and CISM professional certifications.

Lance is also a trained social scientist, holding a Ph.D. in Information Science from the University of Texas, where he teaches courses on Information Security and Surveillance in Society. Lance's research has explored surveillance and security technologies in social and organizational contexts, and he combines quantitative and qualitative data and analysis to understand these challenging research issues holistically. As an academic, Lance has published articles in conference proceedings and peer-reviewed journals. When he is not working, writing, or teaching, Lance enjoys hanging out at home and riding bikes with his son Wyatt.

About the Case Study Authors

Doug Dexter has been with the Cisco Systems Corporate Information Security Department since 1989. During his tenure, he has done everything from maintain the internal firewalls to lead architecture development for a variety of enterprise-wide solutions. As the Team Lead for Cisco's internal PKI deployment, he built a team of people and solutions to provide certificates and sign the production code for IP phones, call managers, and cable modems. Since 2005, Doug has been Cisco's internal Audit Team Lead, responsible for a global team of auditors who handle Cisco's acquisitions, vulnerability assessments, and site assessments. Prior to working at Cisco, Doug was active duty in the U.S. Army for 11 years and is currently a Major in an Army Reserve Information Assurance unit. He holds an MBA from the University of Texas at Austin with a concentration in Information Systems, Controls, and Assurance, and he is a CISM, CISA, and CISSP-ISSMP.

Mike Burg is a Senior Solutions Architect in the Cisco World Wide Security Practice. He has nearly 20 years of experience in the network security field across many different verticals (health care, education, distribution, aeronautical, environmental). Since 2004, Mike has worked for Cisco Systems helping customers assess, measure, and improve their security architectures and operations. Mike has given many presentations on security-related topics at industry events, partner summits, and Cisco Networkers. Mike is currently the Cisco Technical Lead for Identity Services and for Cisco's IT Governance Risk, and Compliance (IT GRC) Practice. He is also a senior advisor with Cisco's Security Posture Assessment Team. Mike graduated from California State University San Bernardino. He is a Cisco Certified Internetwork Expert (CCIE No. 19965).

Caroline Wong manages Strategic Security at Zynga Game Network. She was formerly the Chief of Staff for the Global Information Security Team at eBay, where she built the security metrics program from the ground up. She is well known for her expertise in the area of security metrics and has been a featured speaker at numerous industry conferences, including RSA, Metricon, the Executive Women's Forum, Archer Summits, and the Information Security Forum. Caroline has contributed as a technical reviewer to the Center for Information Security Consensus Metrics Definitions and is actively working with the Cloud Security Alliance to define metrics for the cloud computing space. She has a B.S. in Electrical Engineering and Computer Sciences from U.C. Berkeley, a Certificate in Finance and Accounting from Stanford's Executive Education Program, and is CISSP certified.

Craig Blaha is an IT professional with 15 years of experience in education and information technology, including more than a decade in leadership roles for security-related operations and projects. Craig has managed and coordinated special IT and security projects for most of his professional life, focusing on stakeholder involvement and outreach in support of large-scale IT operations. Currently completing his Ph.D. in Information Science at the University of Texas, his professional expertise has also informed his academic career in that he researches and teaches on security, privacy, and information policy. Craig regularly presents his research and experiences in technology program strategy at academic and industry conferences. He holds a variety of certifications, including credentials for ITIL, Project Management, IT and IT Security Leadership, and Incident Response.

At a Glance

PART III   Exploring Security Measurement Projects

PART IV   Beyond Security Metrics

Contents

Part I

Introducing Security Metrics

Part II

Implementing Security Metrics

PART III

Exploring Security Measurement Projects

PART IV

Beyond Security Metrics

Foreword

B y now it's become cliché to say "You can't secure what you can't measure," or similar variations on Lord Kelvin's original pronouncement about the relationship between measurement and outcomes. Unfortunately, very few organizations follow this mantra effectively. In my view, this is one of the biggest indictments of the security profession as a whole; despite an ever-expanding litany of control frameworks, best practices, and guidance, no one seems yet to have asked (to paraphrase risk metrics guru Douglas Hubbard), "How do we know if any of this stuff is really working?!"

Well, after nearly 15 years of security consulting for Fortune 1000 organizations, I'm here to tell you the dirty little non-secret of IT security: no one really *does* know if any of this stuff is working. Firewalls, vulnerability scanners, intrusion detection/prevention systems, data leak prevention, application security, patch management, encryption, PCI DSS compliance ... the list of "stuff" that IT security invests in grows more and more, but talking about measuring return on this investment is still avoided like the plague. Now that serious money is starting to be spent on security (I know of organizations with upwards of $50M in annual IT security spend, for example), the time is ripe to start confronting the elephant in the room and have a mature conversation about practical, relevant, effective security metrics.

Enter the book you're holding in your hands. Lance Hayden has compiled a thoughtful and fact-based tour of the who, what, when, where, how, and why of security metrics. He disperses myths while illuminating truths, pointing towards better ways for IT to conceptualize, implement, and articulate the value proposition of security activities and investments.

I particularly like Lance's down-to-earth approach in this book: he's clearly been around the block enough times to understand and appreciate the profession's historical attempts at metrics (e.g., annual loss expectancy, ALE), but he's also savvy enough to know that what we've done so far hasn't provided useful decision support to key constituencies, nor has it articulated the value of security activities very well in an age where accountability and scrutiny have only increased for all organizational functions.

This is one of the great differentiators of this book versus others I've read on the topic: there's a strong undercurrent of contrarian thinking that refreshes and enlightens, while at the same time not losing the baby with the bathwater. Too often the desire to innovate and challenge the status quo goes too far in technical fields, and we lose track of some of the fundamentals that keep us working within reasonable arcs. The fundamentals are not overlooked in this book, which is clearly grounded in foundational concepts of risk management, decision support, and basic economics. At the same time, there is a recognition that many of the practices followed by security professionals today are "… a bit lame" (to borrow a phrase from Chapter 1) and that "alchemy" is often employed by "slackers" who want to take shortcuts around data and "hedgers" who would color the results as audiences want to hear them. Somewhere between the stone age and the bleeding edge, we've all become lost and confused; this book is a concise guide back to the middle, that is, a more empirical way to think about information security and measure its progress.

And although "middle-of-the-road" and "security metrics" may sound like a recipe for boredom, this book is quite the opposite. It abounds with practical examples, anecdotes, metaphors, crisp descriptions of difficult concepts, comparisons with other industries, and a just plain entertaining writing style that won't strain your attention span. No punches are pulled either—you won't find baby-talking around tools like the Poisson distribution and Monte Carlo simulation that can be applied to real problems in infosec today, and real math is performed in the examples to illustrate how things work in practice.

The relevance, information density, and readability of this book is top-notch, and I don't say that lightly, having been a technical author for over a dozen years myself. I cribbed numerous good ideas to try in my own work while reading through the chapters herein, which is my own personal metric for value and usefulness. *IT Security Metrics* hits its numbers through and through, and I strongly recommend it to anyone who is passionate and serious about protecting digital assets with better precision and effectiveness.

Joel Scambray

Co-Author, *Hacking Exposed*,

and CEO of Consciere

April 25, 2010

Acknowledgments

I have a lot of people to thank for this book, because without them it would have never been possible. My wife and son have my love and gratitude for their unwavering support through the research and writing process. Their understanding every time I had to disappear into the study for hours on end still amazes me, and I feel very lucky that they had my back.

I wish to sincerely thank all my colleagues who contributed to the book in one way or another. Doug Dexter, Mike Burg, Caroline Wong, and Craig Blaha wrote great case studies, and the book benefits enormously from this diversity of practitioner input. I'm also grateful to Joel Scambray for contributing his thoughts and insights in writing a very generous foreword. Caroline Wong did double duty as my technical reviewer, and I want to thank her for the many insights and constructive critiques she provided as I was writing. Several topics in the book grew out of experiences that Mike Burg and I shared working on various projects, and I owe him big time for his feedback. Thanks also to Pablo Salazar, who runs the SPA team at Cisco, for ideas that emerged from our many conversations on topics as varied as measurement in other industries, translating academia to the real world, human security behaviors, the Panopticon, and numismatics. And finally I want to sincerely thank David Phillips, my boss at Cisco, who steadfastly supported and encouraged me to make this book a reality.

Many of the concepts and techniques in this book grew from my doctoral program experiences at UT Austin, and I owe a debt of gratitude to my dissertation committee, particularly to my co-chairs Dr. Phil Doty and Dr. Mary Lynn-Rice Lively. These scholars taught me to be a social scientist and researcher, and they impressed upon me that exclusively focusing on quantitative or qualitative methods simply commits one to ever understanding only half of a question. The iSchool at the University of Texas has been my academic home for many years, and I want to express my appreciation to the mentors, colleagues, and students who have enriched my thoughts and my life time and time again.

I want to thank the team at McGraw-Hill who brought this book to fruition. My acquisitions editors, Jane Brownlow and Megg Morin, were wonderful, believing in the book and providing constant advice and support. Acquisitions coordinator Joya Anthony ran an incredibly tight ship, keeping me and everyone else on target and on time. And thanks to the excellent copyediting from Lisa Theobald and team who provided sharp eyes and great suggestions for improving the writing in the chapters, as well as to Vastavikta Sharma and everyone at Glyph for bringing the book to print.

Finally, I want to express my gratitude to the many security authors and practitioners who have inspired me and to the readers of the book who are the ultimate arbiters of its success. I hope you find it interesting and useful and that it serves its role as one more voice in the ongoing conversation about measuring and improving our security.

Introduction

I f you want a good measurement problem, watch the movie *Die Hard with a Vengeance*. In the movie, the characters played by Bruce Willis and Samuel L. Jackson are trying to stop the bad guys and find themselves in a crowded park with a five-gallon plastic jug, a three-gallon plastic jug, a water fountain, and a big bomb attached to a scale. To defuse the bomb, they must place four gallons of water (with no more than a few ounces error) on the scale within a certain amount of time; otherwise, everyone dies. They solve the problem, of course, but only after realizing that the jugs and scale are not enough and that they need a precise, logical process to arrive at the necessary measurement. The scene is great. It has a measurement challenge, an acceptable margin of error, and unacceptable consequences should the measurement fail. And in the end, the problem is much less about metrics (volume and weight in this case) and much more about the process of measuring in support of a decision (whether or not to put the jug on the scale and risk going boom).

Measuring IT Security

This book is also about the process of measurement as much as it is about metrics themselves. IT security practitioners, from the CISO down, are increasingly being directed to measure security in their organizations and improve the effectiveness of their data protection activities. From regulatory and industry compliance for Sarbanes-Oxley or PCI DSS to discussions of "Advanced Persistent Threats" posed by nation states and transnational criminal or terrorist organizations, IT security has experienced a dramatic bump in visibility. No less an authority than the President of the United States has weighed in, with a 2009 review of America's cyberspace policy that concluded that the digital infrastructure of the United States was neither secure nor resilient to ongoing attacks. At the top of the report's list of recommendations for improving the security of our infrastructure was the requirement to implement better security measurement and metrics.

This brings us to an important and fundamental question: What is this thing we call security that we are so keen to measure? Our industry often uses words like *security*, *risk*, and *vulnerability* haphazardly, without first even bothering to define our understanding of what the terms mean. We often hear the mantra, *you cannot manage what you do not measure*, and I agree with this. But if you lack definition or consensus regarding the phenomena that you hope to manage (system performance versus human behavior, for example), then jumping straight into metrics is a recipe for frustration and failure. Your understanding of what you are measuring must be specific and agreed upon if your data is to be specific and accepted by everyone. Thus, a corollary to the mantra can be stated like so: *You cannot measure what you do not understand.*

A Rocky Understanding

Some of the most difficult IT security metrics work comes from trying to figure out what you are trying to figure out. After all, security isn't a tangible thing. But forget security for a moment, and let's look at measuring something "easier" like, for instance, a rock. Rock metrics seem pretty straightforward. Rocks have height, width, and depth that you can easily measure with a ruler. Rocks have weight that you can measure by putting a rock on a scale. It would be great if measuring security were this easy, and the way some security pros measure it, you'd think that it was. But even rocks have characteristics that complicate measurement. Rocks have mass, which is different from weight. How do you measure that? Rocks have chemical composition and mineralogy. Rocks have special metrics such as clast size, which is a measure of the size of the rock's individual grains. And there are even more challenging metrics for rocks. Many rocks have social value and financial value that can be measured, although these metrics are far from intrinsic to the properties of the rock.

So it turns out that even measuring something that appears simple and tangible is not a straightforward proposition. If you do not understand what aspects of a rock you are interested in, you'll have a much more difficult time assessing which metrics will increase your knowledge or improve your decisions regarding the rock. Would this rock be better to throw at my enemies or to polish and put into a ring? You might find yourself regretting that you hurled 24-karat diamonds at your adversaries in defense of your stash of iron pyrite. If we can't even measure a rock without agreeing on our process and criteria of inquiry—how much more difficult will it be to measure IT security?

Security experts often fall into a trap of trying to measure security without first understanding what we really want to know. We may think we know, but too often our line of inquiry is simplistic and relates only to our immediate experiences and perceived priorities. How many of us have taken part in discussions about the security of our organization only to discover later (usually when it comes time to implement something) that everyone involved in the discussion had very different ideas about what security meant? This is especially common when business-side security managers are talking to security technologists. Business definitions of security differ from technical definitions, because the things a financial analyst is familiar with and cares about are often very different from what a firewall administrator is familiar with and cares about.

Improving Security with *IT Security Metrics*

As the security industry (and profession) matures, and as security is recognized as a core business process, the need for effective measurement of that process is growing. The IT security metrics movement is growing as well, in response to this need. This book is intended to contribute to the ongoing conversation about security measurement and to help you understand how to put metrics to effective use within your own organization. To this end, I have proposed a framework that helps situate security and security metrics within the context of business process improvement, and I hope to provide you with some ways of looking at measuring IT security that are new, and perhaps different from, what you might see in other metrics books.

How This Book Is Organized

I've divided this book into four parts, which reflect the general content and purpose of the individual chapters. I did not write the parts or chapters as independent modules, but rather as an interconnected narrative that starts at something like a beginning and closes with something like an end. (Of course, you do not have to read it linearly, but that is the way that I laid out the book.) I also constructed the book around the Security Process Management (SPM) Framework, a general methodology for creating a cohesive IT security metrics program that considers both tactical and strategic elements of a measurement program. So all things being equal, I suggest you read the book start to finish and feel free to skip those chapters covering concepts with which you are already proficient.

I have also invited several industry practitioners with experience in one or more aspects of metrics to contribute case studies to the book. Each part closes with one of these contributed case studies, more or less tied to the content of that particular set of chapters. The case studies serve to show how what I discuss may play out in different contexts and environments, and I hope you will find them useful alternative perspectives on measuring security.

Parts

The book has four parts.

Part One: Introducing Security Metrics

Part One discusses the state of IT security metrics today, critiques several existing security metrics and preconceptions regarding how security should be measured, and offers alternative ways of thinking about security metrics. The part also introduces concepts of data that are important in understanding how to measure security.

Part Two: Implementing Security Metrics

Part Two introduces the Security Process Management (SPM) Framework and discusses analytical strategies for security metrics data. This part also explores the concept of the security measurement project (SMP), a bounded metrics exercise that is a key component of the framework.

Part Three: Exploring Security Measurement Projects

Part Three discusses specific, practical examples of SMPs from goals, to data, to analysis. These project examples give readers a concrete introduction to the concepts referred to in earlier chapters, and shows how they can be implemented.

Part Four: Beyond Security Metrics

Part Four explores how to take a security metrics program and adapt it strategically to a variety of organizational contexts and environments, the goal being the continuous improvement of security over time.

Chapters

Each chapter in the book covers specific material germane to the understanding and development of IT security metrics and to the SPM Framework. I have made every effort to make the content of these chapters practical: Instead of just describing concepts, I strive to provide concrete, operational examples of what I am talking about. My goal is for readers to be able to form ideas about how they might operationalize those concepts within their own practices and organizations. To this end, chapters include methods, use cases, and tool descriptions that relate to security metrics and can describe templates and organizational considerations as well. Each chapter also includes a summary and recommendations for further, more in-depth, reading on the chapter concepts and topics discussed.

Final Thoughts

This book was born in an ending. As I finished my Ph.D. program, it became increasingly obvious to me that my industry colleagues could benefit from many of the social science research methodologies and techniques that I had been exploring for several years. My dissertation topic itself was less important. Writing a dissertation in the social sciences can be an exercise in taking an interesting, relevant idea and drilling down into it so deeply that it no longer applies to anything except itself. But the dissertation process is about practice more than inspiration. As I came up for air in the wake of my research, I realized that, while my specific topic wasn't going to change security practices, the techniques and tools I had learned very well might do so. I was reading others' ideas on security metrics and realizing that the security field was at the beginning of a journey that has been made by industries and research fields since the beginning of scientific exploration. We're new at it, and we have a lot to learn. But measurement is not new by any means, and neither are the methodologies of inquiry and empirical observation by which measurement is accomplished. I hope to share some of these methods with you in this book. If I've done my research correctly, you will be unfamiliar with some of them. If I've done my job as an author well, you will find that you can use them to understand and improve your security operations. I hope that I've accomplished both.

PART I | Introducing Security Metrics

CHAPTER 1 | What Is a Security Metric?

So you are ready to set up a security metrics program—or maybe you're not quite ready, but you're curious about how you can better measure and improve the security of your organization. You may be looking for new ways to show the value of security to senior management. Or perhaps you just want more visibility into security operations. You may be worried about compliance with laws or regulations that require your organization to be more accountable for the specifics of security management. Whatever your reason, you are ready to learn more about how to develop and benefit from IT security metrics. Before you dive into those details, however, you need to understand the role of metrics in the security world.

The past few years have seen increasing buzz around security metrics. Several books as well as numerous industry articles, reports, and white papers have been devoted to the benefits of measuring IT security. Security metrics have become a hot topic so quickly that some might assume we have only just discovered that we can measure what we do. But this is not accurate, of course, and well-known security metrics such as annualized loss expectancy (ALE), total cost of ownership (TCO), and quantitative and qualitative risk assessment have been used by security professionals for years.

What is new in security metrics is the growing understanding that many of our traditional efforts at measurement are unsatisfactory. They do not give us the information we really need to support decisions and articulate the value of security activities. And they are not adequate for the changing security landscape of more subtle threats and increased accountability and scrutiny. The growing consensus is that we must measure better and consider new and innovative ways of analyzing the metrics data we already have. The purpose of this book is to add to the IT security metrics conversation and help you achieve the goal of better measuring and articulating the value of information and IT asset protection.

When I advise clients on how to develop an effective security metrics program, I usually face some immediate challenges, not the least of which is that, although people generally understand metrics, it is often localized to their immediate concerns. We tend to measure only those things that we deal with regularly, and eventually we decide those are the only measurements that matter. For example, every morning I make coffee, carefully measuring several scoops of ground coffee and several cups of water into a French press as part of my daily caffeine ingestion ritual. I care about these measurements because they directly affect my morning. I don't think about how these measurements are related to other metrics, such as the proper acidity and nitrogen levels for growing coffee or the optimal temperatures and durations for roasting it. I depend on others for these measurements (although if they are incompetently performed, I find another source for my coffee).

Metrics, both for coffee and for IT security, involve many local and tactical efforts that become increasingly interdependent and strategic as they begin to affect larger systems. I may not perform measurements outside of my local context, but, if I'm smart, I will try to understand more about them so that I can make the best decisions. And others will do the same. Understanding what makes good coffee beyond just grounds-to-water ratios will help me maximize my consumption experience, while understanding how I measure and drink my morning beverage will help coffee producers show value and compete for my business. It is no different for IT security. I may not measure security beyond analyzing the contents of my firewall logs, but if I don't understand how others measure security or other business values, I will be less able to use my data to make (or help others make) good decisions. And if I can learn to understand how other stakeholders in my business measure success, I can use my security metrics data to help them be more successful in their operations, thereby demonstrating the value of my own activities.

As security becomes more complex and pervasive, and security professionals are held responsible not only for protecting company assets but also for contributing to its financial and competitive success, information about how IT security operates will be more globally and strategically relevant. As a consultant, I am exposed to a wide variety of requirements and environments that have proven the value of a broad understanding of security measurement. I advise people to take a big-picture approach to security metrics.

To return to my analogy, if your livelihood depends on coffee, you need to understand more than just the mechanics of a cup of joe. Likewise, if you are a chief information security officer (CISO), you need to know more than just how many events the firewall logged yesterday or how much one vendor's firewall might save you over another. Measurement is also about understanding why we want to measure something in the first place, what it is that we actually want to measure, how we can measure it, and what to do with the data we collect. So let's begin by taking a look at metrics and measurement in general.

Metrics and Measurement

You might want to implement a security metrics program for some immediate reasons, including justifying the value of your activities to management or improving your ability to control and secure your infrastructure. But at the heart of your reasons lies the single reason why we measure anything: we want to understand it better. This is a key point that will inform the rest of the book and your efforts to implement metrics within your own security program.

You measure security to understand security. This statement may seem simple, but it is more difficult to put into practice than it seems. I know clients that have established metrics programs and yet still struggle with understanding their security efforts. This often occurs because a client's metrics program is actually a data collection program and not measurement-driven at all. These metrics programs remind me of the giant warehouse in the Indiana Jones movies, where the government stashed away and subsequently forgot about every cool mystical device that Dr. Jones worked so hard to procure. Collecting security data is critical to any effective metrics program, but without a context for that data and an idea of why you collected it and what you intend to do with it, you might find yourself limited to describing your measurement only in terms of terabytes of log data and the shelf volume occupied by auditor reports.

Metrics Are a Result

One of the common mistakes people make when setting up a security metrics program is to focus too much on the metrics themselves. Some of the blame for this focus can be assigned to semantics, because the industry has adopted the term *metrics* in favor of the term *measurement*, which would better describe what we are trying to accomplish. I'm guilty as well, as evidenced by the title of this book, but I try to choose my battles, and a book on IT security *measurement* would be dissonant and perhaps confusing.

The important point to emphasize is that security metrics are a *journey* and not a *destination*. Once you have established a security metrics program, you must ask yourself how the results of the program have improved your understanding of your security systems and processes. Understanding is not diagnostics. Knowing year after year that some percentage of your users' passwords are easily cracked or that the ratio of vulnerable to secure Internet-facing hosts hasn't dropped below 1-in-4 reduces some of the uncertainty regarding your IT security effectiveness, but if the information has not enabled you to improve that effectiveness, something is missing from the program. Even if the security has improved, if that is all you know and you cannot say why the improvement occurred, your metrics are not giving you any more value than if you were struggling over why your security was getting worse. Metrics are conceptual data repositories—they define and standardize information. Metrics do not organize that information into knowledge, any more than well-defined word entries will transform a dictionary into literature. Only people can accomplish these things.

Measurement Is an Activity

The point of security metrics is not to collect a lot of data. A small set of data, understood well and applied regularly, is much more valuable than a mountain of data left untouched on shelves or hard drives and gathering real or virtual dust. The true benefits of metrics come when the data that they represent is the end result of meaningful activities, actions that we take to accomplish a goal or a task. Metrics are, or at least should be, the records of our observations. Measurement is the activity of making observations and collecting data in an effort to gain practical insight into whatever it is that we are attempting to understand. The distinction is important, because metrics bring not just information about IT security, but also costs and risks.

Collecting metrics data for the sake of collecting metrics data is not measurement unless the purpose of the activity is to mine historical data for interesting patterns as a research exercise. I actually love this type of measurement and think it is valuable, but most of the clients I work with that collect security data do not do so for academic reasons, and their security data is rarely analyzed historically or experimentally. More often, the benefit of collecting security data is directly related to the ability to claim that a lot of security data has been collected. Having great amounts of data at hand can be comforting, providing a reassuring sense that we are on top of things even if we have no real clue about what the data reveals. Collecting all this data may even serve as ammunition in support of organizational rivalries as people strive to collect more data than the peers, supervisors, or groups with whom they interact and compete.

The challenge is that security metrics are inherently risky, as is anything that allows you to understand something better than you understood it before. Knowledge may be power, but it often carries with it certain demands and obligations, not the least of which is that you may have to consider new ways of looking at your environment that can be quite uncomfortable (or expensive). In addition to the simple questions of overhead that come with collecting and storing metrics data, there is the implication that whatever security data you collect now constitutes something that you are aware of as an individual or an organization. Collecting data regarding the vulnerabilities in your systems implies that you now know how vulnerable they are, because that information is in a report, either from an automated tool or from a consultant, that may be sitting on the shelf behind your desk or on your hard drive. In the event of a security breach, those metrics may even become discoverable should your organization face litigation.

Whether you read the report or understood it is immaterial: you collected the data and increased your knowledge. Knowing about the problem and not having acted upon it, leading to a security breach, however, could actually end up more damaging than the ignorance that existed before you ever gathered the data. Many security managers don't consider the idea that the data they collect becomes a matter of corporate record and possibly subject to e-discovery. Unused metrics data simply adds insult to injury. You still get hacked, but you also lose the resulting lawsuit because you "knew" you could get hacked based on your security metrics data. This is an important consideration for security metrics that is only beginning to be discussed in our industry.

My point is not that metrics are too risky and that we should strive to know as little as possible about how our security is functioning. It is that if you collect data and do not use it, you do not have a security metrics program. Measurement without analysis and action wastes time and money and contributes to uncertainty and risk rather than reducing them. We need to know more about our security operations. The value that comes from understanding our security processes far outweighs the risks associated with that knowledge. But metrics must be based on a sound strategy for security measurement and applied understanding, and not about hoarding data that we never intend to look at again, much less put to productive use. Instead, security metrics should be seen as part of a business process that continually seeks to improve the protection of enterprise information assets over time.

If you are undertaking a security metrics program, you should do so with the same eye toward risks, costs, and benefits that you would approach any other business process. For every metric your organization collects, you or someone must understand why that data is being collected and what decisions the data will be used to support. And someone should be assessing the costs and benefits of collecting the data. It is fine (and often useful) to collect exploratory data that is not associated with any particular objective, but research metrics should also be understood and should eventually lead to new knowledge and insight for your company.

As you put metrics into place to explore your security operations, ask yourself whether you are prepared to act on the knowledge you gain through your measurement program, even if it is unexpected or imposes new obligations and requirements on your security operations. If you are not ready to act on what you discover, metrics are only going to compound your problems.

Security Metrics Today

Increased interest in IT security metrics notwithstanding, the security industry already uses several commonly recognized metrics. Some of these metrics are cornerstones of security practice for vendors seeking to market their products and for security managers trying to improve security and reduce risk. The problem is that many of these metrics have limitations that make them misleading indicators of security effectiveness.

There are plenty of arguments about what makes a good or a bad metric, and I will explore some of these arguments throughout this book. I believe that any empirical measurement that helps an organization reduce uncertainty is a good metric. I do not believe that a metric should be discounted simply because it is not quantitative or specific, or that a metric is good simply because it is easy and unambiguous. Any measurement becomes problematic when it is conducted poorly and when those measuring are not sufficiently critical of their own methods. Problems that can arise from unsophisticated attempts at measuring security can include issues of data quality, empirical rigor, or the fact that the metrics are used in immature or misleading ways. The following metrics all suffer from one or more of these problems.

Risk

Risk is a foundational concept in IT security. At the heart of any security-related question is the deeper question of what risks we assume by making a certain decision or taking a particular course of action. Of all the phenomena that we care about understanding as security stakeholders, risk would seem to be at the top of the list. But as critical as an understanding of risk is, it is often one of the most poorly understood concepts. Information security practitioners typically use terms such as *risk assessment*, *risk analysis*, and *risk management* as generalities in which the definition of risk is often assumed or taken for granted. In IT security, risk is typically associated with some harm or loss to systems or data, but this definition is too general and not universally accepted or consistently used. Instead, risk is usually bundled into some combination with other generalized issues of threats, vulnerabilities, and parameters that are often equally imprecise until we are left with a fuzzy concept that can change across organizations and implementations. This makes risk difficult to measure consistently in security, and it doesn't help that many vendors confuse the meaning of the term or misuse it when they try to sell their security products and services.

IT security's approach to risk can reflect the relative immaturity of the industry and our responses to the professional challenges we face. Our understanding of risk is something of a catch-all, and we rarely feel the need to be clear about what we actually mean when we discuss it. We use the term *risk* to describe many different phenomena that we know can affect our security, but that we have not yet explored and defined.

When you mention risk in an IT security context, everyone will nod in agreement, but you can never be sure that everyone is thinking of risk in the same way. Risk can, after all, mean a lot of things. Consider a mature industry such as finance and the definitional problem is put into perspective. Ask a finance person about risk, and she may require more clarification about what you actually mean. Are you referring to *endogenous* or *exogenous* risks—risks from events within your control or risks that come from outside of your control? Or are you talking about *systematic* or *unsystematic* risks—whether or not the risk is subject to chance as defined by some probability curve, or whether the risk is non-probabilistic? These are just a few of the specific characteristics and types of risk that might be referred to in a discussion of formal risk management.

You may find that, in the eyes of your colleague in finance, you need to do a bit more homework before you are ready to consider measuring your risk. Immaturity is a natural thing. Insurance and finance companies didn't always measure risk with the sophistication that they do today (and in the wake of the recent economic crisis, some will argue that they remain immature in some ways). Measurement improves with practice and discipline, and the more security pros actively attempt to measure and understand our operations, the better we will get at our assessments.

Our somewhat naïve definition of risk in the context of IT security is mirrored by the lack of rigor we tend to demonstrate in measuring it. Probably the most common method employed in measuring security risk is to use a variation of the "Likelihood × Severity" matrix shown in Figure 1-1. Some version of this formula and matrix can be found in the

Generic Risk Matrix

		Likelihood of Event		
		High	Medium	Low
Severity of Impact	High	"We're Doomed!"	Bad	Outlier
	Medium	Bad	Not Good	Error
	Low	Annoyance	Typical	"Whatever..."

Figure 1-1.   Generalized risk assessment matrix

majority of discussions, books, and training programs regarding IT security risk assessment. The matrix may be more complex and contain different scales, weighting factors, heat map colors, or other bells and whistles, but they all are derived from the same concept. The idea is that you estimate the likelihood that something (usually a technology system) will experience a negative security event, and then you estimate the severity of that event in terms of how badly the system is impacted. The results are used to populate the matrix and give you a prioritized summary of your risk. The matrix is simple and makes intuitive sense, which is likely why it has persisted for so long. Nevertheless, as an instrument for measuring risk, it is pretty limited, certainly too limited to justify the enormous amount of stock that we put into it in support of some of our security decisions.

While it has problems as a measure of actual risk, the matrix can be quite effective as a targeted opinion poll. It allows security subject matter experts to prototype quickly what they believe to be their biggest security problems. You see this type of assessment used all the time in the media, when experts are brought in to clarify and provide opinion on current affairs and events. These individuals have knowledge and experience that should make them more suitable to comment on the topics under consideration than just anyone off the street. Of course, none of this expertise proves that these people are correct, and in fact experts often disagree. The point is that experts should have more informed opinions regarding the areas of their expertise than the rest of us—this is why we have teachers and doctors and attorneys and security specialists in the first place. Their insights can clarify a subject and remove the confusion and noise surrounding it, allowing us to focus on what really matters.

The important point is to recognize that opinion alone can have value, and not to insist that the opinion also represent a fact in order to have merit. A security risk matrix based on expert judgments can be a useful estimate, but it remains a set of opinions about risk. The biggest security problems identified in the matrix are not necessarily the biggest security problems facing the enterprise. The hope is that the true security risks will correlate in some way with the expert opinions of those responsible for security. As I will describe in later chapters, there are ways to calibrate and refine expert judgment to make these opinions less uncertain, but there will always be a margin for error. When we deliberately ignore this uncertainty because we want to pretend we have identified a fact, we lose track of what we are measuring and our matrix becomes misleading and contributes more, not less, uncertainty to our decisions. This result reflects the first of two fundamental limitations involved in this form of risk assessment.

Security Risk Assessments Don't Measure Risk

Consider the standard security risk assessment methodology. Groups of stakeholders are gathered together or surveyed by questionnaire and asked to provide risk scores for probability and severity of occurrence for their systems and data. These individuals dutifully provide the requested data, which is used to populate the matrix. The result is that a measurement has certainly been conducted. We can even claim that the measurement was more or less empirical because it involved observing some phenomena.

The problem is that where we think we measured security risk, we actually measured human judgments about security risk. In more formal measurement terms, we have just developed what is known as a validity problem—what we think we are observing does not accurately reflect what we are actually observing.

Some critics of this simplified form of risk assessment go to the opposite extreme, believing that since you are not actually measuring risk, the entire assessment matrix exercise is worthless. I tend to disagree. Nothing is intrinsically wrong with measuring someone's opinion of something. If such measurement did not produce valuable results, the marketing and advertising industries (not to mention political consulting groups) would have collapsed long ago. The important consideration is that, when the marketing department of your favorite gadget measures consumer opinions on product quality, they do not make the mistake of thinking that they are actually measuring how good the product really is. Security managers could do a lot to improve the quality of their risk assessment activities by simply recognizing this subtle but important point—that they are measuring opinion rather than risk, but that opinion is also valuable. They might then make the risk assessments more rigorous by focusing efforts on improving the judgments that they elicit, perhaps by calibration exercises and the use of confidence intervals, instead of insisting on turning those opinions into hard numbers that look better in a chart.

Measurement Slackers and "Statistical Alchemy"

A second problem with the current state of security risk assessment results from the fact that, whether consciously or not, we all realize that those assessments are a bit lame. Because we realize this, some security practitioners may feel compelled to try to improve on the method, to make it appear more complex or more rigorous than it really is. At their core, matrix-based assessments take two basic parameters—"how likely?" and "how bad?"—and assign three basic levels—low, medium, or high. And these parameters are derived from data sources that are subjective—namely, people. Anyone thinking about the matrix approach in this light realizes that it makes it difficult to approach senior management with "objective" results based on the exercise. But senior management often isn't interested in opinions; they want facts that they can use to make their decisions, and nonfactual results appear to be less valuable.

The security community has two common responses to this perceived limited value of the risk matrix. The first is to label the risk matrix methodology a "qualitative" risk assessment, which, in IT security terms, tends to translate into "Security is fuzzy stuff; you can't really measure it as you do other things, so you can't blame us if our results prove wildly inaccurate." This is, of course, nonsense. It is the slacker way out of the risk-measurement problem, where we manage to justify the use of the methodology while distancing ourselves from any results we might obtain from it. It also gives qualitative research methods a bad name, implying that they cannot be rigorous or empirical, which is also nonsense. This argument actually functions to relieve security managers and risk-assessment team members from having to critique and improve their own measurement activities.

Even worse is a practice I call "statistical alchemy," which involves transmuting one thing into something completely different that is perceived as more valuable. As I noted earlier, the risk matrix generally involves assigning high, medium, and low levels of likelihood and severity to a particular event under consideration. These levels are on what is known as a *nominal* scale. I will address levels of measurement such as nominal, ordinal, and interval measures later, but for now suffice to say that nominal measures function as discrete categories. Hot and cold, good and bad, and high and low are all nominal, meaning that you cannot compare them in terms of value, scale, or ratio to one another. Business decision-makers tend not to like the inputs to those decisions expressed so categorically; they want to see numbers, to know *how much* hotter or colder, better or worse, or higher or lower something is. Numbers add a sense of certainty and importance to observations, whether or not they actually provide those things. Luckily, when a risk analysis is conducted for someone who is expecting to base decisions on numbers, a simple solution is at hand: Just change all the levels to numbers! Now a high likelihood is a 3, a medium likelihood is a 2, and a low likelihood is a 1. The same goes for high, medium, and low severity. This lets you successfully transform statistical lead (an ordinal measurement) into something that may not be gold, but is closer than you were before. Calculating the average of high and medium (medium-high?) is meaningless, but calculating the average of 3 and 2 is not (it's an unambiguous 2.5).

Most assessments that adopt simple numerical categories would not be portrayed as quantitative. Security folks are smart people, and we would see through such a ploy. But more "sophisticated" risk analysis matrices up the ante. Instead of numbers corresponding to high, medium, or low, perhaps they require the specification of a dollar loss, such as "below $25,000" or "above $500,000" in the severity columns. Likelihood levels may be replaced with probability scores, such as "90% likely" or a "0.25 probability" that an event will occur. Additional columns can be included to simulate numerical weights based on the system's environment or the ratio of system functionality that may be lost. Now the matrix becomes something more like a spreadsheet, with the highest risks expressed in estimates of financial loss. It is our same humble risk matrix now dressed up, Pygmalion-like, as something more than it is. And even if those who conducted the assessment are still reminding everyone that the matrix is qualitative, reflecting human opinions and not real numbers, no one is really listening anymore.

So Why Even Use the Risk Matrix?

The real tragedy of the security risk matrix is not that it is a bad method of measurement, but that it is bad to pretend that the matrix measures actual risk. Unfortunately, most users of the matrix in IT security do not give much thought to the importance of that nuance, and they use the matrix to make "risk-based" decisions. Even considering the hedgers who caveat the matrix with the word "qualitative" (and then often go on to treat the results as factual), the risk matrix has become the engine behind some of the most common security–risk-assessment methodologies today.

It seems that new variations of the matrix are developed every year at significant effort and cost. Often these methodologies are used as the organization's formal risk assessment and management methodology, as required by some compliance frameworks. In these cases, the matrix does not act as an initial prototype of risk measurement that leads to more questions and metrics, but as the end result of the risk assessment process. It is as if an insurance company made underwriting decisions based on the experiences and opinions of a team of actuaries and never bothered to verify whether those opinions were correct before handing out policies. I don't advocate abandoning risk matrices as a means to support security decisions, but I do think that these tools should be used for at least two different purposes than they are used today.

Assessment Prototyping   A security risk matrix is, as I mentioned, a good barometer of people's thoughts and perceptions regarding risk. And since the methodology expects you to ask risk questions of people who are responsible for the systems under review, knowing what these experts think about the risk levels of the systems they manage can be valuable data.

Some of the best value comes when we use the matrix as a means of prototyping further risk assessments. Too often I see organizations that have undertaken a general risk assessment methodology and accept the results without ever asking the all-important question "Why?" Why is this system so likely to be compromised, and why is the impact so severe compared to the other systems? Instead of simply accepting the rating, asking why encourages security managers to think about follow-up questions, which lead to more measurements. Asking these questions does not mean you disagree with or challenge the risk rating, but that you need to understand why the claim was made so that you can effectively respond to it. As the first step in defining the data we need, the tests we must run, and the metrics we must define to assess our risk, a risk matrix can function quite effectively and not be ruined by expectations that should never have been laid upon it in the first place.

Measuring Differences in Agreement   Another great use for a risk assessment matrix is to compare what different people in the organization think about risk. Rather than treating the matrix as a reflection of reality, the scores used to populate the data can be used to identify areas where everyone is in agreement or everyone varies widely in the opinions that they hold. This, too, can provide valuable data, particularly if major disagreements exist over the importance of particular systems or how much the organization would be hurt should they be compromised.

This approach encourages the assessment team to expand the pool of experts from which they collect data. You might find, for instance, that the e-mail administrator is far more concerned with a loss of service to users' inboxes and rates e-mail storage as a relatively low risk, but the compliance officer responsible for records retention and e-discovery is far more concerned with compromises in the e-mail archiving system. As with prototyping, this use of the risk matrix serves primarily as a means to discover where the organization should concentrate its risk assessment efforts, including where to conduct more sophisticated and robust measurement activities.

Security Vulnerability and Incident Statistics

Measure for measure, the data most often collected for the purpose of understanding IT security involves system vulnerabilities and efforts to compromise them. System vulnerability statistics are produced when an organization runs a security scanner on its network, when new exploits are identified and released to vendors and the public, and when organizations release reports resulting from industry surveys they have conducted or analyses of security data they have collected. Incident statistics come from system logs, intrusion detection and prevention systems, and industry surveys and analyses. These numbers are often used as general indicators of the current stat of IT security.

A Parade of Horribles

I recently read a vendor-sponsored industry research report on Internet security trends. The report included a scatter plot chart that showed the number of reported product security vulnerabilities over time. It showed an obvious positive correlation as the number of vulnerabilities increased steadily over the timeline of the graph. The report concluded that Internet security was getting worse (a trend that certainly justified the sponsorship of the security vendors who subsidized the research study). The problem here is that measuring Internet security by the number of reported vulnerabilities each year is like measuring male virility by the number of prescriptions written to treat erectile dysfunction. If I charted these prescriptions on the same chart as security vulnerabilities, it would appear that male reproductive capabilities were in rapid decline during the last decade or so and that the human race might be in trouble. Both analyses ignore more data than they include. From a security perspective, the mere addition of hundreds of new technology products every year could be enough to account for the increase in reported vulnerabilities.

Counting and analyzing technical vulnerabilities and the attempts to exploit them are important aspects of any IT security program. But if you make security vulnerabilities the primary data you use to measure your security, you cannot help but distort and skew the results. Relying too much on vulnerability data contributes to fear, uncertainty, and doubt (FUD) rather than rational attempts to analyze and improve security business processes. When that analysis is also sloppy, as in the security report I found, the problem is compounded.

A Thousand Walled Gardens

Vulnerability and incident data reporting is not problematic only because of its tendency towards hyperbole. As a measurement, it is inconsistent because it occurs in too many places and in too many ways, without sufficient aggregation or normalization of the data. A company running a vulnerability scanner against itself is not likely to share the information it gathers with other companies or even with other groups inside the company. Vendors and consultants publishing this information for a fee or as a way to promote their products and services are unlikely to be forthcoming, because the data represents valuable intellectual property. This reluctance to share data and the lack of effective systems to facilitate sharing among organizations make it that much more difficult for academic researchers and public institutions that might want to distribute the information. The result is that most organizations have no data to rely on other than what they collect and no real way to compare their data with anyone else's data.

The most common question I am asked by clients from a security perspective is how well they stack up compared to their competitors and other companies; I am always forced to admit that I cannot provide a satisfactory answer. Of course, there have been efforts to share security data, with efforts ranging from high-level surveys and studies such as the Computer Security Institute's annual *CSI Computer Crime and Security Survey* and a host of studies by vendors and market analysis firms. Other technical efforts have attempted to normalize vulnerability data, including the Common Vulnerabilities and Exposures (CVE) dictionary and the Common Vulnerability Scoring System (CVSS). But while these resources help with general understanding, they do not reflect anything close to the common metrics and shared data that exist in more mature industries such as insurance, transportation, or manufacturing.

Annualized Loss Expectancy

If vulnerability-related statistics are among the most commonly collected measurement data in security, ALE is the most commonly used conceptual metric. ALE refers to how much you think you will lose as a result of security incidents. Where risk assessment matrices are used to compare and prioritize risks qualitatively into cells in a table, better to identify where to focus security efforts, ALE is pitched as a fully quantitative metric, complete with formulas and other statistical goodness.

The formula is expressed as ALE = ARO × SLE, where ARO is the annualized rate of occurrence (how often you expect to experience the loss in a given year) and SLE is single loss expectancy (how much you expect one incident of the loss to cost you). Suppose, for example, that you have a server worth $10,000 (system and data combined) and you estimate a 25 percent chance that the server will be successfully compromised as the result of a zero-day exploit in the coming year (ARO = 0.25). Each time the server is compromised, you estimate that you will lose $5000 due to remediation costs and the exposure of the data stored there (SLE = $5000). Your expected annual loss is then ALE = 0.25 × $5000, or $1250 each year. Theoretically, you have now identified your security budget for that particular server, as you should not spend more protecting the asset than you would lose should it be compromised.

I find the ALE formula interesting because it is unique to the security industry. You might expect that it was borrowed from the insurance industry, which has a much longer history of risk assessment and management. In fact, as far as I can tell, the metric first emerged in the 1970s as part of Federal Information Processing Standards Publications (FIPS PUBS) published by the National Institute of Standards and Technology (NIST). And in those three decades, the metric and the way it is used have hardly changed, while ALE has developed into perhaps the most common single measurement in IT security. Unfortunately for security managers, ALE is a poor metric.

Expectations vs. Probabilities

I am certainly not the first to critique ALE as a security metric, and it surprises me how the formula continues to gain and maintain acceptance as an IT security standard by professionals who should know better. Like general matrix-based risk assessments, ALE relies on data that is often completely fabricated. This is reflected in its name, which implies human expectations. If it were called Annual Loss Probability, the formula would at least imply that the results were based on more concrete data. Like the risk matrix, ALE measures what people *think* rather than objective reality. The people in question may know a lot about the systems they are asked to review, but when a risk assessment team polls its members to populate the ALE formula, they are soliciting opinions. ALE is a perfect example of statistical alchemy. Unlike the risk matrix, which, though flawed, presents data in a categorical context that does not necessarily imply how things will actually turn out, ALE pretends to show you probable outcomes.

ALE deals in opinions and expectations primarily because IT security does not have the data necessary to define actual probabilities. The discussion of security vulnerability and incident data showed some of the weaknesses involved in collecting meaningful security data. Part of the problem is that most organizations do not have systematic programs for collecting and analyzing historical data even for vulnerability and incident data, much less the impacts and losses that they have experienced as a result of security breaches. In many cases, organizations are not even able to detect or track events that would lead to this data in real time. In those rare cases in which an organization is detecting, collecting, and analyzing this data, there is no collective industry mechanism by which this data can be shared, even assuming that the organization wants to share it. Most do not. Industries such as insurance function because they have made a science of collecting and sharing data regarding the risks that the industry faces as a whole. IT security has not matured to a level at which we are able to do this—one of the many reasons that real, verifiable security metrics are becoming more important to everyone.

What Have We Got to Lose?

The other big problem with ALE is our lack of understanding about what constitutes loss. ALE can function only by assigning dollar costs to events. Therefore, the metric tends to focus on those scenarios in which the system in question is rendered inoperable for some period of time, where time must be spent to clean or repair the system, or when the value of the data residing on the system is negatively impacted through theft or exposure. (Assigning value to our data is a completely different problem that also complicates our ALE results.)

ALE does a poor job of estimating the risks associated with intangible losses to such things as brand or reputation. The model is blunt and inaccurate, and the moment you try to add nuance or sophistication to your analysis, it tends to break down. Part of the problem is a lack of awareness of our security environments. Just as organizations have a hard time gathering data on attacks and events, they often do not have a sophisticated awareness of what losses they might incur.

ALE tends to focus specifically on technology systems, because they are the easiest to model. We mislead ourselves into thinking we can understand our losses based on an analysis of hardware, software, and data because we can calculate their value even if that means only factoring in how much we paid for them. But this valuation is often the least useful for risk assessment, because what we really want to know is not direct replacement cost, but rather how the loss of an asset creates other losses such as those involving productivity, efficiency, or competitiveness. Determining these losses brings us right back to our limitations of data and awareness and forces us to rely not on verifiable data and probabilities but on more or less educated guesswork.

Return on Investment

Return on investment (ROI) is a security metric that has to do with calculating how much benefit (usually described in financial terms) will be gained from an investment. IT security borrowed ROI directly from the business world, where the idea of taking more out of your efforts than you put into them (also known as profit) is of central importance.

From a security perspective, we usually refer to ROI in a couple of ways. First it is related to ALE, which defines the expected security losses incurred in the absence of any preventative action. If an organization takes preventative action, the relationship of the cost of the action to the expected losses defines ROI. If, for example, you expect to lose $10,000 in a security incident and prevent that loss by spending $1000, your ROI is $9000. If you spend $20,000 to prevent the same event, you have a negative return of $10,000. You can beef up the measurement in other, fancier ways, such as weighting or discounting the return over time, but these are the basics.

The second way ROI gets used is by security vendors as a means of marketing products. The vendor builds models to show how an organization that buys its product will end up getting a great ROI. The vendor may include ALE analyses that show how the product reduces loss as well as ways that the customer can benefit from improvements in efficiency or productivity. The vendor can then use these ROI figures in conjunction with pricing and support options to show a customer that the product provides the most bang for the buck.

ROI in an IT security context also qualifies as statistical alchemy, because it misleadingly tries to equate different concepts quantitatively. In the finance industry, for instance, ROI might be reflected in the rate of return on a monetary investment in which a borrower agrees to pay a lender for the use of the lender's money. In capital expenditures in industry, on the other hand, the ROI has to do with profit, the amount of additional money that can be made through the use of a fixed cost asset over time. Security does not really function in either of these ways, because security activities are not undertaken as a profit center (unless they are provided for somebody else as a business). IT security has to do with loss prevention, much like physical security mechanisms such as locks, fences, and guards.

The reason IT security is portrayed as an investment has to do with marketing. The main use of security ROI figures is to convince someone with money to give that money to someone else, and most people feel more comfortable about giving away money if they think they are investing it. This is why security ROI is used a lot by security managers who make business cases and by security vendors that sell products—both have a vested interest in convincing someone to give them money.

As with the security metrics discussed previously, the biggest problem with ROI is the data that goes into the equation. If the data is unreliable, the metric is equally meaningless. ROI has an additional stigma in that, because it is used directly to influence financial decisions, it encourages people to manipulate the data to achieve the outcome most favorable to them. This makes ROI doubly unreliable, because you not only have to account for incomplete and subjective data, but now you must consider whether the metric is not just inaccurate but deliberately misleading.

Total Cost of Ownership

Where ALE attempts to measure losses associated with IT systems and ROI attempts to measure the "profit" derived from them, TCO seeks to quantify the money that must be spent on the system throughout the entire ownership lifecycle, from initial purchase to final disposal.

TCO was first developed by the Gartner Group in the late 1980s as a way of helping its analysis clients compare vendor products. TCO is designed to take a more holistic view of the cost of a particular system and to include factors that may not be reflected in the purchase price, including the following:

- Central system components such as hardware and software
- License and support fees
- Supporting infrastructure (space, power, environmental controls)
- Installation and maintenance
- Training and expertise
- Security and audit
- Hidden costs

TCO in IT security is designed to mirror TCO in other industries. For instance, most of us realize when we buy a new car that we have to factor in long-term costs such as insurance, maintenance, and fuel. Security TCO attempts to make similar costs associated with data protection systems more visible, so that a picture of the actual costs of a system is revealed.

TCO is more likely to bring some quantitative rigor to the results of the metric than ALE and ROI, because some of the parameters of ownership have more supporting data. But this strength also limits the utility of TCO as a broad security metric, because it applies only to security purchases and not to the measurement of the IT security process. TCO can help you to understand how much a security product will cost over its lifetime, but that doesn't tell you whether or not it will meet your security needs.

Security TCO cannot escape the data uncertainties of other common metrics. Since the security world can't agree on how to track or measure the impact of security incidents, many costs remain hidden and unavailable for inclusion in the analysis. TCO, like ROI, has also been co-opted by security vendors that recognize it as a purchasing decision support metric. These vendors spend a lot of time developing TCO statistics to influence CISO purchasing decisions directly as well as to gain CISO buy-in and support for larger infrastructure purchases. As much as TCO can be a tool to help customers compare solutions, it is also a primary means by which vendors compete with other vendors. No vendor is going to claim higher TCO than a rival when chasing the deal and the motivation for manipulating data and conclusions is high.

TCO can be a useful comparative metric. When factored with other measures, it can support some specific security decisions, including larger IT infrastructure purchases where the vendor has had the foresight to include TCO measures from a security perspective. But TCO does not measure security operations, and the fact that it is one of the most common metrics used in the industry speaks to how much we can improve on our current state.

The Dissatisfying State of Security Metrics: Lessons from Other Industries

The limited number of metrics commonly employed in IT security and the limitations presented by the metrics themselves mean that we do not have the appropriate tools to understand or improve our security systems. This bothers me, because there is no reason that we should not be doing better. We are an industry full of smart people who care deeply about protecting our systems and data. We should be able to measure the results of what we do every day more effectively. Security is not the first industry to deal with complexity, uncertainty, or risk, and if you are considering setting up your own security metrics program, it pays to understand how other professions have dealt with challenges similar to our own and how to overcome the shortcomings in our own efforts.

Insurance

The insurance industry has been professionally managing risk for several centuries, and the security industry could learn a lot by taking cues from its older and wiser forebear. The single most important asset in insurance is data. Data allows insurers to understand the probabilities involved in events against which their customers seek to be protected.

Data collection for insurance purposes dates back to the seventeenth century, when information about everything from mortality rates to shipping routes began to be collected and traded, often in London coffeehouses such as that of Edward Lloyd, of Lloyds of London fame. The data that was collected was subjected to relatively new and innovative statistical analyses that allowed insurers to predict the likelihood of loss and thus set policies and insurance rates accordingly. Today insurers can issue policies for just about everything from your car to specific body parts, adjusting rates accordingly based upon probabilities gathered from observations of all aspects of life.

Security managers can find it challenging even to provide current and accurate configuration data for the systems they operate. Without data, you cannot even describe daily security activities, much less generalize to how your security functions across the company or across your industry. It is unsurprising that when I first entered the IT security industry, I heard a lot of talk about insuring security risks, and now, ten years later, we still have not been able to make it happen. The insurance industry provides us with the first lesson of IT security metrics:

Security Metrics Lesson #1   Your security metrics and your subsequent risk-management decisions will improve as you improve your capability to collect, analyze, and understand data regarding your security operations.

Manufacturing

The manufacturing industry depends on processes designed to create similar products on a mass scale. Variation in these products is highly undesirable, because it introduces problems of quality, efficiency, and reliability in that which is produced.

Whether the manufacturing process is the injection molding of plastic drinking cups or the assembly line activities of an automobile plant, manufacturing industries must ensure that each product is free of defects within strict and predefined parameters. At the same time, the manufacturing process must be constantly monitored and improvements made to the efficiency and productivity of operations if the manufacturer hopes to compete with other manufacturers.

The manufacturing industry has been studying how to improve its processes for nearly as long as the insurance industry has been managing risk—at least as far back as the famous economist Adam Smith's description of the benefits of division of labor in the typical English pin factory. In the early twentieth century through the end of World War II, process experts began applying sophisticated statistical models to the manufacturing process in an effort to increase efficiency and quality in the products created. In the decades since, manufacturers have conducted much research into quality management and statistical process control methods that allow for high degrees of consistency and standardization even in highly complex production systems such as microelectronics and biotechnology.

Your security program may not function exactly like an assembly line, but unless your security operations are very different from most others, you are also not treating your security as a true business process. You may have security processes in place, but it is unlikely that these processes have been formally deconstructed, mapped, or analyzed at levels of detail sufficient to implement statistical controls on the activities involved. So it is likely that many of your security activities remain somewhat opaque and unclear even within your own organization. You can and should consider many techniques and methods from the process control research literature to understand and improve these processes. Along with the need to collect more data, a process approach to security is the most important improvement strategy that you can undertake, and this is the goal of the Security Process Management Framework described later in the book. For now, we can take from the manufacturing industry our second lesson in security metrics:

Security Metrics Lesson #2   Security is a business process. If you are not measuring and controlling the process, you are not measuring and controlling security.

Design

I am a social scientist by training, so I sometimes find myself at odds with other security metrics advocates who believe that only "hard facts" expressible as numbers should be counted as effective metrics. It often seems to me that one of the end goals of IT security is to rid ourselves of the "problem" of human behavior—if we could just automate everything, users would have no choice but to behave properly. In academia, this is sometimes referred to as "technological determinism" and reflects a state of affairs in which technology rather than people is the primary driver of human society.

No one understands how misleading this view of the world is better than technology designers who deal every day with the consequences of not understanding how central people are the development and use of that technology. What this means for security metrics is that if you are not making an attempt to understand the social, organizational, and even cultural aspects of your security program, you are missing at least half of the picture.

When qualitative measurement is brought up in the context of security, it is often a euphemism for data that is conceptually too "soft" and unscientific or logistically too difficult to collect to be useful. This represents a gross misunderstanding of the purpose and methods behind the science of qualitative inquiry. Designers rely on a variety of "soft" research methods in their work that would likely make believers in hardcore quantitative security metrics cringe or at least roll their eyes disapprovingly. Designers may talk in terms of context, social norms, and even empathy as part of their measurement process, which they are more likely to refer to as research than measurement. (I'll cover the distinction as it pertains to security in the next chapter.)

Design researchers and the companies that employ them use a variety of rigorous qualitative methods such as survey research, ethnography, and narrative analysis to gain insights into areas of human behavior that simply cannot be analyzed any other way. These researchers study everything from people's shaving habits (to create better razors), to the way people use their kitchens (to create better smart appliances).

In security, we often go the opposite way, studying the technologies in an attempt to create better human behaviors. But IT security is inherently a social and organizational phenomenon that involves the use and misuse of technology by people who are not so easy to understand or control. Understanding does not come from deliberately ignoring what you need to understand, because those things are perceived to be too difficult or expensive to measure or because they do not involve something you can easily count.

The canonical example is social engineering, which has been a bane of security managers since before IT security had to worry about the problem. Whether the deception comes through human interaction or technical hybrids such as phishing attacks, trust trumps technology every time. I find it sadly amusing that our industry recognizes the threat of social engineering but, beyond lip service to training and policy, the main response is often to go right back to an attempt at a technical solution to the problem. So I'll offer a third lesson as you consider your security metrics strategy:

Security Metrics Lesson #3   Security is the result of human activity. Effective measurement programs attempt to understand people as well as technology.

Reassessing Our Ideas About Security Metrics

The security metrics we use today are insufficient to carry us forward into the future of our profession. Security practitioners must develop more sophisticated approaches to security processes in general and measuring and assessing those processes in particular. The experiences of just a sampling of other industries hold valuable lessons regarding how we should think about data, process, and people in approaching our next-generation security metrics. As you develop your own metrics programs, you can and should apply these lessons in several ways to maximize your success.

Thinking Locally

Although it is true that the security industry as a whole is going to need to pull together on metrics, particularly in the areas of common measurement and performance indicators and better sharing of data regarding security operations and incidents, most security managers do not have the luxury of becoming activists. As you develop your own metrics program, you should do so with a keen eye toward your local environment, your organization's specific needs, and the resources that you can bring to bear on your measurement activities.

Metrics programs are not required to be large or comprehensive to be successful; they do need to be better than what was in place before the program. If your organization has no security metrics to speak of, you are in luck, because literally anything that you do will improve the understanding of your security processes. One focused metric, properly analyzed and presented, can be the catalyst for a complete change in the way your organization manages its security. So whether your security program is a tightly run ship or an unorganized mess, it doesn't matter. Metrics can help make it better. You won't accomplish everything overnight, but over the course of this book I will try to help you identify measurement activities that are appropriate to your unique situation and environment and that offer immediate benefits.

Thinking Analytically

Much of this chapter has covered issues of data in regard to metrics: the need for it, where you get it, and why data quality matters. But a security metrics program that collects a lot of data without giving much consideration of what it will do with that data is going to fail. When you build a security metrics program, remember that what you are actually setting up is a program for analyzing the data from your security measurements. If metrics were the end goal, many security organizations would already be finished, and not left wondering why all the data they are collecting is having little real impact on their security. Security metrics analysis means identifying tools and techniques that you can use to create actionable intelligence and organizational learning. Analysis and the sharing of your results widely among the stakeholders that you support becomes the key to transforming your security program from a paradigm of static audit and reactive remediation to one of continuous improvement and innovation.

Thinking Ahead

The thing about measurement is that once you begin, it becomes difficult to stop. Metrics lead to knowledge and insight, which in turn gives you ideas about what else you might be measuring. As your initial metrics efforts gel into a formal process and that process becomes an ongoing program, you should be mindful of what you are hoping to accomplish at the next stage of the game.

As we begin exploring some basic techniques for developing metrics and then more sophisticated tools and methods for analyzing the data that you get, start thinking about what you want to know about your security. Chances are, there's a metric for that. But you may not be able to get to all your security metrics goals immediately. The goal is to stay focused on results. You don't want to drown in a sea of metrics that overloads your ability to analyze the data you have gathered, but you want to begin addressing immediate security measurement goals.

The next chapter offers advice on selecting new security metrics to supplement or replace the traditional and less-satisfying metrics described in this chapter. It provides a methodology for ensuring that your metrics stay focused and aligned to your strategic security and business goals.

Summary

As you consider developing an IT security metrics program, remember that metrics are the result of a measurement process built on human and organizational activities and are not an end in and of themselves. Collecting large amounts of metrics-related data without a cogent plan of analysis and alignment to well-formulated goals is ineffective and can even prove dangerous to the organization, because the argument can be made that any data the organization collects regarding security problems implies awareness of those problems and a responsibility to address them. Your security metrics program should therefore be designed to provide a manageable amount of usable data that your organization is committed to managing and acting upon, including exploratory or experimental research on data collected without explicit purpose.

The security industry already uses several commonly recognized metrics today to measure aspects of organizational IT security:

- Risk matrices
- Security vulnerability and incident statistics
- Annual loss expectancy (ALE)
- Return on investment (ROI)
- Total cost of ownership (TCO)

Although these metrics are widely accepted, they can be severely limited in terms of the value they bring to a security program. Too often, the measures themselves are poorly understood, measuring aspects of security that are quite different from what their users believe they are measuring. Because of the lack of industry-wide information on security practices and incidents, most of these metrics begin with unreliable data that must be supplemented with non-empirical data such as the opinions of specialists. Although this does not mean that the conclusions drawn from this data are false, it does mean that those conclusions must be subjected to more questioning and skepticism than is typically afforded. In some cases, these metrics are abused by those who manipulate the data to provide results more favorable to their individual or organizational goals.

Other industries have faced the same challenges that the security industry now faces in terms of measuring what they do. As you begin your security metrics program, consider the lessons that can be learned from such industries as insurance, manufacturing, and design. The importance of quality data, the focus on security as a business process, and a greater respect for the role of people and social interactions in the security process are all important elements of a successful security metrics program.

Further Reading

Bernstein, P. *Against the Gods: The Remarkable Story of Risk*. Wiley, 1996.

Condamin, L., et al. *Risk Quantification: Management, Diagnosis, and Hedging*. Wiley, 2006.

Fasser, Y., and D. Brettner. *Management for Quality in High-Technology Enterprises*. Wiley, 2002.

Merholz, P., et al. *Subject to Change: Creating Great Products & Services for an Uncertain World*. O'Reilly, 2008.

Taylor, D. "Your Security Log Files Are a Discoverable Liability." www .thecomplianceauthority.com/security-log-files-are-discoverable-liability.php

CHAPTER 2 | Designing Effective Security Metrics

In Chapter 1 I discussed the basics of security measurement, including why some of the security metrics currently used in the industry are insufficient for helping you to understand your security activities. This chapter explores how you can choose more useful security metrics and proposes an approach adapted from empirical software engineering, the Goal-Question-Metric (GQM) method, to create useful security metrics.

Choosing Good Metrics

The security metrics literature often devotes space to defining metrics and discussing what characteristics make a metric good or bad. More often than not, books and articles about security metrics state that good metrics can be expressed only in numbers, and if a metric cannot be expressed in numbers, it is bad by definition. This implies that if you cannot measure something numerically, then you cannot measure it, analyze it, or understand it at all.

Holders of this opinion often invoke a quotation from the nineteenth century scientist William Thomson, a.k.a. Lord Kelvin, who said that unless you can express your measurements in numbers, your knowledge is poor, unsatisfying, and unscientific. Many of the books, articles, and general championing of IT security metrics cite Kelvin to support their preference for quantitative measurement. My response when someone quotes Kelvin to me is to ask them to rephrase their support of quantitative metrics in the form of a number. I have yet to meet anyone who can provide me quantitative evidence that shows why numbers make better metrics and provide more satisfactory knowledge than other forms of measurement. Instead, the person will tell me stories, recount anecdotes, and cite the opinions of others. At that point, depending on my mood, I will decide whether or not to hold the person to their adopted standard and make the case that he doesn't know what he is talking about. If I'm irritated, I might remind him that Lord Kelvin also believed in the existence of the ether and said X-rays would prove to be a hoax, but I usually try not to be a jerk about it. As an academic, my Ph.D. research depended on a blend of quantitative and qualitative methods, which means I often have a different perspective on measurement and research, and questions and answers, than physicists or engineers.

As will be sometimes painfully clear in this book, this multimethod approach to inquiry has carried over significantly into my perspective regarding IT security metrics. I believe not only that nonquantitative approaches to measurement are possible in our world, but that they are necessary and vital, because security is inherently a social process as much as a technical one. The debate between the merits of quantitative and qualitative research and, more generally, between those of the hard sciences and the social sciences, has been ongoing for decades and is well beyond the scope of this book.

I must respectfully disagree with those in the security metrics field who discount nonquantitative metrics out of hand. I find it ironic that the evidence presented against qualitative measurement is itself qualitative. It is ironic because the argument itself shows how people use empirical data: raw facts or numbers do us little good.

Instead, we engage evidence so that we can interpret it, and it is the interpretation of the data rather than the data itself that provides us value.

From a security perspective, understanding how the CISO *thinks* about security or what the e-mail administrator *believes* is the best way to approach a problem is just as important as quantitatively analyzing data produced by logs or tools. Measuring and improving IT security is about asking the right questions to reduce uncertainty and improve operations, not about arbitrarily deciding which questions and answers quite literally count or do not count.

Security metrics should be about choosing the best methods to determine what you need to know about security so that you can understand and improve your operational processes, within the resource constraints you face. Measuring a complex phenomenon such as your IT security requires an equally sophisticated and complex approach. Oversimplification of both the problems and the solutions will introduce more risk rather than removing it.

In Chapter 12, I talk about the characteristics of organizations in high-risk environments and how maintaining an appreciation for complexity is a secret to their successful operations. For now, understand that an appreciation of complexity means realizing that you cannot solve or even measure everything. Your metrics should be about choosing what you will measure and what you will improve while appreciating that you may not know what you may not know. It is not bad to use a few key metrics or to decide that certain metrics are outside of the organization's resources at the time (real qualitative measurement is often more expensive and difficult to do correctly). But if you fall into the trap of always choosing simple or easily obtained answers, this becomes a serious risk for your security.

When metrics are limited or restricted to simplistic categories such as good or bad, people may ignore some measurement methods that would be useful to them simply because some expert said that they were not valuable. Worse, if you believe that only numbers make for good metrics, you may be tempted to numerically label things that have no business being expressed quantitatively. At the end of the day, you must decide what you need to know, regardless of what is recommended by others who are not as familiar with your security environment and challenges. Measurement is always a local activity, performed within the context of individual and organizational understanding. Few arbitrary limits should be placed on how you go about achieving your understanding of security operations if those efforts are rational and methodical. A definition is always a good place to start.

Defining Metrics and Measurement

I define *metric* broadly to mean some standard of measurement. I particularly like this definition because it is meaningless unless it combined with an understanding of the word *measurement*. Recall that metrics are a result and measurement is an activity. Measurement is defined as the act of judging or estimating the qualities of something, including both physical and nonphysical qualities, through comparison to something else. Usually the things being measured are not compared to one another directly, but to some accepted standard of measurement—which circles back around to the original definition of *metric*. Thus metrics are standards of measurement, and measurement is the comparison of things, usually against standards. Often these standards are expressed in numerical units that provide standard metrics for qualities such as length, weight, or quantity. But metrics don't have to be expressed in this way.

Measurement allows us to do more than count and compute things. Remember that measurement did not originate in scientific inquiry, but rather in social relationships between individuals and groups of people. The division of hunt, harvest, or spoils based upon social status and the equivalencies necessary for trade and barter are measurement practices that significantly predate metrics being used for scientific analysis.

In addition to allowing for the rational analysis of security systems and activities, metrics can provide social and organizational benefits:

- Measurement allows us to predict things. The inferential statistical analysis of security data can compare samples and populations, providing generalizations beyond the immediate data.

- Measurement allows us to move beyond subjective language and individual experience by providing a common framework for the observation and comparison.

- Measurement helps us deal with disagreement and error, because it allows us to standardize our criteria and values and then assess our results against these agreed-upon baselines.

- Measurement promotes fairness by requiring everyone to adhere to the same accepted standards, whatever those standards may be.

- Measurement allows us to refine our descriptions of things as our metrics become more sophisticated; over time, the distinctions we can make become more precise.

Nothing Either Good or Bad, but Thinking Makes It So

As you develop your security metrics, you should be less concerned with what makes a metric intrinsically good or bad and much more concerned with how you develop measurement projects that provide value and organizational benefits to your security program. This means taking the time to develop metrics that are based on your unique requirements and not relying on "out-of-the-box" metrics that you apply without thinking about what the measurement is supposed to achieve.

Most security programs today already collect more data than they analyze, and metrics that generate unexamined data just add more to the pile. These are the types of metrics I would consider intrinsically bad, because they add no value to the security program and may even produce additional uncertainty and risk. What makes a metric good has less to do with the innate qualities of the metric and more to do with how you approach the measurement. If you want to know whether or not your metric is good, consider your answers to three basic questions.

Do You Understand the Metric?

Recall the general risk assessment matrix from Chapter 1, placed in the context of the preceding definitions. Can it be described in terms of a security metric? Sure it can. Building a risk matrix is an act of judging or estimating the qualities of something through comparison to something else, to some standard of measurement. The risk matrix is an *instrument* for the measurement.

But what exactly is the something being measured and what is the standard to which that something is compared? Here is where things get tricky. Based on how the matrix is described and used throughout the security world, the something being measured would be the risk to whatever system or organization is the target of the assessment. The standard of measurement therefore would be the combined risk score that determines where in the matrix the risk falls, be it very high, very low, or somewhere in between. But this is not accurate, because the data that has gone into the construction of the matrix does not directly involve the system itself or the threats to the system (some of which may only be the subject of speculation), or the realization of probable loss (which cannot be fully known until after a security incident has occurred). Instead, the data that is used to build the matrix are the statements of the people that (hopefully) understand the system in question and have enough expertise and experience to estimate the risk to the system. These statements do not measure actual risk, but rather what people think the risk may be (or at least what they are willing to say they think).

The problem is not that the risk assessment is bad measurement, but that the way many security professionals using the matrix have defined it guarantees that it will not be used effectively. When you use a tool improperly, it tends to give you poor results. We know that a risk assessment involves human judgment and cannot be completely accurate. The proper approach to the resulting uncertainties is to define, understand, and reduce them.

There are accepted methods for increasing the accuracy of judgment and prediction under uncertainty, including expert calibration and training to make estimates more precise and to leverage large bodies of past event data on which to base future extrapolations. These techniques require expertise and work on the part of the organization measuring the risk.

IT security capabilities are often too immature to effectively handle all the variables. Instead, risk assessments result in a bad mix of turning opinions into numbers (because 1–100 looks more credible than high/medium/low), treating estimates as facts (because you can't tell your boss that your made-up numbers may also be wrong), and then rationalizing away failure by saying that the assessment was qualitative so no one should have expected accuracy to begin with. Poor results do not mean the risk matrix is flawed any more than a disappointing attempt at using a hammer as a can-opener means the hammer is flawed. Improper understanding of a problem increases the probability that you will choose the wrong tool.

When selecting metrics, be sure that you have given adequate thought to what you are trying to accomplish, and this includes more than just the immediate thing that you are trying to measure. You should take into account a number of considerations:

- The underlying reason for the measurement. Metrics designed to understand security are different from metrics designed to respond to a request for metrics.

- The audience for the results of the metrics. Do not assume that everyone thinks of security metrics (or security itself, for that matter) in the same way that you do.

- The qualities or characteristics of your security program that you are trying to judge. It might be easier to measure an increase in attempted insider attacks over a given period of time, but those metrics will probably not explain the conditions that gave rise to the increase.

- The data. You should be able to articulate what observations you made as part of your metrics, and how you made them. Are you actually observing the quality or characteristic you are trying to measure? If not, what *are* you observing, and does that impact your analysis and decisions based on the metrics?

Do You Use the Metric?

I have been involved in delivering security consulting reports to customers for well over a decade, and most of these reports described the results of extensive and detailed measurements of the security vulnerabilities identified in customer networks. These metrics are sought after and usually well received by customers who hope to understand more about their security posture. Most of these customers do something with at least some of the resulting data, but experience has taught me that few customers actually use all the information that they contracted for. The same holds true for many other security-related data sources. Robust logging, monitoring, and event capture are all touted as important features by security product vendors, and security managers now have ready sources for metrics data being piped in from any number of systems. How is all this data used?

I am certainly not saying that you must use every single bit of security data that you collect, in real time, to have a mature measurement program. Measurements will need to be classified and prioritized, just like any other business information asset. But from a security metrics perspective, the point of capturing data is to reduce your uncertainty about aspects of your security activities.

Having no information regarding an element of security represents a certain state of uncertainty in that *you don't know* about that element. But collecting metrics data on the element means that now, technically, *you do know* about that element because you have been making observations regarding it. If you use the data, you eliminate some of your uncertainty about that element. However, when you do not use the metrics data you are collecting, you actually add to your uncertainty and maybe your risk. In Chapter 1 I described how security metrics data is potentially discoverable during litigation. How much worse is a breach when it turns out that you actually knew about the vulnerability that led to the damage and loss in question because it had been identified on two previous network scans but was never remediated?

There are many reasons to collect security data that you may not use immediately, forensics being at the top. In the event of a breach, you want to be able to reconstruct the events leading up to it. Most organizations collect data to be able to reconstruct the past.

Many organizations also implement defined records and document retention policies to provide a balance between the risks of not keeping enough information on hand and those of keeping too much. In the current environment of compliance and e-discovery, it is unwise to keep any information for longer than you need to do so. And if you are not using the information, why keep it at all? Your metrics should follow the same logic, and you should understand all the metrics that you have defined for your security program, why they were selected, and how they are used. The metrics catalog should be regularly reviewed, and if it turns out that some metrics are not utilized or acted upon, you should consider why you are even measuring those aspects of your security program.

Do You Gain Insight or Value from the Metric?

Security metrics are local. While a global set of security metrics with cross-industry adoption would enable companies to compare their performance in a standardized way similar to what occurs in other industries, we are not there yet. Today's security metrics are about individual organizations and enterprises making observations regarding their own environments and attempting to measure those environments accordingly. But there is nothing inherently wrong with this situation, and it has a lot to do with the immaturity of the security industry in general.

Today local metrics are more valuable, but when enough companies have robust local security measurement data, the industry will be ready to improve and mature as a whole by sharing data for mutual benefit. In many ways, the whole current metrics push is indicative that this may be beginning to develop. Your organization likely has security concerns that you need to understand better to make improvements and increase the value of your operations. While it would be nice to know what your main competitor is doing to address its security concerns, this knowledge is currently a luxury. If it turned out the competitor's security was worse than your own, you probably wouldn't consider that justification for lowering your own posture, although you might feel a bit better about what you've done. Until an accepted standard of security performance metrics is available, what your peers and competitors are doing doesn't really matter. You have to do what is necessary to protect your corporate interests and justify your security infrastructure against your own tolerance for risk and reward.

The local nature of security metrics is exactly the reason why blanket categorization of these metrics does not work. Assuming that you understand the metrics you have chosen, including the limitations they may impose on your knowledge, and assuming that you use the metrics that you select, the only real question is whether or not those metrics are giving you more insight than you had before you started using them. You may be collecting hard, quantitative data regarding system vulnerabilities and using that information to track remediation efforts over time. Or you may be using social media to conduct informal opinion surveys of users' security attitudes and behaviors in the workplace. To state that either of these (or any of the myriad other ways that we can acquire information) is better or worse than the other is inappropriate. What matters is that you can assess the value that you get out of the metric and that the value you get is proportionate to the effort that you put into measuring to begin with.

What Do You Want to Know?

Many factors influence how useful a metric will be for a particular organization or purpose. Beneath these factors lies a more fundamental question: What are you trying to understand about your security environment and operations? Your answers will often depend on other, related questions about the nature of your enterprise. What kind of organization are you? What are your corporate goals? What is your business model? What information assets are more or less valuable to you? Surprisingly, figuring out what the organization wants or needs to know is often a neglected step in setting up a security metrics program. Rather than being driven by questions, metrics are often chosen because they are simple or easy to accomplish, or someone else says they are important. The result is that the metrics end up defining the problems and driving the questions. If you have not specifically considered and defined what you want to know through the use of security metrics, everything becomes exploratory, and you will have a much more difficult time assessing how effective your efforts towards knowledge were or are.

To Count or Not to Count

I have already covered the complementary nature of quantitative and qualitative metrics, as well as my arguments with those who believe anything not expressed numerically is a bad metric. Some aspects of security make for excellent quantitative data sources, and this data is also usually the most easily available, cheapest, and least ambiguous data regarding the security environment. In fact, we almost certainly do not leverage this data enough in our security reviews and assessments, and this may explain why the security metrics literature has swung to the side of overemphasizing quantitative metrics as best practice.

In the context of the various benefits of measurement mentioned earlier in the chapter, quantitative data allows for more precise and standardized comparison and even predictive power, with less reliance on the subjective language and interpretations of people doing the measuring. Numbers possess an unmistakable power to persuade, which is probably why we try to turn so many things into numbers. But it is important to remember that numbers must be interpreted just like any other data. They do not speak for themselves but instead must be reconciled with the standards of measurement to which they are associated.

Consider temperature as an example. Say your local weather forecast tells you that tomorrow will be twice as warm as it was today. If you are in the United Kingdom and today it was 10° Celsius, which is a little chilly, then tomorrow is looking to be quite a pleasant day. But in the United States this statement means that today's mild 50° Fahrenheit will give way to a brutal 100° scorcher tomorrow. And if we're speaking in Kelvin, then you should enjoy today's 283° weather while it lasts because tomorrow we are all going to be roasted alive.

Numbers taken out of context can be as misleading and as confusing as any uninformed opinion. Security metrics already suffer from these distortions at times. The example of the vendor-sponsored Internet security report in Chapter 1, which correlated rise in vulnerabilities with a decline in security, shows how a lack of specificity regarding the scales or standards of data can make your findings less credible.

Just because you have an unquestioned quantitative measurement about some state of your security program does not mean that the data means anything. A 100 percent increase in the number of security incidents over a month holds different implications if you had one incident last month or if you had 100 incidents. Numbers may not lie, but the people who use them are under no such restrictions.

Again the problem is often definitional. Some will argue that qualitative metrics are not even possible because *by definition* a metric is expressed in numbers. That's not true, but I understand the argument. Definitions are the way that we standardize the meaning of words, the way we *measure* that meaning if you will. If you have never considered another meaning to a word, then that usage will make no sense to you, regardless of any sense it may make to others. You may recognize the word but not the context.

If your definition of a metric is an easily attainable number that reflects a state of affairs, then much of what I'm going to propose is not going to seem like measurement. But if you apply a definition of metrics that says they are standard expression of the act of comparing things, then what I'm proposing may seem perfectly valid. The question is how married you are to your own definitions. We all face the prospect sometimes of being trapped by our preconceptions.

One way to avoid these traps is to contextualize your metrics with the tried-and-true 5 Ws (and one H) formula: who, what, when, where, why, and how? If you can describe the security knowledge that you want to obtain in terms of these simple questions, it becomes much easier to decide whether quantitative or qualitative metrics are your best bet.

Who, What, When, Where?

If you accept that most of your desired security knowledge will involve knowing issues of who, what, when, where, why, and how in relation to your security program and environment, then you can likely address two-thirds of your knowledge with quantitative metrics. Identities, activities, events, and locations are all highly adaptable to numbers and counting, and can yield very useful data:

- ■ **Who?**   Which users have access to sensitive information? Who in the organization consistently chooses weak passwords?

- ■ **What?**   What ratio of the company's systems is not configured according to company security policy? Is the security training and awareness program effective?

- ■ **When?**   How often does management review the company's security strategy? Are security incidents more likely to occur during or outside of normal business hours?

- ■ **Where?**   Which organizational units have the fewest security policy violations per month? What is the most common source of reconnaissance scans against the corporate network perimeter?

Most diagnostic and operational information regarding security can be obtained using metrics like these, with quantified data that can be analyzed, compared, and even generalized in some cases.

These metrics make up the backbone of a robust security measurement program, assuming that you understand the metrics you choose, that you use them, and that they provide you with insight that makes for more effective decision making. Metrics can often be automated as well, making collection and analysis easier. And because of the relatively unambiguous nature of the questions, the answers can be made equally unambiguous and objective. I'd say every security manager in the industry has some set of metrics that answer who/what/when/where questions. But this leaves a third of our security insight unaccounted for.

How and Why?

If having the facts was all we needed to make decisions, life would probably be a lot less complicated. From criminal investigations, to business school case studies, to historical documentaries, people do not satisfy themselves with just the facts. Facts give us the dots, but we must still connect them if we want to understand anything in our world.

The history of human science is one of collecting data not for the purposes of knowing who, what, when, and where, but because we are really interested at the end of the day with the how and why. Not every IT security decision depends upon understanding the answers to these two remaining questions, but if we do not make an attempt to understand them in some cases, we accept by default that our security will always have blind spots and risks into which we have no visibility.

Security technologies and controls are complex systems, and understanding how they impact security at a systems level involves more than just simple metrics. So do efforts to understand security as a psychological instead of a technical process, one in which people make choices based on whether or not they feel safe taking a particular action. These characteristics become far more interpretive:

- **How?** What are the most expensive bottlenecks in our current patch management process? Which user workflows are most closely aligned with the company's e-discovery strategy?

- **Why?** What is the root cause of the increase in virus infections over the past 12 months? Has the economic downturn made the organization more susceptible to insider threats?

Understanding people and the organizations they create together socially means exploring such things as ethical and behavioral norms, personal motivations, and even individual experiences (commonly known as "stories"). It's enough to make a hardcore objectivist engineer's skin crawl. But qualitative measurement techniques are designed specifically to get at this data in rigorous and verifiable ways. I will be spending much more time in coming chapters describing methods and techniques for qualitative metrics, but for now I will leave it at this: Quantitative metrics can give you a lot of information that you can use to support your security decisions. But you won't fully understand your security environment and its effectiveness until you measure and explore the hows and whys that exist behind the numbers.

Observe!

A legitimate concern of skeptics of qualitative metrics is that that data collected from this type of measurement does not reflect what is actually going on. Asking people about whether or not their system has current virus signatures on a survey, for example, is not the same as assessing the virus signatures to ensure they are up to date. The former leaves a lot of room for guessing, confusion, and misinformation on the part of the person responding to the question. This same concern is equally legitimate when it comes to quantitative metrics, which also produce data that may not reflect what is actually going on.

Where qualitative data may prove inaccurate, quantitative data often proves incomplete. You can set up 50 different quantitative security metrics in the data center, ranging from badge reader access statistics, to login information, to the time reporting data of the operations staff, but these are not the same as knowing the people and the environment that make up that data center. The data will not tell you about culture or interpersonal quirks, perhaps that a few especially security-savvy staffers carry the load for the rest, or that security incident handling differs by business unit based on social networks rather than company policy. These insights might be common knowledge among the staff, but you'll never know about them if you don't ask the right questions. Observation includes listening to people, and security pros have a lot of experience and insights to offer (most are just waiting for someone to ask them what they think). Metrics are about decision support, and any information that helps a decision-maker is valuable—anyone can blindly follow numbers.

My point here is that the main challenge of metrics is not whether we can make them quantitative as often as possible, but whether we can make them *empirical* as often as possible. Empirical metrics, put simply, are based on direct observation and experience. Empirical data is produced when the metric uses methods that rely on our senses, whether as a result of actually looking at (or listening to, or touching) the thing being measured (for instance, measuring configuration errors by reviewing the configuration files and counting them up), or by experiment (changing a security process and observing whether that change affects the outcome of the process). One of my favorite examples of an empirical security metric came during a business impact analysis at a client. As we were asking a system administrator how he knew some of his machines were business critical he explained that, if a particular server's purpose was not documented or known, he would unplug it. He measured criticality based on how quickly the users of the machine freaked out. I don't recommend this as a best practice security metric, but it certainly has the potential to generate a lot of empirical data.

A lot of critics of qualitative metrics make the mistake of assuming that qualitative means "not empirical," but this is actually wrong and shows a lack of understanding of real qualitative research methods. Empirical qualitative measurement is exactly like its quantitative cousin in that it is based on observation and experience. Where the two differ substantially is regarding what is actually being observed.

At the risk of generalizing, where quantitative metrics gather data in regard to anything that can be counted, qualitative metrics focus on measuring the activities, behaviors, and responses of people. Of course, people can be counted, too, but qualitative measurement seeks to understand how and why people do what they do and not just the mechanics of those activities. Qualitative security metrics are concerned with issues of organizational behavior, culture, and politics and with the interactions between people in what, as technical as it may be, is fundamentally a social environment. And to measure these security attributes requires empirical data and methodical techniques.

To return once again to the example of the "qualitative" risk assessment, you cannot say that this activity empirically measures the organization's risks, because those are not observed. But these assessments do collect empirical data every time they ask someone to offer a judgment regarding what that risk may be. The secret is always to remember what it is you are really looking at.

GQM for Better Security Metrics

Up to this point, I have emphasized that, in selecting IT security metrics, it is more important that you know what you are trying to accomplish and to let this drive your measurement efforts than to let the metrics decide this for you. Starting with metrics is akin to hiring a general contractor to start building your house before you have engaged the architect. This is indicative of a common complaint more generally found in security (and IT in general), because it seems that often our infrastructures and systems do not seem to quite align with higher level business strategies.

As you consider developing your security metrics program, it would be nice to have a way to build that alignment in up front, so that you can always be reasonably sure that you are measuring what you should be measuring to meet your specific objectives. Luckily, there is a great way to do just that—one that comes out of the field of empirical software engineering called the *Goal-Question-Metric (GQM) method*.

What is GQM?

GQM is a simple, three-step process for developing security metrics. The first step in the process involves defining specific goals that the organization hopes to achieve. These goals are not measurement goals, but objectives that measurement is supposed to help achieve. The goals are then translated into even more specific questions that must be answered before assessing whether the organization has achieved or is achieving the goals. Finally, these questions are answered by identifying and developing appropriate metrics and collecting empirical data associated with the measurements. The method ensures that the resulting metrics data remains explicitly aligned with the higher level goals and objectives of the measurement sponsors. Figure 2-1 illustrates the basic GQM method.

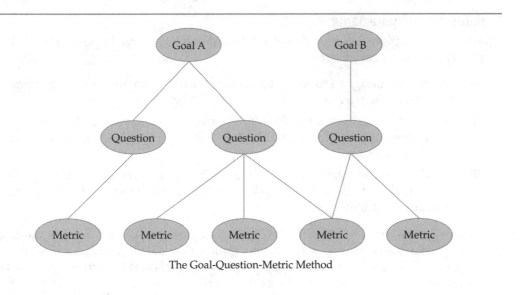

The Goal-Question-Metric Method

Figure 2-1. The GQM method provides direct alignment between metrics and goals. Note that metrics may be shared between goals and questions.

Background

The GQM method traces its roots back through software engineering practices into the 1970s, primarily through the academic and industry research conducted by Victor Basili of the University of Maryland. Originally developed to support NASA, GQM was designed to move testing for software defects from the qualitative and subjective state it was currently in to an empirical model in which defects would be measured against defined goals and objectives that could then be linked to results.

It may be difficult to believe today that software design and testing was ever non-empirical, but every scientific and technical discipline goes through phases of maturing sophistication. IT security is no different—part of the reason this book and others like it are written. But I digress. In developing GQM, Basili and his successors built a simple and elegant framework for aligning software metrics with software goals. Since it was first proposed, GQM has been studied and used to improve software measurement and testing in many environments. And yet, somewhat amazingly, GQM has not suffered any significant methodology bloat or major modification in the nearly three decades that it has been in use. Part of the reason may be because GQM was born and has lived in a primarily academic environment and for whatever reason was not widely adopted by consultants with a vested interest in making something simple and open into something complex and proprietary. But another reason is that very simplicity itself. GQM is immediately intuitive and functional, and any attempt to improve on what it offers would seem to be an attempt to gild the lily.

Benefits and Requirements

Using GQM to build your security metrics provides at least three important benefits to a security measurement program:

- Metrics are designed from the top down, starting with goals and objectives, rather than from the bottom up.

- Measurement activities are inherently constrained and bounded by the goals set for the project, reducing the chances that the project loses focus or suffers from "scope creep."

- Metrics are customized to the unique needs and requirements of the organization, which are reflected in the goals that the organization sets for its security measurement activities.

Achieving the benefits of the GQM method does, however, place certain demands on the organization implementing it. Chief among these demands is the requirement that the organization make the effort to define properly the goals and objectives against which they want to measure. If you are exploring IT security metrics, the first requirement in your efforts should be to understand what you are trying to accomplish. Do you want to have more visibility into your security operations or posture? Are you trying to ensure that you will pass next month's audit against some regulatory requirement? Different goals will naturally involve measuring different aspects of the security program. In some cases, overlap will occur, as some metrics answer multiple questions and some questions support more than one goal, as illustrated in Figure 2-1. But if the goal is not stated, or is vague and unclear, any attempt at measurement becomes problematic.

GQM also encourages a project-oriented measurement activity structure. Goals are specific and bounded, as opposed to broad and open-ended, and must relate back to some system, process, or characteristic of your security program if they are to be measurable and verifiable. Measurement projects allow you to stay focused and in control of the measurement activities you undertake. But these smaller component projects do not have to stand alone and should not. Metrics created through GQM result in catalogs that can be shared and reused across measurement projects over time, and the data analysis and results of individual measurement projects become the building blocks for broad and ongoing security improvement capabilities. I will discuss how GQM supports the larger security improvement program in later chapters, but for now let us concentrate on using the methods to produce solid security metrics.

Setting Goals

Goals give GQM measurements their power, so setting appropriate goals becomes the most important part of the metrics process. But it is not always easy to develop good goals. Effective goals require us to move from abstract ideas to specific commitments. "I'm going to be a better person" is all well and good, but "I'm going to spend ten percent of my free time and income helping people less fortunate than myself" is a different goal entirely. The latter goal provides a set of assumptions and commitments that can be measured and verified. Who's to say whether or not I failed to meet the former?

Many of the goals I see in my security work involve some variation of the goal of being a better person. I see customers setting goals to "improve our security," "protect sensitive information more effectively," or "reduce our vulnerabilities," and then moving on to the methods and activities they think they need to meet those goals. Later these organizations may find that they cannot effectively articulate their success or the value of their efforts, or that a goal proved so open-ended that it has morphed through several iterations and now has little in common with the original objectives that drove those efforts. As we work toward better metrics and improved security, we cannot escape the fact that we need to work on creating good security goals first. And good goals under the GQM method share several common characteristics.

Good Goals Are Specific

The difference between a dream and a goal is that dreams are open-ended. Goals involve nailing down the details. The more you define the attributes and milestones of your goal, the better that goal will be. Making your goal specific also makes it easier to measure your results. Keeping the goal too general or vague reduces the value of your accomplishments even if you succeed.

General success makes it very difficult to tie what you actually did to what you committed to do, or to figure out which of your successes overcame which of your mistakes to get you across the finish line. Success could have simply been a product of dumb luck or other coincidences that had nothing to do with your actions.

The same holds true for failure. Without specific goals, you run a high risk of seeing your goal misinterpreted, or even hijacked, as situations and circumstances change. Goals need to be flexible, but flexibility should be about consciously altering known quantities and not about completely changing course midstream because your goal could be interpreted in several different ways.

Good Goals Are Limited

As the specifics of your goal show you how complex even simple problems can become, it pays to limit what you try to accomplish in a single effort. We often hear two competing pieces of advice coming from the common wisdom. We are told that we shouldn't limit ourselves. Limit yourself artificially and you never know what you could have achieved. But at the same time, paradoxically, we are also told that we should know our limits. Extend your capabilities too far and you risk failure and even disaster. So how do we reconcile the two? These sayings actually reflect two aspects of the same problem.

Good goals are limited in the sense that they involve a bounded scope of accomplishment that is also well understood. Limiting a goal does not mean making the goal so easily achieved that it is no longer challenging. Instead, good goals have defined boundaries, which may include a business unit, a particular system, or a concept such as worm defense or compliance with an industry regulation. You do not have to have all the answers, but a good goal will at least have clearly defined the problem space in which those answers exist.

Limiting your goals does not mean that they lack strategic scope, but rather that strategy is embedded in clear hooks at the boundaries that allow goals to be chained into a series of interrelated tactical activities that becomes greater than the sum of its parts. If a goal is too strategic, details become lost in the grand picture. But as any builder of systems can tell you, if you lose control of the details you lose control of the whole.

Good Goals Are Meaningful

The worst goals you can imagine do not mean anything. Actually, the absolute worst goals are not only meaningless, but also known to be meaningless by most or all of the people involved. When a goal is meaningless, it negatively impacts everything involved. Objectives are not achieved, decisions regarding the goal are uninformed, and participant morale suffers. Two primary ways that you can ensure that your goals have meaning are to construct them so they are both attainable and verifiable.

Attainable   An attainable goal can actually be met. Attainable goals are not open-ended but are developed in the context of a particular project or activity that has a beginning and an ending. At the end of the activity, whether you measure its duration in terms of time or in terms of some other criteria such as project milestones, you assess the activity against your stated goal. Attainable goals also involve deciding how much you want to attempt, your level of commitment, and your tolerance for risk of failure. Attainability involves striking the delicate balance between attempting too little and attempting too much. Developing attainable goals often requires that you do some research to decide where these limits currently exist, and then incorporate those insights into a goal's overall limits and boundaries.

Verifiable   In verifying our goals, we decide up front what criteria will be used to indicate our success or failure at achieving the goals. To make our goals meaningful we must be able to show not only that we have attained some end, but whether we in fact did or did not attain it. Depending on your goals, verification can be accomplished through positive indicators that prove the goals were achieved—for instance, a predetermined increase in the number of users who have formally reviewed and acknowledged the corporate security policy. Or verification can be accomplished through refutation by predefining criteria that indicates the goal was not achieved, such as a failed audit. Verification ensures that everyone knows exactly where they stand in regards to the goal, and it keeps all involved individuals honest about how much was accomplished.

Measurement is implicit in the concept of verification. While some goals may be straightforward (you either pass the audit or you do not), most goals will involve gathering necessary data to help you understand how well the goal was achieved or by how much it was missed. GQM addresses measurement against set goals directly, as you shall see.

Good Goals Have a Context

Few goals are made in a vacuum. Even my New Year's resolution to lose ten pounds involves multiple circumstances including how bloated I'm feeling after holiday season gorging, my wife's off-the-cuff reminder that I'm due for a physical, and my watching a neighbor take his new racing cycle out for a 50-mile ride (showoff…).

When we set goals in an organizational context such as IT security, we are also reacting to various situations and circumstances. Perhaps we suffered a security breach recently, or internal audit is knocking on our door for an annual review, or our peer on the network side just published an internal case study on her success rate against virus outbreaks (showoff…). Effective goals recognize and address the contexts in which they are attempted, from the stakeholders involved and the desired outcomes, to the unique environment in which the goal is being attempted. These are often considerations that we undertake almost unconsciously, knowing the lay of the land in which we operate, but a good goal will have made at least some of these considerations explicit.

Good Goals Are Documented

After you have put the effort into designing effective goals, it makes sense to formalize them. A good goal will demand a level of documentation that captures and organizes all the salient attributes and parameters involved. If your goal doesn't seem to be something that you need to write down ("we're going to implement a data loss prevention strategy…"), it is probably not a well-constructed goal. Documenting your goals also serves as an easy way to capture and solidify the support of multiple stakeholders. Putting a goal into writing and requiring individuals responsible for assigning as well as achieving the goal to review and sign off on its details allows for negotiation and debate before the project begins, instead of recriminations and rationalizations that might occur after it ends.

The GQM method includes a basic template concept for articulating the goals of a security measurement or improvement project quickly and succinctly. Specific information is captured regarding the goal, including explicitly defining the basic attributes and criteria for success. The resulting information is incorporated into the template and used to create a basic statement of the goal. These components are shown in Table 2-1.

Goal Component	Description	Example
Outcome	The purpose of the project, what will be achieved	Improvement, assessment, understanding
Elements	The boundaries and objects (systems, processes, characteristics) involved in or impacted by the goal	Vulnerabilities, network components, regulatory compliance, system users
Perspective	The point of view taken to understand the goal	External attackers, compliance auditors

Table 2-1.   Goal Template for the GQM Method

After the components of the goal are defined, the template provides for the easy creation of a brief goal statement that captures the pertinent information necessary to begin working on the activity.

Let's use the example of a security manager considering a project to improve user compliance with corporate security policies that are not effectively disseminated or enforced by the organization. The goal components for the activity could be broken down as follows:

- **Outcome:** Increase
- **Element:** Enforcement of the corporate security policy
- **Element:** User awareness
- **Element:** User acknowledgement of security policy documents
- **Perspective:** Security manager

These components can then be combined into a simple, yet comprehensive statement: *The goal of this project is to increase the enforcement and awareness of the corporate security policy by increasing user acknowledgement of the company's security policy documents from the perspective of the security manager.*

Constructing goal statements this way forces the stakeholders involved to keep their goals limited, specific, and meaningful. The short format of the statement also makes it much easier to communicate and evaluate the goal, and the natural constraints imposed by limiting the number of attributes and targets reduces the likelihood that multiple goals will become conflated and confused. Multiple goals, such as those for complex projects, are effectively parsed into subcomponents that can be addressed and evaluated individually.

Asking Questions

Developing and documenting good goals is critical to effective security measurement in general, and to the GQM method in particular, but it is just the first step toward effective metrics. Although the goal statements produced by the GQM template enable stakeholders to share and review their goals easily, these documented goals do not contain enough information to allow stakeholders to evaluate whether or not the goal was successfully achieved.

Goal statements are conceptual in nature. They do not define how the attributes and targets of the goal will be operationally addressed. To develop that information, individual goals are translated into a series of questions that enable the components of the goal to be achieved or evaluated for success. These questions articulate the goal and the measurement project in terms of what objects or activities must be observed and what data must be collected to address the individual components of the goal statement.

Using the example of the security policy improvement project, how would you translate the goal statement into operational questions? Several questions are already implied by examining the goal components:

- What is the current level of enforcement of the corporate security policy?
- What is the current structure of the corporate security policy?

- Do employees read and understand the corporate security policy?
- Is enforcement of the security policy increasing?

Through the development of operational questions, the goal of the security improvement project can now be expressed in terms of tangible characteristics of processes, systems, and individuals that can be evaluated and measured. These questions remain tightly integrated with the overall goal of the project and ensure that any resulting data and conclusions remains aligned with the original intent of the stakeholders involved. GQM-derived questions also provide an intuitive second-order analysis of the resources that will be required to meet the goal by outlining the sources of data and resources necessary to provide adequate answers to the questions. The security manager in our example should immediately recognize that these questions mean she will need to understand specific details of the security policy and identify any data sources to which she does not have direct access.

Assigning Metrics

After questions have been developed to define the goal operationally, the goal can begin to be characterized at a data level, and metrics can be assigned that will provide answers. A key strength of GQM is that, by this point, designing metrics becomes much more intuitive, because only certain measurements will produce the data necessary to answer the very specific questions that the goal has produced. Many metrics are potentially able to answer these questions, and more emphasis can be placed on evaluating the feasibility of adopting certain metrics based on how difficult data may be to collect or how detailed the data needs to be. The questions also help the project stakeholders choose appropriate quantitative or qualitative measurement and analysis techniques in a way that is driven by the goal and not subject to arbitrary judgments about the metrics themselves.

Our intrepid security manager knows her goal and knows a few of the questions that she must ask to evaluate whether or not the project is achieving the goal. Now she uses those questions to develop a set of metrics by which she can measure achievement.

What Is the Current Level of Enforcement of the Corporate Security Policy?

Metrics supporting this question will involve data regarding how often security policies are violated within the company and how often the company takes action against these violations:

- Number of reported security policy violations in the previous 12 months
- Number of enforcement actions taken against policy violations in the previous 12 months

If there are fewer enforcement actions taken than there are violations, the policy is not being enforced in all situations. If there are no reported violations, this could mean that no one is violating the policy, but it more likely indicates that, not only is the policy not being enforced, but the company has little visibility even into how often employees are violating the policies. In this case, the goal of increasing enforcement may even develop a dependency on another goal—that of increasing the visibility into security policy violations, spawning another measurement project.

What Is the Current Structure of the Corporate Security Policy?

This question involves data different from measuring the frequency of an event. Understanding the structure of the security policy means measuring aspects of the policy infrastructure:

- Number of documents that make up the corporate security policy
- Format(s) of security policy documents (hard copy, HTML, PDF)
- Location(s) of security policy documents (content management system, static web page, three-ring binder)
- Types of policy acknowledgement mechanisms (e-mail notification of users, electronic acknowledgement of policy access or review, hard copy signoff sheet)
- Length of time since the last security policy review by management

The company's security policy may exist as a single document or as a set of documents that define policies, guidelines, procedures, and even configurations. Knowing the structure of the security policy aids decision-makers by identifying ways to make employee acknowledgment of the policy more efficient and the policy more enforceable.

Do Employees Read and Understand the Corporate Security Policy?

Measuring human understanding and behavior gets interesting and touches on many of the points made in this chapter. Understanding cannot really be observed directly unless you are a neuroscientist studying brain activity, and even then the results are open to interpretation and not particularly useful to our security manager. (Requiring brain scans of all employees will probably not lead to an acceptable return on investment for the policy project.) Instead, we measure understanding by observing how people behave and respond and comparing that data to what we agree is appropriate for someone who understood:

- Ratio of employee job descriptions that specify responsibility for following the corporate security policy
- Number of security policy awareness or training activities conducted in the previous 12 months
- Ratio of employees who have formally acknowledged the corporate security policy in the previous 12 months
- Results of a user survey asking how familiar users are with the policy and how appropriate and usable the policy is judged to be

Metrics of this kind can also provide good opportunities to explore alternative data sources and to combine observations of activities and processes with those of human responses for comparative purposes.

Is Enforcement of the Security Policy Increasing?

The questions and metrics so far have provided data that supports increasing security policy enforcement by describing the current environment. Without developing a sound baseline of performance, there can be no credible or verifiable way of judging whether the project is meeting or has met the goal. After the current performance baseline has been established, it becomes possible to consider metrics to define improvement or progress:

- Increase in security policy enforcement actions over baseline (expressed as either a raw count or a percentage, as appropriate)

- Increase in awareness of corporate security policy (number of awareness activities, number of user acknowledgements of the policy)

- Increase in efficiency of the security policy process (increased policy reviews, reduction in the number of policy documents or locations)

- Improved response from surveyed users on policy familiarity and usability

Using the data provided by these metrics, the security manager can analyze the effects of decisions or activities undertaken over the course of the project, describe how well the project achieved the goal, and produce conclusions and insights that can lead to more measurement and ongoing improvement over repeated activities.

Putting It All Together

Capturing and documenting GQM data for security measurement and improvement activities can be accomplished by expanding upon the GQM template for goal creation (Table 2-1). The full template includes the goal statement and associated goal components along with the questions and metrics necessary for fully implementing the project. This template can then be used as the baseline project charter and documentation. Table 2-2 shows the fully completed GQM template for the security policy enforcement project.

The Metrics Catalog

The GQM method results in a set of specific, documented metrics for a particular measurement project. These metrics are also tied directly to well-understood goals and questions regarding specific systems, processes, and characteristics of an IT security environment. Another strength of GQM is that the outputs of the methodology are naturally suited to the creation of metrics catalogs that can be reused over time and shared across projects as well as security and business organizations and stakeholders.

As seen in Figure 2-1, different goals and questions can rely on the same metrics for the data they need. As the metrics program becomes larger and more sophisticated, the structure and results of preceding measurement projects becomes invaluable in the brainstorming process that leads to the creation of new goals and projects. The new goal might be the direct result of the findings of a previous project. (In the security policy example, for instance, it was possible that the project would reveal not only that policies were not enforced but that violations were not even being reported, a situation requiring exploration.)

Goal Components	Outcome: Increase Element: Enforcement of security policy Element: User awareness Element: User acknowledgement of security policy documents Perspective: Security manager
Goal Statement	*The goal of this project is to increase the enforcement and awareness of the corporate security policy by increasing user acknowledgement of the company's security policy documents from the perspective of the security manager.*
Question	What is the current level of enforcement of the corporate security policy?
Metrics	Number of reported security policy violations in the previous 12 months Number of enforcement actions taken against policy violations in the previous 12 months
Question	What is the current structure of the corporate security policy?
Metrics	Number of documents included in the corporate security policy Format(s) of security policy documents Location(s) of security policy documents Types of policy acknowledgment mechanisms Length of time since the last security policy review by management
Question	Do employees read and understand the corporate security policy?
Metrics	Ratio of employee job descriptions that specify responsibility for following the corporate security policy Number of security policy awareness or training activities conducted in the previous 12 months Ratio of employees who have formally acknowledged the corporate security policy in the previous 12 months Results of a user survey asking how familiar users were with the policy and how appropriate and usable the policy was seen to be
Question	Is enforcement of the security policy increasing?
Metrics	Increase in security policy enforcement actions over baseline Increase in awareness of corporate security policy Increase in efficiency of the security policy process Improved response from surveyed users on policy familiarity and usability

Table 2-2.   GQM Project Definition Template (Security Policy Enforcement)

New measurement projects can also result as security personnel become more comfortable using GQM to develop their metrics and project sponsors become more impressed with the results. In these cases, previous project goals and questions can act as inspiration for new metrics or as easily modified templates to apply to other scenarios.

Managing a metrics catalog does not require any special tools, although you can get as sophisticated as you want. Simple capture of GQM templates for each measurement project in a central archive for use by the security staff is one way of ensuring that everyone's work can be reused and recycled. More sophisticated approaches to metrics cataloging might include building databases that permit more robust links between goals and metrics. Collaboration technology such as wikis are also a good fit for the metrics catalog, because they can be set up to allow metrics users to add content, comment on experiences with measurement projects, and dynamically grow the metrics program around a central repository of security-related data.

More Security Uses for GQM

I have already outlined how you might use GQM to develop goal-driven metrics for a particular project involving security policy enforcement. GQM is applicable to just about any situation in which you want to measure the security environment against some set of goals or objectives. The only limits are the ability of the organization to define specific goals and to commit resources to measurement projects. I will discuss detailed security measurement projects, including what to do after you have collected your metrics data, in later chapters. For now, we'll look at how GQM lets you build defined goals, questions, and metrics for a number of security measurement problems.

Measuring Security Operations

Measuring the day-to-day systems and activities that make up our security and data protection programs is perhaps the most ubiquitous activity of security professionals. We measure things so that we know what is going on, to determine whether immediate fires must be extinguished, and to demonstrate that we are earning our keep. GQM provides a way to structure and standardize operational security measurements. In many cases, this sort of data is already being collected, but applying GQM to the problem ensures that metrics do not end up "orphans" that are unconnected or aligned with specific security goals.

If you have metrics for which you collect data, but they are not tied to specific objectives, GQM can provide the basis for a "ground-up" thought exercise as you ask yourself what the data actually supports. If you can't answer that question, even the most "common sense" data starts to look suspect.

Example: Security-Related Downtime

Understanding how long your systems are up and available to users is a common IT metric. Understanding how security impacts availability is also important, particularly when you need to compare security to other IT challenges. Table 2-3 illustrates an example project for measuring security-related downtime.

Goal Statement	*The goal of this project is to understand security impacts on system availability by comparing security-related downtime to general availability from the perspective of the security team.*
Question	How often is the system down due to failure?
Metrics	Time between failures Failure duration Mean system availability
Question	How often is the system down due to maintenance?
Metrics	Time between maintenance Maintenance duration Mean system availability
Metrics	How often is downtime the result of a security event?
Question	Number of security events in time period Duration of event remediation

Table 2-3.   GQM Project for Security-Related Downtime

This scenario demonstrates the importance of the perspective component of the GQM template. For the security team, understanding how much impact on general availability results from security-related issues would be important. But from the perspective of a system user, downtime is downtime. Users usually don't care that they are grounded as a result of a security problem, a misconfiguration, or the fact that Bob accidentally unplugged the wrong box—they just want the system back up.

General Risk Assessment for Data Loss Prevention

I spent a bit of time in this chapter and the last critiquing general risk assessments as a measurement tool. But I do not believe that these assessments are as completely useless as some critics would contend. The challenge is to make them better; so it makes sense to adapt GQM to the challenge as a way of getting some closure on my arguments. A simplified example of a GQM project involving general risk assessment for data loss prevention (DLP) is illustrated in Table 2-4.

The use of confidence intervals and calibration of expert judgments are analytical techniques that allow you to move away from less-precise ranking scales (low–high, 1–10) that are often employed in security risk assessments. Detailed descriptions of how to use and apply these techniques to security measurement projects will be covered in later chapters.

Measuring Compliance to a Regulation or Standard

Metrics for daily operations are somewhat easier to grasp and are usually directly supported by information produced either by the systems under management or through well-understood metrics such as uptime or throughput. Measuring other environmental

Goal Statement	*The goal of this project is to understand the risks of sensitive data loss for the company by analyzing calibrated confidence intervals (CCIs) for likelihood and severity of losses from the perspective of company HR, legal, and IT experts.*
Question	How calibrated is the risk assessment?
Metric	Number of experts involved who have undergone calibration training
Question	How much sensitive data exists on the corporate network?
Metrics	CCIs for types of sensitive data CCIs for location of sensitive data
Question	What is the value of sensitive data under corporate control?
Metrics	CCIs for data value by type CCIs for external costs (legal, etc.) resulting from loss of data
Question	What vectors are most likely to contribute to data loss (e-mail, network penetration, malicious insider, etc.)?
Metric	CCIs for loss vectors

Table 2-4.   GQM Project for General DLP Risk Assessment

factors, such as regulatory compliance, challenges security managers to create metrics for something conceptual that cannot be directly observed ("compliance") by identifying empirical measurements they can use to find answers. In the case of regulatory controls, this can be accomplished by understanding the requirements promulgated under a particular regulatory framework and extrapolating compliance by measuring how well those requirements are met.

Compliance to Health Insurance Portability and Accountability Act Using NIST SP 800-66 Guidance

The Health Insurance Portability and Accountability Act (HIPAA) is a U.S. law that mandates, among other things, how personally identifiable healthcare information must be protected by healthcare entities covered under the law. Enforced through a series of regulations, including specific regulatory requirements for IT security, HIPAA requires covered entities to undertake a number of activities to achieve compliance. The U.S. National Institute of Standards and Technology (NIST) has developed a special publication, SP 800-66, that provides guidance for meeting these compliance requirements in language that is easier to understand than the formal legal jargon found in the law and accompanying regulations. A possible GQM project for HIPAA compliance is illustrated in Table 2-5.

Goal Statement	*The goal of this project is to evaluate the company's compliance with the HIPAA security regulations by comparing company knowledge and activities to the HIPAA compliance guidance for IT systems provided in NIST SP 800-66 from the perspective of regulatory auditors.*
Question	Does the company have a security management process?
Metrics	Number of assets and information systems that create, receive, transmit, or maintain electronic personal health information (EHPI) Number (percentage) of assets and information systems that have not been assessed for EHPI
Question	What are the risks to EHPI under the company's custodianship?
Metrics	Number of risk assessments performed by the company in previous 12 months Mean time between risk assessments
Question	How does the company manage risks to EHPI?
Metrics	Number of approved controls in the company's security controls baseline Ratio of addressable or supplementary to required security controls and implementation specifications

Table 2-5.   GQM Project for HIPAA Compliance Using NIST SP 800-66

HIPAA and NIST SP 800-66 have too many requirements to complete the entire template in Table 2-5. But the structure of GQM would allow you to create a complete template for the entire SP 800-66 guidance. Or you could choose to divide HIPAA requirements into smaller subprojects based on different aspects of the regulation (policy requirements versus technology requirements, for instance). The flexibility of GQM allows for either method to result in a metrics catalog that is tightly aligned with the overall goals in a formally documented way.

Measuring People and Culture

To close out these introductory examples, let's explore how you can use GQM to create metrics for elements of your security environment that you may have previously thought were relatively unmeasurable such as people, behavior, or motivation.

Measuring Tailgating Behavior and Motivation

My security experiences include physical IT security assessments, and in these situations I've observed a lot of tailgating (people using a secured entrance without authenticating by following another person who authenticates properly). If weak passwords are one of the most common logical banes of the security manager's existence, people tailgating into facilities has to be the physical counterpart. I've tailgated into sensitive buildings while passing and reading large "Don't Allow Tailgaters!" signs, as my accommodating new friend and I crossed the threshold. But I've always found it curious that, when asking why this occurs, organizations tend to throw up their hands. "It's just something you have to deal with," is a common reply. "Who knows why people do it?" is another. So the problem gets written off as, if not unsolvable, then at least not measurable, and efforts are put to find better technical solutions or to make the sign I read going in even larger (and maybe neon). As a social scientist, that strikes me as deliberately ignoring a lot of available empirical data.

Table 2-6 offers a possible GQM project for reclaiming some of that unknown information.

This project, of course, requires a bit of unorthodox thinking. Some of my clients have been reluctant to confront tailgaters at the time of the infraction, because this can be perceived as a disciplinary action or an interrogation. Yet at the same time, organizations recognize that if they cannot control their physical perimeters, they cannot hope to achieve effective information security.

Part of the problem, one that is not addressed in this project, is that most organizations have not measured the loss associated with physical breaches of IT security (another opportunity for metrics excellence!), so the full extent of the problem is unclear. If the organization knew it was losing hundreds of thousands of dollars due to physical breaches, it might decide it was worth confronting a few people on why they

Goal Statement	*The goal of this project is to understand the reasons for tailgating at company facilities by analyzing the perceptions and behaviors of individuals who tailgate from the perspective of the employee.*
Question	What is the general employee perspective on tailgating at the company?
Metric	Results of company-wide survey on opinions regarding motivations and impacts of tailgating on company IT security
Question	What are the common characteristics of tailgating at the company?
Metric	Results of passive observation of tailgating activities at a selection of company facility entrances during a two-week period
Question	Why do individuals engage in tailgating, either by tailgating themselves or by allowing tailgaters to enter?
Metric	Results of brief follow-up interviews (nondisciplinary) with observed tailgaters as part of an experimental IT security assessment

Table 2-6.   GQM Project for Analyzing Tailgating Behaviors

are behaving in this way. And this type of experiment does not need to be necessarily hostile. Often, in academic research, a small reward is given to survey or experiment participants. Tailgaters in this project could be assured that the interview is not disciplinary in nature, and then provided a $10 gift card as proof that their input is valued, even if the infraction is not.

My physical security clients recognized that their awareness campaigns were usually fairly ineffective (yet often expensive—neon signs do not grow on trees, after all). Understanding the real motivations for a person's behavior can provide insights into how to manage that behavior more successfully and can potentially improve the efficiency and return on investment of the security program in the process.

Applying GQM to Your Own Security Measurements

The GQM model does not relieve security professionals of their responsibility to understand what they are trying to accomplish. It is not a magic black box that will spit out good metrics from garbage inputs. Instead, GQM provides a logical and structured process for thinking about security, translating those thoughts into requirements, and then developing the data necessary both to document and meet requirements. GQM is a conceptual tool that reminds me of mind-mapping software. It does not give you ideas, but it helps you organize and structure your ideas in a way that allows them to be more valuable and productive.

You might try to apply GQM to some of your current security projects to determine whether it enhances your perspective on what you are trying to accomplish. At the least, GQM should help you to translate your goals into measurement activities and data in a systematic way and to document that process so that your projects are more precise and success is easier to evaluate. The metrics you create using GQM are the first step and the engine that drives forward movement of a larger framework for IT security improvement and are discussed in the next two chapters.

Summary

Debates exist within the IT security metrics community as to what constitutes a "good" metric, and many measurement proponents believe that only quantitative metrics are suitable or adequate for measuring security. But measurement has a number of definitions, and not all of them depend on using numbers. Measurement provides social as well as scientific benefits and can be defined as the judging of the qualities of a thing against accepted standards that may or may not be quantitative.

More important than deciding whether a metric is good or bad, quantitative or qualitative, security professionals should be more concerned with whether their metrics meet the following goals:

- They are well understood.
- They are used.
- They provide value and insight.

Arguments between quantitative and qualitative metrics may tend to ignore the fact that numbers require interpretation and standards as well and can be as misleading as any subjective statement of opinion when not properly presented or understood. And these different types of measurement address different questions. Who, what, when, and where questions can be more easily answered using quantitative metrics than questions of how and why.

When evaluating your security metrics program, begin by looking at the questions that you want to answer and then choose the best metrics (within your resource limits) to provide data and insight. These metrics, whether qualitative or quantitative, should be supported by empirical data, based upon direct observation of the phenomena at hand. This may require you to rethink what you first believed you were observing.

A valuable method for building security metrics can be found in the field of empirical software testing. The GQM method provides an elegant and intuitive process with which to develop metrics by requiring that the organization first develop goals that are bounded and specific, followed by operational questions that define how the goal is to be achieved and evaluated. These questions then allow a natural progression toward metrics and data that are tightly aligned with the original goals and are documented through easily understood and communicated templates that capture the appropriate GQM components of a measurement project. GQM is applicable across a wide variety of security measurement projects, including policy reviews, security operations, regulatory compliance, and even measuring security in terms of people's motivations and the culture within an organization.

Further Reading

Boehm, B., et al. *Foundations of Empirical Software Engineering: The Legacy of Victor R. Basili*. Springer, 2005.

Bradley, W. James, and K. Schaefer. *The Uses and Misuses of Data and Models: The Mathematization of the Human Sciences*. SAGE Publications, 1998.

Campbell, S. *Flaws and Fallacies in Statistical Thinking*. Dover, 2004.

Kaplan, A., and C. Wolf Jr. *The Conduct of Inquiry: Methodology for Behavioral Science*. Transaction Publishers, 1998.

VanderStoep, S., and D. Johnston. *Research Methods for Everyday Life: Blending Qualitative and Quantitative Approaches*. Jossey-Bass, 2009.

CHAPTER 3 | Understanding Data

E stablishing your goals, asking the questions that help you understand how to achieve those goals, and defining the metrics that allow you to answer your questions all inevitably lead you to the central component of any successful metrics program: data. IT security metrics, like any measurements, are really about collecting and analyzing data based on the observations that you make. The metrics are simply a means of organizing and defining the data. So all the rules of good metrics apply:

- You should understand your data.
- You should use your data.
- You should gain value and insight from your data.

You will learn about detailed methods of analyzing data in later chapters, but for now let's review types of data, possible sources of data that you may encounter or consider, and ways that data can be collected and normalized in support of your security metrics. You need to understand the different types of data, including quantitative and qualitative data, and the divisions that exist even within each of those categories. IT security today suffers from a tendency to mix and match different types of data and to then apply analysis techniques that are completely inappropriate to what is actually being observed, such as using statistical analysis on qualitative data.

What Are Data?

First of all, before we explore any other characteristics or meanings, the word *data* is technically considered to be a plural noun. So this section's header is grammatically correct. It would also be correct to say *your data do not support those security recommendations*. But for many, especially those outside the scientific community, the plural use of data looks awkward, and people prefer to use *data* as a singular noun, as in *data depends on how you look at it*, or *your data does not support those security recommendations*. Even some academics prefer the singular usage, and some insist upon it, such as physicist Norman Gray who posts his argument for the singular use at http://nxg.me.uk/note/2005/singular-data/.

In real life (as opposed to academia), it doesn't much matter—data is used and accepted both ways. But you should know your audience. Use *data* as a singular noun (*the data is...*) in front of a scientist, and you may appear to be less knowledgeable, reducing your credibility. Use it as a plural noun (*the data are…*) in front of your business colleagues, and you may look like you can't speak properly, which also tends to hurt credibility. With that caveat, I will try to use *data* primarily in the singular since I have found that industry audiences tend to be more comfortable with it. I will use it in the plural sense when I actually mean more than one, to avoid making redundant statements such as "data points" or "data observations." I can't promise I will always be consistent, but either way I won't be incorrect.

Definitions of Data

By definition, data is a form of information and is represented by the facts, quantities, figures, statements, symbols, and observations that we use for inquiry, reference, or analysis. We produce data every day as we go about our lives. Our eyes work with our brains to provide basic visual data from the light sources around us, our language capabilities provide more socially complex data as we ask our spouses and children at the dinner table about their days, and we process multi-dimensional data in the course of our jobs configuring our systems or reporting our status to management. Much of our data collection activities are unconscious and transparent to us, things that we just do as human beings. When we get more structured and pay more deliberate attention to the data that we collect because we have a purpose for it, we call those activities *measurement* or *research*, and these activities are typically divided into two broad types: quantitative and qualitative, concepts that I have covered a bit in previous chapters.

Data (points) vary, or differ, as you ask questions and make observations. So you will often see the concept of data going hand-in-hand with the idea of variables, things that can change, such as a person's gender, the OS running on a particular machine, or a system's anti-virus software. Data is the raw material of your metrics program, the stuff that you collect, examine, analyze, and refine to make effective decisions regarding how your security is functioning. We even use the term *raw data* to indicate data that has not been organized or processed, although the concept is relative. Firewall log data processed into a quarterly report might be considered finished by the firewall administrator, but it looks like raw data to the chief information security officer (CISO) preparing his annual report of all security activities for the board.

Data has also been conceptualized as part of a hierarchy that includes information, knowledge, and even wisdom. The general idea is that as data is given context through various analytical processes, it transforms through various states or stages. Also contributing to this increased sophistication are the experiences of those dealing with the data and its higher forms, until ultimately wisdom can appear to be an almost intuitive gift for understanding circumstances derived not only from the data at hand but from the insights generated using previous data, information, and knowledge as well.

The hierarchy, known as DIKW (for data-information-knowledge-wisdom), is often used in information science and other disciplines and is illustrated in Figure 3-1. The DIKW hierarchy is a simple, generalized model for imagining relationships between different ways of understanding the world. It can also be useful to IT security metrics development because it reminds us that data is not the only, or even the most important, aspect of what we are trying to achieve. Metrics and data represent the core of a larger process of understanding in which we try to constantly learn and improve over time. Corporate "wisdom" may not seem like an appropriate term, but sometimes there is no other explanation for those organizations that seem to be able to intuitively avoid situations that wreck others, even when all involved had access to similar data. Moving from metrics data to security wisdom will be one of the goals of the Security Process Management Framework proposed in the next chapter.

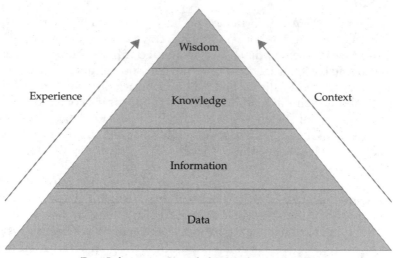

Figure 3-1.   The DIKW hierarchy shows how the context and experience allow data to be transformed into more sophisticated components of the continuum.

Data Types

I've already talked about quantitative and qualitative measurement, and, not surprisingly, these two approaches to security metrics produce different types of data stemming from the observations being made. Just like the research methods used to produce the data, neither type of data is intrinsically better or preferable to the other. Deciding which data is best depends on your understanding the questions that the data is supposed to help you answer. Understanding more about these data types can help you make decisions regarding which might better support your security metrics.

Quantitative Data

Quantitative data is expressed with numbers and analyzed statistically. Numerical data can reflect things that you can actually count, such as the number of installations of a particular OS in your network environment or the number of reconnaissance scans against your network perimeter in the past month. Numbers can also reflect changes in state along some scale, such as the temperature in your data center or the severity rating of an identified vulnerability. Scientific measurement identifies four major types or scales of data: nominal, ordinal, interval, and ratio.

Nominal Data   The nominal scale is the simplest, and sometimes the most misleading, scale for quantitative data. Nominal data is not really about numbers at all, but has to do with categories. Numbers are often used as labels for the categories involved, but this is not required. For example, say you are identifying the types of OS you have in your environment for a security review. You might assign OS type according to the nominal scale in Table 3-1.

The choice of numbers to represent OS types is arbitrary. You could have just as easily used letters (A, B, C…) or abbreviations of the OS name as your data, but numbers are often the first choice for nominal data sets. In nominal data sets, the fact that the data is represented as a number does not convey any meaning regarding the target of observation other than the category to which it is assigned. It does not measure anything intrinsic. But you can count the instances of categorical data, how many of Type 1, Type 2, and so on, are observed. For analytical purposes, this means that you can use nominal data to build frequency distributions and perform cross-tabulation if you have more than one set of nominal data. It is not appropriate to use statistical techniques such as the *mean* (commonly called the average, although the two are different), or the *median* (the middle value) on nominal data directly (how do you average three separate categories?), although *mode* (the most frequent value) works okay. I will cover these analytical techniques in detail in later chapters. For now, remember that the numbers associated with nominal data are used to divide your observations into different "buckets"—they do not indicate anything particularly quantitative about the things that go into those buckets.

Ordinal Data   Ordinal data uses numbers to describe a more complex relationship between the targets of observation than is found in nominal data. Where nominal metrics describe whether or not something falls into the same category as something else, ordinal data involves the rank order of those observations. A simple example is the order in which contestants finished in a race (first, second, third, and so on). A security example includes the risk rankings obtained in a risk matrix analysis (for instance, a 1–3 rating of

Category Value	Operating System
1	Windows XP
2	Windows Vista
3	HP-UX
4	Solaris
5	Linux
6	Mac OS X

Table 3-1.   Nominal Categories for OS Type

risk severity and likelihood scores reflecting low, medium, and high). Ordinal data does not provide any information regarding the amount of difference between the rankings, such as how much faster the winner of the race was compared to the runner up. By the same token, a security risk ranking of 10 does not mean that the risk is twice that of something ranked as a 5. To this extent, ordinal data remains somewhat categorical, but the buckets are now arranged in numerical order in a way that means something in the context of the scale.

Analysis techniques for ordinal data are much like those of nominal data, involving counts of which observations fall into which ranks and the distribution of the data. Although people often do it, it is still inappropriate to apply means or averages to ordinal data, because the ordinal scale does not give any insight into the differences between ordinal rankings. (Think of a race that results in a close finish for first and second place, followed by a distant third.) The mode (the value most often observed) still works fine with ordinal data, and the median (the middle value observed) can be applied as well. Ordinal data may also be compared against other nominal or ordinal data in tabular fashion, as in the example risk scoring summary in Table 3-2, which shows ratings observed in a survey of ten security administrators. Analysis shows the most frequent risk scores given to each data type.

Interval Data   Where ordinal data describes a ranking relationship, but with no real measure of the distance between individual rankings, interval data involves increases in rank in which the distance between the ranks is measured in some sort of standard unit. Thus the amount of difference between ranks means something. Measures of temperature on the Celsius and Fahrenheit scales are good examples of interval data, because the difference between 10 degrees and 20 degrees is the same as the distance between 0 degrees and 10 degrees on each scale (but not necessarily between the scales).

Another example would be the Common Vulnerability Scoring System (CVSS) scores used to measure the severity of security vulnerabilities. Unlike ordinal severity scores that reflect low/medium/high rankings, CVSS scores range from 0 to 10 with the assumption that the difference between 3 and 4 on the scoring scale is mathematically equivalent to the difference between 5 and 6. The reason is pretty simple. If standard

Data Type	Risk of Data Loss or Corruption (Summary of Scores)			
	1 – Low	2 – Medium	3 – High	Mode
User data	3	5	2	2 – Medium
Financial data	1	4	5	3 – High
Customer data	2	7	1	2 – Medium
Intellectual property	5	3	2	1 – Low

Table 3-2.   Cross-Tabular Nominal and Ordinal Data

intervals were not the case and the difference between CVSS scores of 9 and 10 was not the same as the difference between scores of 1 and 2 (or, to use temperature, if the difference between an 80- and 90-degree day was not the same as the difference between a 30- and 40-degree day), then the data loses its comparative meaning.

There is a fine line between ordinal and interval data, as you might infer from the example of the risk matrix scores in the preceding section and the CVSS scores here. You must carefully consider what kind of data you are dealing with, or you risk making errors with regard to what you are measuring. Consider the example of academic grades. The difference between a grade of A and a grade of B is unclear, except that A is ranked higher than B (ordinal data). You cannot find the mean of A and B (or say that an A and a C average to a B). The data does not reflect that level of standardization. By assigning fixed differences between the grades, however, you can move from an ordinal to an interval scale. Now A is defined as a 4.0 on the scale, B as a 3.0, C as a 2.0, and so on. The difference between a 2.5 and a 3.0 is considered equivalent to that between 3.5 and 4.0, because we have added a layer of standardization on our metric.

It is possible to do more analytically with interval data than with nominal or ordinal data because we are now playing with real numbers. We can add, subtract, and multiply measurements. We cannot divide or develop ratios between data, however, since the zero point on an interval scale is arbitrary and it is possible to use negative numbers (as with temperature), although this is not always part of the scale (as with academic grades). But most common statistical techniques become available with interval data, including the mean, the median, the mode, and the standard deviation. Interval data allows us to analyze dispersion, or how "spread out" our data is, and this in turn opens up some interesting probabilistic analysis techniques and the possibility of inferential statistics (those that generalize and predict) rather than more simple descriptive statistics (those that only tell things about the immediate data).

Ratio Data   Ratio data is pretty much the same as interval data, with the addition of an absolute zero point where nothing exists to measure. On a ratio scale, not only is the difference between 0 and 1 the same as the difference between 1 and 2 (as with interval data), but the difference between 0 and 1 is also half the difference between 0 and 2. Measurements such as weight and length are measured on ratio scales. So is the Kelvin scale of temperature since, unlike Celsius or Fahrenheit scales, an absolute zero point is defined.

Analytically, ratio and interval data are very similar, because the data is truly quantitative and allows for a variety of statistical techniques to be performed. Ratio data, by virtue of being divisible and having the zero point, offers a few more statistical techniques in the toolbox, but from an IT security metrics perspective, it is likely that interval and ratio data will look very much the same come analysis time.

A basic visual reminder of the four data types is shown in Figure 3-2. It is important and worthwhile for you to understand differences in data and measurement scales. Scales define the level of analysis that we can perform on data and the limitations regarding what we can assume about or infer from that data. Understanding how numbers can be used within each type of data also inoculates us against the mistaken idea

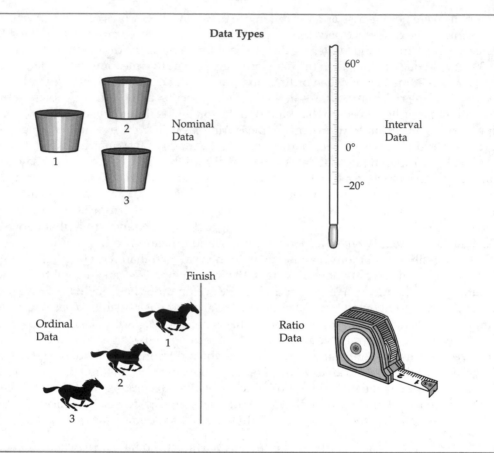

Figure 3-2.   Four data types or scales of measurement commonly associated with quantitative data are nominal, ordinal, interval, and ratio data.

that quantitative data and numbers are all the same. What some security professionals might refer to as qualitative data would be more accurately described as quantitative data on an ordinal scale, a distinction worth considering since qualitative data is considered something quite different by experts in qualitative research methods.

Qualitative Data

In security, confusion over qualitative and quantitative data often occurs when measurement activities involve collecting data from people, and then preparing that data for analysis. For example, you may interview several administrators and analysts for a security risk assessment and ask them to assign value to their assets and explain their rationale. Your interviewees then rate their assets, perhaps on a scale of 1 to 10, and you take notes regarding their justifications. From a research perspective, you now have two sets of related data. On the one hand, you have quantitative, ordinal data that represents each stakeholder's asset value estimates; you can perform certain analyses on this data. You also have notes that reflect that person's feelings and thoughts about how they came up with their numbers. This is qualitative data. If you recorded your interview, the video, audio, and transcripts would also be qualitative data. Analysis of qualitative data is very different than quantitative analysis, as the data is messier, more complex, and requires more interpretation.

IT security often mistakes the actual qualitative data, in the form of documents and recordings, with what the data represents in terms of people's opinions, statements, and actions. In the preceding risk assessment example, the score given by those interviewed is less interesting than the discussion of how they arrived at that score, from a qualitative perspective. Qualitative measurement is about analyzing how people think, feel, and act, not just the record of what they say.

Security risk assessments may produce a rich body of data in the form of meetings, discussions, arguments, and even people changing their minds. But all this qualitative data is then glossed over and only the end result, the final risk estimate, is considered data. This gets confusing, because most qualitative risk assessments then assign numbers to these scores, most often ratings on an ordinal scale, which are then subjected to attempts at statistical calculations such as counting, averaging, and multiplication across risk scores. The result, as I've pointed out, is a misunderstood hybrid of analysis techniques that is misleading and imprecise. Only a tiny fraction of the data, and not even the interesting stuff, gets analyzed. When it turns out to be inaccurate, we distance ourselves from the result by slapping the qualitative label on the analysis which, like fine print, then absolves us of most accountability because the data was never based on "reality" to begin with. All the data that could have helped us understand why our logic was faulty in the first place, all the discussions and debates and rich interaction, were thrown on the scrap heap before our analysis even got started.

Qualitative data is more difficult to pin down and assess. Quantitative data is pretty simple: it involves quantities of something. That naturally means units of measurement and numbers of units. Qualitative data, on the other hand, deals with human action, activity, and psychology. That's a big bucket of possibilities. It is no wonder that many "hard" science types such as physicists, chemists, and computer scientists (or IT engineers) have a difficult time taking qualitative approaches seriously. How can you rigorously deconstruct the world if everything (including what people feel or believe) is part of the equation (or, worse, if there *is no equation*?)

The good news is that qualitative data types can be defined, though not as specifically as would make the quantitative types completely comfortable. A key aspect of qualitative data is that it involves people, at individual and group levels. The activities, behaviors, norms, and social interactions of people are the bread and butter of qualitative research, and qualitative data involves observing and exploring these characteristics. And as security continues to gain visibility elsewhere in the organization, and to impact non-technical outcomes, questions of human psychology and "messy" social relations will play a greater part in IT security operations. Applying false mathematical principles to data and trying to simplify away complex systems with narrow, quantitative performance indicators hurts rather than helps security metrics and operations.

Furthermore, as more security professionals and stakeholders come to the industry from "softer" backgrounds, the inclusion of qualitative measures will become more common and more valuable to your efforts.

Data from Observations   Remember that empirical data is based on direct observation. Qualitative data can be highly empirical. Consider the field of anthropology, for example, in which researchers study entire cultures in order to understand them. The techniques of direct observation are known as *ethnography*, and these studies are accomplished by direct observations of the culture under study, by specially trained experts who go and live among its members (or in some cases observe from a distance). By observing and meticulously documenting various aspects of the culture, data is obtained that contributes to understanding. Qualitative data of this kind may include written research notes, photographs and drawings, video or audio recordings, and transcriptions of such data.

Data from Responses   Response data comes from interviews and interactions with people as individuals and as groups. This type of qualitative data is in the form of records of these interactions, with one person asking questions that are answered by others. The data is still empirical, based on direct observation of the interviewees' responses, but response data tends to be more structured and specific than ethnographic observations, although interviews may also be a part of such a study. Interview data also reflects an attempt by those measuring the responses to drill down and explore areas of interest to the measurement project, including the thoughts, speculations, and stories provided by those being interviewed. These responses are encouraged and can be used to guide the interview into new areas of interest.

Response data, like observational data, can take the form of transcriptions of recorded interviews, interviewer notes, and video and audio recordings. In some qualitative settings such as academia or market research, it is more acceptable and easier to record the entire interaction. In other business settings, such as IT security, interviewees may be uncomfortable with being recorded, especially if they have not volunteered but rather are participating in an assessment or audit. In these situations, the notes taken by the interviewer may be the only record of the interaction. It is critical that the interviewer be well trained, capable, and equipped with appropriate interview techniques and templates to facilitate the capture of the data. Knowing who to ask is also key, as choosing the proper people to interview or observe can mean the difference between measuring what you think you are measuring and measuring the wrong things.

Data from Records and Artifacts   The third type of qualitative data comprises information produced by our activities. Written documents and texts are common examples of qualitative data, from books and periodicals, to policy documents and corporate reports, to HTML pages and source code. This type of data reflects what you are measuring or observing. If you are observing herder activities on a botnet command and control net, for instance, the logs of those activities could be considered direct observational data, even though they are texts. The same goes for the notes on the interview you conduct with a bot herder you met online for the project, which are considered interview data.

But let's say that later you decide to analyze the most effective botnet research techniques across several projects. Now those logs and interview notes themselves become the target of analysis and are therefore a different kind of data.

Objects and artifacts can also provide qualitative data. When I conduct physical security assessments, one of my data collection activities is to conduct site surveys; I walk perimeters, noting entrances and badge readers and cameras, and perhaps photographing possible entry points or dumpsters that may be good targets for diving. This is inherently qualitative measurement work, as is the data I collect. The perimeters, structures, and countermeasures that I observe are the direct result of human planning and activity, and all that data helps me analyze and reconstruct those individual and organizational behaviors. Like other empirical data, these may take the form of notes, pictures, and video or audio recordings.

Analyzing Qualitative Data Qualitative data requires very different analytical approaches than quantitative data. The statistical techniques I describe for ordinal, interval, and ratio data in the preceding section are not immediately appropriate. Part of the distinction involves the differences between the data types themselves. Quantitative data is narrow, specific, and unambiguous: things are counted and the counts and quantities of those things (that is, dollars, hours, tons, or positive vs. negative responses to a survey) are analyzed. Assigning meaning comes later. Meaning comes first in qualitative data, which is broad and general, filled with latent information that must be separated from the rest of the data before analysis can even begin. It is the difference between counting the digitally encoded bits on a DVD to reconstruct a movie and deciding whether or not the movie was an example of good filmmaking. The tools to reconstruct the signal may be sophisticated, but they don't concern themselves with the film's direction, cinematography, or screenwriting. Deciding how well the film was made, on the other hand, cannot take place until you decide what aspects you are interested in measuring (were the edits too choppy or did the script average five clichés per minute?) and your standard for comparison (*Casablanca* vs. *Plan 9 from Outer Space*). Interpretation is everything with qualitative data, and for some people this makes qualitative analysis seem impossible. For others it holds out the possibility of much richer analysis with more applicability to the way "the real world" and the people in it work.

At the heart of qualitative data analysis is the concept of categorization, commonly known as *coding* of the data. Documents, sections of text, interview responses, recorded activities, or any of the other myriad elements of the data are bracketed and assigned codes that reflect themes, commonalities, or other characteristics of interest. As more codes are assigned to the data, patterns may begin to emerge across the mass of collected observations.

Qualitative coding can be every bit as complex as quantitative statistical analysis, and equally sophisticated automated tools have been developed for markets ranging from academia, to market research, to software engineering. These tools are known as Computer Assisted Qualitative Data Analysis Software (CAQDAS) systems and include commercial products such as ATLAS.ti and NVivo, which are enterprise-grade CAQDAS that allow for complex coding, annotating, modeling, and searching of large data sets.

These software packages are used by large companies and research institutions to understand complex problems that cannot be analyzed through quantitative methods, and they have price tags to match. A number of open source CAQDAS tools are also available, such as TAMS Analyzer, which I describe in the next example. Qualitative analysis tools are used in market research, product design, and technology consulting settings across many industries where measurement and performance improvement must take into account the activities and behaviors of people.

The easiest way to explain qualitative data analysis is with an example of a very basic qualitative metrics project. IT security shops often conduct security policy reviews to evaluate how effective and how current their policies may be. A security policy document is a typical example of qualitative data, specifically a record of human activity (the planning, development, and publication of the policy at the least). When an organization undertakes a security policy review, it undertakes an exercise in qualitative measurement and analysis. Often the process for the review is nothing more strenuous than to read the document (or hire a consultant to do so) and identify any components that might be out of date or that are poorly written (in the judgment of the reader). These reviews are usually not rigorous or structured in the way that a quantitative assessment might be conducted, which is unfortunate and diminishes their value. Qualitative analysis can provide much more insight than this.

Consider this example of more in-depth analysis from a sample review of a company's security policies. In this case, the company was concerned because some users believed that the security policies were hostile and condescending, and that the policies existed only to give management an excuse if they wanted to discipline people. Not everyone felt this way, however, and the company was curious about whether this was a real problem. Qualitative analysis is wonderful in such a situation due to its ability to extract themes from data that might otherwise go unnoticed or unanalyzed.

In the case of the policy review, a coding system was developed that identified statements within the policy that fell into the following categories:

- **Benefit**   The policy statement describes how the policy benefits the user or reader.

- **Punishment**   The policy statement describes circumstances or criteria in which policy violations will face disciplinary actions.

- **Requirement**   The policy statement describes an action, activity, or configuration that must be performed or present.

- **Prohibition**   The policy statement describes an action, activity, or configuration that may not be performed or present.

Figure 3-3 shows the cross-referenced results of this analysis, showing how many examples of each coded statement were identified in three sample policy documents covering acceptable use, endpoint systems, and network devices. Coding and analysis was done using TAMS Analyzer, an open source application that has many sophisticated features for analyzing qualitative data. Looking at the results window, you can see thematic differences between the three policy documents. The Acceptable Use

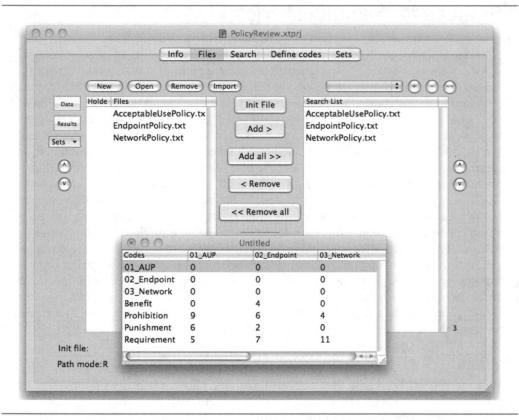

Figure 3-3.   Some coding summary results of a security policy review using TAMS Analyzer, an open source CAQDAS tool

Policy document is much more likely to contain statements involving punishment for infractions of the policy, but with no real mention of benefits to the users. Conversely, the Network Policy document is more focused on requirements, particularly configurations, and less likely to beat users of the policy over the head with negative consequences for not adhering to the document. The results of the analysis would indicate that those who thought that the Acceptable Use Policy was draconian may have had a point.

This policy example is a simple illustration of how you can use qualitative data and analysis to answer questions that quantitative work is ill-equipped to address. It also demonstrates that qualitative data is not just about opinions or "anything goes" analytical techniques. For certain security questions, particularly those that examine how and why people do what they do, qualitative metrics can be uniquely valuable. And when conducted properly, qualitative measurement projects are just as empirical and methodical as their quantitative brethren. I will go into more depth regarding qualitative measurement projects for IT security in later chapters.

Data Sources for Security Metrics

Having covered quite a bit of ground regarding how data is defined, we can turn our attention to how we go about getting it. Here again I must respectfully disagree with some of my security colleagues, particularly those that would put artificial constraints on what makes good or bad data. I do not believe there is such a thing as data that is inherently good or bad, only data that is good or bad in the context of the measurement at hand. I like to use the metaphor of using natural materials such as oil or water to create energy. Neither oil nor water are inherently good or bad energy sources, but both must be considered in the context of how much it will take to access, process, and benefit from the resource. You could build a hydroelectric plant in the middle of the Saudi Arabian peninsula, but you would spend more energy getting the water to it than you would recoup from your plant. Much easier to tap into the ocean of oil just beneath your feet.

Data works a bit like this, too, as some data is easier and cheaper to acquire, process, and benefit from. If you have immediately available data that answers your questions, it would be silly and counterproductive to look elsewhere. But to ignore or discount the data that answers your questions because it is not easy to gather or analyze is shortsighted and amounts to surrendering without a fight. Security metrics are about answering questions and understanding our processes. Discovery is much more difficult when you are allowed to look only in the same places every time. There are a lot of possible sources of security data to consider.

System Data

IT systems, especially security devices, are a natural choice for security metrics data. Most of these systems are already preconfigured to collect and report a variety of data about their operations, either directly or through interfaces with tools such as security information and event management (SIEM) systems or configuration and application lifecycle management tools. In addition to being accessible and increasingly easy to collect, system data usually lends itself well to quantitative analysis techniques and longitudinal measurement (measurement that is conducted to understand how things operate over time).

For early metrics initiatives and proof-of-concept activities, system data can let you show the value of describing your security operations in new and more rigorous ways. These descriptive metrics may not answer the questions of how or why some aspect of security is working the way it does, but they can often generate these questions and provide you with more buy-in to go and find out. System data is also useful for immediate decision support, when you are required to articulate elements of the security process or justify what you have done in the past or what you may want to do in the future. Some common examples of system-related data include these:

- System and event logs
- System configurations
- Source code
- Test results such as vulnerability assessments or patch testing

Process Data

System data shows us what our machines and applications are up to, and by extension what the users and operators of those systems may (or may not) be doing. But security is more than just technical processes. It also includes organizational and business processes that manage and guide everyday activities as well as exceptional circumstances. Process data usually involves the more active inclusion and participation of people than system data, which often does little more than monitor (and maybe automatically respond to) predefined behaviors.

Process data can prove a bit more difficult to collect and analyze than system data, although many automated processes have embedded data that is as easy to access as any other IT system. But process data in IT security is also, in my experience, less well understood than system data, and it is underutilized. Analyzing security process data requires more initial thought about what you want to know and accomplish using the data, and it may need to be correlated with other data to provide intelligence and understanding. In the case of actual process mapping or workflow analysis, the data may not even exist within the IT security program, as many programs do not take a process-based view of security. In these situations, it may be necessary to create the data from scratch by documenting and analyzing the IT security processes in place. The upside is that process data also holds some of the greatest potential as an untapped source of metrics for security programs. A few example sources of process data include these:

- Activity reporting (budgets, time tracking, training records, meeting minutes)
- Process tracking (trouble tickets, support call records, compliance monitoring)
- Workflow breakdowns
- Business process diagrams

Documentary Data

If system- and process-generated data are the best and most readily measurable indicators of technical and organizational operational details, then organizationally generated documents and records provide the best measures of "big picture" activities.

We live in a bureaucratic society, and the lifeblood of bureaucracies is documentation. We may complain about the burdens such bureaucracy places on us in our public and personal lives, but few of us can imagine how we would function in a world where nothing was ever written down, where no records about us or what we do existed. The system and process data in the preceding sections are forms of documentary data as well, but what I am referring to here are documents that provide structure and context to our IT security programs and activities.

Somewhat ironically, many of my experiences with security clients have shown me that many security programs are like a world with no records and that many systems and processes are not formally documented. However, in almost every security shop, some form of documentation exists as a place to begin, and if you really do have zero documentation regarding your program, your first critical remediation activity is clear.

Documentary data does not necessarily have to be IT security–specific or directly created by security stakeholders, but it can include everything that effects, impacts, or provides insight into the security program.

Collection and analysis of documentary data is more complex than either system or process data, for two reasons: First, the data is usually qualitative and made up of electronic as well as print text that is almost never centrally located. You have to go looking for documentary data, and that means you must have some idea up front of what you are looking for. There is no "generate report" button for this kind of data, and the closest you may get to one is a search engine. Second, documentary data is not usually specific, so even if you do know what you are looking for, you will have to analyze a larger set of data to extract what you are interested in, and then perform another analysis on that data. So measurement projects involving documentary data tend to be more involved and require different resource commitments. This is the natural tradeoff in security metrics work between easy measurements that give you narrow results and harder measurements that give you wider insights. Examples of documentary data can be found in the following:

- Security policies and procedures
- Other policies (which might have an impact on security operations)
- Audit and review reports
- Project plans and stakeholder documents
- Corporate records (financial statements, customer lists, contracts, e-mail)
- Corporate documents (annual reports, shareholders briefings, SEC filings)
- Industry reports (analyst research, government reports, market research)

People Data

Collecting data on people directly (as opposed to process data that collects data on how people behave within rigidly defined structures) can be the most challenging measurement activity, which is one of the reasons it often gets discounted out of hand. This is not because the data collection is all that difficult or expensive in this era of online survey tools and web conferencing. Nor does the difficulty come from not having any skills or experience with the research techniques. Most of us participate in, if not conduct, people-related research every day in the form of staff meetings, customer briefings, design requirements whiteboard sessions, and good-old-fashioned people watching in the park over the weekend with our families.

The challenges of collecting and analyzing people data concern how to do it methodically and scientifically so that the results are as credible and reliable as possible. You must also understand the data and the methods you employ so that you recognize any problems with credibility and reliability and can explain them. We've all had experiences coming out of a staff meeting or other group activity and telling our peers how great or how terrible the experience had been. We've all shared water cooler banter with colleagues about how "everyone" knows that the organization's security was compromised, or how "no one" takes the policy against personal use of the Internet seriously. The challenge (and expense) of people data is how we transform this general, vague data into something usable and explainable. This type of data will not always be appropriate, and may begin to make sense only after you have generated enough of the other kinds of data to realize that certain questions keep emerging but cannot be answered.

People data can come from many empirical sources:

- Surveys and questionnaires (internal and external)
- Interviews and focus groups
- Case studies
- Direct observations

As corporations become more globalized and grow into complex hybrids of employees and outsourced resourcing that cross different cultures and organizational boundaries, the scope of data collection can get complicated. It is important to consider your scope and your goals in these situations so that measuring the social and psychological aspects of your security operations is not impeded by different values and norms that you may not have considered.

We Have Metrics and Data—Now What?

Metrics are vital to a successful security program. We need to make sure that they are developed to support defined goals, and we need to identify and collect appropriate data to make the metrics meaningful. They are the engine of effective security. So if metrics are the engine, what are they driving? And where is everything going? Even well-defined goals and the best metrics will remain limited if they remain tactical. We must apply the engine to a bigger purpose.

This book is about IT security metrics. But. more important, this book is about treating IT security as a true business process. If metrics are the engine, the security business process is the vehicle that the engine supports. And if I may indulge in yet another extended metaphor (my Ph.D. work was about how metaphors are used in technology, and I find now that I like to use them a lot), improving and managing the security process over time becomes the road, the journey, and the destination. When we talk about security metrics, we do not mean that we are measuring security in the same way we measure a physical force. Security is not gravity. When we say we are going to measure security, we mean that we are going to apply metrics and indicators to the security process, to our security management systems (in both the technical and business senses of management), and to our understanding and improvement of security policies, security activities, and security infrastructures. To achieve these goals, we must move beyond metrics, beyond the GQM method, and explore a more comprehensive framework for implementing our strategy. This framework and its components will be the subject of the next chapter.

Summary

Security metrics rely on data collected in support of measurement activities, and data can be described and defined in several ways. At its most general, data is a form of information and can be described as the facts, quantities, figures, statements, symbols, and observations that we use for inquiry, reference, and analysis. Data can also be described as existing at one end of a continuum that, by adding context and experience, results in increasingly sophisticated forms of understanding including data, information, knowledge, and wisdom. As data is analyzed, used, and incorporated into individual and organizational learning, it grows more powerful and applicable to general situations.

Data can also be described in terms of quantitative data that relies on numbers and statistical analysis, and qualitative data that is not numerical and requires more interpretive (but equally rigorous, when performed correctly) analytical techniques. Quantitative data is often combined with measurement scales that represent standardized units and embedded information regarding the data, such as nominal, ordinal, interval, and ratio data types. As the scale increases in sophistication, more sophisticated mathematical and statistical operations may be performed on the data. Qualitative data refers to such things as documents and other artifacts of human activity, direct human responses to interview questions and surveys, and direct observation of (usually) human activity and behavior. The quantitative and qualitative distinction is less important than the distinction between empirical data, which is based on observation, and nonempirical data, which is not. Knowing what you are actually observing thus becomes critical for both quantitative and qualitative metrics.

Sources of IT security data to support metrics projects and programs are everywhere, although you should recognize what data and which analysis techniques will work best within the resource constraints of any particular measurement initiative. Data sources can include systems, processes, documents, and people—to name a few. Some data sources are better understood and more easily analyzed than others, but a trade-off always exists between the ease of the data and the requirements for answers. Metrics and data are central to security, but they function most effectively when they are used within a larger framework of security business process management and improvement.

Further Reading

Adams, J., et al. *Research Methods for Graduate Business and Social Science Students*. Response Books, 2007.

Babbie, E. *The Practice of Social Research*, 12th Ed. Wadsworth Publishing, 2009.

Denzin, N., and Y. Lincoln, eds. *The SAGE Handbook of Qualitative Research*, 3rd Ed. SAGE Publications, 2005.

Knoke, D., et al. *Statistics for Social Data Analysis*, 4th Ed. Wadsworth Publishing, 2002.

Case Study 1 | In Search of Enterprise Metrics

Doug Dexter's case study is a good starting place and an example of how IT security metrics are a journey and not a destination. Doug's experiences at Cisco put him at the heart of one of the most dynamic and complex IT security environments in the world. This complexity becomes apparent as Doug and team attempt to measure their risks, threats, and operational activities. Doug peels back the onion, so to speak, and shows how metrics at an organizational level cannot be something that you decide to do on a whim. Metrics take effort and a nuanced understanding of the goals and questions necessary even to define and articulate that which will be measured.

Doug offers a practitioner's lessons in the benefits and pitfalls of measuring IT security that parallel the advice and examples you will read about throughout this book. One of the takeaways from Doug's case study that I find most valuable is the need to question the value and positioning of your security metrics continually, both for yourself and for any stakeholders you may be trying to reach or sway. A careful and self-critical approach to security metrics that continually requires you to justify the data you collect and the analyses you perform on them is the best way to ensure that your metrics program provides long-term value for your organization.

Case Study 1: In Search of Enterprise Metrics

by Doug Dexter

I'm the team leader for Cisco's corporate security audit team. My team is responsible for performing assessments, audits, and acquisition integrations for the Corporate Security Programs Office (CSPO). With a team mission to proactively identify, prioritize, and communicate threats, vulnerabilities, and other risks to the confidentiality, integrity, and availability of Cisco's information and computing assets, we're responsible for the corporation's vulnerability scanning, web application scanning, and penetration testing programs. Communicating the results of these programs has put us squarely on the path to find and deliver the best set of security metrics to the people responsible for addressing the issues we discover.

We began our journey to find a set of enterprise security metrics five years ago, at the close of a project to procure and deploy a vulnerability scanning system capable of scanning all of Cisco. Yes, I said "close" of the project, because it wasn't until after we had the scanning product in-house that we really started to understand just how large and difficult the issue of metrics was going to be for us.

Prior to that time, we had no enterprise-level ability to scan for security vulnerabilities. Some of the engineers had installed Nessus on their laptops and were using that on an ad hoc basis. But for a corporation our size, we knew we needed a "real" system. And in the back of our minds, we knew that we'd have to generate reports and use those reports to show the system administrators that they needed to patch this host or that one. Certainly we knew we needed metrics of some type, but we didn't have a clue as to what we were really getting into.

To help visualize and provide some background about what we're working with internally at Cisco, I've provided a couple of figures. Figure 1 shows the standard view

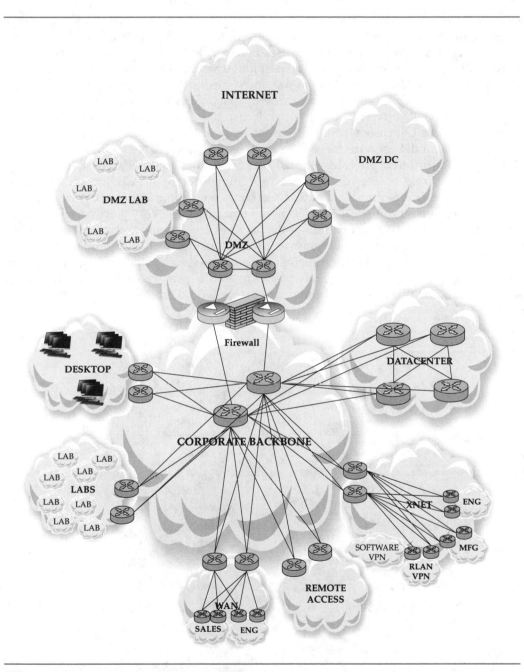

Figure 1.   How Cisco views itself conceptually

of how an enterprise describes itself. The view contains internal networks, external networks, and others, all contained in clouds and connected by clearly defined lines. This is a high-level, conceptual view of the Cisco network. It doesn't provide details about how anything is connected, or how any part interoperates with any other part, but it does show a "20,000-foot view" of the size and complexity of our network.

Figure 2 shows a more realistic picture of Cisco. This view was created with network modeling software, and although it displays basically the same contents shown in Figure 1, it clearly demonstrates just how intricate modern networks have become. This model contains more than 27,000 router and switch configurations. Although Figure 2 also provides a broad view, with this model it's possible to zoom into a specific zone, or even deeper into a specific router, or an ACL line on a router. In raw form, it's more than 4 GB of text. Certainly we all know that networks are complex. But it isn't until you create a model that includes every piece of equipment and defines how the different zones of the network communicate that you begin to comprehend just how overwhelmingly complex your network environment really is.

Cisco has more than 30 million available IP addresses, subdivided into approximately 56,000 networks that change on a daily basis. The Audit Team realized that due to Cisco's size and complexity, any systems and processes we would create had to be automated.

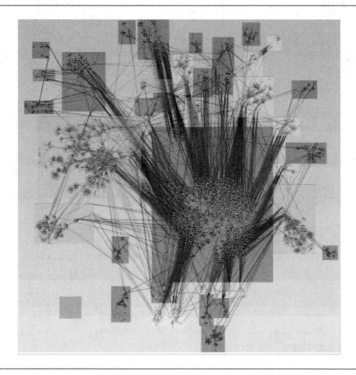

Figure 2.   How Cisco actually looks

There was no sane way we could manually update this amount of information, let alone begin to comprehend it. And with that automation, we needed a set of metrics that would assist us in describing the threats and vulnerabilities in the devices that lived on our network and that would help us prioritize remediation efforts by identifying which vulnerabilities and hosts were likeliest to be attacked.

This case study consists of five scenarios that describe real-world situations we encountered. My team has learned a number of lessons from these experiences, and our goal is to share them.

Over the course of the past few years, the audit team has accomplished some things well, and we've made some mistakes. This case study isn't written with the notion of teaching you everything you need to know about creating your own metrics. On the contrary, it consists of some of the more memorable mistakes we've made and the lessons we've learned on our journey toward finding a credible set of realistic, reliable, and reproducible metrics. The team is still not there yet, but we are getting closer.

Scenario One: Our New Vulnerability Management Program

On the first day of using our new vulnerability management system (scanners), we ran a series of scans and eagerly awaited the report. We had decided to focus on DMZ-based hosts, as they are the most accessible to an attacker. We ran the report and found a large number of hosts with easily exploited vulnerabilities on our DMZ. Our initial metrics looked like this:

- Total number of hosts scanned
- Total number of hosts vulnerable by severity (low, medium, high)
- Percentage of hosts vulnerable

We put together a couple of slides and used them to brief our CSO, who looked at the slides and said, "So how many of these hosts are on the production DMZ, and how many are in lab DMZs?" We didn't know. Not a clue. Not even a hint. We had gone to our boss with metrics that said, "There are *this* many vulnerabilities on our DMZ hosts," when we really didn't know how many were serious and how many were not.

For background, at that time, Cisco had more than 5000 labs and more than 600 hosts on DMZ networks. We did have a very good network management tool. However, no one had ever made a distinction between a "production DMZ" and a "lab DMZ." They were all just labeled "DMZ" in the network management tool. Even the underlying system that maintained the inventory of all our networks didn't have the ability to distinguish between the two. No one had ever thought about them in that manner before. They were all just DMZ networks.

Lesson One: Verify that the data you're presenting accurately describes the conclusions you reach with the data. We mixed the two types of data (DMZ production and DMZ lab), and we couldn't tell the two apart. While any issues in our production DMZ would be addressed immediately, issues in our labs aren't revenue impacting so they're not addressed as quickly. To make matters worse, we had no easy way to delineate the production networks from the lab networks. It took another three months for us to review all the hosts and their applications, mark the networks, add a new field in the database, and update the related tables. During this time, our CSO kept asking us for more information about the Production DMZ—information we simply couldn't separate from the rest of the DMZ networks. It was a very long three months.

Lesson Two: Manage executive expectations about the accuracy of initial metrics, and solicit their input on metric creation. Executives at any company probably expect that a system just purchased will immediately begin providing very accurate information about the enterprise, and they will have an idea of which areas they want more information about. However, the tool will be only as accurate as the data it receives (see Lesson One).

You must explain to executives that the tool will need to be checked and tuned, prior to making any major decisions from the information it presents. Solicit executives' input about which areas they want more information, or what questions they'd like answered. Consider that input and think through the metrics you'll likely need to create to provide that information or answer those questions. Then think through what additional information will be necessary to act on the results you've just produced. If that additional information is not available, or accurate, it will affect your ability to act upon your initial results.

Scenario Two: Who's on First?

Once we separated the two sets of networks, we ran our scans again and put together new slides. Most hosts were in very good shape, but a few hosts needed to be checked to verify whether their vulnerabilities were valid or if they were false positives. This is when we discovered another set of issues:

- Some hosts didn't have anyone registered as the owner.
- Some host owners were no longer at the company.
- Some host owners had moved on to other positions, but were still with the company (leaving us to follow up with someone who could possibly identify the current owner).

Overall, we had a significant portion of our hosts with either a "zombie" owner (the name provided was someone who didn't exist in the company anymore) or with no owner at all. Much to our chagrin, our initial set of metrics no longer described the real issues. Our new vulnerability scanning tool worked fine and could easily identify hosts with vulnerabilities. It was our internal processes and inventory control systems that were lacking, and they couldn't tell us who was responsible for the hosts with vulnerabilities. The effectiveness of our scanning tool was hampered by our inability to contact a host owner to begin remediation.

Lesson Three: Knowing who owns a host is more valuable than knowing what vulnerabilities are on a host.   It was at that point we realized we needed to create a new set of metrics based on ownership. Learning from our previous mistake, we included the subsets of DMZ(s) and datacenter(s):

- Hosts with valid owners (separated by DMZ and by datacenter)
- Hosts with zombie owners (separated by DMZ and by datacenter)
- Hosts with no owners (separated by DMZ and by datacenter)

This new set of metrics helped us define the new problem of host ownership (or lack thereof). To help us gauge this new aspect of our situation, we added the category of Registration to our initial set of metrics and came up with a more accurate vulnerability management list:

- Total number of hosts scanned
  - Total number of registered hosts
  - Total number of unregistered hosts
- Total number of hosts vulnerable (low, medium, high)
  - Total number of registered hosts vulnerable (low, medium, high)
  - Total number of unregistered hosts vulnerable (low, medium, high)
- Percentage of hosts vulnerable (low, medium, high)
  - Percentage of registered hosts vulnerable (low, medium, high)
  - Percentage of unregistered hosts vulnerable (low, medium, high)

As we studied these categories, we realized that the most dangerous hosts in our organization were those that were unregistered and had high severity vulnerabilities. Vulnerable hosts with valid owners were easy to contact and correct. Vulnerable hosts with no owners were difficult, if not impossible, to remediate. We couldn't "blackhole" them (disconnect them from the network), because we didn't know whether they were still providing mission-critical services. They became our most urgent priority, and we began to sleuth out the owners.

Scenario Three: The Value of a Slide

As we worked our way through the issues, we started developing more accurate information from our scanning systems. This helped us build a relationship with our executives, and with the administrators tasked with remediating the issues found with the hosts. But there was a side effect—the ability to display too much information that added little or no value.

As we started considering which metrics to brief, we created tons of slides—most of which we discarded, because, although they were very cool looking, they really didn't

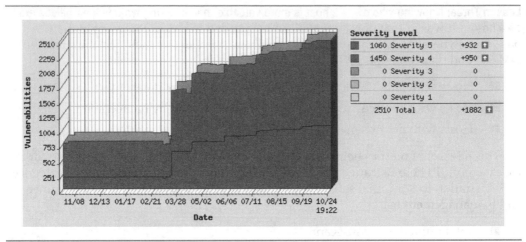

Figure 3.   DMZ vulnerabilities across time

say much of anything. Figure 3 shows one of the automatically created graphs from our vulnerability management tool. The chart displays the total DMZ vulnerabilities by month over the course of the previous year.

At first glance, this is quite an informative chart. There appears to be an increase in vulnerabilities across time. That is a fairly simple message. But the graph is missing so many items that it really doesn't say anything, and it actually hides more important questions:

- It needs a key that explains Severity levels (for reference, 1 is low, and 5 is high).

- It needs to explain why there aren't any Severity 1, 2, or 3 vulnerabilities. (They were omitted for clarity.)

- It needs to explain whether these vulnerabilities are confirmed as definitely exploitable, or confirmed as potentially exploitable. (This chart included both confirmed and potential vulnerabilities.)

One important question that should be asked is, why did the vulnerabilities triple in March? March was the month we moved from development to production and started scanning all, rather than only part, of our DMZ networks.

The other important question that is not readily apparent is, why do we have only an increase in vulnerabilities? Actually, many vulnerabilities were being remediated by decommissioning hosts and consolidating their services to other systems. But for the vulnerability management tool to remove a vulnerability, it needed to rescan the host and ensure that the vulnerability had been addressed. If there was no host to scan (that is, it had been decommissioned), the vulnerability would remain in the database until it was manually removed.

Lesson Four: You'll be tempted to create and brief exciting slides. Don't do it. Metrics aren't about being pretty; they're about inciting corrective action.   Metrics exist to assure a process owner that a process is functioning correctly. If a metric indicates the process isn't functioning correctly, the process owner needs to determine what is affecting the process and address the underlying issues. That's simple enough. But if the metric is causing a belief that an issue exists when it actually doesn't, then it's not a good metric. In this case, the impression was that vulnerabilities had increased across the year, when actually they had decreased, but we hadn't tuned out results from the decommissioned hosts. With Figure 3, we have a very good looking, easy-to-produce, and interesting looking chart that also happens to be horribly misleading.

Lesson Five: Don't trend your data until you have a solid baseline.   The graph in Figure 3 purported to display a trend in Severity 4 and Severity 5 vulnerabilities over the course of the previous year. But that trend actually presented data from initial product testing, initial deployment, and subsequent incremental additions to the overall pool of hosts being scanned. As a result, the total vulnerability count skewed upward, with no sign of any effort to reduce the vulnerabilities that had occurred the previous year.

More to the point is the question "How many vulnerabilities do we have?" a very good one? Does it really represent what we're hoping to capture about our efforts at remediating vulnerabilities on our hosts? Certainly, we could compare how many vulnerabilities we have per month, as is demonstrated in Figure 3. As long as the trend is down, we must be appropriately addressing issues on our hosts, right? But, really, that question simply describes a point in time. It's sort of a dipstick into the gas tank of total corporate vulnerabilities. A measurement like this describes only one facet of an issue (How much gas is in the tank?), and it often doesn't answer the real question (Do I have enough gas to make it to the next filling station?). In this case, our metric failed to take into account how long it takes to remediate a vulnerability, what category of host requires remediation, and who is doing the remediation. As we realized this, we changed the question from "How many vulnerabilities do we have?" to a series of more accurate questions:

- What is the lifespan for a vulnerability on a production DMZ host?
- What is the lifespan for a vulnerability on a production datacenter host?

And even as good as these two questions may be, they become even more accurate once they have been reworded to include the responsible support teams. So here are those same questions, with their accuracy improved by defining who is doing the remediation:

- What is the lifespan for a vulnerability on a production DMZ host maintained by the e-mail team?
- What is the lifespan for a vulnerability on a production DMZ host maintained by the Windows Sysadmin team?
- What is the lifespan for a vulnerability on a production DMZ host maintained by the UNIX Sysadmin team?

As we informed the teams about the vulnerabilities on their systems, and included the trend of how long remediation was taking, we encountered an interesting side effect: The metrics had spurred the teams to try and outperform one another. This is discussed in more detail at the end of the case study.

Scenario Four: The Monitoring Program

The Cisco Security Incident Response Team (CSIRT) is a sister to the Audit Team. As the name implies, this team is responsible for handling more reactive security tasks, such as incident response, while the Audit team handles more proactive security tasks, such as compliance audits. Of course, this is an oversimplification, because both teams perform proactive and reactive security tasks, and some overlap occurs between the teams.

A major task for the CSIRT team is to monitor botnet activity on the internal network via a network monitoring tool called NetFlow. Data is fed to this tool via a SPAN port on each datacenter switch. A SPAN port is a port whose purpose is to mirror the data flowing across all the other ports on that switch. (SPAN stands for Switched Port Analyzer, but this is Cisco's specific name for this functionality. Other vendors provide this same port-mirroring ability with their own name for the feature.) So in a nutshell, all the traffic on every datacenter switch is mapped to a port on that switch, and all that traffic is sent through a series of NetFlow filters that recognize and identify botnet activity.

Over time, CSIRT has discovered a variety of malware, including botnets, on our internal network. As these malware-infected hosts are identified, they are not allowed to route traffic on the network via a technique commonly called *BGP Blackholing*. CSIRT worked with the network team to create an application that can easily deploy instructions to our routers to ignore traffic from these hosts. (For more information on this technique, go to www.cisco.com/web/about/security/intelligence/worm-mitigation-whitepaper.html.)

With these tools in place, the CSIRT team began detailed tracking of malware and botnet activity, kicking infected hosts off of the network and not allowing them back until the sysadmin said the infection had been removed from the hosts and that the hosts had been patched against reinfection. Hosts that were reinfected were repetitively denied access.

Figure 4 shows how this program ran over the course of two years. You'll notice a gradual decrease in activity over the first year and a half, with a small increase in April 2009, followed by another decrease.

When this project began in February 2008, a large information awareness campaign was associated with it. The campaign was designed to inform our lab administrators that Cisco did have malware and botnets, and that entire lab networks had been removed from the Cisco network until they were fully patched. The program was largely successful; malware activity decreased in eight months from a high of more than 1000 botnet-infected hosts, to a low of 50 botnet-infected hosts. But after that time, the awareness campaign ended, and after four months of very few issues, the numbers started increasing again in February 2009. It seems that something must have happened to lower the total of botnet-infected hosts (perhaps a second awareness campaign?), but that's not what really happened.

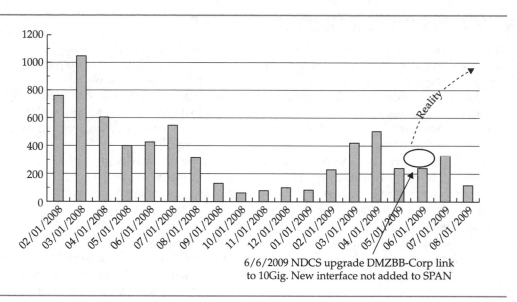

6/6/2009 NDCS upgrade DMZBB-Corp link
to 10Gig. New interface not added to SPAN

Figure 4.   The disappearing interface

Cisco, like most large organizations, has a very large and distributed workforce. Unknown to the CSIRT team, the Network Operations team (NDCS) had been upgrading many corporate interconnection links from 1GB to 10GB. A ten-fold increase in bandwidth is usually a very good thing, but while performing the upgrade, the NDCS team neglected to reconnect the SPAN port for some of the links. In effect, this made our monitoring systems blind to traffic handled by those links. As for the metrics, it made it look like the CSIRT team was being very effective at addressing the malware and botnets. The CSIRT team discovered this four months later when they saw botnet traffic on a filter on a different network segment than the source of the traffic. That traffic should have been detected by a filter on that network segment. After reconnecting the SPAN ports so the filters could review the missing traffic, we saw a huge increase in malware activity.

Lesson Six: Create a sanity check on automated metric-generating processes.   Automation is absolutely essential to managing and maintaining an enterprise network, and automating data collection and analysis is just as essential. In this case, an automated flow that had been running for over a year fell out of the total group of flows that CSIRT was measuring. Although a number of mechanisms were in place to determine whether the NetFlow collectors were functioning correctly, no mechanism was used to determine whether a NetFlow collector was up, but not doing anything. If all of our NetFlow collectors had been dropped, it would have been noticed immediately. But we lost only a few, so although the system was broken, it still appeared to be functioning correctly. This was an easy issue to fix, but it made us reexamine all our automated processes to look for gaps in how they functioned that could lead to an incorrectly generated metric.

Scenario Five: What Cost, the Truth?

This scenario looks more closely at the message we're communicating from the data contained in one of our slides. We'd been running the vulnerability scanning program for more than a year and were providing more accurate information based on the metrics data we were capturing and the lessons we'd learned. Figure 5 shows a slide with vulnerability details about one of our datacenters. It lists the operating systems, the number of Severity 5 vulnerabilities, the number of hosts with Severity 5 vulnerabilities, and the percentage of hosts with Severity 5 vulnerabilities.

My team had marked the Windows OS row and the Solaris OS rows of this slide, because we thought that having 8.2 percent and 5.2 percent (respectively) of our managed hosts exhibiting high-severity vulnerabilities was too many. We went into an executive meeting to discuss these findings.

What was interesting was how this information was absorbed, evaluated, and repurposed by the executives. Everyone agreed that too many vulnerabilities appeared on the Windows and Solaris hosts, and we spent very little time discussing what my team had assumed would be the gist of the meeting. Basically, the executives knew that the hosts would be remediated and that the remediation effort would cost the company in time and resources. So that part of the meeting was quick and easy. The time-consuming part was the discussion around how many or what percentage of high-severity vulnerabilities was acceptable. One executive called out the Linux OS and Cisco OS categories and said that since both had less than 1 percent of their hosts with high-severity vulnerabilities, those teams must be spending too much time, effort, and resources on patching their hosts. Now that was an interesting thought. The executive didn't realize it, but he was describing the law of diminishing returns and was applying it to vulnerability remediation.

Operating System Count & Urgent Vulnerabilities

	# Hosts	# Sev5s	# Hosts with 5	% Hosts with 5
Windows	4212	593	347	8.2
Linux	8026	62	41	<1
Solaris	2733	216	143	5.2
Cisco	4626	6	6	<1
HP-UX	468	7	7	1.5
HP ILO/RILO	3113	1	1	<1
NetApp	311	0	0	0
Other	3008	44	39	1.3
Total	26497	929	584	2.2

Sev 5s are the most serious vulnerabilities and include remote root exploits

Figure 5.   Operating System Count & Urgent Vulnerabilities graph

Lesson Seven: There is a trade-off between the money spent to remediate vulnerabilities and the increase in security posture.   This balance between the money spent and the increase in security posture is the most important principle in information security. Certainly, if an organization had unlimited funds, it could spend those funds to create an "unhackable" environment. But the rest of us have to show that the money we're spending is actually improving the overall security posture in the organization. We don't have unlimited funds. Nobody does (except perhaps the government, or financial institutions such as banks). Even if we did spend more money (time, effort, resources) on remediating every vulnerability, it doesn't necessarily follow that we would receive an increase in the overall security to the company. It's quite possible that by patching every vulnerability, a critical vendor-supported application would fail because it wouldn't be able to function with the latest operating system patch. At that point, you'd have to consider a mitigating strategy that maintained and defended the vulnerable critical system until the vendors figured out a patch, or you'd have to migrate your application to a more defendable system. Given that there are any number of complex situations like this that require a significant commitment in time, effort, and resources to address, it's safe to say that some vulnerabilities are easier to patch than others. We can also infer that the more time and effort we have to remediate a vulnerability, the more it costs to repair.

So how much do you want to pay for security? How many vulnerabilities is too many? For that matter, how many vulnerabilities is too few? Is zero the right amount? And if zero is the right amount for your organization, are your executives willing to spend the money to ensure that there are zero vulnerabilities on their systems? Admittedly, some organizations are willing to spend more money on addressing vulnerabilities (such as banks, hospitals, and governments). But many other organizations are willing to accept the risk trade-off of balancing vulnerabilities with cost savings.

For Cisco, we decided that zero, for any of these, would be an awfully expensive number to maintain. From there, we decided to use a different metric. After listening to the executives describe the balance between money and security posture, we realized that the question we wanted answered wasn't "How many hosts have high-severity vulnerabilities in this datacenter, sorted by OS Support team?" The question was, "How long does it take us to address vulnerabilities on hosts in this datacenter, sorted by OS Support team?" You may remember these questions from a couple of sections ago:

- What is the lifespan for a vulnerability on a datacenter host maintained by the e-mail team?

- What is the lifespan for a vulnerability on a datacenter host maintained by the Windows Sysadmin team?

- What is the lifespan for a vulnerability on a datacenter host maintained by the UNIX Sysadmin team?

This set of questions was created following the meeting with those executives. The questions reflect our realization that in a large enterprise, many different teams led by different executives are responsible for remediating issues. These executives are very focused on the issues they can control and that directly concern them.

They are not interested in a metric that contains issues outside of their area of control. For instance, a slide that describes all UNIX-based vulnerabilities is mildly interesting, but it's always followed by questions along the lines of "How many of these hosts are mine?" or "What action should I take from this data?" or "Why are you telling me this? It doesn't concern me."

Lesson Eight: Tailor your metrics to each executive and team you're soliciting for remediation.   To support the remediation effort fully, you must make sure that your analytic systems can not only narrow down the responsible owner or support team, but can also aggregate those support teams into a larger, more comprehensive view for executives to understand issues their teams are responsible to remediate. These larger views can be briefed to more senior executive management and display trends between and among teams.

For instance, dividing out the Windows Active Directory support team from the Windows Call Manager support team provides more detailed remediation data for the individual teams to address issues. But based on the principle of "everybody has a boss," aggregating those same teams provides a view that allows a "very senior executive" to compare the executive-led Windows team to the executive-led UNIX team and review how those teams are doing. These comparisons, at the executive and more senior executive level, are what drive teams to address issues. There's an old audit saying that goes like this: "That which is not inspected is neglected." In this case, by creating metrics that are directly attributable to a team, and providing those metrics to the executives responsible for those teams, we've created an inspection process that is helping the corporation address host vulnerabilities.

Summary

In this case study I've attempted to illustrate a series of issues that we have encountered while trying to develop a set of enterprise metrics. Perhaps you were already aware of these pitfalls—if so, we're jealous, because we've fallen headlong into every one of them, though we learned a lot in the process. If these pitfalls were new to you, we share them generously, in the hope that you and your organization won't learn the same painful lessons that we learned and in quite the same way that we learned them.

PART II | Implementing Security Metrics

CHAPTER 4 | The Security Process Management Framework

In the preceding three chapters I explored the case for IT security metrics and provided advice for choosing and designing effective measurement strategies and addressing the data requirements of those strategies. At this point, you should have a good idea of how to methodically select the security metrics you may be interested in exploring. But I have not yet discussed the larger context of these metrics beyond the idea that goals are important to measuring security, as illustrated in the Goal-Question-Metric (GQM) method described in Chapter 2.

Metrics are not nearly as effective when taken out of context, analyzed in piecemeal fashion, or undertaken as stand-alone exercises. The real power and value of metrics emerge when they are considered as part of a larger and ongoing programmatic approach to security that views IT security as a true business process and not simply an exercise in controls or technology. The Security Process Management (SPM) Framework that I propose in this chapter is designed to help you to look at your security metrics program in just this way.

Managing Security as a Business Process

In some ways, IT security challenges today mirror the challenges faced by IT a decade or more ago. Security skills and techniques have become more prominent, but they are still fairly esoteric. Security professionals are often seen as eccentric and paranoid, with special abilities that are less well understood than mainstream IT pros. In the old days, IT was staffed by the oddball techies in the backrooms of the corporation, hidden from view and poorly understood. Today the security experts have seemingly mystical knowledge on which the now-common IT infrastructure depends.

Like IT staffs of the past, today's security professionals also struggle to demonstrate the value of what they do—you can't ignore them, but it can be difficult to articulate what they bring to the table in tangible terms. Security is viewed more as protection or insurance, implemented to prevent bad things from happening. Measuring success, therefore, involves proving a negative: did nothing bad happen? What bad thing could have happened but didn't because of the activities of your security team?

Although CISOs are beginning to enjoy more visibility and participation at the same levels as other executives, I still hear many complaints that security teams are relegated to the roles of providing supporting statistics to others and acting as a punching bag when things go wrong. Less often are IT security activities discussed in terms of the corporate value and bottom-line contributions they make to the organization. Focus tends to be on how the security function protects the value of others' contributions rather than actually making its own.

I've had many conversations with security managers who are frustrated by their seeming inability to articulate their value to the rest of the organization, or who complain that they are not taken seriously as contributors to the corporate bottom line. Instead, they believe they are viewed as a necessary evil at best and, at worst, as active obstructionists who use fear, uncertainty, and doubt to make people's jobs more difficult and complex. Part of this problem exists because IT security has not yet learned to translate its activities into the language of value used elsewhere in the business, just as other IT functions had to be expressed in different terms as they matured. Although the role of today's CIO is still subject to political and organizational turf battles, most of these conflicts are couched in terms of how the CIO can stay competitive at the table with other CXO-level players and not whether the CIO has any right to be sitting at the table in the first place.

Some of the frustration about security's lack of influence has resulted from the profession's implied claims of exceptionalism—the idea that security is somehow different from other business activities. I've heard many times from security experts that what we do is as much, if not more, art than science. Not surprisingly, this is also a common argument against measuring security, given the belief that what we do somehow defies description, observation, or deconstruction. This approach to our professional activities does have its rewards, however. It is difficult to hold someone truly accountable for something that carries no hard criteria for success or failure. It is difficult enough for security management to deal with budget battles, political battles, and winning the hearts and minds of users without wanting to concern ourselves with the hard task of self-assessment and self-criticism. I believe that this can be a motivation against measuring our activities that is, unfortunately, difficult to resist. And the flipside is the frustration of not being able to explain ourselves fully to others and of not being recognized as real contributors to the success of our respective organizations.

But just as IT grew to be recognized as an independent business process of its own and not simply a technological enabler of other business processes, security is about more than simply protecting the activities and contributions of other, productive, parts of an organization. Security is an activity that consumes resources and produces outputs that are in turn consumed by the rest of the enterprise. This is the definition of a business process, and where business processes exist, so do opportunities to support the organization productively in tangible terms. But to manage security as a business process, security managers and CISOs will have to extend themselves beyond the technical aspects of security and take an interest in defining and measuring how security works in terms of the human, organizational, and economic characteristics of security and the associated costs and benefits that these activities bring to the organization as a whole.

Defining a Business Process

The first characteristic of a business process is that it involves activity, which means that it involves things happening and getting done as people and technologies interact. This may seem rather obvious, but it is an important concept. Activities are dynamic, implying action, interaction, and change. Activities are not static things. Think about how security is usually described within your organization. You probably hear statements such as "our security is good," "security needs to improve," or "the security posture of the network is weak." These do not describe activities, however, and it is far less common to hear that the security of the organization as a whole is "acting according to plan," or even "working properly," although the latter may be heard when referring to a particular IT system. We just don't talk about security as a set of activities unless we have to, preferring instead to abstract security to some general thing or force that is difficult to pin down.

Business process experts, however, understand that any process, including IT security, is in fact a structured series of activities that are conducted by individuals, groups, and machines working in concert. You cannot describe a business process as a single thing or an abstraction, because the process is always in flux as the activities that it comprises are accomplished. Instead, the process is described in terms of how well those activities function in support of the organization's goals and objectives.

Consider human resources (HR) as another example of a business process. HR is usually not understood to be a single thing, but a collection of activities and people within an organization. It would be unusual to hear "our HR is good" unless the comment referred to the HR department and not some general state of HR goodness. If you want to test the theory that security does not typically refer to itself as a business process, just search the Web for "HR business process" and then for "security business process." In the top hits for HR, you will find that human resources is described as a process of its own, whereas the top hits for security mostly appear as advice on how to incorporate security into the development of other business processes.

Security Processes

Looking at security as a set of activities helps IT security organizations better understand the low-level interactions that are necessary for security to function at all, from the activities of the firewall administrator, to the online habits of users, to the development of corporate strategy by the executive board. Any activity that either directly or indirectly impacts the security of the organization as a whole becomes part of the security business process and therefore subject to analysis.

From an IT security perspective, problems of coordination and collaboration that hinder the mission have always existed. In more than a decade of working with security clients, I have seen many examples of an almost willful failure to align the different stakeholders necessary for successful security programs. The divisions between the business and technical activities supporting enterprise security can be huge even within a single IT security organization. Getting the department to coordinate with other divisions of the organization such as Legal or HR is even more challenging. Consider the area of physical and logical security convergence. If a strong collaboration between common activity was to be found anywhere within a company, one would think it would be found in the joint development of corporate and IT security programs. But I have found that IT security teams are often no more closely aligned with facilities and physical security teams than they are with other organizational entities. This silo effect impairs the overall effectiveness of security operations by creating an environment in which no one really understands IT security and IT security doesn't really understand anyone else.

IT security metrics require that the organization collect measurement data from a variety of sources. Protecting data and resources from harm and abuse cannot be localized to a single organizational unit, regardless of whether or not that unit is responsible for the protection. The activities that define whether or not a company is protected take place everywhere and they must be suitably addressed. A business process management approach demands that all activities that can impact enterprise security be subject to appropriate measurement and analysis. To this end, security managers must involve many other stakeholders and process participants in the overall security program if they are to continue to demonstrate the value of their unique activities.

Process Management over Time

The good news is that a long history and an equally large body of literature are devoted to the practice of managing business processes, and IT security can leverage all of this historical experience and expertise to articulate and promote the value of the security process.

Early Studies

Process management practices date back several hundred years to the beginning of the industrial revolution and involved the detailed analysis and restructuring of labor processes to introduce standardization and new efficiencies to the work performed in factories. In 1776, for instance, economist Adam Smith wrote about the division of labor in a pin factory as part of *The Wealth of Nations*. Smith described how, instead of one laborer being responsible for the entire construction of a pin, a team of workers each were given their own separate tasks in the manufacturing process. Smith calculated that this division of the assembly process enabled a single worker to contribute to the manufacture of hundreds of pins, on average, whereas that individual worker might find it difficult to manufacture a complete single pin on their own.

Scientific Management and Manufacturing

In the late nineteenth century, American engineer Frederick Winslow Taylor began to apply rigorous scientific principles to the study of workflows in shops and factories. Taylor's principles of scientific management refined the division of labor into highly organized, machine-like assembly lines of workers. The workflows and activities of these laborers were then extensively observed and studied to understand empirically how work was conducted and where inefficiencies or insufficient oversight might exist. As the factory process became more understood and controlled, work was then optimized to achieve maximum productivity for managers and owners, including such industrial giants as Henry Ford. Taylorism, as scientific management is also called, has been widely criticized for its overly mechanistic view of human beings as expendable parts of the factory "machine," but Taylor's influence is unmistakable and remains at the core of much of the working world today.

Process Analysis and Control

In the mid-twentieth century, a new approach to business process management began to emerge in the works of process and workflow researchers such as W. Edwards Deming, Walter Shewhart, and Joseph Juran. Working both in academia and in industry, these men developed new approaches to process analysis and management that built upon

Taylor's scientific management principles of empirical observation and methodical testing, adding concepts such as quality control and applying innovative statistical methods to the understanding and improvement of the processes and workflows they studied. Recognizing the importance of social and interpersonal factors in the business process, they also moved away from some of the more dehumanizing elements of Taylorism. Where Taylor's work had served to separate managers and workers, consolidating power into the hands of the former so as to better control and manipulate the activities of the latter, the new view of business processes was more holistic and recognized the contributions of all sides to successful process improvement.

Another important aspect of process control was the concept of continual improvement of the processes being managed. Deming in particular contributed significantly to the promotion of continual process improvement through his creation of the Plan-Do-Check-Act (PDCA) cycle, which remains widely used to this day. PDCA is even used in the security industry as the formal basis for the ISO 27001 international security standard. In creating PDCA, Deming drew from the scientific method, which involves hypothesis formation, testing, and analysis, as an inspiration. And like scientific progress in general, he emphasized the PDCA cycle as an iterative and continual activity occurring over time. Deming constructed PDCA, shown in Figure 4-1, as a wheel-shaped model that started and ended in the same place, articulating that the end of one iteration of the process was the beginning of the next iteration. The Deming Cycle, as PDCA is also known, can be recognized at the root of many improvement cycles today across a variety of industries, including security. Andrew Jaquith, who wrote one of the first books on security metrics, describes a funny and perverse variant of the cycle in which the phases remain but the original intent of continual improvement has been forgotten. Organizations on this "hamster wheel of pain" simply run around and around, repeating process phases without understanding what they are trying to accomplish, and getting nowhere fast.

Quality Control

Deming began his work in the United States, but it was in Japan that he enjoyed his greatest success. In the years following World War II, Deming was working to help the Japanese government recover and rebuild its destroyed industrial capabilities. By the 1950s, Deming had conducted extensive training of Japanese businessmen and engineers on his ideas for process improvement. These techniques primarily involved the use of statistical measures to analyze and control business processes empirically. Deming also introduced the concept of quality, tying increases in the quality of products to lowered costs and increased productivity and financial success. By continually monitoring and improving quality, Japanese businesses could make themselves more competitive and successful in the marketplace.

The Japanese embraced Deming's work and advice enthusiastically, and during the next three decades, Japan grew into an economic superpower, successfully competing with and even surpassing other nations around the world, including the United

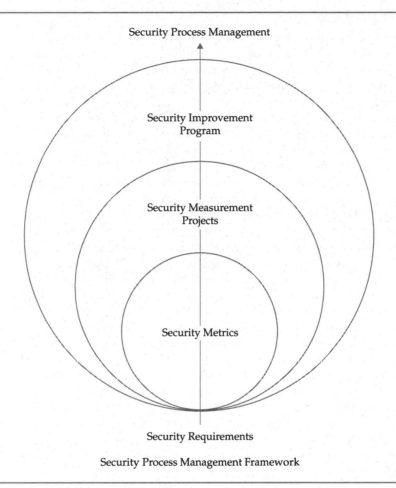

Security Process Management

Security Improvement
Program

Security Measurement
Projects

Security Metrics

Security Requirements

Security Process Management Framework

Figure 4-1.   The SPM Framework includes security metrics, security measurement projects, and the security improvement program.

States. In the 1980s, as a direct result of Japan's success, Deming's work was embraced and expanded upon in the United States, as American industry sought to compete more effectively with their Japanese rivals. Driven by the results of the improvements experienced in Japan, concepts such as quality management and process improvement became hot business concepts for the decade, as "Total Quality Management," "Just in Time" manufacturing, the ISO 9001 quality standard, and other frameworks were implemented and adopted on the Japanese model.

Business Process Reengineering

You may see a pattern emerging here. As the analysis and improvement of business processes emerged historically, researchers continued to expand and develop the ideas and techniques that came before. The 1990s were no different, as the next phase of process improvement took shape. Business process reengineering was a response to the idea that continual process improvement frameworks such as TQM and process control were not sufficiently radical. Process improvement experts such as Michael Hammer and James Champy were concerned that the attempts to improve process efficiencies were inefficient themselves, concentrating more on automation through technology and streamlining workflows. They argued instead that processes needed to be completely reengineered, and those processes that were not valuable completely done away with. Similar arguments were made by other reengineering proponents such as Thomas Davenport, who believed that only by completely rethinking the business process (as opposed to simply improving the one in place) could an organization achieve the gains in activity that were needed to compete in an increasingly technological and global marketplace.

In the case of process reengineering, technology began to play an increasing role as both a driver and an enabler of change. New information technologies were beginning to displace traditional manual processes, and the reengineers looked for ways to leverage these technologies to reshape the workplace completely rather than be satisfied with incremental improvements to business as usual. In a similar fashion, the availability of new technology allowed for more sophisticated analyses of the processes themselves. Organizational activities could be tracked, charted, analyzed, and monitored through the use of technology in ways that transformed the older, manual ways of accomplishing the task. As a result, organizations could afford to build process improvement into the workflows themselves, rather than depending on outside experts to conduct more expensive and disruptive reviews periodically. This allowed for the capability to collect more "real-time" continual feedback on processes and more input from everyday workers, although not everyone implemented such improvements in the same way or to the same degree of effectiveness.

Business Process Management

By the late 1990s, business process reengineering had also taken some hits, as companies used the concept as an excuse to cut costs, jobs, and benefits in the name of efficiency and productivity. Many of the same critiques of Taylor's scientific management were applied to business process reengineering as a way of ignoring the human aspects of the organization in favor of a more mechanical view.

And so the history of business process improvement continues. As I write this book, the current preferred term for referring to the analysis and improvement of business processes is simply "business process management." At its most basic level, business process management involves the active measurement and analysis of the activities of the business to understand and improve them. Some process improvement techniques are about identifying redundant activities and eliminating or combining them through automation. Some are about understanding where the process may yield opportunities for growth or additional value.

Many frameworks are available for managing business processes, all building upon the historical development I have outlined here, dating back to Smith's description of the pin factory. Some are proprietary frameworks promoted by consulting companies and others are more generic guidelines for tracking activities. The framework outlined in this chapter is an application of business process management for IT security and is designed to be both usable and practical, and I specifically address security process improvement in examples later in the book. My recommendations are not a revolutionary new twist on how to do this sort of work. They represent one way that you can adapt these ideas to measuring and improving your security over time.

The SPM Framework

The SPM Framework allows you to structure your security measurement activities into a structured yet holistic approach to improving security over time. The framework is iterative and built upon several components that are then structured into a continuous program for managing security as a business process. The SPM Framework is illustrated in Figure 4-1. At the lowest level of the framework are the security metrics you identify to enable the measurement, analysis, and assessment of your security process activities. But, as I've discussed, metrics are far less effective when they are ad hoc or unstructured aspects of the security program. The GQM method described in Chapter 2 is an elegant and easily understood way of bounding and aligning metrics with a specific goal, but even GQM-derived metrics remain relatively tactical and more suited for specific projects than as strategic activities.

The project-specific nature of GQM can be carried a step further. Strategies are never accomplished at once, but are the result of well-coordinated sets of interrelated objectives and actions. The SPM Framework's strategic approach to security involves the coordination of many different project-level activities, somewhat obviously called security measurement projects (SMPs), in which bounded security measurement initiatives are undertaken, tracked, and coordinated into a larger system. These projects allow you to tackle security improvements in manageable increments that document and align the specific goals of the project with the larger goals that exist across projects as part of an overall program to improve the organization's security.

This modular approach to security measurement supports a larger, strategic Security Improvement Program (SIP) that works to combine, coordinate, and align the activities of all the various measurement projects into a system of continuous measurement, analysis, and improvement of enterprise IT security. Under the SIP, metrics and project results are cataloged and retained for future reuse and projects are cross-referenced and incorporated into organizational learning systems to create security knowledge management and experience sharing across the organization. The end result is SPM, a capability maturity in which a broad selection of IT security characteristics, including people and organizational process as well as technology, is understood, measured, and continuously improved.

Security Metrics

I have spent several chapters digging into the topic of IT security metrics, so instead of rehashing that material, let's just leave it at the fact that your metrics are the engine that drives your SPM Framework initiatives. In fact, SPM exists primarily as a way to organize, structure, and keep track of the various activities that you are doing to measure your security. The framework ensures that metrics are developed and addressed in a bounded, manageable way over time and that the results of these activities can be remembered, learned, and used by the organization long after the original project is completed.

Think of the growth of human knowledge, moving slowly along on a foundation of observations, experiments, and analysis. Experiments and observations may have been the core of the process, but it took the conceptual framework of the scientific method in the seventeenth century to kick-start that growth, standardize it, and make the results available to others who may have wanted to replicate and build on preexisting work. Metrics without a structure for long-term exploitation of the measurements will never allow you to reap the full benefits of your efforts.

The GQM method keeps your metrics bounded in the service of specific goals and provides a good organizing principle of its own, acting as a natural way of designing security measurement projects around particular metrics goals. GQM also represents a good mechanism for classifying and cataloging your metrics for future use. Constructing a metrics catalog with cross-referenced goals and questions can enable you to build institutional memory and avoid repeating steps unnecessarily. A metrics catalog does not have to be anything fancy so long as it keeps track of the metrics you have already developed and used, organizes them in some way, and is easily available for your team (and possibly others) to use and draw upon. A process of review should also exist, in which metrics are assessed, updated, or removed. Wikis are a great way to develop a metrics catalog that can be easily shared and updated in a collaborative environment, but a simple document such as the one shown in Figure 4-2, posted to an internal server where it can be found and downloaded, can also work quite well with minimal overhead.

Security Measurement Projects

SMPs are the building blocks of your security process management. I will cover the process of setting up measurement projects in detail later in the book. For now, you should know that SMPs allow you to break down the complexity and size of IT security into manageable chunks of inquiry that can be defined and observed in a realistic way. SMPs can be applied to anything you want to explore or understand. If you can articulate a desire to know something, then you can build a measurement project to delve into it, using the GQM method to figure out what you want to accomplish and what metrics you have to develop and explore to get there. In this way, the SMP concept adds to the practicality of metrics in general as projects are naturally customized to the unique needs and goals of your organization. At its core, the measurement project is just the logistical and organizational structure that you employ with regard to your security goals, questions, and metrics to see them to completion.

Security Metrics Catalog

Goals and Projects	#	Associated Metrics
Perimeter Security	1	Time between perimeter security assessments (months)
	2	Count of vulnerable hosts (# or %)
	3	Mean CVSS score and standard deviation
	...	Additional Metrics
Endpoint Security	1	Count of hosts without required security patches (# or %)
	2	Count of hosts without current AV signatures (# or %)
	3	Count of hosts running unapproved user applications (# or %)
	...	Additional Metrics
Security Policy	1	Time between security policy reviews (months)
	2	Count of security policy violations reported over previous 6 months
	3	Readability of security policy documents (lexical density)
	...	Additional Metrics
PCI DSS Compliance	1	Count of non-conformance issues identified
	2	Count of security staff with documented PCI DSS responsibility
	3	Count of users without unique system ID assigned
	...	Additional Metrics

Figure 4-2.   A simplified security metrics catalog organized by previous projects and listing the metrics that have been used for those projects adds value by allowing you to track and reuse what you have already built.

SMPs create context and documentation for your metrics and tie together your measurement efforts. For most organizations, this is less about actual projects and more about a state of mind. Every organization has security projects, just as every organization collects metrics-related data. The challenge is looking at these projects as links in a chain of effort that naturally lead to other links, other projects, and other findings. I see this most often in customer consulting engagements when it comes to remediating the problems identified during an assessment or a review. The two tasks are viewed as different activities rather than as two components of the same activity. The results are delivered and the consultants leave, at which point a separate project must be set up to address the issues. Under the SPM Framework, all projects are components of an integrated activity, with inputs from some projects and outputs to others. Smaller goals are rolled up into larger goals, metrics into broader understanding, and security capabilities mature and grow more embedded over time.

The Security Improvement Program

The strategic goals of every security team include reducing the risks posed by security threats, improving the effectiveness of their security operations, and adding value to the organization. These goals drive security staffs to assess and improve what they do. But improvement often competes with day-to-day operational management of those systems and the security program in general. It is difficult to stay focused on the future when the present is constantly calling the help desk or showing up at your office door to ask where your budget inputs are prior to the upcoming ops review. And it never helps that there are not enough people or funds to go around. As a result, many security programs remain rooted in the immediate, tactical requirements of daily security operations.

Continuous improvement of anything, including IT security, requires that the efforts to make things better be done in a consistent and coordinated way, not as piecemeal exercises that could be easily forgotten or neglected as the next task appears in our inbox. You do not train for a marathon by running whenever you have the time, nor do you get an advanced degree or certification by taking classes and studying when it is convenient. All genuine improvement in the quality of effort requires a commitment to that improvement.

The SIP works within the SPM Framework to provide a structure for that commitment, just as the GQM method structures your design of metrics and a security measurement project structures your enactment of those metrics. The goal of the SIP is the explicit linking and coordination of individual measurement projects over time, as illustrated in Figure 4-3. The SIP accomplishes this coordination by leveraging documentation, activities, and feedback tools to facilitate organizational learning and capabilities maturity. Like the rest of the framework components, I will discuss techniques for SIP development later in the book. For now, the key takeaway is that the improvement program functions as an organizational control plane for measurement projects, metrics, and data. Under the SIP, projects are coordinated with other projects, with collaboration across project teams, and documented through measurement project catalogs much like the metrics catalogs discussed in the preceding section. Over time, data becomes information, information becomes knowledge, and (hopefully) we all end up wiser as well.

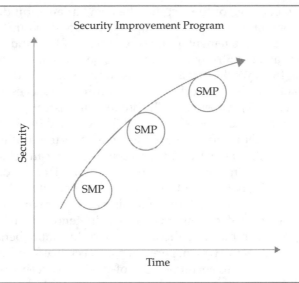

Figure 4-3. The SIP links and coordinates individual measurement projects over time for continuous security improvement.

Security Process Management

At the top level of the SPM Framework, supported by all the work occurring in the phases and activities below it, is the attainment of ongoing security process management and continuous improvement of your operations and initiatives. The benefits that result from measuring and coordinating security processes and from sharing and reusing the results can be profound. From an operational standpoint, SPM gives more insight into the mechanics of security and backs up these insights with empirical data that can be used to support budget and resource requests, audits, and reporting requirements. Better understanding of the security process also contributes to decreased risks and losses due to security breaches and incidents. Perhaps even more powerfully, SPM can enable security management to articulate the value of their efforts and activities in language that is understood and accepted by business stakeholders outside of the security group.

Whether metrics let you better quantify the losses that your program prevented or, by analyzing and improving the efficiency of your security processes, allow you to cut costs and increase productivity in existing operations, you'll find that you can describe and explain how security supports the business beyond being just an insurance policy.

Research has also shown that effectively managed processes pay off for organizations in more ways than just preventing security problems. A 2008 research study by the IT Policy Compliance Group (available at www.itpolicycompliance.com/research_ reports) found that managing IT processes (including security processes) effectively provided double-digit increases in revenue, profit, and customer satisfaction and retention. Such increases make sense when you consider that they do not result from new product implementation, or the fact that the firm has an audit done every year, but rather from a true commitment to process improvement and maturity.

Continuous process management and improvement of the kind attainable through the SPM Framework and the SIP structure are the objectives of a number of process-oriented conceptual frameworks that are increasingly being considered by security managers and consultants. Frameworks such as Control Objectives for Information and related Technology (COBIT), Information Technology Infrastructure Library (ITIL), Six Sigma, and several of the special publications of the National Institute of Standards and Technology (NIST) all promote the need for more mature, continuously improving security processes and offer paths by which an organization can achieve sustainable improvements. The SPM Framework is not intended to replace or compete with these other frameworks, should they be in place. But as I have developed the idea for the framework over time, I saw the need for something a bit more practical and easier to grasp. Other potential process frameworks for security tend to be proprietary (and expensive), increasingly complex and theoretical (and thus more beneficial to consultants than to operational security managers), or too specialized and focused on checklists and standard techniques to encourage out-of-the-box experimentation.

To recap the SPM Framework in simple terms, the general idea is this:

1. Develop metrics, ensuring that your measurements are appropriate and well-designed using the GQM method or a similar alternative.

2. Collect and analyze your metrics data through bounded, well-defined security measurement projects. Projects can be built around anything you want to measure and can include quantitative metrics, qualitative studies, experiments, or documentation exercises as meets your needs. Share and save the results.

3. Make a commitment to treating measurement projects as components of a larger security improvement program and not just separate or stand-alone activities. Document them, make the results easily accessible, and build upon them to create new projects based on what you have learned.

4. As you gain insight into how your security programs are working, employ processes to analyze and improve how you measure as well as what you measure, so that you achieve continual, sustainable management of security as a business process just like any other in the enterprise.

As much as I would enjoy claiming credit for discovering some new truth about IT security management, the SPM Framework and the techniques for implementing it are not revolutionary. Many of you are already performing some of these activities in your own programs. I don't claim that the SPM Framework is the only way to measure and improve security. If you are already doing things in a certain way, and those things provide some of the same results as those I discuss in this chapter, you should not change them just because I describe how to do those activities differently. But I do believe that any security program that does not include well-designed metrics and a variety of different measurements of different aspects of security, or that does not undertake those measurements within the context of a larger program of continual process improvement, is going to be much less effective. I also believe that if you do not explicitly understand and treat your security management as a business process just like HR, manufacturing, or sales, with associated input sources, products, and customers, you are missing opportunities to be taken more seriously and articulate the true value of your security efforts. The SPM Framework is meant to be a fairly straightforward and practical method for structuring your security to achieve both of these goals. Adopt it, tweak it, or discard it in favor of some other framework that meets your unique institutional needs, but put something in place if you don't already have that structure.

Before You Begin SPM

One of the ideas behind security process management and the SPM Framework is that you can start anywhere. Implementing SPM does not mean that you have to launch a formal, company-wide initiative with all the associated trumpets and internal memos. In fact, I'd recommend against that approach for most security organizations, unless you already have support and resources from senior management (or you are the senior management and you have the ability to make the program happen yourself).

A successful SPM program will address only as much as can be immediately influenced by the stakeholders of the program. You cannot expect others to buy into your vision strictly on the basis of that vision—most will want to see some results first. Of course, once you can produce those results, you may want to begin bringing other stakeholders such as internal audit into your efforts, as these teams are more likely to "get" what you are doing and can act as a force multiplier as you take the security message to others.

By keeping initial SPM efforts local, limited perhaps to a security measurement project or two, you can keep control of the effort and build a pilot program with results that you can use to justify expansion into a larger initiative. This approach is not much different from deploying a new technology or starting a new branch of scientific exploration. You don't change everything and rewrite all the textbooks until you have built up your credibility through initial stages of development. Security metrics are no exception.

Getting Buy-in: Where's the Forest?

A standard mantra of process improvement and project management of all stripes is that you have to have some level of sponsorship and support to be successful. Pick up almost any book on the subject and you'll read very early about the need to get management buy-in for your efforts. This is certainly true as you work to improve security across the organization. The first question you should ask yourself when considering security metrics or SPM is "what large-scale issues am I attempting to address?" Metrics are usually local. They tend to be specific sources of data and of primary interest to those closest to them. But to make a metrics program work beyond the immediacy of security operations—for instance, to argue for bigger budgets or more clout at the executive table—your security metrics must mean something to more than members of the security audience. Understanding the boundaries of the impact you want to make with your security metrics and process improvements will define the scope of your process management program.

It is easy to get bogged down in all the cool data that is available through measuring various aspects of your security. You begin to gain visibility into your operations that you might have only dreamed about. But a much more detailed operational knowledge of security, thanks to your metrics, is not a guarantee that anyone else will care. Deciding on the scope of your efforts before planning your security metrics program can save you a lot of frustration and false starts. For many stakeholders elsewhere in the organization, the nuances (or even new characteristics) of system or security performance that you discover will not be relevant to the things they care about. If you want to make security important to these people, you must understand what they consider to be important and then figure out how security affects those things. In other words, security is often about understanding how security *does not* help the business, whether this is due to lack of direct support to a business need or because those benefits have not been articulated effectively. Show stakeholders how security can improve their personal, political, and economic situations and you will find that you suddenly have a lot of support.

In the beginning, you may not even be able to see all the trees, much less the forest. The challenge sometimes facing those looking to improve security is that it is difficult to describe how your efforts will meet the needs of others if you don't understand those efforts yourself. How do you get buy-in to accomplish something you cannot fully explain?

One of the benefits of starting small in SPM is that you don't need a lot of buy-in. The metrics, projects, and process improvement described by the framework can be accomplished even if you don't manage anything but your own daily activities. One friend of mine, for example, began a new job in a consulting practice, delivering security assessments. As he finished his training program and started conducting his own engagements, he found several areas of the process inefficient, negatively impacting his productivity. Being the kind of engineer that he was, he quietly set about analyzing and changing his own workflow. He didn't complain about the old way of doing things or propose a study—he simply figured out a better way to do the work. Then he showed others what he had done. Within a couple months, management had gotten involved, the entire practice had adopted his changes, and he was being asked to analyze other elements of the practice. Buy-in follows results.

Requirements Analysis

Understanding what you want to achieve and how that integrates with what others want to achieve can be an important first exercise for an SPM program. The analysis does not have to be formal or particularly methodical, although as your program grows and you gain more experience, you may find it valuable to capture and refine this data through a formal process. But at first, your goal should be simply to help yourself understand what you want to accomplish and who you might need to sell on your vision in order to see it to completion.

Drivers   Like the goals that lie behind our metrics, we often neglect to consider fully why we are doing something. The risk assessment is a classic example, in that we will often talk about the primary driver being improved security when, in fact, the primary driver of the assessment is that some authority (a law or standard, an auditor, or our boss) told us we have to do one. Understanding the motivations and reasons behind our security activities makes them much easier to analyze and improve, but getting there can be difficult.

Sometimes, the reason we claim to do something is not really why we do it. A company might implement only enough security to meet minimum regulatory requirements, but it is not politically correct for management to say they don't care about security as much as they do passing an audit. The public story will always be that protecting company information is paramount. This is not a book on corporate ethics, so I'm not going to address the philosophical problems here. My point is that misleading yourself and misleading others about motivations and drivers creates inefficiencies, requires extra work, and costs money. Realistic analysis of the goals behind your security processes and measurements allows you to identify actual areas of improvement. Consider some of the high-profile security breaches in which companies that claimed to take security very seriously, and were even certified as doing just that, became victims, because it turned out that much of their security was on paper. It doesn't matter whether or not a particular company behaved badly—what is important is that any savings they might have achieved by skimping on some aspect of security was offset by the costs incurred when their security failed.

What are you really trying to accomplish? If you want improved security in some form, that requirement should drive your SPM efforts in a certain direction. If you need more budget, a successful audit, or a particular certification, those needs serve to define what you need to do. Realistically assessing your drivers and motivations also allows you to consider other questions and ramifications of your program, such as the politics involved with taking resources from other parts of the business or the consequences of a security breach on your reputation if you have been doing lots of audits but failing to remediate the problems you found.

Stakeholders   Stakeholders are those who stand to benefit from (or lose as a result of) your efforts. These are the people you will depend on for resources or data, the individuals who will make money or save time because of what you discover, as well as those who may be threatened or inconvenienced by changes in the security program. If you are a security manager implementing metrics for your immediate team and processes, your main stakeholders might be limited to your own group. But it always pays to consider the bigger picture. Thinking about how you can win new support from nontraditional areas of the business by adapting your SPM program can give you new ideas on how to construct goals, questions, and metrics. Likewise, understanding potential conflicts with other teams can help you work through problems before they become a risk to your security program activities.

Stakeholder analysis is one of those areas where security practitioners within an organization can really improve their efforts by developing novel approaches to security measurement and process improvement that meet the needs of others. Reaching out to peers in areas such as HR, finance, or sales and asking, sincerely, how the security team can support them and then working to provide those benefits can prove very valuable.

Of course, don't expect these stakeholders to be waiting for your call. You may have to explain exactly what you do, and you may have to listen to complaints about how security makes their jobs more difficult. But if you can get others talking to you and you listen to what they have to say, you may get some new ideas about where your program can meet your own needs and result in alliances with other parts of the organization.

Resources   Resources are never as abundant as we would like, and in today's economic climate they are positively scarce. One of the reasons for launching an SPM initiative is to justify the resources being spent on security (and, hopefully, to make the case that more resources are justified). But, as the saying goes, you have to spend money to make money, and adding new metrics and data analysis to your program is going to require resource commitments.

Depending on what kind of security measurement projects you attempt, you may need to leverage resources outside of your own immediate team. It is important to understand the resource requirements of any metrics or data gathering activities you undertake as well as the requirements of the security measurement projects that are ongoing. As your program expands into continual process improvement, you will find that you need additional resources to ensure that the program can function (although at that point the goal is to have so thoroughly demonstrated the value of continual security improvement that you do not need to argue very hard for these resources). Some things to consider:

- What data sources will you need? Do you control them? What are the costs of accessing these sources, either to you or to other owners?

- How will you analyze data from measurement activities or security processes? Do you have the tools and skills in house for statistical or other types of analysis?

- Have you considered the resources involved in addressing any findings you may develop through your program efforts? If you find major risks or opportunities for improvement, do you have the ability to act on them quickly?

- How will you present your findings and recommendations? How will you use your measurement results to convince stakeholders, particularly those who have provided you with data to begin with, that changing their security behaviors and activities will be to their benefit?

Setting Expectations

The end goal of the SPM Framework is nothing short of a transformation of your security operations into a better managed and more mature business process. This transformation may be huge or it may be specific to particular areas, depending on how well your security program is currently governed. But in either case, the transformation will and should be gradual. A potential trap of any business process improvement initiative is that the organization tries to do too much, too fast. Someone attends a conference, takes a training course, or reads an article or book (oh my!) on implementing a process improvement framework and the next day comes into the office fired up to change everything. But turning an entrenched process on a dime doesn't work in real life and it will not work for your security program. From oil tankers to our personal lifestyle habits, you don't just decide "now I'm going that way" and instantly alter your circumstances. I have even see this occur with security metrics, as one or more individuals within the firm decide metrics are the answer to improved IT security and thus begin to measure everything without even thinking very much about what they really want to achieve. Usually these efforts end up unsustainable, putting out more light than heat and fading quickly. While it may feel more gratifying to dive into action in the face of a problem, it is more important to put a process into place that has staying power derived from clear definitions and well-formulated planning.

So expectation setting is key to successful metrics and to implementing SPM successfully. You have to set expectations for others and, equally important, you have to set them for yourself. On the one hand, measuring and improving security is going to require you to expend resources. However small you start, you are probably going to have to do some new things and learn some new skills. And as you tackle bigger questions requiring more (and different kinds of) data, or as you employ the structures for security improvement and continual process management, those resource commitments may increase. It helps to be ready for this. You also must make others ready for what you are going to do, and this often means explaining how massive transformation and savings is not going to occur overnight. Working with your stakeholders to identify clear, attainable objectives for measurement that you can build upon going forward is the best strategy when starting your program.

I think that one of the reasons IT professionals in general like big, broad transformation projects is that incremental change is at odds with our belief in how smart we are and how cool our technology is. Everyone wants to start a revolution, it seems, but revolutions can be violent and messy (just ask anyone at the heart of a large, failing enterprise resource planning [ERP] implementation). I prefer knowing each day that I am a bit better than I was the day before, that I have every expectation that I will be a little better tomorrow, and that I can keep it up indefinitely.

Showing Results

Setting realistic expectations is important, and just as important is the need to meet those expectations with tangible results. Earlier in the chapter I discussed how security managers often struggle with a lack of credibility with other business owners given the difficulty in expressing the value of security in terms those owners understand and care about. The upside of this challenge is that as long as nothing blows up, the security team can make the argument that they have delivered the results expected. But such absence of true accountability is not optimal or sustainable, and it certainly does not survive the first failed audit or high profile breach. The downside, of course, is that the security manager is never able to bring real value to the table. At worst, he or she becomes a functionary, making reports and keeping track of logs in an effort to prove that the security team is actually doing anything productive at all.

Results of IT security metrics and process management can take many forms, including these:

- Visibility into the real costs of protecting systems and data, and reductions of those costs in direct support of the bottom line

- Demonstrating to other business units and stakeholders the value of information and the associated real costs of protecting corporate assets

- Positively affecting corporate goals such as productivity, revenue, and profit through improved compliance and IT governance

- Building internal and external customer satisfaction on the basis of understanding markets for security improvement, attitudes towards protecting corporate assets, and motivations for why people do or do not exhibit good security practices

The Security Research Program

Many of the security practitioners with whom I've discussed metrics and process get a little hesitant when I begin talking about that exploration as a research program. This is one of those cases where having a Ph.D. actually adds to the problem, because I say "research" and people start to think I mean academic activities that are complex, theory-heavy, and unlikely to provide the immediate benefits they are looking for or need. Even in security, "research" tends to refer to work that is separate from daily operational activities, unless you are a security researcher looking into specific areas of interest such as vulnerability discovery or botnet tracking. The discoveries made through this research may benefit day-to-day operations, but probably not directly and not immediately.

The security research program I advocate is more practical and relevant, involving far more applied research (research geared toward solving a real problem and not just for the sake of new knowledge) than basic research. In this way, it is more like the research programs for marketing, advertising, or manufacturing. The goal of a security research program is to understand the security environment and the forces that govern it so that you can better influence and control them. There may be a place for exploratory research within your security program, but you will probably find as you begin to measure and manage your security that there is plenty of low-hanging fruit available in terms of process improvement without getting overly creative with your research. You should think of your research as supporting the understanding and improvement of your business, as though you were an entrepreneur looking to attract potential venture capital or a consumer product firm hoping to capture a new market.

The point of considering your activities as a research program instead of, say, just a security metrics program is that a focus on metrics is simply a focus on data. With metrics, all you need to do is measure. Looking at what you do as research keeps you focused on the prize: new information and knowledge that you can apply to a greater purpose. The SPM Framework provides a good structure around which to build the research program, to document and champion your security management agenda, and to benefit from your results.

I like the research program trope because I have an academic streak and I think research is enjoyable. If the research program is not working for you or does not keep you engaged, then find another way of looking at it. If you have an entrepreneurial spirit, treat your security process management as a new business venture and draw up a SPM-aligned business plan for your program rather than a research agenda. If you are more of the artistic or literary type, use the metaphor of a novel or a screenplay in which you have to tell the story of security for your organization, including characters, motivations, and ongoing plotlines. The point is to develop a way of thinking about security holistically that gets you literally "out of the box" and gets the processes your organization uses to drive business into people's heads. In any of these examples, you will find that you still need to understand your resource needs, drivers, and stakeholders and to organize your metrics, projects, and improvement program to make your new venture successful. Whatever helps you to do it, you want to take a big-picture approach to how you comprehend your security, building on the metrics you develop to ensure that you have a structured and coordinated means of putting them to use.

Summary

Effective metrics are an engine for improved security, but taken on their own they can lead to an overemphasis on measuring and data collection without a larger contextual framework to guide and coordinate the work. To be successful in an increasingly challenging environment of compliance and business accountability, you should treat and manage security as a business process rather than primarily a technology issue. Security managers and CSOs today often struggle with an inability to articulate the value of their activities and hold themselves accountable to the same metrics and priorities as other business owners. Understanding and managing security as a business process can help your security organization improve both operational and organizational success.

Business processes, including security processes, are activities that combine the efforts of people and technology working in concert toward organizational goals. Understanding these processes includes measuring and analyzing social and organizational aspects of the business environment in addition to the technological components of these processes. The analysis and improvement of business processes has a history dating back centuries to the beginning of the industrial revolution. Over its history, business process analysis has included increasingly sophisticated methods of observing factory work, scientific management theories, statistical process analysis, quality improvement, and most currently the reengineering and management of business processes to achieve continuous improvement over time.

The SPM Framework offers a practical, flexible structure on which you can build more effective security operations. The framework includes well-designed metrics, the analysis of which is accomplished through independent, focused SMPs that provide a vehicle for coordinating metrics within a standard project management plan. Measurement projects are not conducted in a vacuum, however, and the framework includes a SIP that builds organizational learning and knowledge management to enable metrics and projects to be leveraged and reused over time. As these processes improve, your security program achieves greater capability maturity and continuous improvement, while meeting management requirements for the data and insight necessary to demonstrate value and accountability throughout the business.

Before beginning an SPM Framework initiative, it is important that you consider issues of buy-in, including understanding the drivers, stakeholders, and requirements for security and security knowledge beyond your immediate security stakeholders. Setting proper expectations and delivering results can help you gain support and cooperation from areas of the business that may not have previously supported or given credibility to security.

Further Reading

2008 Annual Report: IT Governance, Risk, and Compliance—Improving Business Results and Mitigating Financial Risk. IT Policy Compliance Group, 2008. Available from www.itpolicycompliance.com/research_reports.

Jaquith, A. *Security Metrics: Replacing Fear, Uncertainty, and Doubt*. Addison-Wesley, 2007.

CHAPTER 5 | Analyzing Security Metrics Data

As you implement the Security Process Management (SPM) Framework, selecting metrics and launching security measurement projects, you will accumulate data—the raw material of the framework. It may come from familiar sources and repositories that are regular sources of security data, or it may come from new sources as different data are needed to answer emergent questions that have developed in support of your goals. In many cases, it will be a combination of data sources as you start to use existing data in innovative ways, mapping it to and correlating it with new sources that allow you to explore your security program in more detail or in different directions. Whatever the means by which you collect it, your data will require analysis. This chapter explores several techniques and considerations for that analysis.

The Most Important Step

I have had many interactions with security practitioners who collect metrics data on their operations. Modern security systems offer a variety of ways to generate data in the form of logs, reports, and summaries of system activities. The data is usually saved or archived somewhere, for some period of time, and pulled into regular reports, presentations, and various other articulations by which the security team can demonstrate what occurred during some previous time period. Although I see plenty of security organizations that collect and store operational data, many of these teams do not analyze their data thoroughly or by means of a formal process. Analysis typically involves the development of general charts that show the values of particular metrics for some recent time period but offer little additional insight. Are security incidents up or down this month? How many exceptions to the security policy were requested through the change management system in the last quarter? Did our penetration test consultants detect fewer problems this year than when they did their assessment last year? This data may certainly prove valuable in a specific context, but it really only allows you to describe specific current events. Without more sophisticated analyses, you are unlikely to develop the kinds of insights that allow you to transform security into a more effective business process and to build a program that has continual growth and improvement built into that process. As you begin to develop more mature and process-oriented security capabilities, you will find that effective analysis will be a key to continued success and management of your security program over time.

Analysis is also important because, as I discussed earlier in the book, the simple act of collecting security data carries risk. If you collect data, then, as an organization, you know something. Even if you don't know you know something, that data becomes a record of events that took place and actions undertaken to monitor those events. If those events are bad, such as security breaches, the loss of personal data, or evidence of fraud or harassment, the organization may have incurred an ethical or legal responsibility to take action. If that action is neglected, the firm can put itself at risk from legal discovery or regulatory scrutiny.

The point is not simply to collect data, but to ensure that data collection includes a plan for analysis and a commitment to addressing any problems or risks that may result from the data. Given two bad options, I would rather be viewed as foolish because I didn't collect the data that showed I had a security problem than to be viewed as negligent and liable because I did collect the data, had evidence that I had a security problem, but took no action because I did no analysis. Of course the best choice would be to avoid both of these situations by collecting data, analyzing it, and making informed decisions based upon the results.

Reasons for Analysis

Data associated with security metrics can be analyzed in many ways, but before we can explore specific techniques, I need to talk about two basic reasons for analyzing data that you should consider.

Applied Analysis

When your security metrics data analysis is designed to answer a known, specific question about an aspect of the security program, this is *applied* analysis. Examples include analyses such as those mentioned in the preceding section, in which statistics on events or security operations are needed for reporting or compliance purposes. In applied analysis, you often already know what you want to know and probably have some insight about the answer.

Consider a situation in which a firewall administrator must report monthly on the number of accepted and rejected connections through the corporate perimeter. Table 5-1 shows a simplified breakdown of such data collected from the firewall logs.

In this case, analysis may be as simple as counting the number of accepted or rejected connections, the most common IP addresses or services, and the averages for a given time period. Other analyses may be more involved—for instance, tracking the weekly hours spent by the security staff against particular projects for purposes of internal billing to departments and general resource allocation, as in Table 5-2. In this case, the data may be used to calculate follow-on metrics such as overall utilization of staff members, how well time budgets are met for particular projects, or compliance against contractual or regulatory requirements for employment.

Date	Time	Action	IN/OUT	Source IP	Destination IP	Service
Oct 28	09:34:20	Accept	OUT	xxx.xxx.110.25	xxx.xxx.200.33	HTTP
Oct 28	09:34:50	Deny	IN	xxx.xxx.66.78	xxx.xxx.110.119	ICMP
Oct 28	09:35:01	Accept	OUT	xxx.xxx.110.25	xxx.xxx.200.33	HTTP
Oct 28	09:35:15	Drop	OUT	xxx.xxx.66.92	xxx.xxx.125.10	FTP
...						

Table 5-1. Firewall Log Data

Name	Project Hours (HR)	Project Hours (CFO)	Admin Tasks	Training	PTO	Week Total
Jane	8	12	30	0	0	50
Bob	16	12	40	0	8	68
Tim	20	0	10	16	0	46

Table 5-2.   Employee Time Tracking

Applied analysis implies that the end result of the analysis is already understood, and all that is required is that the analysis "fill in the blanks" with the information necessary to complete the task.

Exploratory Analysis

When you analyze data for the purposes of answering new questions, or even for developing those new questions on the basis of existing information or knowledge, you begin to move from applied analysis to *exploratory analysis*. Exploratory analysis does not mean that your research and analysis activities have no practical application. The difference between applied and exploratory analysis is that in the case of the former you are typically dealing with known and well-understood questions and answers, whereas the latter is focused on adding to or expanding upon existing knowledge.

Revisiting the firewall example of the preceding section, perhaps the CIO wants to review and update the organization's policy regarding acceptable use of the Internet during work hours. She asks the security staff to generate a report of the web sites most commonly visited by employees during the workday and gets the information shown in Figure 5-1. The results of the analysis allow the CIO to make more informed decisions regarding how to update the use policy. In this case, even if personal use of the Internet is permitted, the CIO is likely to update the policy and impose severe penalties on those who use corporate resources to access adult-oriented material, which amounted to 5 percent of employee web use.

In the case of time tracking for the security staff, the data can be used to produce reports on overall utilization of employees assigned to projects, how well projects are meeting time budgets, and general levels of work effort. For organizations with formal project management programs, these metrics may represent cases of applied analysis, as the organization already tracks such figures. For those organizations that do not have such programs, the analyses could be used as an exploration to gain greater insight into time management and efficiency. And for both types of organization, exploratory analysis will develop as efforts are made to determine why projects are not being completed within scope or why some personnel have higher utilization rates for their projects.

Most analysis of qualitative metrics data is exploratory in nature as well, because these techniques tend to explore more complex characteristics of security that are

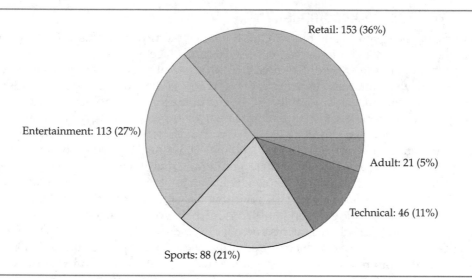

Figure 5-1.   Most commonly accessed web sites

subject to interpretation and are designed to reveal abstract relationships and characteristics of people and organizations. Qualitative metrics will often be explorations into characteristics of a security program that cannot be measured in a way that provides one "answer" to a question. Instead, they are exercises not only in pattern recognition, but in pattern development, including the construction of new concepts that can support different ways of looking at security. Lots of experienced security experts already do this sort of inductive analysis, even if they do not call it qualitative or even measurement. The changing nature of security threats and vulnerabilities, as well as shifting organizational and political priorities, means that success depends on reading the patterns before they become a problem. Exploratory and qualitative techniques are simply formally structured methods for doing what many of us undertake naturally as we navigate our environments.

The differences between applied and exploratory analysis are dependent upon the needs and routine metrics used by various people and groups. When the data is being analyzed to support requirements or decisions that are already well established, with little new information needed beyond what is expected, then you are dealing with applied analysis. When the data analysis is designed to develop new insights, add new information to an existing process or decision, or help in the development of new questions and analytical requirements, then the data can be seen as exploratory in nature. It is useful to be able to understand and articulate the differences between applied and exploratory analyses so that you can better market and promote particular measurement projects and metrics efforts to various stakeholders that need to understand the reasons for and the potential benefits from any particular metrics effort.

What Do You Want to Accomplish?

I have made the point several times in this book that metrics programs are most effective when they are considered in the context of goals and objectives for the development and use of those metrics over time. This holds true in terms of data analysis as well. As you prepare to develop analysis strategies for your metrics data, you should be considering what it is that you hope to accomplish at the end of the analysis process. Is your analysis in support of a specific decision or a requirement, or are you looking for new knowledge and insight? Is your goal simply to understand and describe the data you have collected, or do you want to use your data to predict things about your security program?

Before beginning to analyze your data, you should revisit how you developed the metrics and data that you are using and how you intend to fit them into your activities once analysis is completed. For the first task, revisiting the GQM process that you used to align your metrics with specific goals and questions can help you ensure that your analyses will also contribute to your original intents and objectives. Similarly, you should review your analytical strategies in the context of the security measurement project in which they will take place. Are your resources sufficient for the analysis that you are undertaking? Are there any risks involved with that analysis? And have you fully articulated and gained buy-in from the various stakeholders that will be the beneficiaries of the results?

It is worth taking some time to revisit your previous steps and strategies before the heavy lifting of analysis begins. By doing so, you allow yourself some flexibility to revisit your metrics goals and designs, to incorporate any new issues or considerations, and to ensure that as you begin analyzing the data you can continue to be comfortable that you are achieving the outcomes you want. This is an important intermediary step because you will find that your data is usually going to require some expenditure of effort to get it in a form that is ready for analyzing.

Preparing for Data Analysis

Most people getting into data analysis for the first time underestimate the amount of time and effort that is necessary to prepare data before you are even ready to begin analyzing it. Preparing and cleaning your data so that your analyses are functional and reliable can add quite a bit of time even to a straightforward analysis, and this process should not be underestimated or taken lightly. There is no point going to the trouble of building insights out of your security metrics data if those insights are faulty because the data was messy or incomplete going into the analysis. You should take several issues into consideration as you pull together the data from the metrics you collect.

What Is the Source of the Data?

Even in situations involving very basic analysis, it is important that you understand and keep track of where your data is coming from. There are many potential sources of security-related data, including the following:

- System logs
- Security event and incident management (SEIM) systems

- Scanners and analysis tools
- Audit reports
- User surveys
- Company databases (operational and historical)
- Policies and other records and documents

In some cases, you may be pulling data from one source that has been collected or aggregated from another source. As you begin preparing for the analysis phase of the project, keep a log or other record of where each type of data you will be using originated. If the origin is not the same as the source from which you pulled the data (for instance, if you are pulling aggregated data from an SEIM tool), you should note the difference between these secondary and primary sources. Some tools for aggregating or analyzing security information, and certainly reports and historical records that already contain a degree of analysis, may alter or transform data to provide unified presentation, and you will want to understand how, if at all, such data normalization affects the original sources.

The key point for data sourcing is that, as the analyst responsible for turning metrics data into security knowledge that supports decisions, you must be able to trace any finding or conclusion based on your data back to original sources and observations. The most effective metrics are empirical, developed from direct observations of some activity or characteristic that can be explained, articulated, and repeated. When you are asked to justify a particular recommendation (especially when what you recommend may involve spending more money or changing the way things are done), you should be ready and able to "show your work" by following the data trail back to the original observations on which you based your conclusions. If you cannot ground the advice you offer empirically, your analysis can face a serious loss of credibility. In many cases, the analyst will not own or control the data sources, which will change and even vanish over time. So documentation of data as well as analysis is important. Replicating every bit of data analyzed, especially in the case of very large repositories, can become impractical and may even violate backup and retention policies. But just using the data is not sufficient. You should be documenting sources of the data, the times of access, owners of the data, and the data types used in any analysis as part of the project. This is a very important element of data sourcing activities.

What Is the Scale of the Data?

In Chapter 3, I described the different scales of measurement that can be applied to security metrics:

- **Nominal**   Names or labels only, with no quantitative meaning involved even if numbers are used; "bucket" categories.
- **Ordinal**   Indicates ranking order, but with no insight into the differences between rankings; first, second, and third place race results.

- **Interval** The distance between measurements does have quantitative meaning, but there is no zero point to compare with; temperature on the Fahrenheit or Celsius scales.

- **Ratio** The distance between measurements has quantitative meaning, and there is a zero point, so the distances between measurements can be compared as well; length, weight, money, temperature on the Kelvin scale, and so on.

It is likely that your collection efforts will produce data sets that are measured on different scales. Some analytical techniques can be conducted only using data from certain scales, so it is important that you know what scales you are dealing with in your data and what scales you must be using to conduct the analyses you want to complete. It may be necessary for you to change data from one scale to another before you can use it.

We have already seen examples of changing scales in the case of qualitative risk assessments where nominal scores such as high, medium, or low are changed to an ordinal scale using a set of numbers. If you want to understand the average scores provided for the risks assessed, this becomes a necessary transformation. But changing scales should always be handled with care and should be well documented prior to the analysis. Changing scales involves potentially changing the amount and quality of information you are getting from the metric, and the decision to do so should always be driven by the goals and questions of the metric rather than from an effort to "fit" the measurement to a desired outcome. In the case of the risk assessment example, it is acceptable to change scales if you want to understand what people generally had to say about risk, but if you change the scale in an attempt to compute the average risk to the organization, you have engaged in statistical alchemy and turned the data into something that it is not.

Does the Data Require Cleaning or Normalizing?

When your security data comes from different sources, you will want to make sure that any comparisons you make regarding the data are valid. Data may have been coded or collected differently across multiple systems, and any discrepancies between measurements of criteria from one source to another can introduce errors into your analysis. It may also be necessary to remove or transform data that is missing, inconsistently coded, or superfluous to the analysis at hand and that can add error or impact the general analysis. This step can take up significant data preparation time, but it's important to complete to be sure that you are making apples-to-apples comparisons across data sets or drawing proper conclusions from the metrics you have employed.

Consistency and Accuracy One of the first steps in preparing your data is to ensure that the data is accurate and consistent, particularly across different sources. Let's say you are analyzing vulnerability assessments conducted across your company during the course of several years. As you examine the assessment reports, you notice the following descriptions of operating systems assessed:

- Windows
- Windows 2000

- Win2k
- Win2k3
- XPsp2
- WinXP
- Windows XP

These seven data entries may refer to a few or to many different operating systems, and they should be standardized before you begin data analysis. It may be necessary in such situations to approach the original owner of the data or others who are closer to the data sources for clarification and assistance in identifying what these data labels mean. It is unclear which systems may be running server versions, and there is ambiguity between which service pack levels the different XP machines were running at the time of analysis. The goal of the exercise is to maximize the accuracy and insight of the analysis; it's important that you understand what is being measured in detail.

Missing Data and Outliers   You may find that your data contains values that are missing from the set or values that fall far outside the normal ranges occupied by most of the data. In such cases, you need to make decisions about how you will handle these situations, beginning with trying to understand why the values appear in the data to begin with. Missing data can occur due to errors, processing failures, or coding conventions (for instance, when a blank or "N/A" value is automatically converted to or interpreted as "missing"). Outliers can also result from mistakes in collecting or measuring data, but they can also be accurate and indicate one or more values that are simply outside of the normal range.

Table 5-3 shows an example of missing data in a subset of simplified vulnerability scanning results. You can see that some data is not applicable or has not been entered. If values are missing from the data, it might be necessary to create a special variable as a placeholder (for instance "000" to reflect a missing value), or it might be possible to remove missing values altogether.

Figure 5-2 illustrates outlier examples for vulnerability scan data and shows the number of systems with particular maximum Common Vulnerability Scoring System (CVSS) scores. While most of the systems scored in the 3–8 range, one system had a

IP	OS	Version	SP	Scan date	Max CVSS
xxx.xxx.201.150	WinXP	Pro	2	03/04/2008	7.5
xxx.xxx.204.121	Red Hat Enterprise	5.4	—	06/30/2009	6.8
xxx.xxx.205.113	Windows Server 2003	—	4	04/04/2009	5.3
xxx.xxx.210.110	OS X	10.5	—	10/20/2006	4.6

Table 5-3.   Missing Values for Vulnerability Scan Results

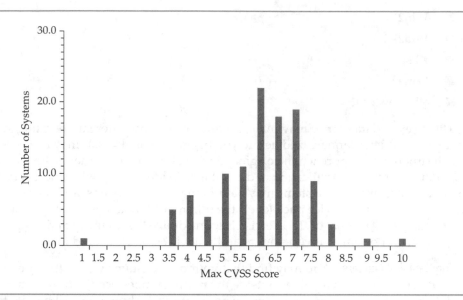

Figure 5-2.   Outlier CVSS scores in vulnerability assessment data

maximum CVSS score of 1, while a couple of systems scored near 10. It might be necessary to revisit the data to determine whether or not the outliers represent errors or real
data. You can also decide, based on the judgment of those knowledgeable about the
systems or on the reasons for the assessment, whether you want to eliminate any of
the observed systems from the analysis. You might, for example, decide that the CVSS
score of 1 was too low and is a potential error, while the higher scores are legitimate
based on what you know about the systems in question.

When faced with missing data or outliers, you will often need to make judgment
calls on whether to explore further, remove problematic data, or attempt other analyses
to incorporate what you have measured. Knowing why you included or excluded certain data, observations, or values is critical to being able to explain and defend the conclusions and recommendations that you generate from your analysis. As you become
more comfortable with your data and your metrics and security process management
programs improve and mature, you will find that few arguments are more convincing than knowing your stuff and having the data to back up your claims. Credibility
becomes even more of an issue as you begin to explore qualitative and interpretive
security metrics that may not have the luxury of falling back on numbers system data.
But if you have ever followed opinion polls during an election or watched economic
reporting on the state of the economy, you will quickly understand that even supposedly "hard" quantitative data is interpreted, argued over, and requires that those
making claims be able to articulate how they got their numbers. The best defense for
your security metrics data is to understand your data in minute detail and to be able to
deflect any criticisms or answer any questions because you have already applied those
critiques and asked those questions of the data yourself.

Transforming Data   Sometimes it is necessary to change data from one scale or format to another to accomplish the analysis you require. This can happen because data values are measured on different scales or have confusing or incompatible ranges that could influence the analysis. In some cases, transforming data may make the results easier to understand than using the original data, while in other cases the analysis techniques you choose may dictate that the data conform to certain characteristics or be measured on a certain scale before the analysis will work.

You can use numerous techniques for normalizing, cleaning, smoothing, and otherwise transforming data to aid analysis, and I will cover some of these techniques in later chapters and examples. Here are some examples:

- Changing data values to decimals or percentages for ease of comparison
- Grouping and aggregating raw data into categories or bins to facilitate analysis
- Reversing value orders or standardizing value scores for data sets that use different coding structures
- Employing descriptive statistics such as mean, median, mode, or z-scores to compare values
- Techniques such as min-max transformation, which fits all observed values into a new range of predefined minimum and maximum values

It's difficult to understate the value you derive from properly understanding and preparing your data prior to analysis. Effective data preparation does not necessarily mean that you have to invest large amounts of time into sophisticated data transformation techniques when they are unnecessary. But keeping with a central theme of the book, you need to understand what you hope to achieve and to accomplish with any security metrics efforts, and these requirements will in turn drive the level of depth and complexity that you should be considering for how you look at your data. Trending monthly reports from your SEIM system over the past five years to establish a baseline is likely more straightforward than embarking on a large data mining project to build a security data warehouse that the organization can use to build predictive models of emerging risks or threats. The purpose of using methodologies such as GQM and the SPM Framework to build a structured metrics program is that these tools can help you assess and choose the best metrics, data, and analysis strategies for what you want to achieve with your security program. Having talked a lot about what you will do before you analyze your data, I can now turn to some techniques for performing an analysis.

Analysis Tools and Techniques

I discussed two reasons for conducting data analysis, including applying analysis to a particular problem or decision and using analysis to explore the functions and characteristics of your security program. In addition, you might choose several types of analyses when conducting applied or exploratory security metrics research. These include analyses to describe data, analyses to infer or predict from data, and analyses to make sense of qualitative data or to combine quantitative data with other analyses to create models or to correlate data and identify patterns that can reveal more insights than is apparent in the raw data.

As a general analogy, analysis can be seen as exploring data in two ways. In the first direction, analysis moves from simply describing the data, showing only what is present in the actual data collected, to providing some level of predictive capability based on the data. Predictive analyses, sometimes referred to as *inferential statistics*, seek to use a sample set of data to infer things about the larger population from which the sample is drawn. Predictive analyses can also be used to develop patterns and models that may allow an analyst to draw conclusions about some future state of the object under analysis, such as in data mining techniques.

In the second direction, data analysis moves from working with raw data toward the identification and development of patterns within the data that provide analytical value. Pattern recognition may be accomplished through mechanisms such as summarizing raw data into tables of sums, totals, or cross-tabulations. Techniques also exist for categorizing and grouping data to reveal hidden relationships, as well as for mapping data into process flows or relationship networks. In the case of qualitative analysis, where grouping and pattern development is a central analytical process, there are tools and techniques for structuring interpretive pattern generation from data that is not quantitative at all and may be highly subjective and personal, such as field notes or interview responses. Figure 5-3 provides a basic visual illustration of the directions of analysis.

Descriptive Statistics

At a basic level, data analysis involves summarizing and describing the results of observations and measurements that you have undertaken. But descriptive statistics are by no means less valuable for being foundational. If you have a security metrics program in place or are seeking to build one, descriptive statistics will likely represent the lion's share of the analysis you will conduct. One reason for this is the currently nascent state of security metrics generally within the industry. Most security organizations, if they are measuring their security programs at all, are not using the full toolbox of descriptive statistics against their data. In my experience, security metrics tend to focus on totals and frequency distributions across categories. Measures of central tendency or dispersion are not used with much sophistication. This is okay, because it represents a great opportunity to improve our security metrics analysis without even getting into the more problematic world of inferential statistics or predictive models.

Distribution

As the name implies, the distribution of data involves where and how particular observations and measurements fall along some scale in the overall data set. Distribution does not involve much more sophisticated statistical processing than counting, but figuring out how data is distributed creates an important foundation for further analysis of the data. Some measures of distribution apply to all data scales, meaning that they can be used to analyze categorical as well as numerical data, which makes

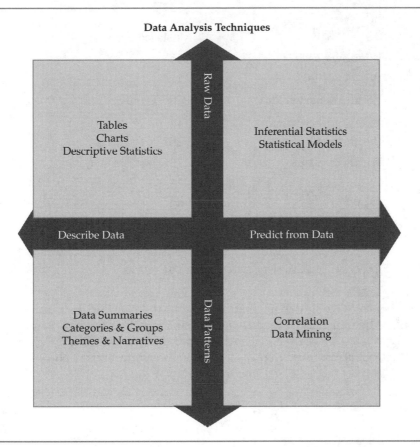

Figure 5-3.   Analysis techniques may involve moving from description to prediction, from raw data to patterns, or a combination of both.

sense given that the primary means of analysis is to count occurrences of any particular value or observation.

Data analysis begins by counting the individual observations or values contained in the measurement data. The most common result of such counting is a frequency distribution in which all the values are tallied and presented. Consider a data set containing a number of different operating systems installed within a business location. Table 5-4 shows one way of presenting the frequency distribution of the OSs.

Another way of showing frequency distribution is through the use of a bar chart, also known as a *histogram*, which shows the same data graphically, as shown in Figure 5-4. Whether presented textually or graphically, the data analysis is a straightforward count by category. Depending on the purpose of the analysis, the data could have also been expressed as a percentage of installed total systems.

OS	Installed Systems
Windows 2000	15
Win2k Server	11
Windows Server 2003	20
Windows Server 2008	14
Windows XP	257
Windows Vista	131
Windows 7	15
OS X	83
Red Hat Enterprise 5.4	17

Table 5-4.   Frequency Distribution for Installed Operating Systems

My experiences have shown me that identifying and charting distributions are the primary means by which most security groups analyze their metrics. Sometimes the analysis may involve more than just adding up the totals, but usually it's not much more than that. Security metrics reports tend to involve questions of counting incidents,

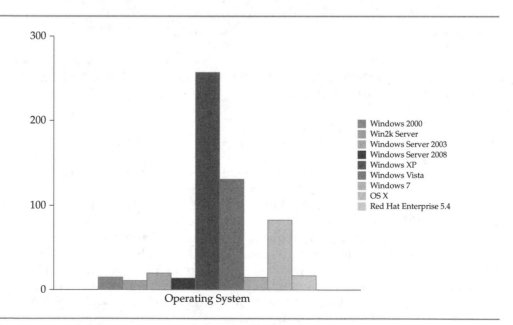

Figure 5-4.   Histogram showing frequency distribution of installed operating systems

changes, vulnerabilities, and other observations and then presenting summarized data on a periodic basis. If more sophisticated analysis occurs, it is usually just to state whether those totals went up or down over some period of time (usually since the last time the report was given) and may involve a graph to show trending as well as a histogram.

These analyses can be useful in helping to prioritize immediate efforts and to meet the needs of quarterly ops reviews, but they don't generate the comprehensive understanding of security operations that we need to establish going forward. From an analytical perspective, the industry's practice of security metrics is on the ground floor and can only go up in terms of sophistication and effectiveness.

Central Tendency

As you consider the distribution of your data, it is often valuable to understand what values in that data are most representative, most average, or most expected for the overall data set. Statistics that allow you to describe these qualities in your data are referred to as "measures of central tendency" because they help you identify values that tend to fall in the middle of the data. These characteristics of quantitative data are at the heart of most statistical analyses, particularly those that involve "normal" distributions (those that take the shape of a bell curve), and it is useful for you to understand some basic concepts around these measures.

You are probably already familiar with the mean, or average. But the mean is not the only measure of central tendency. To explore these statistical tools, let's look at a sample set of data based on change requests submitted to a firewall administration team each week over the course of six months. Table 5-5 lists the weekly number of requests submitted to the administrators.

Mode   The mode is the most commonly reported value for the data under analysis. In the case of the firewall change requests, if you put all the data values into order, you get the following sequence:

19, 20, 21, 21, 22, 22, 22, 26, 27, 27, 27, 27, 28, 28, 29, 31, 34, 35, 35, 37, 41, 46, 61, 65

| | Change Requests | | | |
Month	Week 1	Week 2	Week 3	Week 4
Jan	29	27	41	22
Feb	27	35	21	27
Mar	22	31	46	61
Apr	65	35	28	22
May	19	27	26	37
Jun	20	28	34	21

Table 5-5.   Example Firewall Change Request Data for Analysis of Central Tendency

Looking at the sequence, we can simply count the most commonly occurring number of change requests, which is 27 and occurs 4 times. This means that the mode of the firewall data is 27:

19, 20, 21, 21, 22, 22, 22, 26, **27, 27, 27, 27**, 28, 28, 29, 31, 34, 35, 35, 37, 41, 46, 61, 65

In some cases, multiple values are tied for the most frequent occurrence; in these cases, the data is said to be *multimodal* and the mode is shared among all the highest frequency values. With a multimodal data set, the mode would include all of the most frequently occurring numbers—you would not take an average of the numbers and call that number the mode. The mode is particularly useful for analyzing central tendency involving data on the nominal scale (categorical data), since this scale is non-numerical (even when numbers are used as the category labels) and cannot legitimately be analyzed using the median or the mean.

Median   The median represents the middle of the data distribution, where half of the observed values fall above the median and half fall below it. For the sequenced firewall data, you would identify the median by finding the number in the exact middle of the data set. Averaging does apply with the median, and since you have an even number of values the point in the exact middle is halfway between (or the mean of) the twelfth and thirteenth observations, or 27.5. Had the data been an odd number of values, the median would be the middle number of the set. So the median number of firewall change requests is 27.5.

19, 20, 21, 21, 22, 22, 22, 26, 27, 27, 27, **27, 28**, 28, 29, 31, 34, 35, 35, 37, 41, 46, 61, 65

Median values can be calculated for data on the ordinal, interval, or ratio scales. One advantage of the median comes when your data has outliers or skewed data that might affect the mean (discussed next). The median can provide an alternative measure of central tendency that is not as affected by these values and provides a more accurate picture of central tendency. This is why data reports such as household income often rely on the median rather than the mean. If large discrepancies exist between household incomes (to use this example), then mean household income could be misleadingly inflated or depressed, whereas the mean would better reflect the center of the distribution. In the case of the firewall data, suppose you had a couple of very anomalous months, one in which no change requests occurred and one in which 200 occurred. The median for the data set would not change, even with these outliers present.

Mean   Most of us are more familiar with the common term "average" than "mean," and the terms are often used interchangeably. For clarity, I will use *mean* when I refer to the statistic and I'll use *average* in the more colloquial sense of common expectations of something.

The mean is one of the most commonly applied statistical techniques, even when people don't think about using statistics. The mean is the sum of all the values in a set divided by the number of values in the set. For the example data, the mean number of weekly firewall change requests over the time period observed is the total number of requests divided by the number of weeks: 751 / 16 = 31.3. So over the time period observed, mean change requests were a little more than 31 per week. You can see an example of differences between median and mean scores in these results, as the mean weekly number of change requests is somewhat higher than the median weekly value of 27.5. Adding in the outliers from the median example makes the difference even starker. The median did not change with the addition of the outliers because the middle number remained in the same position in the sequence. The mean, however, is now 951 / 18 = 52.8, which is a significant increase as a result of the two extreme months.

The measures of central tendency I've outlined can help you understand where to find the middle of your data set, those observations that are most common or most typical. You can also continue to build upon these analyses to tell yourself more about the security metrics data you collect.

Dispersion

While measures of central tendency focus on the middle of your data, measures of dispersion explore how the data is distributed across observations. Dispersion is as important, if not more important, than central tendency in understanding your data, particularly as the questions you ask and the insights you seek to develop become more sophisticated. Means and medians do not help you understand how your data varies across observations or, more importantly, why they may vary. To understand these questions, you have to dig deeper into the data. Dispersion also applies most to data on interval and ratio scales, which deal with continuous variables. While statistical techniques for measuring dispersion for nominal and ordinal scale metrics are available, the differences and variations in these measurements are best handled in other ways.

Range   The range measures the dispersion of data by calculating the difference between the highest and lowest observed values in your data set. In the firewall change data, the range of change control requests is expressed as the highest value minus the lowest value, or 65 – 19 = 46.

19, 20, 21, 21, 22, 22, 22, 26, 27, 27, 27, 27, 28, 28, 29, 31, 34, 35, 35, 37, 41, 46, 61, **65**

Quartiles and Interquartile Range   Quartiles involve dividing your data into four sections, each containing 25 percent of the observed values for the data. An easy way to calculate the quartile ranges is to use the same technique you used in defining the median for the data. In fact, the median and quartile 2 will be the same value (27.5):

19, 20, 21, 21, 22, 22, 22, 26, 27, 27, 27, **27**, **28**, 28, 29, 31, 34, 35, 35, 37, 41, 46, 61, 65

To identify quartile 1, you would find the middle value for the first half of the data values, or 22:

19, 20, 21, 21, 22, **22**, **22**, 26, 27, 27, 27, 27, 28, 28, 29, 31, 34, 35, 35, 37, 41, 46, 61, 65

For quartile 3, the quartile measurement would be the middle value for the second half of the data values, or 35:

19, 20, 21, 21, 22, 22, 22, 26, 27, 27, 27, 27, 28, 28, 29, 31, 34, **35**, **35**, 37, 41, 46, 61, 65

We now have quartiles 1, 2, and 3 equaling 22, 27.5, and 35, respectively. Quartile ranges can be used as basic descriptors, buckets that allow us to identify low ranges and high ranges quickly in our data. If we want to get more statistical, we can use quartiles to calculate the interquartile range, which is the difference between the first and third quartiles. For the preceding data, the interquartile range is calculated as $35 - 22 = 13$.

Variance   When you determine variance of data, you are describing how variable, or spread out, the data is compared to the mean of the data. Another way of looking at variance is how far from the center of the data (the mean is a measure of central tendency) you may observe values. At this point, we begin to get into issues of whether we are talking about samples of data versus the entire population from which a sample was taken. In our firewall change request data, for instance, we are looking at a sample of the request data over a period of six months as opposed to the population of all firewall change requests. I will talk about samples and populations later in the section "Inferential Statistics." For now, I will use variance and standard deviation to refer to samples only.

In discussing variance, we also move out of relatively simple formulas for calculation of these statistics and into more complex mathematical functions. For example, variance can be defined as "the mean of the sum of squared deviations from the mean for a sample" and is described with a rather impressive looking statistical formula. This book is a primer on security metrics and not a textbook on statistics (of which there are many excellent examples that I have to refer to often). And, as one of my statistics professors told me, not even statistics professors worry about formulas when actually conducting research—that's what statistical analysis software is for. It may be that variance and the following techniques may prove quite useful to your security metrics program, but if you use them, you will not be calculating these measures by hand. I'll discuss tools shortly in the section "Tools for Descriptive Statistics," after I finish describing descriptive statistics.

Standard Deviation   Variance ultimately leads us to the most common measure of variability and dispersion in a data sample: the standard deviation. While many people may not be familiar with variance as a concept, most of us have heard of standard deviation as a measure of how likely or unlikely is the occurrence of a particular observation or value. The formula for the standard deviation is to take the square root of the variance. Increases in the standard deviation of a data set indicate increases in the spread of values around the mean of the data sample. The frequency distribution of data around the mean also takes particular shapes. The most familiar shape, the one that many common statistical methods assume in their calculations, is the normal distribution or the bell curve. In a normal distribution, approximately 68 percent of all observed values will be found within one standard deviation of the mean (half on each side), and approximately 95 percent of all observed values will fall within two standard deviations of the mean (half on each side). By the time you reach three standard deviations from the mean, less than one-half of one percent of observed values remains unaccounted for. Figure 5-5 shows standard deviations for a normal distribution, with the mean at 0 standard deviations and the number of observed values (expressed as a percentage) that are included as standard deviation increases.

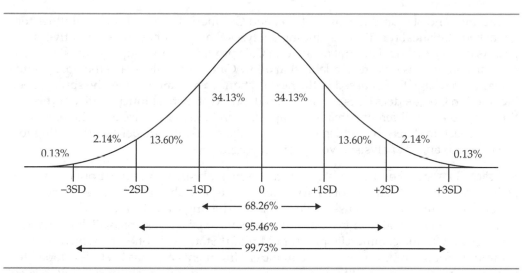

Figure 5-5.   Standard deviations in a normal distribution of data

The statistical methods I've described can help you get more value out of your metrics analysis than just counting up totals. Using the right measures of central tendency such as the median instead of the mean can help you reduce the uncertainty introduced by outliers and extreme variations in your data. Measures of dispersion can help you understand just what constitutes extreme values in the first place, and it can tell you whether a certain observation is seriously at odds with the general shape of your overall security data. You may not use these techniques every time you analyze your metrics data, but they represent the basic statistical tools upon which analysts in every field and industry rely to make sense of their numbers.

Tools for Descriptive Statistics

Many tools are available for describing security metrics data, and most security professionals are familiar with at least a few of them. Reporting and analysis features are built into various security products and are capable of providing statistics regarding incidents, events, and other metrics. If you are working with metrics data that you have collected and need to analyze yourself, you can choose from among several options.

Spreadsheets   Most of us are accustomed to running spreadsheets, and many spreadsheet applications are available. Some, such as Microsoft Excel, are proprietary, but open source and free spreadsheet tools are available as well, including Calc (part of the OpenOffice application suite), Gnumeric, and the spreadsheet program available as part of Google docs. Spreadsheets allow you to create data tables and summarize data, and they provide capabilities for charting and graphing of the results. Most of the quantitative analysis I see conducted around security metrics heavily leverages spreadsheet applications.

Some spreadsheet applications also let you conduct statistical analysis that goes beyond basic mathematical functions, with capabilities for calculating statistics such as variance and standard deviation. Excel and Gnumeric have built-in capabilities for advanced statistical functions, including analyses that go far beyond descriptive statistics. As of this writing, I am not aware that Calc provides native support for statistical analysis, but extensions are available that allow Calc users to leverage the open source statistical package R, discussed in the next section. To my knowledge, the spreadsheet included in Google docs does not support advanced statistical functionality at this time. If you use a different spreadsheet application than I have discussed here, you should check to determine which statistical analyses it supports before attempting to use it for advanced analysis in your metrics program.

Statistical Software   For more advanced statistical analysis, a variety of applications go beyond the capabilities of ordinary spreadsheets, and they are designed to be easier and more intuitive to use while you're conducting statistical research. As with spreadsheets, both commercial and open source programs are available. I have experience with the commercial program Minitab® Statistical Software, which is commonly found in business and academic environments and has been developed to be relatively easy to use and to provide advanced analytical capabilities. Minitab is not the only product for statistical analysis, but I find it quite usable.

A well-regarded open source statistical analysis package, R, is extremely powerful and as capable as any commercial package. R, however, is not as intuitive as most commercial packages and requires a longer learning curve, especially for users who are accustomed to graphical interfaces and point/click/drag/drop workflows (R functions primarily at a command line interface). R is typically found more often in academia and scientific research institutions than in the average corporate business unit. Users of the commercial packages such as Minitab will notice the similarities to spreadsheet interfaces, with the familiar cell format. But statistics programs allow a user to access many more analytical functions and visualization techniques easily just by accessing a menu. Figure 5-6 shows a graphical display of various descriptive statistics produced in Minitab for the weekly firewall data we have been exploring throughout this section.

Inferential Statistics

You can bring an extraordinary level of improvement and sophistication to your security metrics program by using the full toolbox of descriptive statistics available to you. I described basic statistical techniques in the preceding section, and I would encourage you to explore these tools. But descriptive statistics address only the immediate data with which you are working. You cannot assume that your descriptive findings automatically apply to other areas that you have not observed, or to the same areas you have observed under different circumstances. You cannot automatically generalize or predict based on a single data point or data set, although many people often do for a variety of reasons (just look at politicians, for example).

To use data to generalize findings into areas for which there is no data, or to predict an outcome based on a limited data set, requires different techniques and analytical methods. These methods are referred to as *inferential statistics,* because they involve

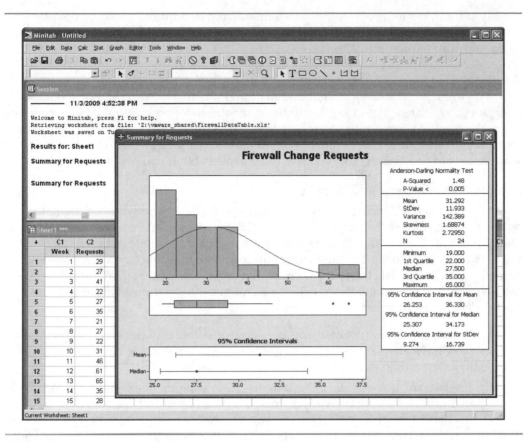

Figure 5-6. Descriptive statistical summary in Minitab

drawing conclusions or making inferences about something you have not observed on the basis of those things that you have observed.

At this stage, I want to provide more context to the discussion of techniques and tools provided in this chapter. I am not a statistician (I just played one in grad school), a fact that will be obvious to any real statisticians reading this book. I am a security professional with some analytical training (both quantitative and qualitative). As I learned to apply these techniques during my doctoral studies, I came to realize the value that they could bring to measuring and analyzing IT security programs. Inferential analysis is already used in a variety of industries for process and quality control, and there are definite applications for these techniques in IT security. Some techniques are more applicable than others to security challenges in general, and to your security challenges in particular. As I describe these statistics, I will take a more general approach, since it is difficult to apply specifics to each of these techniques without describing an entire security metrics project. I will reserve detailed explanations of these techniques until the chapter examples.

My second, related, point is that as we move from descriptive statistics into other techniques, it will become increasingly critical that you understand what you are trying to do with any particular analysis. Descriptive statistics are easy, frankly, because we are already accustomed to counting things, summarizing them, and charting them up for the next management review. The techniques in the preceding section help you to do that with more methodological rigor and in more sophisticated formulations. Inferential statistics (and the techniques in later sections) require that you start out by knowing more about what you want to know. And they require that you be more self-critical and thoughtful in your analysis, because you will have to decide how sure of something you want to be and how much risk you are willing to accept that you may be wrong.

Inference, Prediction, and Simulation

I have always had a difficult time understanding the nuances between inferential statistics, predictive models, and simulations. All three types of analysis can use statistical techniques and have similar aims of getting at insights that are greater than the sum of the data producing them. But they are not quite interchangeable, and I have not found a good explanation that clearly shows how they are delineated. So I am forced to take my own crack at separating them, because techniques for all three goals might prove useful to your security metrics program:

- **Inference**   The most easily described from a statistical perspective, because inferential statistics involve commonly used ways of generalizing from a sample to a population from which the sample was taken.

- **Prediction**   A bit more difficult to describe, as predictive techniques can include anything that gives you insight into what *might* happen based on what *has* happened. Inferential statistics are somewhat predictive in that they extend existing observations out to that which has not yet been observed, but prediction can also involve findings patterns and themes in your data, or even be used to forecast future events or phenomenon in ways that are different from the sample/population analogy.

- **Simulation**   This is also a bit difficult to describe because both inference and prediction involve elements of similarity between the data and the insight produced through the data. But simulation, for my purposes, involves the mapping of things that are difficult to observe or understand into things that are easier to observe and understand—for instance, simulating future risk through Monte Carlo techniques.

In this section, I focus specifically on inferential statistical analysis. I will discuss techniques for prediction and simulation in subsequent sections.

Samples and Populations

We are all familiar with the polling that occurs around political elections. The media and political groups conduct polls that tell us what voters are thinking, how they will vote, who is likely to win or lose. Obviously, these polls do not question everyone eligible to vote before making their determinations, but instead rely on more or less random samples of voters and statistical analysis to provide the results (usually with some margin of error regarding the poll). Manufacturing uses the same techniques to assess standardization and quality of products. If a factory is producing widgets, for example, and each widget is designed to weigh one pound, a manufacturer can sample widgets from the assembly line and determine how well the factory is meeting the weight criteria for the widgets. The factory does not have to weigh every widget, which could be quite costly. These processes work because we understand relationships between samples and between samples and the population of all voters or all widgets. For instance, if we sample properly, we have to sample only a few dozen values for our frequency distribution to be normal, or bell-curve shaped. As I described earlier in the chapter, if we know we are dealing with a normal curve, then we know a lot about how observed values will fall within our data and we can begin to make inferences about the larger population.

IT security has its own populations. We have populations of users, populations of systems, and populations of vulnerabilities, attackers, and threats that we hope to understand. Inferential statistical analysis can help get at these populations—but we rarely use them properly, if at all, in my experience. I have witnessed generalized security decisions made on the basis of horrific sampling strategies. Almost as often, I hear arguments that these kind of insights can't be developed in security because organizations don't have access to or share security information. This is often the argument used for why security is uninsurable. That jury is still out, but if you look back on the history and origins of insurance and risk management, you might be surprised at the quality of data available to early actuaries. The fact is that a population is what you make it, literally. If you decide you want to know about all the desktop systems in your organization, you have just defined the population. You don't have to know or care about all desktops everywhere—that would be a different population. You have to determine how to draw inferences regarding only your own population.

Hypothesis Testing

Central to the concept of inferential statistics is testing hypotheses regarding a population based on sample data collected from that population. A *hypothesis* is a fancy term for an explanation. More specifically, a hypothesis is an explanation that may or may not be true. To determine whether the hypothesis under consideration is the correct explanation for whatever needs explaining, you must test the hypothesis. One way to test a hypothesis is to use statistics to determine how likely it is that the hypothesis is true or false, whether it should be accepted as truth or rejected.

The basic method for hypothesis testing can be described in four steps:

1. *Create two related hypotheses, the null hypothesis and an alternate hypothesis.* The null hypothesis is sort of a statement of the status quo, a nonexplanation as it were, for example, stating that all observed values you are trying to explain are the results of random chance. You may believe, for instance, that security incidents among business units in your company are a matter of chance and do not mean that security is different among the BUs. Competing with the null

hypothesis is your alternate hypothesis, an explanation that you want to put forward to challenge the null hypothesis that there is nothing special about your data. In response to the security null hypothesis, you might formulate an alternate hypothesis that security is managed differently between BUs, thus resulting in more or fewer incidents. The goal of the test is to reject one of the hypotheses and to accept the other. If you accept the null hypothesis, you reject your own alternate explanation.

2. *Build your test method.*   The test method will depend on the type of data and your analysis goals, and it includes the details of your analysis, including which test statistic you will use and the level of significance necessary to reject the null hypothesis (in other words, the degree to which you are willing to be wrong). The test method should always be completed before analysis, to avoid the temptation to retrofit your method to the end results (in other words, to cheat).

3. *Conduct your analysis, using sample data.*   The test is used to produce a P-value, a statistical term of art that represents the probability that you would obtain an observed value were the null hypothesis true. Smaller P-values indicate smaller chances that you would get such an observation, and thus a smaller likelihood that the null hypothesis is true.

4. *Draw conclusions from the test.*   If the probability of occurrence of a value is less than that of your predetermined level of significance, you have statistically significant findings, and you may reject the null hypothesis, thus accepting your own alternate explanation. If the probability of occurrence of a value is greater than the significance level, you cannot show significant difference between your data and the status quo, and you must accept the null hypothesis and reject your alternate explanation.

From a security perspective, there is nothing magical about hypothesis testing—it is simply a question that is answered. But the formalized and logical structure of the question is specific and inflexible, which can take some getting used to. Many statistics can be used for hypothesis testing. Two very common ones are a t-test and a chi-square test, both of which have potentially useful applications to security metrics analysis.

T-test   Simply put, a t-test compares the mean of a data sample against the mean of the population, or it compares the means of two sets of data to determine whether they are significantly different. Applications for security metrics could include observing a random sample of endpoint systems for instances of malware, and then using a t-test to infer from the sample the mean instances of malware across all endpoint systems in the company. Another use of the t-test statistic could be to compare the results of an experiment that compared the effects of a new security procedure in one random sample of systems against a control sample in which no new procedures were implemented.

Chi-Square Test   If the data being analyzed is categorical (on either a nominal or ordinal scale), a chi-square test can be used to determine whether a relationship exists between data variables. The chi-square test is sometimes referred to as a *goodness of fit* test when it compares an observed frequency distribution with an expected frequency distribution to see how well they match up. Another use of the chi-square test is as a *test of independence*, where variables in a contingency table are analyzed to determine whether they are independent of one another. An example of this use of a chi-square test could be our preceding example, in which security incidents are compared across several different business units. The null hypothesis might be that differences between types of security incidents across BUs are the result of chance. The alternate hypothesis is that observations are independent of one another, indicating that a relationship exists between types of security incidents and the BU in which they occur. A chi-square test can be used to reject or accept the null hypothesis in this case.

Tools for Inferential Statistics

The tools available for analysis of inferential statistics are much the same as the tools for descriptive statistics. Both Excel and Gnumeric can conduct inferential analysis and hypothesis testing, including t-tests and chi-square tests. Statistical programs such as Minitab and R also have these abilities, along with the extra bells and whistles such as charting and reporting features that are common to dedicated statistical software.

Other Statistical Techniques

Inferential techniques add a lot of flexibility to your security metrics analysis toolbox, but other techniques that don't fall neatly into either category can be used to leverage the statistical concepts we have discussed in the last two sections. Once again, these are just a sampling of the techniques that are available to extend traditional metrics analysis into new areas of sophistication. The only real limits are your imagination and the resources you can bring to bear.

Confidence Intervals and Decision Making   One of the issues I discussed regarding traditional, matrix-based risk assessments was that instead of measuring risk, they measured people's thoughts about risk. This is problematic for two reasons. First, results in these assessments are often used as if they measured something more tangible than opinions. Second, the development and articulation of those opinions are imprecise and usually do not equate to more than a basic "high, medium, low" rating that is, at best, ordinal (despite all sort of gimmicks to replace the words with numbers, weights, multiples, and other alchemist tricks). It is almost as if, because the assessment deals with subjective opinions, there is no need (or way) to try to be exact.

Opinions can be made more precise, just as can any other measurement, as we experience every day. Suppose I were to ask you the exact amount in your savings account at this moment. Chances are you don't have that information immediately at hand. But you could certainly give me a rough estimate, based on your opinion. Now suppose I were to ask you the same question about my savings account. You could still express an opinion, but you are likely to be much less confident about that opinion. Now suppose I asked you to give me, instead, a range of amounts for each account that you would be 90 percent certain contained the correct figure. You know about how much you have in your own account, so that range might only be a few (or a few hundred) dollars in order to give you 90 percent confidence in your opinion. For my account, you would have to come up with a much broader range, perhaps in the thousands or even millions of dollars to be 90 percent sure that you were right.

These associated estimates and ranges form the basis of what is called a "confidence interval," which is a statistical term for a range that has some specified chance of containing a certain value. Confidence intervals are at the heart of many statistical analyses, such as hypothesis testing, where we determine a level of significance that allows us to be confident that a particular value does or does not allow us to reject the null hypothesis. The use of confidence intervals in decision-making comes out of the fields of psychology and decision science and can be used to improve the kinds of assessments that traditional security risk analyses are supposed to provide.

Imagine replacing high, medium, and low threats in a risk assessment with confidence intervals for actual losses based on the experience and expertise of the IT staff involved in the assessment. The outcomes have the potential to be far more precise expressions of risk, with more rigorous supporting evidence, than the overused red-yellow-green heat maps security professionals are accustomed to using. Of course, like any other statistical analysis, these assessments must be conducted properly. One of the critical factors in these sorts of judgment exercises is the calibration of experts who will provide the opinions. Calibration is the process by which experts are trained to express their opinions in terms of confidence intervals and to select appropriate confidence intervals so that they are being neither too conservative nor too broad in measuring their own opinions.

Inter-rater Reliability   Another problem associated with opinions, expert or otherwise, is how to determine the extent to which people agree, or the amount of consensus on a given question or challenge. Think about a situation for which system criticality is being measured, perhaps as part of the risk assessment example used previously. All the experts involved in the assessment are given a list of corporate IT assets and asked to categorize them along some scale of business impact should the system be compromised or inaccessible. Odds are that not everyone is going to rate every system identically, but the question becomes one of how much general consensus (or lack of such consensus) exists? If everyone generally rates systems the same way, the assessment shows a higher level of agreement between raters and the rating scale is valid. If there is low agreement between raters, something is wrong either with the scale or with the raters. Note that neither result means that the scale is accurate or inaccurate in terms of business impact! It is very possible that everyone will rate that impact as low when it is in fact very high. The test measures only whether the scale is or is not understood in the same way by everyone using it. Everyone can be in complete agreement and still be wrong. Inter-rater reliability is useful in reducing uncertainty by ensuring that at least everyone is on the same sheet of music in understanding how they have agreed to evaluate something.

Numerous statistical tests of inter-rater reliability can be used, with cool-sounding names such as Fleiss's kappa and Krippendorf's alpha. They are often used in academic research to assess whether researchers assigning codes to data are using codes and categories in the same way, or if there are differences in the way they are assigning them that could negatively impact the research findings. But inter-rater reliability tests can support security metrics programs as well, particularly in measurement projects that involve groups collaborating to measure or otherwise attempt to answer questions about various aspects of the security program.

Correlation Analysis *Correlation* refers to the presence of relationships between things—for instance, there may be a correlation (I haven't tested it scientifically) between the number of cups of coffee I have had and the number of pages of this book I can produce in an hour (as well as the number of fat-fingered typos that exist on each page). Correlation is measured by calculating a *correlation coefficient,* which describes the relationship between two variables in a data set on a scale of –1.0 to +1.0. A correlation coefficient of 0 indicates that no relationship exists between the variables.

Correlation is often best described visually, using scatterplots that show whether correlation is positive or negative and how strong or weak the correlation may be. Suppose, for example, that I decided to test the correlation between my coffee consumption and three other variables: the number of pages I produce in the hour after I drink each successive cup, the number of typo-free paragraphs I produce in the hour after each cup, and the number of e-mails I receive in the hour after each successive cup. For simplicity's sake, assume that I drink about one cup per hour during the course of a half-day of writing and checking e-mail. Figure 5-7 shows scatterplots for the results, with the correlation coefficient of each test. The results are apparent visually as well as mathematically. As I drink more coffee, my productivity increases almost linearly, while my accuracy decreases just as dramatically. The e-mails I receive seem to have little to do with how much coffee I've drunk, as one might expect.

Correlation is a technique that is already widely adopted in IT security, particularly among SEIM and log analysis vendors who seek to understand relationships between security events and other variables, such as sources and destinations, categories of attack, and risk or severity scores.

I would caution you against blind acceptance or dependence on these features for a couple reasons, however. As I've said, security metrics analysis must be goal-driven. Correlation data as a bell and/or whistle, with no understanding of why you are correlating or what you will do with the results, is not a recipe for good security. Correlation data may be an excellent source for exploratory analysis, so don't think you have to know what you are looking for before you go looking. But you should have some idea of why you are doing it. And you should always keep in mind a famous dictum in statistics: *correlation is not causality.* This means that just because something correlates with something else, you cannot simply assume one thing causes the other. In my coffee example, it may be that some force other than coffee is at work, affecting my productivity and accuracy. Perhaps I take time to establish a groove in my writing, and my speed increases as the day progresses along with my typos because I am writing faster for longer periods. Correlation can provide valuable insight, but you should always stand ready to question your assumptions.

Longitudinal Analysis Think about the way your organization collects, analyzes, and uses security data today. In many, if not most, cases, I would be willing to bet that data is collected for a particular set of systems or criteria for a particular time period—perhaps

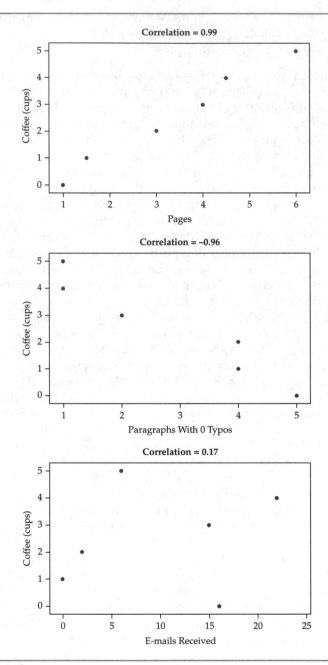

Figure 5-7.   Correlation coefficients for three data sets

all the firewall or IDS events over the last month. This data is used to produce reports or charts, perhaps for the monthly CISO staff meeting, and then everyone moves on. In some cases, trending or baselines may be associated with the data, but this usually involves simple calculations of whether things are going up or down, or otherwise meeting a pre-established threshold. And even these trending exercises are usually conducted as snapshots taken at the same time as other analyses. One area that I have a lot of experience in this regard is in vulnerability assessments conducted for clients, which are often taken as point-in-time analyses of a security posture and provided very little context or follow-up, sometimes not even holding the client's attention long enough to develop a proper remediation plan.

Longitudinal analysis is about moving from snapshots to motion pictures, if I may borrow another metaphor. Longitudinal studies include such things as security baselines and trending over time, but true longitudinal analysis involves setting up measurement projects that are designed to be conducted over months or years from the beginning of the project. This requires understanding goals and metrics in the context of time, which usually means more forethought (and sometimes foresight) must be applied. Longitudinal study does not lend itself easily to corporate environments, where short-term focus on cyclical requirements often drives activities, or where personnel and management turnover can make taking a long view difficult or even politically dangerous. But one of the major problems with IT security today is that we are often so busy managing the pressures of the moment that we have no time or motivation to develop greater situational awareness or strategic planning.

Adding longitudinal components to your security metrics program can be a game changer, when done correctly. And as with other techniques I've covered, fairly simple methods for such analysis as well as complex techniques for collecting and testing data over time are both available. But the main takeaway from longitudinal capabilities is to move your security metrics program into a real, applied research program that is not only concerned with what is happening now, but with how security current state is connected with past and future states.

Tools for Other Techniques

As with the previous statistical analysis methods, the techniques described in this section will benefit from analytical software, including spreadsheets and dedicated statistics applications. For some techniques such as correlation and longitudinal analysis, it may also be desirable or necessary to incorporate databases or to use features built into existing security vendor tools designed to detect relationships or to store and analyze data from archival or historical sources. If your data is coming from several sources, or your security measurement project demands it, you may have to create the database yourself.

The main point to remember is that as you move further away from relatively straightforward counting exercises, the success of your analyses will depend more and more on your ability to articulate and manage your goals and objectives, preferably from some point before the project even starts. At the point at which these techniques become valuable in your metrics program, you should come to realize that you are no longer counting security beans but have become a full-blown security researcher. Whether you choose to share that fact with anyone else is up to you.

Qualitative and Mixed Method Analysis

As we move further away from traditional approaches to analyzing security activities and metrics data, we eventually move into territories that are completely unfamiliar to most security professionals. I have described the reasons for implementing true qualitative metrics and the benefits to be gained from their analysis as I've led up to this chapter, and now I will discuss these techniques and tools in more detail.

I should first reiterate that these approaches are not widely adopted in the security industry, although they are used very successfully in other industries, including advertising and design. They are also not widely accepted by security practitioners, partly because they are poorly understood and because they often seem to violate the sensibilities of security pros with backgrounds in engineering, finance, or the hard sciences. People who discount qualitative measures tend to want to rely on "facts" and "objective data" rather than on opinions and fuzzy data such as people's personal descriptions, activities, and stories. I won't get into any epistemological arguments about the merits of one set of methods over the other. But as I've expressed several times, I strongly believe that some security challenges cannot be addressed by quantitative analysis. And to argue that a security question that cannot be answered with numbers is not even a real question to begin with is to be willfully ignorant both of the history of science and the daily realities of life. So stepping once again off my philosophical soap box, let's talk a bit about qualitative techniques.

Coding and Interpreting Data

The general purposes of both quantitative and qualitative data analysis are similar: to identify patterns and make conclusions regarding a set of observations. Where they differ is in how they go about the identification and what conclusions can be drawn. Table 5-6 breaks down some basic differences between the approaches.

Qualitative analysis seeks to...	Quantitative analysis seeks to...
Construct narratives (stories) from data	Assign numbers to data
Identify the people, places, actions, and themes important to the story	Describe and test statistically
Paint a broad, holistic, detailed picture from the data	Provide very specific explanations of particular aspects of the data
"Go deep" and provide insights into an issue that may not apply elsewhere	"Go long" and provide insights into an issue that can be generalized to other areas

Table 5-6.   Differences in Qualitative and Quantitative Goals

In qualitative analysis, it becomes the role of the analyst to identify themes and build the case for findings and conclusions based on the analysis. The process is naturally and explicitly interpretive, which means that it not only involves the opinions of the people providing the data but also the opinions of those collecting and analyzing the data. All these layers of opinion can breed skepticism in people who like their facts to feel more raw and rational. But skepticism is itself an opinion and an interpretation, one that is difficult to express quantitatively. The only way to express disdain for qualitative analysis is to build a believable story around why it doesn't work, and the better constructed and explained the components of that story are, the more likely people are to accept its conclusions. Ironically, this is exactly the way that qualitative analysts approach their data. The goal is to make reasonable, well-considered arguments about the data and to be able to show how and why those arguments were developed. If most people agree that they are reasonable, they gain credibility and acceptance. You may never be able to "prove" something is true, but proof is not really the end goal.

The heart of qualitative analytical techniques is the concept of *coding*, or assigning themes and categories to the data and increasingly specific levels of analysis. For instance, if you are coding interview transcripts from a security measurement project involving users' online habits, you might start assigning themes such as "personal" or "job related" to categorize different user activities or responses. Later, the coding might become more specific with other subcategories and themes added. Qualitative coding can be applied to any text, from interview transcripts to source code, and is used to identify themes that can be interpreted as existing in the data. As the codebook grows, relationships and patterns between coded themes and categories grow more rich and sophisticated, allowing for higher order conclusions to be reached about the narratives contained in the data.

Mixing Qualitative and Quantitative Techniques

Using purely qualitative approaches to security metrics analysis will be appropriate in some measurement projects, but often the best approach may be a blended analysis that includes both qualitative and quantitative techniques. As I have shown, a lot of security data lends itself to quantitative analysis both generally and as a way to develop bigger questions. Qualitative methods can be added to these quantitative techniques to gain understanding of security practices and results that may not be readily apparent from the numbers. Likewise, some qualitative metrics can be greatly enhanced by adding quantitative elements and criteria based on other data sources.

Process Mapping and Analysis   I have stated that security should be treated and analyzed as a business process. One of the most common means of process analysis is to develop a *process map*, which is a flowchart diagram that shows each activity and the relationships between activities for a given process, as illustrated in the simple diagram in Figure 5-8. Process mapping is widely employed by many organizations, including security programs, but those who use it do not tend to think of it as the exercise in qualitative data analysis that it represents. Process maps are generated by gathering input from people who describe their thoughts and opinions regarding the process, and

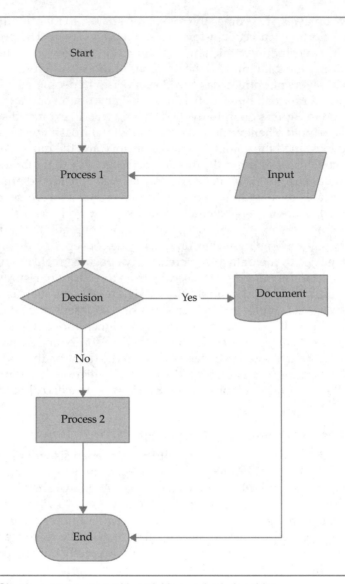

Figure 5-8.   Simple process map with activities and relationships

this data is then coded visually into specific shapes and symbols that are interpreted by the process analyst. The final result is a representation of an intangible thing that can be more easily understood and that can drive decisions.

Process mapping becomes more powerful when combined with quantitative data regarding the stages and steps included in the process. As metrics such as time to complete a process, delays between steps, or the costs associated with each step are added to the process map, the potential for statistical analysis grows. Descriptive statistics can help you understand where bottlenecks or inefficiencies may occur in the qualitative process map, and inferential statistics can be employed as part of experiments or hypothesis tests to determine whether changing parts of the process will improve the results for a given metric. In many industries, the practice of statistical process control is one of the key metrics-based analyses used to improve the business. The Six Sigma methodology, for instance, is designed to facilitate statistical process control and well-known in IT, although it is used less in security. Business process analysis, whether qualitative or quantitative, represents a metrics practice that can be immediately and fruitfully deployed as part of a security program.

Surveys and Interviews   Another excellent source of qualitative security metrics data are people, including the users, technologists, managers, partners, and customers who drive and influence our security programs. Far too often, particularly in vendor marketing, users and other people are described as a big part of the "problem" that security needs to address. I often see headlines in trade news articles and vendor advertisements that state flat out the threats that people pose to the organization, as if the organization were somehow separate from and exclusive of those same people. Of course, people can be and often are security risks, but in the techno-romantic world that some security pros seem to live in, the organization's employees and clients are just more components of a larger system that can be manipulated and managed through product. Even if that were true (and it is definitely not), one of the quickest ways to find out something about a person is simply to ask them questions. You may not get a correct answer, or even an honest one, but you can use the responses as part of a larger data set to get more accurate and valuable knowledge.

Everyone is familiar with doing this sort of work in support of metrics such as customer satisfaction, product marketing, and even performance reviews. It is also a technique that should be considered for security metrics. Survey work, interview analysis, and focus groups can be expedient ways to get a lot of information quickly. And some analytical techniques combine qualitative coding and quantitative analysis to identify patterns and themes in the resulting data. I like to think of this sort of data analysis in terms of usability testing, except instead of asking individuals and groups about how easy a particular technical product is to use, I am considering aspects of the security program as the product. A great example is the security policy—is it usable? Can you read the policies and understand them? Can you follow them easily without making your life miserable? If the answer to these questions is no, then the security program has produced a poor product and you shouldn't be surprised when that product fails in the marketplace.

Content and Text Analysis   Text is central to the security process. The term *text* can refer to writing (digital or otherwise), but the term *texts* also refers generally to the artifacts produced through writing, from documents, to records, to books. Security texts that can be analyzed include our policies and procedures, our budgets and reports, and even our source code and configuration files. Analysis can be purely quantitative, purely qualitative, or a combination of both techniques.

Textual analysis can include cataloging word frequencies and assessing grammatical structures, techniques that are often employed in the publishing industry to determine how complex or readable books and articles may be. These techniques are also applied to documents such as technical manuals, particularly those by the military, where the ability of readers to comprehend the text is critical. I have used these measures in conducting security policy analyses, sometimes demonstrating to a client that the reason no one follows the security policy is not because users don't care, but because the policy is so difficult to read that it requires an advanced degree to understand it.

Content analysis can also be used to identify themes and positions in texts, and content analysis studies have explored everything from how the use of metaphors in speeches makes politicians seem more credible to the analysis of how language in company annual reports give clues that the company is failing over time. Some of these themes can be assessed automatically using certain algorithms and statistical approaches, while others require manual coding on the part of an analyst. But whether you are interested in how friendly your security policy is or how much independent expressions of style exist in your source code, textual analysis provides useful tools for exploring these metrics.

Ethnography and Fieldwork   Some of the most pure qualitative analysis comes from in-depth studies of individuals, organizations, and communities. These techniques involve an analyst working in close quarters with the participants in the study, carefully documenting everything that occurs in the environment. The term for this sort of data collection and analysis is *ethnography*, and *fieldwork* refers to the methodologies used for collecting the data in ways that will be structured, rigorous, and credible when it comes time to present findings. Another term often used for this sort of study is *participant observation*—the analyst will both participate in and observe the environment.

Ethnographic analysis can be resource-intensive. To conduct fieldwork successfully, the analyst must have time to devote to observation (one day of watching is unlikely to paint a full picture; participant observation studies can take anywhere from a few weeks to several years), and he or she must have access to the environment to observe. Once the data is collected, he or she then must properly code and interpret what was observed, identifying themes and building interpretations and conclusions from the results. If the data set includes video or audio data (and many do), this data must be specially annotated, coded, and analyzed.

So if ethnography is that much work, and if the results are so broad and interpretive, why would anyone outside of academia even think about doing it? Ethnography seems more suited to anthropologists who study isolated indigenous villages in the rainforest than to security practitioners. But think about the similarities between that isolated village—complete with its own culture, language, and seemingly strange daily practices—and what it is like for most members of an organization to visit the security operations center (SOC)—that strange, isolated compound with big screens and odd people that have their own culture, language, and daily practices. You don't have to go outside the country to find different cultures; sometimes you don't even have to leave the company.

Consider the questions that you (or your CEO) might be asking about the SOC: What do those folks do every day? Now try to answer that question with a set of descriptive statistics and inferential hypotheses. It is like building a picture from scratch out of pixels rather than taking a photograph and looking for the details that interest you in the whole. Building this kind of knowledge from quantitative metrics, if it is even possible, will prove far more costly in terms of time and resources than a six-week security measurement project in the form of a participant observation exercise.

Companies, including technology companies, use this technique quite a bit. Many design companies rely on ethnography to understand how creations, from web pages to consumer products, are used in daily practice, rather than just in the designers' predictions. Product manufacturers use ethnography to improve their bottom line and conceptualize new offerings. Whether a consumer products company makes razors and wants to understand how the average person shaves, or a high-tech company analyzes how people use their kitchens so that they can create better smart appliances, ethnographic research is an important metrics tool that IT security operations should consider exploring.

Tools for Qualitative and Mixed Analysis

Quantitative analysis tools are often variations on a theme, primarily in the form of spreadsheets and statistical software. The question is not so much functionality, but which product is the most powerful, most specialized, least expensive, or easiest to use for a particular purpose. Qualitative tools are much more diverse, although some of the same criteria apply. Some good commercial packages and good free (not always open source, and vice versa) tools are available. Your choice of tool will depend on your choice of analysis, which of course depends on your choice of metrics, and by extension your goals and objectives—and so the cycle of analysis within the SPM Framework continues.

Academics   Before I get into specific tools, I want to mention a resource that often goes untapped when it comes to more sophisticated analysis. Nearly every major company, and a good portion of small to medium-sized companies, operate within 50 miles of some sort of academic institution—be it a private university, a state college, or a community college. These institutions are filled with specialists who know a lot about conducting well-designed, innovative research on any number of mainstream as well as fringe topics and questions. These researchers have access to literatures, tools, and cheap labor in the form of graduate students and research assistants. What they often lack, however, is data. Access to quality data sources to observe and study is one of the most challenging parts of scholarly research. Most researchers I know would be ecstatic if a company came to them and asked if they were interested in helping conduct research on various aspects of the organization.

Companies are often reluctant to engage academia in research, however, because they fear the loss of intellectual property or confidential information, but this fear is often misplaced. Academic researchers want two things (other than access to data): publications and money to continue their research. Unlike consultants, academics do not usually care about posting the trophy names of the companies they have worked for and should have no problem agreeing to restrictions on the level of detail they can reveal, through non-disclosure agreements (NDAs) or other means, so long as they can use the general results to get published. And the publications themselves are typically in scholarly peer-reviewed journals or at academic conferences rather than industry trade publications. As for money, the costs of conducting an academic study will often pale in comparison to what a consulting firm would charge for the same sort of work (and often the consulting company may contract out to an academic if specialized skills are required). It may not even be necessary to pay for the study, particularly if working with the company might help the academic secure a grant or funding from elsewhere.

If you are thinking about this sort of analysis for your metrics program, consider visiting the nearest university's web site and exploring the fields and disciplines represented. You may find that you have an opportunity to leverage such research without having to build an entire analytical capability.

As I have indicated, far too many tools are available for qualitative and mixed method analysis to catalog them all properly here. Instead, I will present an overview of some of the tools available for various types of analysis, including open source options when they are available.

Computer Assisted Qualitative Data Analysis Software (CAQDAS)   Before computers, qualitative analysis often involved intensely manual exercises in which notes and observations would be recorded on index cards and manually organized, coded, and arranged into patterns. Sometimes it still happens this way. I've seen pictures of entire walls or floors devoted to some poor graduate student's qualitative methods dissertation, and heaven help the small child or pet that comes running through the room and scatters the cards! Today a variety of software tools allow for the effective coding of texts as well as audio and visual data. These tools not only allow the analyst or researcher to mark up the data with codes and tags in the text, but the researcher can also run sophisticated analyses to look for patterns and develop themes from the data.

- **ATLAS.ti**   A commercial qualitative analysis package with a rich set of features for coding, annotating, and analyzing a variety of data; includes sophisticated features and is used by industry as well as academia.

- **NVivo**   Sold by QSR International, this is a sophisticated and feature-rich commercial CAQDAS product that is used in companies, universities, and research institutions.

- **TAMS Analyzer**   An open source qualitative analysis tool with many of the same capabilities as the commercial tools; TAMS is not as sophisticated as the big vendor products and the interface isn't as pretty, but for basic qualitative analysis, you cannot beat the price.

- **Weft QDA**   Another open source qualitative tool; easy to use but with fewer features than TAMS.

- **Transana**   An open source tool (but not free in current version) specifically designed for coding and analyzing video and audio data.

Process Mapping and Analysis Tools   A variety of tools can help you map, chart, and analyze business processes and workflows, although, in my experience, most of these tools are commercial with fewer high-quality open source options, particularly at the level of stand-alone desktop tools. This limitation is somewhat tempered, however, by the fact that a number of standard office productivity suite applications include tools that can be more or less effectively applied to business process mapping.

- Office suites including Microsoft Office and OpenOffice both offer graphics and presentation tools that can be used to create flowcharts and business process maps.

- Specialty diagramming and drawing programs such as Microsoft Visio, Smart-Draw, and OmniGraffle provide advanced flowcharting and process-mapping capabilities.

- Some vendors have developed specialized applications for mapping and analyzing business processes. These tools permit an analyst to model rather than simply map or chart business processes, adding other data and allowing the analyst to simulate the process from beginning to end.

Content and Text Analysis Tools   If you are analyzing text or document content for themes and patterns, you can choose from among the major CAQDAS tools listed in the preceding section; most of them offer advanced capabilities for coding and analysis. Other available tools are more linguistically focused and offer tests and measurements around the structural, lexical, and grammatical elements of textual data. Some of these tools, such as WordStat and WordSmith are commercial products, but Yoshikoder, an open source content analysis application, is also available.

These tools can provide word frequency counts, advanced dictionary and pattern matching features, and they can be used to create *keyword in context* (KWIC) concordances that will take a target word or phrase and arrange all instances of the phrase into a column with the text that precedes and follows it. KWIC concordances provide a quick and visual way to identify themes and patterns of use around specific words or phrases.

Summary

Analysis of the security metrics data that you will produce as you create measurement projects will be a critical component of your success. Your analysis may be applied in support of particular problems or questions, or it may be exploratory and intended to provide further insight into new questions and new areas of security measurement. Whatever your reason for analysis, it is vital that you consider what you want to accomplish with your metrics, leveraging methods, and frameworks such as GQM and SPM to guide and organize your program.

As you prepare for analysis, you will likely be working with data drawn from different sources, measured along different scales, and collected for different purposes.

Cleaning and normalizing data so that it can be analyzed appropriately is a necessary, if sometimes time-consuming, phase of the analytical process and cannot be ignored if you hope to get good insights from your observations and measurements. Many methods can be used for cleaning data and mapping different data sources to one another to ensure "apples-to-apples" comparisons.

Analysis techniques for security metrics data include statistical methods, qualitative methods, and combinations of both. When considering statistical analysis, the measurement scale becomes very important, because some statistics will apply only to interval and ratio data. You should be very clear when considering your statistical tests whether you are dealing with real numbers or with categories. Statistical analysis can also be subdivided into descriptive and inferential techniques. Descriptive statistics apply only to the immediate data at hand and provide analysis of patterns and characteristics of that data, including calculations of the mode, median, and mean, as well as variance and standard deviation. Inferential statistics attempt to compare sample data to a population from which the sample is drawn, the goal being to make generalizations about factors that have not been directly observed. Related to inferential statistics are techniques for hypothesis testing, in which specific explanations are tested against one another to see which may or may not be accepted or must be rejected.

Qualitative analysis involves nonquantitative data, including texts, human responses, and the behavior of people in particular contexts. Qualitative analysis uses methods for structured interpretive coding by a trained analyst or researcher to build patterns and themes from large, broad data sets; it provide insights that are extremely rich but apply only to the phenomenon under observation (that is, they cannot be generalized). Qualitative and quantitative analyses seek to understand data in different ways and for different purposes, so it is often useful to combine them.

The analysis of business processes, documents such as policies and corporate records, and organizational behaviors and practices are all examples of attempts to gain insight into areas where quantitative analysis cannot provide much benefit. But quantitative techniques can be used to supplement and extend qualitative analysis, and the reverse holds true as well, such as when business process mapping includes quantitative measures allowing for experiments and hypothesis testing to determine whether changes to processes actually improve those processes.

Tools for both quantitative and qualitative analysis are widely available, both commercially and through open source projects. The availability of these tools and of techniques for such analysis make it fairly easy to add a great deal of sophistication to existing security metrics initiatives.

This chapter has covered a lot of ground quickly. Entire textbooks have been written about data analysis techniques to which I have been able to dedicate only a few paragraphs; my treatment has been necessarily light. But the purpose of the chapter was not to teach you to be a seasoned ethnographer or statistician. These tools are just that—tools—and as when using any tool, you must consider its merits in the context of your own needs and then learn what you need to learn to apply them skillfully.

I would restate my case that anyone seeking to improve or extend their security metrics program into truly sophisticated analysis could do worse than to partner with local academic institutions, where these sorts of skills are common. But these tools and techniques are available to anyone, and the availability and strength of the open source solutions available for analysis make it that much easier to get started incorporating advanced analytical practices into your security metrics initiatives and projects.

Further Reading

Dalgaard, P. *Introductory Statistics with R.* Springer, 2008.

Graham, B. *Detail Process Charting: Speaking the Language of Process.* Wiley, 2004.

Hubbard, D. *How to Measure Anything: Finding the Value of "Intangibles" in Business.* Wiley, 2007.

Kahneman, D., et al., eds. *Judgment Under Uncertainty: Heuristics and Biases.* Cambridge University Press, 1982.

Minitab, Inc. *Meet Minitab 15.* 2007.

Myatt, G. *Making Sense of Data: A Practical Guide to Exploratory Data Analysis and Data Mining.* Wiley, 2007.

Saldaña, J. *The Coding Manual for Qualitative Researchers.* SAGE, 2009.

Smith, R. *Cumulative Social Inquiry: Transforming Novelty into Innovation.* The Guilford Press, 2008.

VanderStoep, S., and D. Johnston. *Research Methods for Everyday Life: Blending Qualitative and Quantitative Approaches.* Jossey-Bass, 2009.

Winston, W. *Excel 2007: Data Analysis and Business Modeling.* Microsoft Press, 2007.

CHAPTER 6 | Designing the Security Measurement Project

Metrics are the engine of security measurement, as I described in Chapter 4, but engines are not usually capable of independent motion. Instead, engines are used to power other things—and security metrics are no different in this regard. You need a vehicle for your metrics, a way to harness their power and benefits toward a larger goal. Security measurement projects (SMPs) are the organizing structures that contain and channel the process of collecting security metrics. They allow you to modularize metrics activities and create more easily manageable building blocks for long-term security improvement. Like any IT project, successful SMPs benefit from forethought and planning as well as organized and effective management throughout the project lifecycle.

Before the Project Begins

The success or failure of many projects are often determined before the kick-off meeting even takes place. Poor planning and inadequate understanding of what a project is supposed to accomplish has killed the potential of many otherwise well-intentioned efforts to improve IT security. Too often, particularly in reactive IT security organizations, a project is synonymous with a firefighting exercise designed to complete an otherwise neglected task in a short amount of time before the auditors or some other authority figure demands accountability. As a result, the implicit purpose of some projects is not much more elaborate than showing that the project (for instance a risk assessment or a policy review) has been completed. If risks are accurately identified, security vulnerabilities are really mitigated, or policies are actually made more robust and usable, this is icing on the cake. The main objective is to cross that task off the team's to-do list.

In an environment of tight budgets, overworked staff, and increased regulatory scrutiny, we can understand these "do what we can" strategies, but security staff and company leadership should not fool themselves into thinking that sustainable security improvement is a result of the effort. More likely, the organization ends up with check-the-box compliance management and the same false sense of security that plagues other aspects of data protection.

An effective way to avoid these project pitfalls is to adopt an approach to security management projects that does the following:

- *Emphasizes manageable, measureable projects over vague initiatives.*   Successful SMPs should be tightly bounded (even exploratory projects) and clearly understood by all involved.

- *Treats projects as individual links in a chain rather than self-contained activities.*   A series of smaller, focused projects conducted regularly and coordinated over the course of a year has a better chance of success than a large project that tries to accomplish everything at once and is then forgotten for the rest of the year.

■ *Seeks to expand the project beyond the project team or even the sponsoring organization.* Security metrics projects impact the entire organization; there-fore, the security project team should actively seek ways to evangelize the results of the project to other areas of the organization. This may involve the project team actively engaging nontraditional stakeholders to determine what the project can do for them.

Project Prerequisites

Before project kickoff, you should have already gathered certain information that will be useful, if not critical, to the success of your SMP. This is the point in the project at which the needs and requirements of the CISO or security organization are at the fore, although these requirements may be dictated from elsewhere in the enterprise (compli-ance officers, the CFO, manufacturing, and so on).

Goal-Question-Metric Analysis

The pre-project stage is the perfect place to conduct your GQM analysis, if you have not already done so. You likely will have high-level goals in mind, or you probably would not be considering a project, but GQM is the means by which these broad goals are nar-rowed and contextualized, and the supporting information and measurements needed to meet the goal are identified. The GQM analysis should be formally documented and included as a foundational document in a project-specific repository.

Review of Previous Efforts

In academia, when you write a thesis, dissertation, or other long research study, you are usually required to conduct what is known as a literature review. The lit review, as it is colloquially known, is a thorough examination of (ideally) everything else that has been written on the topic of your research. The purpose of the lit review is to demonstrate that you understand the background of your topic and to ensure that you are not wasting your readers' time by rehashing existing work or mislead-ing them by taking credit for ideas that are not new. It isn't a perfect system (and the more difficult the subject, the more literature there is to review), but it is a time-tested means of moving knowledge forward. This concept also has a lot to offer security analysts and project managers.

As you prepare for your project, you should attempt to learn about everything that has already been done relative to the project goals and metrics. If you are assessing some aspect of security, find out whether it has been assessed previously. If you are working on a compliance-related issue, try to understand who else in the company has worked on that particular compliance goal. You may find that the goals, questions, and metrics that you have identified for your project have already been identified in whole or in part elsewhere, even if for a different purpose or organizational unit. You may even find that your own group has already worked on them, but the report has been sitting for several years on the shelves of several successive employees.

By finding and reviewing this data, you can save time and get valuable insights into where to put the effort of the current project. The data you collect may also let you quickly transform your metrics analysis into something more sophisticated, by adding baselines, longitudinal aspects, or other advanced analyses given that you now have existing data to compare with the data that you collect as part of the project. Importantly, understanding what has or has not already been undertaken can help you respond more effectively to concerns or critiques on the part of project stakeholders and sponsors.

Data and Analysis

Since you have already developed GQM criteria for the project, you should give some thought to data sources and analysis that will be necessary for the measurement project. You may not have all the answers at this stage, but some thoughts on how you will develop your metrics data collection strategies and what analysis techniques you think can be useful for the metrics you have selected can help you as you prepare the project plan and begin to assign resource requirements.

When considering data, remember that in many cases you will not own or control access to the repositories or other sources of data that you need to collect. Your planning process should include consideration of stakeholders you will need to work with to get data in the first place, whether that means an administrator giving you access to the systems she controls or a manager giving you access to staff members for purposes of interviews and discussions.

Deciding on a Project Type

Another way that you can begin getting specific and anticipating how the project will progress is to think early about what kind of measurement project you will actually conduct. We talk about projects in a generic sense all the time in IT, but there can be serious differences between one project and the next and one type of project and another. Some of these considerations will emerge from your goals and questions, but it can be helpful to consider the structural limitations and necessities that are involved in different project types, which might include the following examples.

Descriptive Projects

The most common projects we deal with in IT security are those that describe a current state in some aspect of security, and then perhaps we use the results to make an effort to improve security in a future state. If you gather data regarding event and incident statistics for a management meeting, you have completed a descriptive SMP. Measurement projects of this type require you to think about where you will get your data and what descriptions will be of the most use to you and to your audience, and they may involve analysis and recommendations for future improvements, particularly if the description is not favorable to the goals of the project stakeholders or sponsors.

Experimental Projects

Experiments are defined as tests or procedures that are carried out to further knowledge, expand capabilities, or analyze preexisting information. We do not usually think of ourselves as conducting experiments in security operations, and in fact we may specifically deny that we do so, because experimentation carries the implication of unknown results and possible wasted effort. (For instance, we might not call implementing a new secure e-mail system an experiment.) But most scientific experiments are not blind attempts to do something new, but rather very detailed and sophisticated tests of what is expected in a process—just as most IT security implementations have a chance of failure after they go into production, despite our best efforts and intentions. Pilot projects can be a kind of experiment in IT environments, but pilots tend to be limited to small implementations of a new system or technology to see how it functions (it would be quite common to have a pilot project for the new e-mail system I mentioned previously). Real experiments are a bit different in their purpose and methodology.

From a security metrics perspective, experimental projects can be any project in which comparing observations leads to conclusions about some state of affairs. Just because a project is experimental does not mean that it is a research project instead of an operations project. The manufacturing industry, for example, regularly uses statistical quality control experiments to determine whether production is uniform and efficient, and to shed light on causes when this is not the case. Security teams can and should use experimental designs to measure operational activities as well. This can include using inferential statistics to gain insight into a population, or fielding new configurations or technologies to effect security changes.

At the end of the project, you will have knowledge of how things may be or actually are different between your control groups and your experimental groups, and you can test null and alternative hypotheses through observation. One of the objectives of successful experimental projects is to manage your analysis and findings adequately so that you have some idea of why differences exist between those states, so you can intelligently articulate those results to your project stakeholders.

Compliance Projects

Compliance projects demand that the security program adhere to criteria or specifications developed by authorities usually external to the program. These projects involve meeting legal and regulatory requirements, aligning the program to industry standards, or fulfilling contractual or other business obligations. The interesting aspect of compliance projects is that you will usually not be able to self-assign criteria for a successful project, other than whether or not compliance was achieved. The details and specifics of what defines that success are mandated upon the security group from outside. This means that in order to be successful in these projects, you will need to understand in detail what someone else cares about, and what they care about may be documented in formats or languages that you are not accustomed to or experienced with. (Reading government regulations or legal contracts for comprehension is a discipline all its own.) So when considering compliance projects, you should immediately begin deciding which outside stakeholders you need to include to improve your chances for success. Your data and analyses may demand special insights and skills that exist outside of the security program.

Of course, these are not the only types of projects that you will encounter or develop. I have described each of these in quite general terms. Different project types will overlap, and others will not fall into any of the preceding categories. The main takeaway for this preparatory stage is to think about the structure of your measurement project and the unique aspects that any given structure may carry with it. This will help you anticipate challenges and potential problems and help you understand where the most value can emerge from any given activity.

Tying Projects Together

SMPs are one more intermediate component of the Security Process Management (SPM) Framework. As measurement projects and the metrics and data that they encompass are completed and incorporated into the organization's experience and knowledge, they begin to form the next level structure, the Security Improvement Program (SIP), which is described in detail later in the book. But the SIP cannot spontaneously emerge from measurement projects any more than measurement projects spontaneously emerge from goals, questions, and metrics. Projects must be designed so that they link with other projects, providing input to some projects and receiving outputs from others. These inputs and outputs may be direct or indirect, and they may be limited to historical context only. But even historical context would be an improvement in many security programs, where it seems that the ravages of time and reorganization can make it difficult to understand what transpired one or two years ago, much less over the life of the security program.

You can build cross-project functionality into your metrics program in a number of ways, but all of them require that the owners and stakeholders of the projects first make a commitment to ensure that the projects remain linked and cross-referenced. This commitment need not come from senior management, although it certainly helps if it does—and senior management commitment is necessary when the scope of the project crosses team or functional boundaries. But any security manager or analyst working on their own projects can take the initiative and build continuity into their projects just by demanding (from themselves and from others as they are able) that projects be documented and that documentation be maintained for whomever wants to review it.

Building a project catalog can help significantly in such cases, and the catalog does not need to be fancy, although it must be usable. (I always find spreadsheet-based catalogs difficult to use. I prefer narrative documents in which more information can be captured, with tables for more structured data as needed.) The catalog should be as complete as possible and as available as necessary. This could mean assigning a project catalog owner who is tasked with passing on the responsibility if he or she moves on to other jobs.

Getting Buy-in and Resources

The adage that "you can't get something for nothing" is a cornerstone of security, although the industry does not always remember it. Perhaps more than other aspects of IT, security is almost all about tradeoffs and compromise (in both senses of the word), and this applies to SMP management, too. Security professionals know a lot about what needs to be done to improve the posture of their programs and their infrastructure, and we know firsthand the consequences that can result from not having protections and controls in place. Where we have less success is in understanding that everyone else may not understand or share our experiences and insights. Nothing is more frustrating than watching people behave in ways you know are self-defeating—nothing except, perhaps, trying to convince them to change.

So when it comes time to get the support and resources for SMPs, it will not be enough for you to make appeals based on what you know to be correct or valuable as a security specialist. At the time of this writing, the economic downturn has exerted pressure on businesses that make it challenging to get the resources necessary simply to do what they have always done, and budgets even for daily operations have been drastically cut. But even in the wake of a recovery, there will always be competition for limited resources within organizations. To ask for more money, people, or tools means you're going to have to up your game, and that means you need to ask yourself, to paraphrase the famous line, "not what your organization can do for you, but what you can do for your organization."

Identifying Stakeholders and Sponsors

The success of most projects is directly proportional to the number of people who believe the project needs to be done and done correctly. It is a given (in fact, a cliché) in IT security that you must have management support to have success. Management support ideally refers to senior leadership support at the CXO or board level, but in practice, such support is more of a formality unless mandated by a compliance requirement such as Sarbanes-Oxley or ISO 27001 (and sometimes even then it can be difficult).

My philosophy on management support is that depending upon senior management buy-in as a prerequisite for action is the wrong way to approach the challenge. Instead, I advocate a broad approach by which you attempt to influence operational management and the front-line and mid-management levels, where value can still be tangibly measured and expressed. If you can convince peers, particularly peers outside the security realm, that a project will add value to their bottom-line management needs, this support will begin to be expressed upward. Eventually, senior leadership in the enterprise will find they are fielding security project requests not from the security team, but from the managers and stakeholders in their own areas. As security becomes a priority for more than just security people, it will get the attention of leaders who are more attuned to detecting trends and generalizing across the enterprise than to evaluating and comparing individual cross-functional needs and requests.

Approaching projects in this way will require a bit of a change on the part of security teams as well. We can be an insular and suspicious lot, not accustomed to or comfortable with diplomacy and putting others' priorities ahead of our own. But the security world needs to get better at helping others understand what we do and, more important, why we do it, and we need to express these things in terms of the language and requirements of other groups and functions. Security pros who are good at this will find opportunities for expanding their influence and prestige across the enterprise.

Estimating Resources

Few things will kill the buzz of a good security metrics project faster than going over budget or coming in late due to a lack of effective planning. In the case of compliance, the results can be worse, particularly if the auditors are ready to walk in the door and you are not adequately prepared. So measurement project managers will do well to consider and analyze project resources seriously before you begin. One of the benefits of taking a framework-based approached to security metrics, one that recognizes that security is being assessed continually rather than periodically, is that you can afford to be more conservative with your projects. It is better to develop a project of limited scope, which is manageable and which can provide incremental security value, than to attempt to take on too much and fail in execution, follow-up on the results, or both. Small, well-coordinated projects allow for much more granular control over the security program and have the benefit of being easier to scope and easier to complete.

When estimating measurement project resources, you need to consider questions of data collection and analysis. As I discussed in previous chapters, preparing data for analysis can be very time consuming, and if you are choosing new analytical techniques, unforeseen learning curves can be associated with new tools and practices. If you are partnering with other stakeholders, especially those outside the security group, you should also consider that it may be necessary to explain your progress and to ensure that their goals continue to be aligned with your own. And always consider the impact of other duties and daily operations on the measurement project. Your plan should include an implicit recognition that nothing ever goes exactly as planned.

Borrowing from project management methodology, it is advisable to conduct a risk analysis on your measurement project that can help you identify areas of uncertainty and potential problems that could arise over the course of the project. Interestingly enough, risk analyses in project management often look a lot like risk analyses in IT security and usually involve the project team qualitatively discussing and attempting to categorize and prioritize subjective understandings of risk. If your organization does not have defined project management methodologies, it may be necessary to guess a bit in the beginning, but in security metrics everything has the potential to become data, and you should be documenting project progress, including problems, overruns, and delays, so that the next project risk analysis has more than just opinion on which to operate. Specific resource issues to consider as part of the risk analysis include the following:

- **People**   What risks are presented by the project stakeholders themselves? What happens to the project if a stakeholder withdraws support? What happens if you lose a resource due to unforeseen circumstances?

- **Material and operational resources**   Which resources are critical to the project's success? Could certain data sources, tools, locations, or monetary resources significantly impact the measurement project if they were altered or became unavailable?

- **Technical and analytical resources**   What risks are imposed by the techniques and tools that you have selected? Are you choosing commercial or open source tools to complete the project? What happens if a new tool is needed during the project?

- **Contingency planning**   For all the risks associated with the project, what are the contingency plans for dealing with any particular risk? Are workarounds available, or will certain risks threaten the completion or success of the project? Have all risks and contingencies been communicated to project stakeholders?

Managing projects is a discipline and craft unto itself, and as you consider setting up a formal security management program, you should also look at setting up formal project management programs to facilitate your metrics. Not only will this help with individual projects, but it will facilitate and improve the collaboration and coordination of SMPs that takes place as part of the SIP, described later in the book.

Presenting a Business Case for Metrics

After the project has been defined, the security metrics team should develop a formal business case around the measurement project for several reasons: A business case is a good method by which to document the project and archive it for future use. But equally important, documenting a business case allows you to articulate to all stakeholders and sponsors exactly what is to be accomplished through the measurement project, and what each of them can hope to get out of it. There is no set template or best practice for the project business case, but it should be readable and as brief as possible while still being adequately descriptive. Here are some things to include in the business case:

- **Stakeholders and sponsors**   The business case should describe everyone who has a stake in the project and what that stake is. It is important that participants feel included in the process, and it is also important that they see others' involvement. A business case that includes several sponsors and offers cross-functional support can add immediate credibility to a project.

- **Goals, questions, and metrics**   The business case should clearly articulate the results of the GQM analysis and should tie the results to the goals and requirements of specific stakeholders.

- **Project cost and project benefits**   The business case should tell each reader why establishing and analyzing these security metrics are important and what it will take to realize the value that they provide. It may not be possible to forecast financial benefits of the project immediately (that may be exactly what the metrics are designed to reveal), and in these cases the business case should explain this.

- **Risk analysis results**   The measurement project team should be up front about risks and contingencies identified during the project risk analysis. There should be few surprises over the course of the project, even if something goes wrong.

- **Formal acceptance**   At the conclusion of the business case, a process for acceptance of the SMP by all associated stakeholders should be defined. It is best if this includes formal sign-off by sponsors and those providing project resources.

Having set the stage and done your best to consider the criteria for success of your measurement project, the operational phases of your metrics activities can begin.

Phase One: Build a Project Plan and Assemble the Team

The business case documented the project for sponsors and stakeholders. The project plan is the formal documentation of the project for those operationally involved in its execution. It guides the project team members in their efforts to complete the project.

The Project Plan

A project plan is a documented operational map of the entire project that is designed to record all pertinent details in one place. Many resources are available for project managers, including a variety of templates for project plans, so I will not attempt to reinvent the wheel for this chapter. But at a minimum, the project plan should capture the project goals, deliverables, and milestones at a level of detail that exceeds the project business case and allows the project to be effectively managed. The project plan should also be included in the project catalog developed in support of the SIP. The plan should also be reviewed and consulted regularly during the operational life of the project to ensure that milestones are met and deliverables meet project stakeholders' expectations.

Project Goals

The description of the project goals in the project plan may be derived from the project business case, and the need for more detail is perhaps less imperative than the need for milestones and deliverables. But the project goals should include descriptions of stakeholders and the associated stakeholder priorities that were reflected in the business case. Documenting these goals in the project plan enables baseline development and goal tracking over time when projects are linked and cross-referenced, and the inclusion of the goals in the operational details of the project serve as a guidepost to the project team as the work effort progresses.

Project Deliverables

The associated project deliverables should be directly mapped to the goals identified in the project plan. Deliverables can include descriptive reports, findings from experiments or inferential analyses, readiness to pass an audit, or the establishment of other projects as part of the improvement program. Whatever the deliverables are, they should be documented and explicitly aligned with the goals they meet and support. The project plan should specify the expected format and approximate structure of each deliverable and should identify specific stakeholder requirements for deliverables. For instance, in vulnerability assessment projects, there may be requirements to deliver a higher-level report to a project business sponsor, but the technical stakeholders in a project may be more interested in the raw metrics data. The project team should understand different needs and develop customized deliverables accordingly.

Project Milestones

Milestones should be established for all project deliverables, taking into account the resources available to the project and the complexity of the deliverable product. Milestones should be developed on an individual basis for each task and subtask of the measurement project, and these tasks should be assigned to owners within the team.

Project timelines should also be established and developed in conjunction with the milestones. Where dependencies exist between deliverables or related activities, these should be noted within the project plan.

Project milestone development can be a manual process, but the evolution of project management software has removed much of the heavy lifting involved with planning and executing on project schedules. Milestones and timelines are important not only for the project goals, but also as data sources for empirically assessing the project's effectiveness. Like any other data, knowing where you succeeded and where you failed to achieve a milestone within a set time period can generate new questions and insights about your security operations. Many organizations will have access to dedicated project management tools and resources, and project teams should take advantage of these tools, a few of which I discuss at the end of the chapter.

Project Details

In addition to pre-established details, the project plan should give team members the ability to add details and track the project as it proceeds. Records of decisions, activities, and problems that occur during the course of the project should be noted and be included as working notes within the project plan. If regular project meetings occur, the minutes or meeting notes from these sessions should also be included, as should descriptions of metrics activities including data collection and analysis.

Documenting project details can often seem like extra work for little gain, but the effective recording of a project journal can prove invaluable when it comes time to analyze data and articulate findings to stakeholder audiences and sponsors. Project details also serve as supporting data in the project catalog, providing project managers and security analysts the benefit of the team's experience even after the details of the project are lost from memory. This movement from tacit project team knowledge (that which is informal and undocumented) to explicit knowledge (that which is documented and preserved) helps the project to achieve an impact on organizational knowledge management and not just the security issue immediately at hand.

The Project Team

In most cases, the staffing of the project team will not be very flexible. Security staff will be assigned to projects based on roles and ownership of the resources that the project is designed to measure. Outside resources, when included, will be contingent on the availability of people and perhaps on skills and expertise (usually the former will trump the latter, unless a sponsor is truly invested in the results of the project). So when the SMP manager assembles the project team, often the best that he or she can do is to try to ensure that the available resources are appropriately tasked.

Skills

The first thing to consider when assigning project resources is the mapping of team members' skills to the tasks associated with the project. These assignments become more important as particular data collection and analysis techniques are selected and implemented. Asking project team members to perform tasks that are difficult or uncomfortable for them can threaten both the team dynamic and the project results.

If some team members are shy or reserved, it may not be the best idea to send them out to interview managers in other business units. Similarly, asking a very gregarious and social team member to sit in a cube and learn to crunch statistics may not be the best use of that individual's unique skills.

At minimum, make an effort to map people to those project tasks to which they are best suited. This may seem like common sense, but I've been involved in a lot of projects where it seems that tasks were randomly assigned to project participants with no real thought of whether that assignment was smart. Naturally, there may not always be the luxury of choice on a security project, but at the very least the project lead should spend some time developing a skills matrix for the team so that people believe that an attempt was made to make the best use of each individual's talents and strengths. Even if there is no way to assign each member of the team that one task that they are most capable of doing or are most interested in, taking an inclusive and sympathetic approach to assigning project duties can have a positive effect on morale and the project working environment.

Commitment

Along with creating a skills matrix, my experiences have taught me that it pays to recognize up front that not all project members are equally committed to the task at hand. This doesn't mean that some of your team will be slackers, although they might very well be, but reflects the fact that in any dynamic environment, some people will be struggling with conflicting schedules and requirements that mean they will not always be able to dedicate themselves to the SMP. You can prevent a lot of animosity and wasted effort by recognizing this fact up front, not taking it personally, and simply dealing with it. Asking the team up front to provide estimates of their ability to commit their time over the course of the project can identify problems before they grow acute. If a project team member knows, for instance, that he will be on vacation for the last quarter of the project or that he is currently finishing up a different project and won't be able to engage fully yet, then recognizing such facts can go a long way toward making sure these issues don't result in a delay.

Collaboration

Another aspect of the project that should be decided up front is how the team will collaborate. Today's work environments allow for many more options in this regard, as there may be less need for physical meetings or co-location of the team members over the course of the project. Communication and collaboration mechanisms should be discussed and decided upon at the beginning of the project, preferably during the project kickoff meeting at the latest, and should be documented in the project plan. Collaboration tools and processes should take into account the need to share information and project data, as well as any differences in location or time zones (in today's global environment this can be especially important).

One important aspect of collaboration is making sure that important project information is documented as part of the project catalog. Commonly used collaboration mechanisms such as e-mail and instant messaging can make it difficult to archive and share project interactions. The measurement project lead should put some thought into the types of project information that need to be recorded, the level of detail necessary for this information, and how to ensure that any interactions by team members are properly documented and included in the project working papers.

Phase Two: Gather the Metrics Data

Once the project plan and team members are in place, the project can move forward with answering the questions and gathering the metrics data necessary to support the project goals. Several important considerations are required in this phase of the project, most of them concerning the appropriate ways in which data is collected, stored, and protected.

Collecting Metrics Data

The data that you collect will vary, perhaps widely, according to the goals and metrics that you have developed. Some data collection, particularly that in support of descriptive measurement projects, will not require changes to existing practices, and you will use the same tools and sources you used previously, even if you end up conducting more advanced analysis on that data. But if you are incorporating other goals, such as prediction, longitudinal study, or qualitative approaches, you may have to develop new means of collecting as well as analyzing your security metrics data.

The first thing to consider is whether or not the data you need is immediately available through existing systems and resources. The more your project draws from different groups within the enterprise, the less likely it is you will be able to gather the data you need centrally. The same holds true for metrics that do not rely only on system-generated information. Even with system data, you may need to go through archives and historical data repositories to find what you need. You will need to identify and get authorization to use data from any sources not under your immediate administrative control, and your project business case and project plan can help you justify these requests. If your data depends on interactions with people, whether through surveys, interviews, or other interactions, you will need to identify who you must talk with and get the appropriate approvals as well.

Herding all these cats can be a big challenge and time-consuming in and of itself, taking away from the time you actually have to collect and analyze the data that is core to your measurement project. You may track down the data only to realize that you now have to devote significant time to cleaning it up to get it into a usable form. Or if your data has been generated by some customized or home-brewed system, you may need to go back and forth with the owner to translate what exactly the data points or outputs represent. Sometimes you may even discover that the data you're looking for doesn't exist and you are forced to look for a different repository or change requirements and goals based on data sources that you actually can find.

When it comes to interpersonal data collection such as interviews and ethnographic analysis in which you are interacting with a colleague or a group within the organization, there are important concerns. In most research using these techniques, it is common for these observations to be recorded, including interview conversations and even visual recording of the groups under analysis. In industry settings, this can be difficult to do. People are naturally nervous about being recorded in the workplace, and while the data is much more complete when fully recorded, it can be offset by the tendency for people to be less honest or forthcoming. If you cannot record the data you collect, and most of the time you will not be able to, then you must fall back on detailed note-taking as your primary means of collection. In interviews, it often helps if two analysts work together—one conducting the interview and taking some notes while the other is responsible for collecting as much data as possible.

Storing and Protecting Metrics Data

After data is collected, it is important that you give thought to how it will be stored and accessed. You want to make sure that the data you will be using for your project remain in the same state they were when you observed them, and you want to ensure that they are properly controlled and secured, particularly when they involve sensitive data such as information about security operations or personally identifiable data about interview or survey participants. It is best to have a dedicated, secure location (physical or electronic) in which to store the collected data and to limit access to the data only to the project team. If data cleaning or normalization takes place, or if different versions of the data are being used as the measurement project progresses, it is important that someone keep track of these changes. Nothing is worse than getting halfway through an analysis only to realize that you are using a different data set than the one you intended. Even worse is never to catch the mistake and have it influence your findings and conclusions. Security metrics are all about the data, and ensuring that you have access to the correct data and that you can easily document and justify your analysis process at the data level represents an important level of project governance.

Business, legal, and even ethical concerns may also be associated with the data that you have collected. Recall previous statements I have made about data retention and the need to take action on findings. Collecting metrics data often means that you are creating new knowledge and new corporate records. If these records involve particular systems, groups, or individuals, they should be assessed as part of the company's records retention schedule and included as official company documents. At the end of the measurement project, a decision should be made, in accordance with the retention schedule, regarding which project documents should be kept and which should be archived or destroyed. Project business cases, plans, and final deliverables should always be retained as part of the SIP (again, within the guidance of the company's retention schedule), but the data collected as part of the process should be considered on a case-by-case basis and kept as necessary to support the security program.

Phase Three: Analyze the Metrics Data and Build Conclusions

Chapter 5 described security metrics analysis techniques in detail. After you have successfully collected your data, it is time to put one or more of these techniques to use. Once again, if your analysis is primarily descriptive, you may not need to change much in terms of how you undertake this phase of the project, other than perhaps approaching your analysis with a broader understanding of the roles that metrics, data, and analysis play in your security program. If, however, you have collected data for predictive analysis, experimentation, or hypothesis testing, you will have to deal with additional tasks and requirements in analysis. The most important of these, particularly in cases of using data to generalize or compare and test competing explanations of aspects of security, is that your analysis plan should be developed ahead of time and explicitly included in your project plan. The reasons for this pre-determination are worth revisiting.

Central to the concept of inferential statistics is that you develop criteria and thresholds for acceptance regarding explanations and generalizations that answer your questions objectively. In other words, you want to avoid any temptation to cheat by altering the conclusions based on what you wanted to find. It is much easier to avoid getting into these situations if you have decided those criteria and thresholds, and documented them, before you begin collecting and analyzing your evidence. If these parameters of the analysis are part of the project plan, just like the deliverables and milestones, then any changes become obvious and must be discussed with the team and possibly with stakeholders and sponsors. Conversely, if you have developed these criteria and thresholds as part of an approved and accepted project plan, then you can more easily defend any surprising or unpopular findings or conclusions to your project stakeholders. A well-defined analysis plan is like a contract between analysts and audience. It may not always protect you from requests to change your conclusions based on politics or personal feelings, but it puts you in a better position to defend your case should such requests be made.

Another consideration for analysis that should be included in your project plan is to ensure that you have included adequate time to explore the data and develop your conclusions. Analysis takes time, and stakeholders often will be looking for your findings within days of your completing data collection. One researcher I know, an anthropologist who conducts qualitative research for a major technology company, described how every time she came back from fieldwork, her product teams would begin pressuring her for results. And every time she had to explain that they could get the raw data, which would be useless to them, quickly, or they could allow her to complete her analysis and actually get something that would add value to their efforts. You can ward off some of this impatience by realistically building the analysis into your project schedule, but you should also consider the actual resources it will require for your analysis. It may not be necessary for the entire project team to be involved in the analysis, especially when the skills and tools for specialized analysis are in the hands of only a few members. In these situations, you should consider releasing team members back to normal duties and continuing the project with a core analytical team. If you choose this option, I recommend continuing to keep the larger team in the loop, and bringing the entire team together when it is time to present your results to sponsors and stakeholders. This way, everyone is still able to participate in and take deserved credit for their roles in the measurement project.

Phase Four: Present the Results

While collecting and analyzing security metrics data carry unique challenges and obstacles that must be overcome, presenting the results of your metrics analysis presents its own challenges. When you have put a great deal of effort into developing information that is valuable and can contribute to the improvement and success of the organization, you obviously will want everyone to take that information as seriously as you do. But you cannot assume that this will happen simply on the merits of the results. The presentation of metrics findings always has elements of marketing and sales to it, and the wise security metrics professional will realize that even the best data analysis in the world is less useful if you can't get anyone to read it. Sometimes a slide deck is just not enough, and nothing is worse than watching excellent measurement and analysis fail to impact because the results were not presented correctly. For very important projects you may even consider hiring outside communications or marketing specialists to assist your security metrics efforts by enhancing presentation and dissemination of results. This may be a particularly attractive option if these skills are lacking within the existing security organization.

If you have worked closely to get buy-in and support from your stakeholders, and you've done a decent job of showing those stakeholders how your metrics benefit them directly, it will probably less difficult to keep their interest in your results. The goals, questions, and metrics that you have developed prior to beginning the project will go a long way in guiding how you present results. Nevertheless, you should not assume that every audience has the same interests or needs regarding the analyses you have conducted and the conclusions that you have made. It helps to perform a bit of market segmentation work on your larger audience to ensure that you are meeting these different needs.

Some of the groups to which you will likely be presenting information include the following:

- **Nontechnical management** If you have developed stakeholders outside of the security group, or if your conclusions are being presented up the leadership chain, it is likely that your audience will include nontechnical people who have little interest in technical details or even security, except as these things impact issues such as dollars, productivity, or compliance.

- **Technical management** In many cases, you will be working with people who do have technical skills but are also concerned with how to translate technical details into business value and articulate that value to nontechnical peers and supervisors.

- **Operational staff** When your conclusions involve actions such as remediation or system configuration changes, the technical personnel responsible for implementing these recommendations will often be interested in detailed technical and analysis data from your project.

- **Users** In some cases, your data will drive changes in organizational behavior, including the development of new policies or training and awareness programs. You should be able to present your findings to these groups in ways that are understandable and that explain why these changes are necessary.

- **Outside entities** If SMPs have been conducted to support audit or compliance objectives, it may be necessary for you to translate the results into the specific language of the auditors, regulators, and consultants that you will work with to meet your larger organizational goals.

Textual Presentations

Written reports are a mainstay of all research, whether in business or academia. Unless you are dealing with very specific goals and analysis, you will almost certainly develop some sort of written report for your project, even if it serves mainly as background information. You have already developed some documents to this end, including your project business case and project plan. Although it's common, I recommend against shoving all your results into PowerPoint, which is unsuitable for presenting large chunks of text. Instead, take the time to develop at least a written summary of the results of your project. This document does not have to be long, but it should be detailed and in narrative form so that someone down the line can read it and get a richer understanding of the project results. You may disseminate this overview before the presentation to add context to the shorter slide summations, or make it available afterward to add more depth. This becomes especially important in the context of the SIP and the project catalog, when the goal is to build connectivity and context between projects over time.

As you build project documents, you should strongly consider using a standardized style guide and to take issues of readability into consideration. A style guide is a reference document (often a book) that defines standard and accepted ways of producing written communication. *The MLA Style Guide* is a well-known example of such a reference that provides advice on grammar, structure, citations, and other necessities of effective writing. Numerous useful style guides are available for business writing, a few of which I list at the end of this chapter. The sad fact is that a lot of business writing today puts little or no effort into ensuring that the writing is consistent, correct, and readable, an avoidable mistake that can severely limit the usefulness of your metrics reporting.

Visual Presentations

We are all taught that a picture is worth a thousand words, and, whether or not this is true, you will certainly benefit from visual presentations of your data and findings as you proceed with your measurement projects and your security metrics program. You probably already have experience building charts and graphs in spreadsheets and presentations and tables in word processing documents. These are all useful tools for presenting your metrics analysis results. If you are using advanced statistical or qualitative analysis software, you will want to explore the capabilities that these tools offer for visual representation of your results as well.

I will explore examples of visual data presentation techniques in subsequent chapters and case studies, but for now consider some basic visualization techniques:

- **Charts and graphs** The workhorses of visual presentation, these can include histograms and other bar charts, pie charts, line graphs, and a variety of other visual aids. Even simple red/yellow/green matrices can be very useful in conveying data visually and intuitively, so long as you can adequately explain the complexities and nuances that may lurk behind the colors.

- **Maps**   A map is a representation of just about anything, including geographic areas, technologies, people, or concepts, built with some navigational purpose in mind. Maps can help you visually describe processes, social networks, and the relationships between your data sources and results. Maps can even be used to represent themes, stories, and histories that emerge from qualitative data analysis.

- **Scorecards and matrices**   Designed as ways to summarize and visualize disparate concepts and reveal relationships, these visual tools include balanced scorecards for presenting performance indicators as well as diagrams such as SWOT (strengths, weaknesses, opportunities, and threats), force field diagrams, and positioning matrices.

Disseminating the Results

An important question that the measurement project team must answer is how the results of the project will be disseminated to the various stakeholders and sponsors involved. It is preferable, when possible, to have some face-to-face interaction with all the stakeholder groups involved in the project. Sending results over e-mail or posting to a server can eliminate a great deal of useful interaction and runs the risk that the results will be reviewed in a cursory fashion, if at all. You want to try to get in front of the people you have sold on the project so that you can explain to them how you met their needs, understanding that this may not always be an option.

Group presentations can be useful, and are often conducted at the close of a measurement project. If you are presenting to a group, you need to understand who is represented and adjust your content accordingly. If you have limited time and results that include both technical and nontechnical conclusions, you may want to consider having more than one results meeting, perhaps hosting several meetings with individual stakeholder audiences. This can have some limiting effects, as there is benefit to getting all the stakeholders into the same room, but it may be unavoidable.

Whatever dissemination mechanism you choose, you should also build into the project plan a capability for following up with project stakeholders and sponsors over time, both to elicit their feedback on how they used the results of the project, and to maintain a network of potential supporters of ongoing projects and initiatives around the security metrics program.

Phase Five: Reuse the Results

Security metrics are most beneficial when they are developed and maintained over time within the context of continual improvement such as the SPM Framework. The most common mistake I see in security programs throughout the industry is the lack of continuity and reuse of security data across projects and throughout the life of the organization. The idea of reusable and consistent measurement of security processes over time is embedded into the idea and implementation of security capabilities maturity, but many organizations remain at the low, ad hoc end of the maturity scale.

I will cover the reuse of security metrics, measurement project results, and the development of structures to facilitate continuous organizational learning later in the book, but building the hooks for reuse into your SMPs is an important prerequisite to realizing a long-term vision for your security program. In every project you develop, explicit questions and follow-up actions should extend beyond the immediate life of the project. These can be as simple as periodic follow-ups with the project team members and key stakeholders to review how the results of the project were incorporated into the organization's activities, or they can be more formal reviews conducted as part of compliance or management initiatives. But at the end of the day, it will be the security team and the CISO that must take primary ownership for ensuring that the efforts made to measure security are not neglected or eclipsed in favor of the daily grind of security operations. The need to move from tactical to strategic thinking in security begins with those tactics themselves, in the form of the security projects we conduct every day.

Project Management Tools

Project management is an enormous discipline and a thorough discussion is outside the scope of this book. Many resources are available for guidance on how to manage SMPs, and your own organization may already have resources for effective, standardized project management. If not, there is no shortage of good places to look to improve your project management skills and capabilities, none of which are necessarily specific to IT security:

- **Project management software** Many vendors, from Microsoft to cloud start-ups, offer advanced project management tools that include features such as scheduling and resource allocation, milestone tracking, and project risk analysis. Some are expensive, but several open source project management tools are available as well, including Open Workbench, Project.net, and Project Open.

- **Project management organizations** Professional associations dedicated to project management exist globally, including the Project Management Institute, which provides international certification for project management professionals.

- **Project management training and skill building** There are many books, courses, and classes that can help you or your team improve project management skills. A quick web search on "project management resources" is a good place to start if you are interesting in building these skills personally or within your team.

Summary

The SMP is the primary vehicle for operational analysis of the security metrics you develop within the SPM Framework. Measurement projects allow you to create a modular metrics program around tightly bounded goals that are linked and reused over time to facilitate continual security improvement for the organization.

Your measurement project work begins before the project itself ever kicks off, and includes aligning the project with GQM analysis, reviewing what has been done before in regard to the work being conducted, and developing and identifying stakeholders and sponsors for the project. Supporting individuals and groups will all have different goals and requirements for security, and for stakeholders outside of the security group these goals may not even be described in terms of security.

If the program is to be truly successful, it is incumbent upon the security team to promote and champion security metrics on the basis of more than just the needs of the security organization. To accomplish this, the team should build a formal project business case that can be used to communicate and promote the project activities and goals.

Once a SMP begins, it consists of five basic stages:

1. Building the project plan and assembling the project team.
2. Gathering the metrics data.
3. Analyzing the metrics data and building conclusions.
4. Presenting the results.
5. Reusing the results.

Different projects will have different approaches, data sources, analytical techniques, and results. Wherever possible, the project team should use existing organizational resources to keep the projects standardized. If standards for project management or results presentation do not exist, the security metrics team should consider developing standards, including style manuals and project management tools and skills to ensure that the value of the measurement projects are maximized and utilized by the widest possible audience.

Further Reading

Alred, G., et al. *The Business Writer's Handbook*, 9th Ed. St. Martin's Press, 2008.

Modern Language Association of America. *MLA Handbook for Writers of Research Papers*, 7th Ed. 2009.

Project Management Institute. *A Guide to the Project Management Body of Knowledge (PMBOK Guide)*, 4th Ed. 2008. Available from www.pmi.org.

Case Study 2 | Normalizing Tool Data in a Security Posture Assessment

This case study from Mike Burg shows how difficult it can be to get to the point at which you have something meaningful to measure. Mike has been involved in vulnerability assessments for many years and was extremely proficient in delivering results based on the data outputs of a variety of tools. It was only when he was asked to perform some analyses that involved synthesizing (rather than reporting) different data sets that Mike discovered how intractable some problems can be. We often neglect to consider our data before we begin measuring something, but unless our data is completely homogenous (which almost never happens), our analysis and conclusions can suffer significantly.

Mike provides some good examples of "hacking" data sources to make them work better together. Mike is one of the most tenacious problem solvers I know, and when he sinks his teeth into a challenge, he rarely lets go. Understanding how he recursively solved his data normalization problems, where each breakthrough seemed to lead only to a new hurdle to be overcome, is a fascinating story. Hopefully, you will benefit from Mike's examples and save yourself some of the heartburn he experienced.

Case Study 2: Normalizing Tool Data in a Security Posture Assessment

by Mike Burg

One of the challenges that many organizations face in the course of implementing a security program based on metrics is cleaning and normalizing the enormous amount of data collected by today's security tools so that it can be effectively analyzed and used. Whether they realize it or not, most organizations collect disparate types of security-centric technical data. Each of the different data types output by different tools has its own structure and is often output in different formats (XML, CSV, HTML, or proprietary formats). This case study considers one specific type of data—vulnerability assessment data—and outlines the problems associated with normalizing the data output by these diverse toolsets without negatively affecting its integrity. This case study specifically focuses on Cisco's Security Posture Assessment (SPA) team's experiences with handling and analyzing vulnerability assessment data.

Background: Overview of the SPA Service

In 1997, Cisco Systems acquired the Wheel Group, a small independent security company based in San Antonio, Texas. The Wheel Group had a small penetration testing team mainly composed of ex-military information security officers from the U.S. Air Force. This team developed a SPA methodology based on their work at the Air Force and the private sector, and Cisco Systems has continued to offer this SPA service for the 11 years since the acquisition.

The SPA is a vulnerability assessment/penetration testing service that aims to discover and enumerate vulnerabilities in servers, workstations, and network devices on an IP network. SPA engineers then make recommendations as to how to prioritize resources to address these vulnerabilities based on business objectives and risk. Although the service has changed and developed since the Wheel Group was acquired, the main objective of the SPA is still the same. Cisco offers five different types of SPA: Internal, Internet Perimeter, Wireless, Dial, and Web Application.

The Internal and Internet Perimeter SPAs are still the most common assessments performed, and the examples in this case study focus on these services. The assessments are similar in nature except for their attack vectors: the Internal SPA is performed from the perspective of an average corporate user connected to the internal network, whereas the Internet Perimeter SPA is performed from outside the corporate network perimeter, assuming the same view as the average Internet user. The only information (other than logistics) that is provided by the customer prior to the SPA engineers arriving onsite at the client location (if an internal assessment) are the network address ranges that are to be assessed.

Assessments are accomplished in four phases:

1. Discovery.

2. Confirm.

3. Analysis.

4. Report.

The four phases are the same for all of the SPA offerings. Cisco SPA engineers use a variety of different tools in each one of these phases that are described in the following sections.

The Discovery phase of the assessment is where the process begins. The goal of this phase is to gain an understanding of how the network is designed and what types of devices and services are present on the network. During this phase, all IP addresses that are in scope of the assessment are scanned to discover information including the following:

■ Determining whether a device is present at the scanned IP address

■ Determining on what TCP/UDP ports the device is listening

■ Determining what type of device it is (server, workstation, network device, printer)

■ Determining the operating system

This information is then used as input for the next tests that will be run against the active devices.

Phase two of the process is the Confirm phase. The goal of this phase is to use the information that was obtained in the Discovery phase and attempt to compromise any exploitable vulnerability that may exist. The key objective in this phase is not only to try and exploit vulnerabilities but, just as important, to confirm manually whether or not the identified potential vulnerabilities actually exist. The manual confirmation of the vulnerabilities removes uncertainty about the findings and uncovers false positives reported from the toolset.

Following are some of the activities that are performed in this phase:

- Brute force login attempts
- Default username and password login attempts
- SNMP easily guessable read and write strings
- Cross-site scripting web sites
- Buffer overflows attempts

After the SPA team gains access to a device, they search for information that may help to exploit the network further. This information might be obtained from unsecured sensitive files that contain passwords, by observing users on their desktops via an exploited or unsecured remote control program, or by dumping the username/password databases and then cracking passwords. Armed with this new data, secondary and tertiary exploitation takes place.

The third phase of the process is the Analysis phase. The objective of this phase is to document the process and steps that were used to compromise the network and analyze the data from the tools using up-to-date security intelligence. Generating descriptive statistics from the obtained data is a primary function of this phase. The SPA team uses these statistics to help the client understand the types of information and vulnerabilities that were discovered during the assessment. They also use the information to help prioritize the vulnerabilities based upon stated business objectives and risks.

The final phase of the process is the Report phase. A detailed report is created that contains a full summary of the assessment. Included in the report is information about each device that was assessed as well as methods to use to mitigate the risks that were present. A final set of CSV (comma-separated values) files are provided to the customers that contain all the information that was gathered from the tools. These files can then be incorporated into the organization's existing metrics programs.

Many customers have us perform Security Posture Assessments on a periodic basis (usually annually). In general, three different outcomes are associated with repeated SPAs. Some organizations look to identify the root cause of the discovered vulnerabilities and attempt to correct those causes (which are usually process or governance related) in addition to remediating the discrete vulnerabilities. These companies are generally very successful in increasing their security posture, and follow-on assessments usually uncover fewer vulnerabilities. The second type of organization looks only to correct the discrete vulnerabilities that were identified and nothing else (for example, by applying security patches to fix the identified vulnerabilities, not attempting to determine or correct why or how the process broke down). More often than not, subsequent assessments performed for this type of customer uncover the same classes of vulnerabilities uncovered in the previous assessment (even if the previously identified vulnerabilities were fixed), because little or nothing was done to correct the process failures that allowed the introduction of the vulnerabilities in the first place. The final type of customer simply looks to satisfy a requirement to have an assessment performed and does little or nothing to correct even the technical (as opposed to process) weaknesses that were identified.

SPA Tools

Several different tools are used during the four phases of the process. These tools are a combination of open source (a few of which are described in the following sections) and custom programs written in Perl, Python, and Bourne shell scripts. One advantage of using open source tools is that you can modify them. Because the SPA service has evolved over time, so has the toolset, including added third-party tools.

Nmap is one of the primary open source tools used during the Discovery phase. Nmap is specifically used to determine active IP addresses, to fingerprint operating systems, and to enumerate open ports. The SPA team has modified Nmap and other open source tools better to align with the SPA methodology. Where possible, these modifications are submitted to the relevant open source project maintaining the tool so that they can be eventually incorporated into future releases.

Metasploit is another open source tool used during the Confirm phase. The SPA team created a detailed process for researching, identifying, coding, and testing exploits, and Metasploit is used to supplement this process. This community-maintained tool includes many different types of exploits that are usable against network-accessible services. Each of these exploits is rigorously tested in the SPA labs against target devices and validated for expected operation.

The SPA team also uses third-party tools for the Discovery, Confirm, and Analysis phases. One of these tools offers built-in vulnerability identification and classification information. A key advantage of using the third-party tool is that the vendor is dedicated to identifying the most current threats and has resources to incorporate new vulnerability checks and exploits into the tool. Each of the tools described has its own unique challenges when it comes to data output; these are described in detail in the following section.

Data Structures

The primary challenge we faced when integrating many different types of tools into a complex process such as the SPA was to understand the data structure's output by each tool. In the case of open source software, this can be challenging, because numerous developers often contribute to the code. Third-party tools can also be problematic, because their data structures may be obscure and not easy to manipulate, and the vendors do not provide source code.

To deal with all these different tool outputs during the course of a SPA, we decided to normalize all the different output into a CSV type format. A different set of tools was developed for the SPA service to parse the data output of each vulnerability tool and normalize it.

We needed to understand the type of information to be analyzed and reported on. This was the second challenge that was addressed by the team. The SPA methodology focuses on 14 major items, each containing subsections. Figure 1 displays these sections and some examples of the metadata contained within them. In most cases, the metadata within the subsections is structured, but as you will see, this did not always hold true.

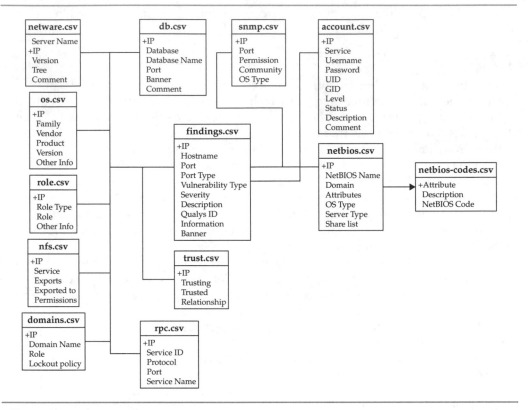

Figure 1.   SPA data structure

Objectives of the Case Study

In an effort to improve the SPA service and as a result of some specific customer need, we needed to change and expand our data analysis efforts and process. Our customer requested that we build more measurement and trending capabilities into the service and the findings of our relatively "snapshot-like" assessments. They also wanted more insight into how different entities and systems could be compared against one another and against developed baselines. This case study explores some of the data normalization and analysis challenges that we experienced as we attempted to bring together output from multiple tools in multiple formats and to make that data usable for analysis and "apples-to-apples" comparisons.

The first phase of this assessment focused on two different business units in one country. One of the key requirements from the customer was an analysis of the differences (if any) of the security posture and vulnerability severity of the different business units using the SPA data.

Methodology

The SPA service includes several ways of characterizing identified vulnerabilities, including severity metrics based on the Common Vulnerability Scoring System (CVSS), an industry-recognized framework for assessing the severity of identified security vulnerabilities. CVSS scores describe how severe an IT system vulnerability is considered to be based on a cross-industry consensus of security experts. These scores determine how much concern a particular vulnerability warrants and support efforts to prioritize vulnerability remediation.

Three CVSS metrics exist (although the Cisco assessment team used only Base and Temporal scores for this assessment):

- **Base**   Intrinsic qualities of the vulnerability
- **Temporal**   Qualities that evolve over the lifetime of the vulnerability
- **Environmental**   Qualities that depend upon environment or implementation

Challenges

Having provided background regarding the service, I can now discuss some of the data normalization challenges that we encountered. In particular I will focus on challenges related to the scoring system and the data structures.

Scoring

Using CVSS scores presented certain challenges when we tried to pull this information from several different sources; we discovered that the links between vulnerability identification information and the CVSS scores themselves were not always directly linked. In some instances, items that we classified as vulnerabilities within the SPA tools were not represented in the CVSS database. Many of these unscored vulnerabilities were exploited in the assessment, and we had to decide whether or not to include the findings in the analysis. If these findings were disregarded, we would be missing out on a large chunk of data for both states that were assessed; if they were included, we would need to assign CVSS scores. We ultimately decided that the vulnerabilities would be included in the findings.

A complex formula and scoring guideline can be used to determine Base, Temporal, and Environmental scores. Using these guidelines, we were able to assign custom scores for both Base and Temporal Metrics to the unscored vulnerabilities. To ensure that the new scores were reasonable, we compared them to similar types of vulnerabilities with assigned CVSS scores. After this sanity check was complete, the new values were entered into our vulnerability data set. Unfortunately, any score that we generated would not be industry recognized, but a full write-up of the adjusted CVSS scores was included in the final report to the customer.

The scoring challenge illustrates the problem that occurs when data is not standardized completely across sources. Different data sources in the assessment treated CVSS scores in different ways and the result was that some links between vulnerabilities and CVSS scores were not present or not reliable. In this case, we could either omit any non-standard data or map that data to CVSS. Our solution was to include rather than disregard non-standard data even if that meant creating CVSS scores that were not industry recognized. The benefit of creating these scores for vulnerabilities was that the data could be normalized against the CVSS standard, but it was very important that we explained what we had done and provided details on how we created the non-standard scores so that the customer was aware of why we scored vulnerabilities in certain ways.

Data Structure

While scoring was a challenge for normalizing what data meant, the harder challenge was normalizing data sources that were structured differently. As discussed earlier, the outputs of the SPA tools are flat CSV-formatted files. The SPA tools are designed to combine the CSV files and generate an HTML report, which is structured so that specific details about the individual hosts and vulnerabilities can be accessed for detailed analysis. While this HTML structure works well for traditional SPA analyses, it did not work so well for this specialized SPA analysis, because the structure of HTML does not lend itself to efficient data management and manipulation.

We decided that the specialized SPA analysis would include the following variables:

- IP address
- Operating system type
- Location
- Vulnerability
- SPA identification number
- Vulnerability name
- CVSS base
- CVSS temporal scores

Each variable for a SPA is normally stored as metadata within multiple CSV files. We encountered problems with this type of native structure. First, the flat file nature of CSV does not present the most efficient way to handle large sets of data. If the CSV files were used for the service, a script would have to be created to gather the data that was needed from the appropriate files. Second, comparing and contrasting different CSV files across multiple customers can be quite cumbersome.

While a CSV file could work fine for smaller or single stand-alone engagements, we decided instead to use a MySQL database for this customer. MySQL is an open source relational database management system (RDBMS) that has made its source code available using the GNU general public license. MySQL can import raw CSV files into tables, which makes the move from CSV file format to a database format much easier.

After we decided to use a relational database, we next created the database structure. The customer database contained tables that included the data from each of the CSV files that the SPA tools generated. Everything seemed straightforward enough to proceed with the creation of the database according to our new structure. After the database was created, we began to populate the tables with the appropriate corresponding CSV file, and at this point, we began running into issues with several of the vulnerability data files.

The first file that we imported into the database was called findings.csv, and contained the following five fields that we were interested in analyzing:

- IP Address
- Port
- Vulnerability Type
- Description
- Vulnerability ID

Two of the five fields in this CSV did not cause any problems (IP Address and Description). Port, Vulnerability Type, and Vulnerability ID, however, were different stories. Some of our tools ended up contributing to our data normalization challenges due to the way they reported services and vulnerabilities.

findings.csv File (Port)   The Port field of the findings.csv file is designed to provide a listing of the open TCP/IP ports on an IP-connected device. The field lists TCP and UDP ports that are represented by up to five digits followed by the protocol. For example, 111TCP represents TCP port 111. Unfortunately, there were exceptions to this structure that we discovered as we populated the database. One of the tools that we used to determine ports not only classified ports by numbers (which is standard), but could also classify them as a vulnerability type or service. One of our tools refers to this type of classification as "pseudo ports." Although these designations are not standard ports as previously discussed, the tool makes use of them in an attempt to identify the nature of the service for the vulnerabilities identified.

One of the reasons the tool listed out the nature of the service or vulnerability as opposed to the port on which it was received was that, in many cases, the service or vulnerability was gathered from many different ports that had been scanned, and then a backend process was run to group the ports together into a single service or vulnerability.

To understand this, let's take a closer look at this port identification process. During the Discovery phase of a SPA, information is sent to listening network services on hosts, which may cause the backend service to return some type of information. A clear and easy example that will illustrate this is to take a look at the response from a Windows XP client machine. This example uses the open source tool Nmap:

```
sh-3.2$ nmap -sC smb-enum-sessions 172.16.2.128
Starting Nmap 5.00 ( http://nmap.org ) at 2009-12-17 10:25 MST
Interesting ports on xp-machine (172.16.2.128):
Not shown: 997 closed ports
PORT    STATE SERVICE
135/tcp open  msrpc
139/tcp open  netbios-ssn
445/tcp open  microsoft-ds
```

```
Host script results:
|_ nbstat: NetBIOS name: REDZVM, NetBIOS user: <unknown>, NetBIOS MAC:
00:0c:29:91:e9:ee
|  smb-os-discovery: Windows XP
|  LAN Manager: Windows 2000 LAN Manager
|  Name: WORKGROUP\REDZVM
|_ System time: 2009-12-17 10:25:28 UTC-7
Nmap done: 1 IP address (1 host up) scanned in 1.28 seconds
```

A few items are important in this scan. Note that both TCP port 139 and TCP port 445 are open. These are Microsoft NetBIOS ports. NetBIOS provides a mechanism that allows applications on different Windows hosts to communicate with each other over the network.

```
139/tcp open   netbios-ssn
445/tcp open   microsoft-ds
```

The remaining information from the scan is obtained from the same tool connecting to those ports.

```
|_ nbstat: NetBIOS name: REDZVM, NetBIOS user: <unknown>, NetBIOS MAC:
00:0c:29:91:e9:ee
|  smb-os-discovery: Windows XP
|  LAN Manager: Windows 2000 LAN Manager
|  Name: WORKGROUP\REDZVM
|_ System time: 2009-12-17 10:25:28 UTC-7
```

In this example, it is possible to access the NetBIOS service anonymously to enumerate potentially sensitive information about system resources present on the host, including items such as user accounts or shared resources, as shown. This sort of vulnerability can be exploited on both TCP ports 139 and 445. The third-party tool we used would classify this as a pseudo service called "Windows" as opposed to individually listing the ports and associating the vulnerability with each of them.

Another example of a pseudo service is easily guessable TCP sequence numbers. This sort of vulnerability is a result of a poorly written TCP/IP stack for an operating system. If the TCP sequence numbers are guessed by an attacker while two other IP-connected hosts are communicating, the only difference between the legitimate connection and a malicious connection initiated by the attacker is that the attacker will not see the replies returned to the authorized user whose IP address was forged. This type of vulnerability is not tied to any single specific TCP port; instead, it would affect all ports because it is a problem with the underlying TCP/IP stack. The pseudo service that the third-party tool assigns to this vulnerability is "TCP/IP".

Another reason the tool we use focuses on the service rather than the port during analysis has to do with the tool's methodology and design. Some tools take a "vulnerability-centric" approach to reporting vulnerabilities. This vulnerability-centric approach means that declaring on what port a particular vulnerability was identified is not as important as the vulnerability itself. The SPA philosophy for reporting vulnerabilities differs from this: it is a "port-centric" assessment. There is no necessarily right or wrong answer regarding how to classify vulnerabilities from a philosophical point of view—these are just two different ways of approaching that classification.

As you can see from the examples, the pseudo services created a normalization problem and we were faced with an important decision: whether or not to include pseudo services in our analysis. We had three different options, of which only two seemed reasonable. The first option was to try to determine the actual port or ports on which a given vulnerability was identified and then replace the vendor information (pseudo service) with standard port numbers and protocols. Unfortunately, this was impossible because some of our tools were proprietary and we could not access this information.

The second option was simply to remove any row that contained anything other than the standard TCP/IP port and protocol. Remember that the "nature of the services or vulnerability" designators may have vulnerabilities associated with them in the same manner as a line that had the standard TCP/IP ports. If these rows were removed, we would also be removing any potential vulnerability/vulnerabilities that were associated with them, which in turn might skew the data.

The final option (which was the one that we settled on) was simply to include the information in that data set. The decision not to alter the data enabled us to report on all the vulnerabilities without sacrificing anything. This decision did require us to put a detailed explanation of the pseudo services in the final SPA service report delivered to customers. In this case we kept data regarding ports that was not normalized in order to be comprehensive and we provided the customer with extra information to help them understand the pseudo services descriptions.

findings.csv File (Vulnerability Type)   The Vulnerability Type field presented a unique challenge within the data set. The format of the data in our findings.csv file was standard for a CSV file. The file contained columns, or fields, separated by rows that contained the appropriate information gathered from the tool. Each column within the CSV file showed quotation marks around the data in that column, which represented a separate field for the SPA data. But it turned out that it was possible to have values within the Vulnerability Type field that contained commas. Having commas within a field was a problem. To input data into a MySQL database, you must declare how the fields are separated. CSV columns are separated by commas, and if commas appear within a field (as opposed to separating the field only), each item on either side of the comma is treated as a new field, which can throw off the whole structure of the import.

Here's an example to demonstrate this problem. Suppose that a CSV file is located at /tmp/import-data.csv and has three fields (IP Address, OS, Vulnerability Name). This file contains the following values:

```
"1.1.1.1","windows","ISAPI Extension Service Buffer Overflow"
"2.2.2.2","windows","iisadmin Directory Present Vulnerability"
```

In addition, we create a MySQL database called *test* with columns for IP address, OS, and vulnerability name that contains a table called *values*.

```
mysql>create database test;
mysql>use test;
mysql>create table test_values (ip varchar(15), os varchar(20),
vulnerability varchar(60), id int not null auto_increment, primary key
(id));
```

Next, we load the CSV file into the newly created table. The following command will parse through the CSV file, split the file based on the commas, and then enter the values into the appropriate field of the table in the database. In this case, the data will be imported without issue into the tables:

```
 mysql>load data local infile '/tmp/import-data.csv' into table
values fields terminated by ',' lines terminated by '\n' (ip, os,
vulnerability);
```

The table will appear as shown in Figure 2.

Now let's modify our CSV file and add a comma into the vulnerability column. Our new CSV file looks like this:

```
"1.1.1.1","windows","ISAPI, Extension for Windows Media Service Buffer
Overflow"
"2.2.2.2","windows","iisadmin Directory Present Vulnerability"
```

Notice the comma after *ISAPI* in the vulnerability column. When this CSV is imported into the database, it will generate a warning stating that the row was truncated because it contained more data than there were input columns. The value in the vulnerability field for the first row in the table contains only *ISAPI* and one quotation mark. The rest of the data in the column is truncated. If we were to select everything in the table, the results would look like Figure 3.

As you can imagine from the example, this outcome represented a problem for the SPA and we needed to come up with a solution on how to fix the CSV import.

```
mysql> select * from test_values;
+-----------+-----------+--------------------------------------------------------+-----+
| ip        | os        | vulnerability                                          | id  |
+-----------+-----------+--------------------------------------------------------+-----+
| "1.1.1.1" | "windows" | "ISAPI Extension for Windows Media Service Buffer Overflow" | 1   |
| "2.2.2.2" | "windows" | "iisadmin Directory Present Vulnerability"             | 2   |
+-----------+-----------+--------------------------------------------------------+-----+
2 rows in set (0.01 sec)
```

Figure 2. MySQL clean CSV import

```
mysql> select * from test_values;
+-----------+-----------+------------------------------------------+------+
| ip        | os        | vulnerability                            | id   |
+-----------+-----------+------------------------------------------+------+
| "1.1.1.1" | "windows" | "ISAPI"                                  | 1    |
| "2.2.2.2" | "windows" | "iisadmin Directory Present Vulnerability" | 2  |
+-----------+-----------+------------------------------------------+------+
2 rows in set (0.00 sec)
```

Figure 3.   MySQL truncated CSV import

To overcome this issue with our data, we decided to write a quick script to open the file and delete any commas that followed an alphabetic character. The regex substitution string looked like this:

`` `s/[a-zA-Z],//g` ``

This script worked well, and we were finally in a position to import the CSV files into the database cleanly. As much as I wish that this was the end of our difficulties, we quickly ran into another issue.

findings.csv File (VID)   One of the key fields that we wanted to analyze was the CVSS score discussed previously. Two important files were needed to obtain this information. The findings.csv contained information such as IP address, hostname, confirmation status, and vid (a field containing an identification number). The vulns-vids.csv file contained a mapping of vid identification numbers to vulnerabilities. This file also contained, among other things, the vulnerability name, the CVSS base scores, and CVSS temporal scores.

With these two files imported into the database, it should have been simple enough to cross-reference the two tables matching on vid. It turns out that it was simple, but it also revealed another problem with the data: inside the findings.csv file, it was possible to have more than one vid per IP address. This would have been acceptable if each vid was represented on a separate line of its own. But that would not have made for a very interesting case study. In fact, the vid column in the findings.csv could contain multiple vids separated by a semicolon. Although this did not present an error during the import, it did present a problem when running a query. The query would always match on the first entry in the string and ignore the rest.

Let's take a look at another example that helps illustrates this new issue. We will start with two CSV files that contain the type of data I just described. Building from our previous CSV files, the first CSV file will be the test_findings.csv file, which contains the following information:

```
"1.1.1.1","windows","ISAPI Extension for Windows Media Service Buffer
Overflow","1234"
"2.2.2.2","windows","iisadmin Directory Present Vulnerability","4321"
```

```
mysql> select test_findings.vid, test_findings.vulnerability, test_vids.cvss_base, test_vids.cvss_temporal from
    test_findings, test_vids where test_findings.vid = test_vids.vid;
+----------+----------------------------------------------------------+-----------+---------------+
| vid      | vulnerability                                            | cvss_base | cvss_temporal |
+----------+----------------------------------------------------------+-----------+---------------+
| "1234"   | "ISAPI Extension for Windows Media Service Buffer Overflow" | "5"       | "5"           |
| "4321"   | "iisadmin Directory Present Vulnerability"               | "4"       | "4"           |
+----------+----------------------------------------------------------+-----------+---------------+
2 rows in set (0.00 sec)
```

Figure 4.   MySQL query matching vid field

The second CSV file will be the test_vids.csv and it contains the following information.

```
"1234","ISAPI Extension for Windows Media Service Buffer
Overflow","5","5"
"4321","iisadmin Directory Present Vulnerability","4 ","4"
```

A simple query in the database that matches up the vid field in both tables will work correctly and display two rows as is shown in Figure 4.

Now we will modify the test_findings.csv file such that multiple vids appear in the vid column separated by a semicolon:

```
"1.1.1.1","windows","ISAPI Extension for Windows Media Service Buffer
Overflow","1234;4321"
"2.2.2.2","windows","iisadmin Directory Present Vulnerability","4321"
```

In a perfect world, we would like to see a result with three rows, because now three total vulnerabilities appear across two hosts. Unfortunately, the query returns only one row, as can be seen in Figure 5. The match only occurs where the vids match exactly, which in this example occurs only on the second line.

Once again the example illustrates a real problem that we were having with the data in our SPA that we had to fix. Our solution was to write a script that parsed through each row of the CSV file and created a new line containing a duplicate of the data in the row and one of the vids. The script ran through each row until they all had only one vid.

```
mysql> select test_findings.vid, test_findings.vulnerability, test_vids.cvss_base, test_vids.cvss_temporal from
    test_findings, test_vids where test_findings.vid = test_vids.vid;
+----------+----------------------------------------------------------+-----------+---------------+
| vid      | vulnerability                                            | cvss_base | cvss_temporal |
+----------+----------------------------------------------------------+-----------+---------------+
| "4321"   | "iisadmin Directory Present Vulnerability"               | "4"       | "4"           |
+----------+----------------------------------------------------------+-----------+---------------+
1 row in set (0.00 sec)
```

Figure 5.   MySQL query matching vid field truncated

```
mysql> select test_findings.vid, test_findings.vulnerability, test_vids.cvss_base, test_vids.cvss_temporal from
    test_findings, test_vids where test_findings.vid = test_vids.vid;
+----------+---------------------------------------------------------------+-----------+---------------+
| vid      | vulnerability                                                 | cvss_base | cvss_temporal |
+----------+---------------------------------------------------------------+-----------+---------------+
| "1234"   | "ISAPI Extension for Windows Media Service Buffer Overflow"    | "5"       | "5"           |
| "4321"   | "ISAPI Extension for Windows Media Service Buffer Overflow"    | "4"       | "4"           |
| "4321"   | "iisadmin Directory Present Vulnerability"                     | "4"       | "4"           |
+----------+---------------------------------------------------------------+-----------+---------------+
3 rows in set (0.00 sec)
```

Figure 6. MySQL query matching vid field final

Applied to our example here, the results of the script are seen in our new
test_findings.csv file:

```
"1.1.1.1","windows","ISAPI Extension for Windows Media Service Buffer
Overflow","1234"
"1.1.1.1","windows","ISAPI Extension for Windows Media Service Buffer
Overflow","4321"
"2.2.2.2","windows","iisadmin Directory Present Vulnerability","4321"
```

With the data in the proper format, we can import it back into the database. This
time when the query is run the results are in the expected three rows, as shown in
Figure 6. We used this script in the SPA to overcome our data import problems in much
the same way.

os.csv and role.csv Files   A last piece of the equation for our SPA data efforts was to add
a bit more data about the hosts. We wanted to be able to report on the primary function
of the devices that were scanned as well as what type of operating system they were
running. This information was split into two different CSV files: os.csv and role.csv.
The issues with operating systems and roles were not as bad as the structural issues
we encountered but they still required us to make some normalization decisions about
how we would handle the data.

A few different methods can be used to obtain the operating system and role of a
machine during a SPA. One of the easiest ways is to banner grab from an open TCP
port. A quick example of this would be to connect to an open port on a machine and
then make a judgment of the operating system based on the returned output.

For this example, I will simulate a web browser connection using the open source
tool Netcat to connect to www.mhprofessional.com on port 80. Netcat is a feature-rich
networking utility that is used to establish connections to network services.

```
sh-3.2$ nc www.mhprofessional.com 80
HEAD / HTTP/1.0
HTTP/1.1 301 Moved Permanently
Date: Thu, 17 Dec 2009 19:35:27 GMT
```

```
Server: Apache
Location: http://www.mhprofessional.com/
Connection: close
Content-Type: text/html; charset=iso-8859-1
```

Notice in this example that the server has declared itself as Apache, which is a type of web server that can run on many different operating systems:

```
Server: Apache
```

This field will also often contain the version number of the service that is running. Sometimes it is easy to identify the operating system (or at least the manufacturer) based on the banner. For instance if the Server field returned "Microsoft-IIS/5.0," we could assume that the device was running a flavor of Microsoft Windows (as that is all that IIS will run on). It is also important to understand for this example that the Server field is a configurable parameter and may not be representative of the type of server that is actually running. It would be difficult to determine the primary role for this host with just the banner. A host may be running web services for many reasons. For instance, the web services could be for remote monitoring or could be embedded in another type of software for remote control purposes, as opposed to strictly serving web pages.

Another way to obtain operating system and role information from a system is to use OS fingerprinting, a technique that sends TCP and UDP packets to a host and then examines the return traffic for patterns. The TCP stacks on operating systems are not all built alike, and many of them have their own unique way of responding to packets that are sent to it. Tools that have fingerprinting capabilities match the response patterns to a backend database for OS identification.

The following example demonstrates OS fingerprinting of a host using Nmap:

```
sh-3.2$ sudo nmap -O 192.168.105.76
Interesting ports on 192.168.105.76:
Not shown: 964 closed ports, 31 filtered ports
PORT      STATE SERVICE
22/tcp    open  ssh
88/tcp    open  kerberos-sec
3306/tcp open  mysql
3689/tcp open  rendezvous
5900/tcp open  vnc
MAC Address: 00:26:BB:1D:E9:F3 (Unknown)
Device type: general purpose
Running: Apple Mac OS X 10.5.X
OS details: Apple Mac OS X 10.5 - 10.5.6 (Leopard)
Network Distance: 1 hop
Nmap done: 1 IP address (1 host up) scanned in 8.05 seconds
```

The results of this fingerprint show that the host is an Apple workstation running Mac OS 10.5.X:

```
Running: Apple Mac OS X 10.5.X
OS details: Apple Mac OS X 10.5 - 10.5.6 (Leopard)
```

What is unclear, though, is the role or function this device serves. This could be a database server, because it is running MySQL (TCP/3306) and also has SSH (TCP/22) running on it. It could also be just a workstation that happens to be running those services as well.

These examples show that there are multiple ways to get OS and role data for machines, using different tools and different types of data. In our SPA we had to decide how to normalize the data from any tool we used in order to produce standard OS and role information. Our toolset contains logic that determines the OS and role of a device from the data gathered, but the downside to the identification process is that there are many different possible results from the tool. As the SPA engineer reviews and confirms the results of the scans, they also enter information about the host, which hopefully should, but may not always conform to standard SPA notation.

Some of the results for the role and OS are very generic, while others may be very detailed and include such data as version numbers such as those displayed in the preceding example. Another good example of this is to consider how a UNIX device may be displayed in the role.csv file. While the device role would be "Server" and the role type would be "UNIX," it could have detailed values such as "Linux," "Redhat Linux 7.2 kernel-2.4.20-28.7," "Solaris," "9.3.1," or even "None."

To normalize the data in our SPA that went into identifying role and OS, and to overcome the challenge of multiple data sources in the previous examples we had to determine how much information we wanted to include about the operating system and role of identified systems in our SPA reporting. Ultimately, we decided that a more generic approach would suffice. We kept the role and OS data general, removing any detailed information about operating system versions or specific role functions from our data set. We only used data that was the same across any particular tool output. This ensured that we had normalized data, because the generic role and OS information from our tools was always populated and consistent. You can compare this strategy with our decision to include inconsistent data regarding the pseudo services I described previously. In that case we deliberately kept data in the set even if it was non-standard because we felt it was needed to understand the results. In the case of role and OS information only general data was necessary to understand the results.

I am happy to tell you that this was the last of the data issues that we encountered for this part of the SPA. We had gone through a difficult process of deciding what we needed and then trying to make the data meet those needs. As each new need was identified it seemed that we found structural problems in our data gathering tools and methods that made it difficult for us to use our data to meet the need. The biggest team takeaway from these activities was that our initial assumptions about the structure of our data were wrong. It seemed logical for us to assume that, because the process works flawlessly inside the current toolset for the SPA service, it would not be much of a leap to produce new data and statistics.

As a result of the difficulties in making our data work for this new type of SPA, I became interested to learn how the tool manages the individual flat files and the logic behind parsing the data. A large portion of the tool code was solely dedicated to normalizing the data to generate the specific output and format for SPA reports, which were always done a certain way. As new tools were and are incorporated into the toolset, the SPA developers add new sections of data manipulation code to compensate for the specific output structure. What this means is that every time the SPA team added a new tool, someone had to go through an exercise like I had done to figure out what data they needed and then create hacks and workarounds to make sure all the data worked properly. I suppose it was a little reassuring to find out that I was not alone in the data normalization game, but it also showed just how much time and effort had to go into making our data useful. The SPA engineers only had to make data work with a well-understood analysis and reporting format, so it was easier. When I had tried to create new metrics and reports that were different from the traditional SPA, normalization became a real nightmare.

A Final Objective

You might think that after all this effort I would have wanted to stop worrying about data altogether. But we had a final objective in the project that was completely new for the SPA: developing a way to let customers know how they ranked from a security standpoint compared to their peers. We needed a solid foundation of data from which to draw upon for the comparison. To begin with, we needed to determine how many years of past data we needed to collect for our baseline. For the data, we would use a general, sanitized archive of historical SPA information that included the types and quantities of vulnerabilities and where/how they were found (internal or Internet Perimeter).

We decided that five years of historical data would be sufficient for correlation. This sample size allowed us to have a large base that still contained data that was relevant in today's environment.

 NOTE   Although it might be hard to believe, we still find vulnerabilities in many customer environments that are five years old. This is usually due to a failure of process, procedures, and governance at a much higher level—but, alas, that is a story for another day.

With the historical timeframe selected, we began to parse through the data in the archive and classify it into a few different categories including the following:

- Internal or Internet perimeter assessment
- Size of the engagement

- Recurring client assessments
- Integrity of the data

Sorting through the data in this manner was a lengthy task, but it did not require any sort of data manipulation. However, other problems soon became apparent.

I already talked about how the SPA toolset has evolved over time and with these changes came changes to the format of the data. Many different types of vulnerabilities in the past were perhaps classified one way (from a severity point of view) in older versions of our tools, but would be classified much differently in more recent versions of the toolset, because of the age of the vulnerability and newer ways to mitigate the threats. Fortunately, the categories of the vulnerabilities have remained consistent over time. The categories include information such as the type of vulnerability (for example, buffer overflow, cross-site scripting, default accounts), and the operating system on which it was found and exploited.

In the current version of the toolset, many types of files contain information about assessed hosts that did not exist a few years back. In some cases, the file structures were the same but new columns had been added to include these new types of information. The next challenge of our data analysis was to determine which values to use from the data sets and whether they had been consistent through the years or would require normalization. Some of the values that we chose to use for a historical baseline and statistical analysis were the following:

- Operating system
- Vulnerabilities
- Role
- Vulnerability severity

These values covered technical details, but did not give information that let us compare different types of organizations. The next thing to sort out was how to classify organizations so that we could compare vulnerabilities within the same industry. This type of information was not being gathered by the toolset, which meant that we would have to determine the different parameters we needed to compare and then determine where to obtain the information we needed. We wanted to be able to answer the question, "How do I compare to my peers?" that is often asked by our clients. It was important that we gathered enough data about the organization to create a useful classification system. We believed that the following categories would provide the correct amount of data for classification:

- Company Vertical
- Total Annual Revenue
- Geographical Locations
- Total Number of Employees

The next step was to create the classification system. In other words, we needed to populate each one of the categories with metadata. Consider Company Vertical for example. Examples of metadata in this category include

- Health Care
- Retail
- Service Provider
- Manufacturing
- Education

Total Annual Revenue and Total Number of Employees would need to have ranges associated with them. Examples of these ranges include

- 1–100
- 100–5000
- 5000–10,000
- 10,000–20,000

And Geographical Locations could have metadata including:

- Country
- State
- Region

The last step in creating the new classification system was to group together each of the categories and their metadata and provide a unique identifier, in this case an alphanumeric ID system. For example, a healthcare company with 50,000 employees in the United States that does $8.4 million in sales was classified as HC5USM. A retail company with 133,000 employees, a global presence, and $19 million in sales would be classified as RT9GLM. The IDs themselves were just our notation and are not important except to show that they allowed us to classify each company in a way that we could use for comparison. The classification matrix then needed to be stored in a new table of the database that we previously created for the new SPA.

Finally, we needed to assign these same classifications to all of the historical data in the archive. This part required some time, as each SPA in the historical archive would have to be looked up so that we could gather the appropriate information for classification. This was a long and tedious process but was ultimately worth the time. We were able to provide our customer with the additional analysis and trending information that they needed. We then added code to the SPA toolset that automatically gathered this type of information at the beginning of an assessment and added it to the data files.

Summary

Companies today are faced with an increasing amount of data that comes from a variety of sources, including security tools or devices, and each may have a different standard for output format. This case study describes in detail the process that we undertook to solve a particular data challenge. Many different types of obstacles needed to be overcome as they related to the data with which we had to work.

When embarking on a project such as this, your most important thing to remember is that patience is the key to success. Start with well-defined goals and realize that along the way, you may have to make decisions about whether or not the data will support those goals. Many factors need to be considered, and you will have to become very familiar with the type and format of the data that you are looking to normalize.

Many important questions regarding the data will need to be answered. Here are examples of some of these questions:

- What format do I need my data in for analysis?
- From how many different sources do I need to pull data?
- Do the fields in the data sources contain unexpected characters?
- Do all of the data sources contain the appropriate variables?
- Will the manipulations that are needed compromise the integrity of the data?

Hopefully, you now understand that normalizing data is not rocket science, but it requires a keen eye and plenty of patience.

PART III | Exploring Security Measurement Projects

CHAPTER 7 | Measuring Security Operations

The preceding chapters have outlined the Security Process Management (SPM) Framework, including the role of security measurement projects (SMPs) as a component of the framework. I also spent quite a bit of time describing various types of data and techniques for their analysis. The next few chapters will dive into the details of SMPs by way of examples drawn from a number of areas, beginning with the measurement of security operational activities.

Data analysis can be daunting, as literally hundreds of statistical tests and methods can be employed to make sense of your observations. The purpose of these chapters and examples is to show you how the concepts covered so far in the book can play out in actual practice, using several more commonly employed techniques. If you are looking to move beyond descriptive methods or to explore qualitative analysis in your security metrics program, I offer some starting points in the pages that follow.

The metrics, data, and analysis methods described in the coming chapters are just suggestions and they may not be appropriate to every organization. But hopefully they can give you some ideas on how you might approach metrics projects and data analysis in your own security programs.

Sample Metrics for Security Operations

The Goal-Question-Metric (GQM) method is a good way to develop security metrics that are targeted to specific needs and initiatives, and it takes into account the unique requirements of a particular organization or environment. But it can also be useful to have a set of predeveloped metrics that can be used "off the shelf" or as inspiration for developing other, similar measurement activities and projects. Most organizations will already have security metrics that they collect and analyze, usually through descriptive methods, and these metrics can be included in developing a sample catalog.

Table 7-1 lists a number of operational IT security metrics that can be used as a starting point for data collection and analysis. I have divided these metrics into four basic areas: budget & personnel, processes & projects, systems & vulnerabilities, and change & remediation. This is certainly not an exhaustive list and only scratches the surface of possible measurements. If you have your own metrics, you should add them to the list or replace those metrics that may not be appropriate to your security goals. And as your SMPs and GQM exercises produce new metrics, you should incorporate these as well into a documented and dynamic security metrics catalog.

These metrics provide just a few ideas for sources of security data that can be used to drive measurement and improvement of the security process over time. Most security organizations are already regularly collecting data on events, vulnerabilities, and other facets of their operational activities to support requests for information from supervisors and senior management. This data is important, but security really begins to benefit from the metrics program when analysis extends beyond the immediate data. This benefit may be brought about simply by collecting and collating data over time to provide baselines and more longitudinal insight, which already takes place in many IT

Goal	Metric
Budget & Personnel	
Understand the prioritization of and investment in security as a function of IT operations.	Percent of IT budget devoted to IT security
Understand the connection between IT security activities and the business.	Percent of IT security budget covered through internal charge back, by unit
Understand the prioritization of and investment in security as a function of IT operations.	Ratio of full-time IT staff resources devoted to IT security
Understand one general level of security personnel expertise.	Ratio of certified to noncertified IT security staff members
Processes & Projects	
Understand the level of visibility into routine security operational activities.	Ratio of security business processes that are documented
Understand the utilization of existing IT security staff.	Number of security measurement or improvement projects undertaken during time period
Understand the prioritization of and investment in security as a function of IT operations.	Ratio of security measurement or improvement projects to overall IT measurement or improvement projects
Understand project size and duration for IT security projects.	Average resource utilization (in staff hours) for security measurement or improvement projects undertaken during time period
Systems & Vulnerabilities	
Understand deviation from established baselines.	Percent of systems compliant with current configuration standards
Understand gaps in existing security posture.	Number or ratio of systems containing vulnerabilities as a result of assessment
Understand threat levels for vulnerable systems.	Average count and severity of vulnerabilities per assessed system or defined set of systems
Understand threat levels for vulnerable systems.	Number of probes, attempted attacks, and penetrations during time period
Understand vulnerabilities posed by wireless connectivity.	Ratio of secured to unsecured wireless access points present on network

Table 7-1. Sample Metrics for Security Operations

Change & Remediation

Understand systemic changes to security baseline over time.	Number of configuration change or exception requests per time period
Understand security reaction posture and impact on IT security staff.	Number of security incidents (escalated or investigated) per time period
Understand what kind of security vulnerabilities are most prevalent in the environment.	Ratio of vulnerability types identified (access, denial-of-service, data loss or corruption, fraud, and so on)
Understand lag time between vulnerability discovery and mitigation.	Average time required to remediate identified security vulnerabilities

Table 7-1.   Sample Metrics for Security Operations (*Continued*)

security shops. But there are other creative ways to approach measurement and analysis projects that are not as commonly applied to IT security today, and I will explore a few examples in this chapter.

Sample Measurement Projects for Security Operations

The following four projects provide some practical examples of how security metrics can be used in the context of SMPs to meet defined measurement goals. For each project, I have developed a basic GQM template to define the goal of the project, the questions the project is intended to answer, and the metrics used to provide those answers.

SMP: General Risk Assessment

The first project is designed to improve upon the annual loss expectancy and risk matrix methods of risk analysis that I critiqued in previous chapters. Estimations of annual loss expectancy have been critiqued because the numbers used are often completely made up, based on little or no supportable evidence.

Risk matrix analysis involves asking IT security stakeholders to assign simple ordinal values to the probabilities and costs of certain security threats. These values are usually a variation on high, medium, or low, although they may be expressed in numerical scales (1–3, 1–10, 1–100, and so on). These analyses are problematic because they measure perception of risk rather than actual risk, and they disconnect the risk metric from real numbers and costs in favor of a heat map. In both techniques, the assessments often introduce as much uncertainty to the risk question as they remove.

We continue to perform these risk assessments for many reasons, including familiarity and the fact that they are pretty easy to perform. We also perform them because of a perception that no viable alternatives exist. We need some way of estimating and judging risk even though we are uncertain about what the actual risk is. But how do you improve the accuracy of an educated guess? Assessing security risks is difficult in part because of a lack of solid, empirical data on which to base estimates. Without that data, it may seem hopeless that we can get any closer than experience and "gut" in our guessing.

Fortunately, a substantial body of literature is available on judgments in situations of uncertainty and of more rigorously analyzing the opinions of experts in the context of those situations. This measurement project used some of these techniques to improve on a company's existing, matrix-based risk assessments to gain insight and reduce existing uncertainties regarding the annual financial costs of several threats. The GQM template for the project is listed in Table 7-2.

Using Confidence Intervals (CIs) for Analyzing Expert Judgments

A full treatment of the methods for analyzing human judgment under uncertainty is beyond the scope of this measurement project, but the implications of these techniques for IT security are interesting because they provide a balance between the estimates of an annualized loss expectancy (ALE) assessment and the construction of a risk matrix, all while focusing on maintaining sound methodological and statistical practices.

Goal Components	*Outcome* – Improve, understand *Element* – Costs *Element* – Threats (unauthorized access, DOS, data loss) *Element* – Confidence Intervals (CIs) *Perspective* – Internal security experts
Goal Statement	*The goal of this project is to improve the understanding of annual financial costs of unauthorized access, DOS, and data loss by developing formal CIs from the perspective of internal security experts.*
Question	How many incidents of unauthorized access, DOS, and data loss will the organization experience in the coming year?
Metrics	CIs based on elicitation of judgment from calibrated internal experts
Question	What costs will be incurred from each incident of unauthorized access, DOS, and data loss experienced?
Metrics	CIs based on elicitation of judgment from calibrated internal experts

Table 7-2.   GQM Template for General Risk Assessment Project

Rather than attempting to develop numbers or scores that can be plugged into an equation or a matrix, these techniques focus on building CIs around the measurements under analysis. A CI is a range of values that is predicted to contain the true value sought at some level of assuredness. For instance, a 90 percent CI is a range of values that is predicted to contain the actual value you are seeking nine out of ten times. CIs allow expert opinion to be articulated in a way that is not absolute, but they eliminate a predefined amount of uncertainty.

Earlier in the book I described building a CI using the example of estimating the balance of your checking account. We each have enough information and expertise about our finances to be more precise than simply saying our balances are low, medium, or high, even if we cannot give an exact amount. CI construction leverages expertise and experience in order to give a range that we are reasonably sure is correct. The level of reasonableness we need or want may vary—in some cases we may want to be 95 percent confident of a result while in others a 70 percent CI may be sufficient for our goals. The trick is to combine the proper level of available information with our experience and opinions at an appropriate level of certainty. Harnessing informed opinion is the core principle of developing expert CIs and can be effectively employed in IT security as an alternative to traditional ALE or matrix assessments.

One advantage of CI construction for security is that the practice of articulating risk as an expected interval with a certain probability reduces the tendency to treat the risk numbers as absolutes. Forcing yourself to consider the chances that you are wrong in your estimates adds a bit more rigor to your analysis, and thinking in terms of ranges helps you to avoid fixating or anchoring on a particular value. Another advantage to CI construction is that the treatment of risk in terms of a range of probabilities can open up further analysis, using techniques to model the various scenarios that you envision within the range. Finally, by building CIs in the context of an ongoing Security Improvement Program (SIP), you are able to check estimates against actual occurrence and use these comparisons to refine further estimates. Over time, this data can then be used to build more sophisticated risk models for the organization than a series of heat maps or a wildly dispersed set of ALE-to-actual loss figures.

CIs for Security Risks

The approach of this project was much the same as that of a more conventional security risk assessment, but the goal was to substitute a CI of 80 percent for the values under examination, rather than attempt to estimate a single best value or to score risks in some other way.

Four expert stakeholders participated in the project, all either members of the company's IT security staff or risk management specialists with IT experience working in the office of the chief financial officer. The task assigned these individuals was to develop 80 percent CIs for the following risk criteria:

- Number of security events over the next 12 months (unauthorized access, DOS, virus outbreak, and data loss)
- Total cost of each security incident of each type

For each CI, the experts were to estimate a minimum value, a maximum value, and a most likely value that would represent the CI. The participants were to base their judgments on their experience and knowledge, such that they were 80 percent certain that the actual risk values (which were unknown) fell somewhere within the expressed range. The structure of the generic CI is illustrated visually in Figure 7-1.

Eliciting and Validating the Expert Judgments

Of course, the central problem of this metrics exercise is not much different from that of ALE or matrix assessments: How do we trust that these expert opinions are valid and useful for decision-making? To ensure that the developed CIs removed more uncertainty from the risk assessment than they added to it, several exercises drawn from decision sciences research were used during the project. In essence, attempts were made to "calibrate" the expert stakeholders' judgments to ensure that they were justified. This task was accomplished by breaking the risk assessment into three phases, each involving the construction of a set of CIs. Each phase was accomplished using a facilitator with skills in eliciting expert judgments and conducted in the form of an exercise:

1. In the first exercise, each participant constructed his or her CIs based on his or her opinions and experiences, with no other input. Participants chose an estimated low, an estimated high, and an estimated most likely value for each risk and cost.

2. In the second exercise, each participant was asked to list three reasons that his or her original 80 percent confidence estimates were correct, and three reasons why the estimates might be wrong. After listing these justifications, the participants were asked to construct a second set of CIs for the risks.

3. In the third exercise, each participant was asked to compare his or her estimated values with a game of chance that involved spinning a wheel and winning a prize. Based on participant responses, each was asked to revisit his or her estimated values.

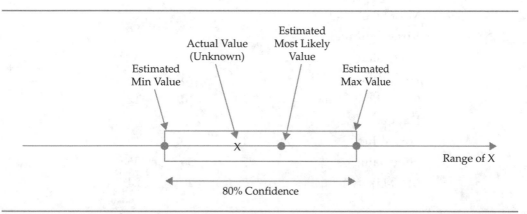

Figure 7-1. Illustration of general 80 percent CI

Table 7-3 shows the results of the CI calibration exercises for one participant in the assessment.

The changes in the estimates of the participants are accounted for by the nature of each exercise that they were asked to complete as part of the risk assessment. In the first exercise, the estimated values represent a more or less "gut" estimate. Each participant had his or her own reasons for choosing the numbers, such as a simple extrapolation of the number of each incident with which the participant was familiar from the previous year. In the second exercise, in which the participants were asked to make formal justifications for their estimated measurements and to consider reasons that they might have been mistaken, the process of reasoning through the numbers made it more likely that each participant would revise his or her estimates. These revisions were not based on new information, of course, but rather on a refinement of each participant's own expertise as each worked to reduce the uncertainty regarding opinions.

The third exercise demands a bit more explanation. Several studies on expert calibration discuss the effects of using games to explore how confident an expert really is

Risk	CI Construction Phase		
	One	Two	Three
Unauthorized Access			
Low Value	0	5	3
High Value	25	20	15
Most Likely Value	10	10	8
DOS			
Low Value	0	2	0
High Value	10	5	3
Most Likely Value	5	3	1
Virus Outbreak			
Low Value	5	5	8
High Value	40	25	20
Most Likely Value	20	10	12
Data Loss			
Low Value	12	10	18
High Value	52	36	36
Most Likely Value	24	20	24

Table 7-3.   Value Estimates for Single Risk Assessment Participant

in the estimates that he or she makes. In the case of this project, the game used was a simple one in which the participants imagined that they would spin a wheel and possibly win a prize. The wheel used for the game is illustrated in Figure 7-2. Remember that the stakeholders participating in the assessment were asked to construct an 80 percent CI for their estimates, meaning that eight out of ten times they would expect the actual value for the risk to fall within their estimated range. To test this confidence, each participant was asked to choose one of two options:

1. Assume the actual value of each risk is known. The participant could choose to be given that value and, if the value fell within the range estimated by the participant (regardless of whether or not it matched the estimated most likely value), the participant would win a prize.

2. Instead of finding out the actual value, the participant could instead spin the wheel. If the pointer landed on one of the "win" sections, the participant would win the prize.

In many cases, the participants chose one or the other of the game options in the exercise, usually choosing to spin the wheel rather than take the risk that their estimates were incorrect. But an examination of the wheel reveals ten sections, two of which cause the spinner to lose the prize, meaning that the wheel provides an 80 percent CI for winning. The 80 percent CI for the wheel game is the same as the 80 percent CI that the participants were asked to construct. If the participants were 80 percent confident of their choices, taking a chance with their own estimates or spinning the wheel should

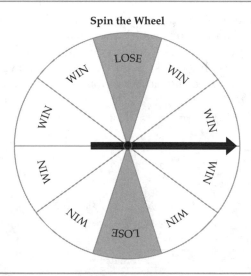

Spin the Wheel

Figure 7-2.   Wheel of chance used for calibration of CIs

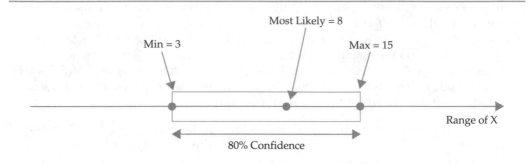

Figure 7-3. CI for estimated incidents of unauthorized access

instill exactly the same level of confidence—in other words, whether to play the estimated value or play the wheel is a wash. If a participant favored one or the other action in the context of an estimate, this is evidence that his or her estimate is one of the following:

- Higher than 80 percent, thus a participant is over-confident (if he or she chose the estimate over the wheel)
- Lower than 80 percent, thus a participant is under-confident (if he or she chose the wheel over their estimate)

Based on the results of the wheel exercise, each participant was asked to revisit his or her estimates and adjust them upward or downward until the participant was equally confident of the estimated values and of the chance of winning if he or she spun the wheel. This last CI was used as the final estimate. Figure 7-3 shows the visual CI for incidents of unauthorized access constructed by the participant scores in Table 7-3. CI construction and calibration exercises were carried out for all risks as well as for the estimated costs associated with the risks. Figure 7-4 shows the visual CI for the same participant's estimated cost of each incident of unauthorized access.

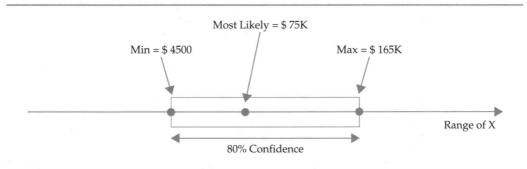

Figure 7-4. CI for estimated cost per incident of unauthorized access

Estimating Distributions Across Stakeholder Judgments

The results of the risk assessment were a set of estimates at an 80 percent level of confidence for each of the four participants. These estimates involved no more actual, known data than the ALE or risk matrix scores that were calculated during previous risk assessments conducted by the company. But the method for this risk assessment deliberately prioritized the analysis and documentation of uncertainty on the part of the participants. By looking at the problem as a probable set of ranges rather than single numbers (whether that number was a monetary figure or a risk score), the assessment characterized the risks in a more realistic way that was less likely to be mistaken for an absolute value by decision-makers.

The analysis was made more interesting by the substitution of the security heat map graph with a different visualization of risk. A common visualization technique for this type of CI data is a basic triangle distribution that shows the lower, upper, and most likely scores for the assessed risk CI. Figure 7-5 shows the triangle distribution for our example stakeholder. This distribution provides a very roughly shaped probability curve

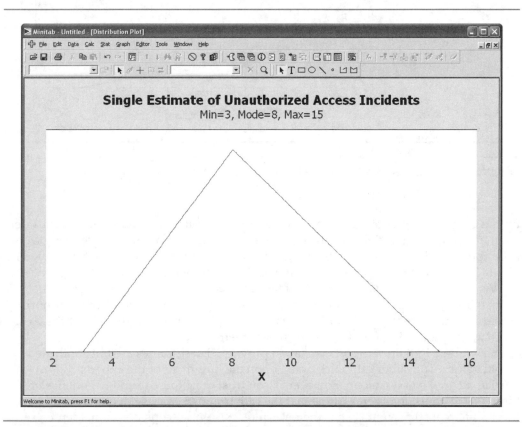

Figure 7-5.   Triangle distribution for single participant's estimate of unauthorized access

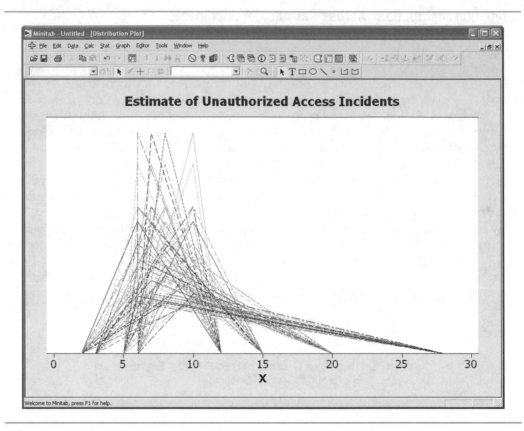

Figure 7-6. Triangle distribution for all participants' estimates of unauthorized access

for the CI, although the single graph does not provide much visual insight. But consider what happened when all four participants' CIs were calculated into a single triangle distribution. The distribution for estimated incidents of unauthorized access is presented in Figure 7-6, while the distribution for estimated cost per incident is shown in Figure 7-7.

Visually, the individual CI distributions now begin to look a lot more like actual probability curves. In the case of Figure 7-6, the estimates for incidents of unauthorized access form a curve that is decidedly positive, or right-skewed. In the case of the cost estimates in Figure 7-7, the skew is negative, or left-skewed.

So what insight does this visualization provide? These values are not confirmed actual values, but rather estimates based upon the judgment of the experts chosen to participate in the assessment. However, if you trust the expertise and experience of these participants, and you assume that the calibration exercises have succeeded in producing real 80 percent CIs for the risks and costs under consideration, then these curves can begin to function as a model for what the organization can expect. The graphs also provide valuable insight into how the experts collectively thought of the

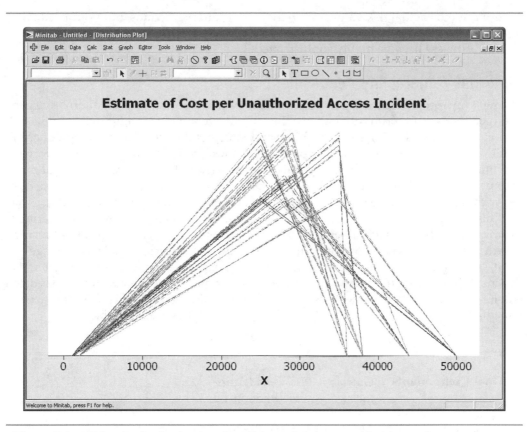

Figure 7-7.   Triangle distribution for all participants' estimates of incident cost

risks. In the case of estimated incidents, the most likely values are bunched to the left of the distribution, with a longer right tail. This would seem to indicate that the participants believed there could possibly be a large number of incidents during the year, but that they generally expected fewer to occur. In the case of cost per incident, the opposite held true. While the participants acknowledged the possibility that the costs of incidents could be low, the longer left tail indicated that they expected each incident to be rather expensive for the company.

The purpose of this measurement project example was to describe how some of the metrics and techniques described in this book could be used even in the context of uncertain measurement analysis such as generalized risk assessments in situations of uncertainty about true probabilities and costs. As these measurement projects are then coordinated and added to a continual security improvement program, your organization can collect actual values for these estimates over time and add them to the assessment model. Actual probability distributions can then be compared to expert estimated distributions and factored back into the calibration exercises for the assessment. You'll never know the actual risk values when making future predictions, but your predictive power for estimating those risk values and for basing decisions upon your estimates can nevertheless become highly sophisticated.

SMP: Internal Vulnerability Assessment

The next few projects are less complex than the previous example of an alternative general risk assessment, primarily because they involve relatively straightforward data collection and analysis. The need to calibrate and interpret the data sources is less onerous in these cases, because most of the work can be automated. This is not to say, however, that blind dependence on automated data is recommended. As I've said plenty of times before, you need to understand where your data is coming from and what you are doing with it if you are to be confident in the validity of your measurement results.

This next measurement project was an analysis of vulnerability data gathered during a security assessment of internal servers within a large public agency. Two groups of servers were assessed, each with its own administration team that was responsible for management, security, and maintenance of the machines. As part of a security improvement initiative instituted in response to new government rules, senior agency management mandated that internal system vulnerabilities be identified and mitigated according to a prioritized remediation plan. The GQM template for the resulting SMP is listed in Table 7-4.

Goal Components	*Outcomes* – Assess, identify *Element* – Remediation priorities *Element* – Vulnerabilities *Element* – Vulnerability severity *Perspective* – Server administrators
Goal Statement	*The goal of this project is to assess the remediation priorities for internal servers by identifying the presence and severity of vulnerabilities on internal servers from the perspective of the server administrators.*
Question	How vulnerable are the internal servers?
Metrics	Security vulnerability counts for assessed internal servers (from scanning) Ratios of vulnerabilities by type, OS, owner, and so on
Question	How severe are the vulnerabilities found on the internal servers?
Metrics	CVSS scores for all identified vulnerabilities present on internal servers

Table 7-4.   GQM Template for Internal Vulnerability Assessment Project

An internal assessment team was assembled to conduct the security vulnerability analysis, using a standard commercial tool to scan the servers for security holes. At the end of the data collection phase, 55 individual servers had been identified and assessed. From the tool data, a basic set of criteria was developed for further analysis that included IP address, operating system, the admin team responsible for the system, and the information regarding the type and severity of each vulnerability identified. Table 7-5 shows a selection of the resulting vulnerability measurement data.

Descriptive Statistics for Internal Vulnerability Data

Having collected a variety of data regarding the internal servers' security posture, the assessment team was ready to perform some analysis. The team relied on descriptive statistics to meet most of the goals of the measurement project.

Counts and Ratios   The assessment team relied quite a bit on counts to understand much of the data, particularly in describing the server environment:

- Fifty-five servers were deployed within the assessed environment.
- Five different operating systems were in use.

IP	OS	Admin Team	Vulnerability Type	Threat Category	Severity (CVSS Score)
x.x.x.1	Windows 2003	Bravo	Telnet	Compromise	3.6
x.x.x.1	Windows 2003	Bravo	SMB/NetBIOS	Recon	4.7
x.x.x.10	Windows 2008	Bravo	SMB/NetBIOS	Compromise	6.1
x.x.x.12	Windows 2003	Bravo	Web Server	Compromise	7.8
x.x.x.12	Windows 2003	Bravo	FTP	DOS	5.7
x.x.x.12	Windows 2003	Bravo	SMB/NetBIOS	Recon	4.7
x.x.x.43	AIX	Alpha	SMTP	Compromise	9.0
x.x.x.43	AIX	Alpha	Remote Services	DOS	4.2
x.x.x.43	AIX	Alpha	TCP	DOS	4.2
x.x.x.43	AIX	Alpha	NFS	Recon	5.7
x.x.x.43	AIX	Alpha	Remote Services	Recon	4.2
x.x.x.43	AIX	Alpha	Web Server	Recon	7.1

Table 7-5.   Sample Vulnerability Data for Server Assessment

- One hundred thirty-six vulnerabilities were identified on the assessed systems.

- Admin team Alpha administered 20 of the assessed systems, while team Bravo administered the remaining 35.

In addition to straight counts, ratios were established to help understand the breakdown of the criteria assessed. Table 7-6 shows selected ratios of OS, vulnerability type, and threat category.

The descriptive summaries in Table 7-6 are common ways of characterizing data in a security assessment and provided information on the vulnerability environment. The summaries showed that the server environment was mostly Windows, that the greatest risks (by count) were those that could lead to compromise of a system, and that two types of vulnerabilities accounted for nearly half of all those identified. So the project benefited from a basic analysis of the metrics data. But the project was also directly concerned with understanding the severity of the identified vulnerabilities so as to prioritize remediation efforts, and this required a bit more than simple addition and division.

Criteria	Ratio
OS	
Windows 2003	58%
Windows 2000	16%
Red Hat Linux	11%
Windows 2008	10%
AIX	5%
Vulnerability Type (Top Five)	
Web Server	25%
SMB/NetBIOS	20.6%
SMTP	8.8%
User Accounts	6.6%
Remote Services	6.6%
Threat Category	
Compromise	56%
Recon	35%
DOS	9%

Table 7-6.   Ratios of Various Vulnerability Criteria for Server Assessment

Severity Scores: Means and Dispersion   The agency chose to measure the severity of the vulnerabilities identified during the assessment by using CVSS scores. Recall that the CVSS is an industry standard for assigning severity to particular security vulnerabilities. CVSS scores range from 0 (the lowest severity) to 10 (the highest). CVSS scores and the methodology used to derive the scores are open and have been adopted by a variety of institutions and vendors, including the vendor of the commercial scanner used by the agency to conduct this assessment, thus making it a logical choice for prioritizing the findings of the assessment. Findings aside, CVSS scores are not the only consideration when remediating vulnerabilities, of course. Other security and business concerns such as business impact, location and role of vulnerable systems, and productivity costs of remediation must also be considered when deciding what to fix first.

Using CVSS scores, the project team was able to gain information about the severity of security problems across the assessed systems, including the mean, or average, severity of the vulnerabilities identified and how much the severity of the problems varied between the systems. I discussed measures of central tendency such as the mean and the median, and measures of dispersion such as the standard deviation, in Chapter 5. Calculating the mean, variance, and standard deviation of the CVSS scores identified during the server assessment provided the assessment team with insights into how serious and how varied the identified security problems were.

When calculating these descriptive statistics based on CVSS scores, you should keep in mind that CVSS is an interval scale, meaning that there is an assumed standard distance between the numbers. CVSS scores are not on a ratio scale, so there is no conceptual zero point (although there is a score of zero) and you cannot assume any proportions between scores. It would be incorrect to use these scores to describe a server with a mean CVSS score of 3.5 as "twice as secure" or "half as vulnerable" as a server with a mean score of 7. Using CVSS scores to prioritize remediation is fine, but using them to make comparative judgments about relative security would be a misinterpretation of the metric.

Table 7-7 lists basic descriptive statistics for the CVSS scores for all vulnerabilities identified during the vulnerability assessment (rounded to two decimal places).

These statistics offer some insights into how the CVSS scores for the assessment were grouped and how spread out they were. Since the mode and median were both somewhat

Statistic	Value
Mode (most frequent score)	4.70
Median (middle score)	5.20
Mean (average score)	5.69
Standard Deviation	1.82

Table 7-7.   Descriptive Statistics for Server Assessment CVSS Scores

lower than the mean, several higher severity scores must have increased the average for the overall data set. Figure 7-8 shows a graphical output of these calculations from Minitab and includes several other descriptive statistics at greater precision than Table 7-7.

Differences in Server Administration   The vulnerability assessment project yielded more than enough information to support the agency's decision-making process regarding remediation plans. But an interesting development arose during the assessment when tensions appeared between the two server administration teams over the results. Admin teams Alpha and Bravo each maintained different portions of the installed server base, stemming from reorganizations under previous agency leadership. A rivalry had developed between the teams, and the vulnerability assessment brought the political situation to the foreground as the two teams argued over which was doing the better job securing the agency's servers. With senior management support, the assessment team responded by separating the server groups administered by each team and calculating the descriptive statistics for each group.

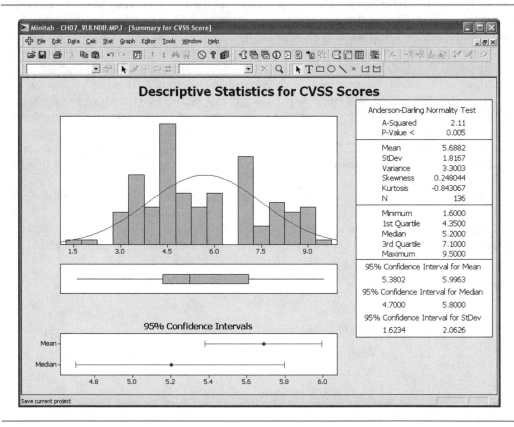

Figure 7-8.   Graphical descriptive statistics for server assessment CVSS scores

The severity of the vulnerabilities identified in the servers under each group's control exhibited similar characteristics, with means and standard deviations for the scores appearing to be roughly similar to a visual inspection, and is shown in Figure 7-9. It would be difficult to tell whether there were actual differences between Alpha and Bravo's success in weeding out particularly bad vulnerabilities, much less why one team was more successful than the other.

The number of vulnerabilities that the administration teams were allowing on their systems was another story. The statistics appeared to show that Bravo was more successful at managing server vulnerabilities overall, with a mean vulnerability count that was less than half of Alpha's. Visually, the difference is a bit striking as can be seen in Figure 7-10.

Actually proving this difference was more than random chance would require more sophisticated statistical tests. But there was strong circumstantial evidence that, while the vulnerabilities managed between the teams were equally bad, Bravo was letting

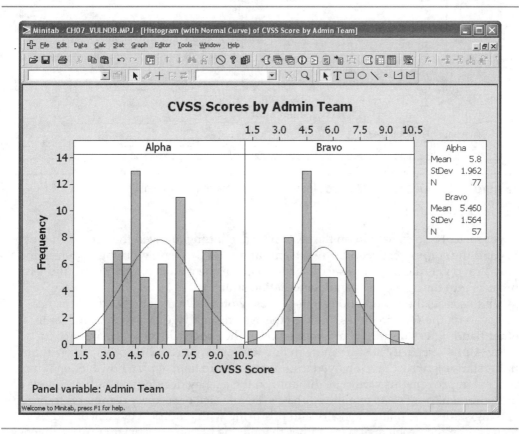

Figure 7-9.   Descriptive statistics for CVSS scores by administration team

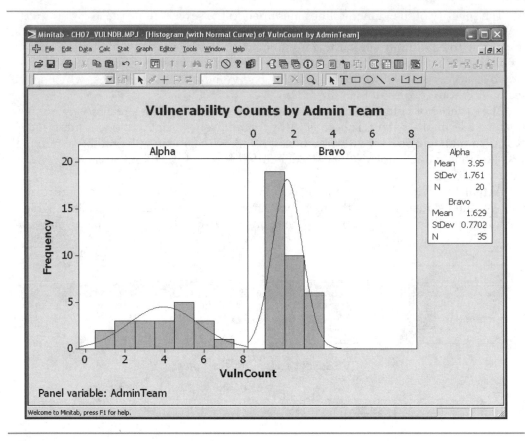

Figure 7-10. Descriptive statistics for vulnerability counts by administration team

fewer security holes remain on the systems. This finding allowed the agency to move beyond the sniping between the two teams and actually begin working to determine why Bravo was having more success, and to factor the results of those measurement projects into the agency's overall remediation strategy.

In this case, the remediation strategy was twofold. On the one hand, it was necessary to fix the security holes found in the systems managed by each team. On the other hand, it was decided that remediation at the process level was necessary to bring Alpha's security posture more in line with what Bravo was achieving. Without understanding why Bravo enjoyed a stronger posture than Alpha, however, making process improvements would be difficult. So the agency decided to conduct follow-on measurement projects to explore Alpha's systemic lack of security compared to Bravo. Having settled the political rivalry and posturing with empirical evidence, and by focusing on the problem at hand rather than laying blame or criticizing Alpha, agency management was able to convince both teams that working together to improve overall IT security was beneficial to both groups.

SMP: Inferential Analysis

The preceding measurement project shows that descriptive statistics can provide a lot of information about your security environment, but it also shows that there are limits to what those numbers can tell you. In the case of the differences between how the admin teams were managing the security of their servers, it was only because one of the metrics was so obviously different under visual inspection that the assessment team could make any judgments. And they still could not "prove" that there was a difference beyond the evidence of their own eyes. The final two projects discussed in this chapter take these analyses one step further, using tests to provide statistical evidence that things are functioning differently within a single security environment.

One-Way ANOVA for Datacenter Perimeter Attacks

The first measurement project involves a large, multinational corporation that ran several Internet-facing datacenters across the globe. As the company considered security management and budget for the overall organizations, the CISO wanted to know whether certain areas of the company's perimeter were at greater risk of attack than others. A measurement project was set up to determine whether perimeter security events were evenly distributed among the four datacenter locations. Table 7-8 shows the TQM template for the project.

Goal Components	*Outcomes* – Optimize, understand *Element* – Security resource allocation *Element* – Perimeter security events *Element* – Corporate datacenters *Perspective* – Datacenter security staff
Goal Statement	*The goal of this project is to optimize the allocation of security resources by understanding the distribution of perimeter security events among corporate datacenters from the perspective of the datacenter security staff.*
Question	What is the breakdown of perimeter-related security events against all the corporate datacenters?
Metrics	Perimeter security events by datacenter; ratio of perimeter security events between datacenters
Question	Are there any differences in how individual datacenters are being threatened?
Metrics	Analysis of variance between reported datacenter perimeter event data

Table 7-8. GQM Template for Datacenter Perimeter Security Project

The company's datacenters were all roughly the same size and configuration, and they had been set up to offer redundant operations across time zones. To determine whether there were differences between the threat environments in which the datacenters operated, the project team analyzed the monthly levels of malicious activity, such as probes and attempted attacks, detected against the outside of the corporate Internet perimeter. The project team looked at the data for the previous year at each of the four datacenter locations. Table 7-9 lists the number of identified malicious activities by month and datacenter.

As you can see from the table, it is difficult to tell by looking how different the numbers of events were between the four datacenters. There are, however, statistical tests that can determine, with a certain level of confidence, whether differences existed between the locations. The event data is measured on a ratio scale, meaning that they reflect real numbers with an absolute zero point. This meant that the project team could select an inferential test statistic that used measures of central tendency and dispersion. The project team decided to use a one-way analysis of variance (ANOVA) test to compare the mean events between the four datacenters and determine whether they were different beyond a certain degree of certainty.

To conduct the analysis, the project team had to construct a hypothesis test. The test was fairly simple: The null hypothesis (the explanation assumed to be true in the absence of any alternative explanations) stated that there was no difference between the events across the four datacenters that could not be accounted for by random fluctuations in the data. In other words, the null hypothesis stated that the datacenters were

	San Jose	New York	Dublin	Bangalore
Jan	4069	4403	3965	4606
Feb	4560	4622	4298	4695
Mar	4856	4630	4537	4102
Apr	4539	4530	4003	4829
May	4420	4380	3846	4650
Jun	4989	4367	4938	4513
Jul	5021	4751	4017	4995
Aug	3993	4610	3981	4847
Sep	5004	4478	4974	4308
Oct	4203	5021	4284	5427
Nov	4444	4518	4129	4674
Dec	4103	4702	3873	4964

Table 7-9. Perimeter-Related Datacenter Security Events

all experiencing about the same number of events on average over time. The project team then constructed a second explanation, the alternative hypothesis, which simply stated that that there was a difference between the average number of events at the data-centers that could not be accounted for by random chance. It is important to note that the alternative hypothesis did not give a cause for the difference, but stated only that the average number of events over time were not the same. Finally, the project team selected a p-value, or a level at which they could claim they had "proved" that the difference existed. They selected a p-value of 0.05, which was the threshold at which they would be 95 percent certain that they had not been in error (although there was still a 5 percent chance that the differences could be random). P-values of 0.05 are a common threshold for statistical significance in the scientific community.

All that remained was to conduct the test, using statistical software. If the test generated a p-value of less than 0.05, then the project team could reject the null hypothesis that there were no differences in the number of events and accept their alternative explanation that the datacenters were facing different security environments. The test would not tell the project team what was causing the differences in the number of events, but it would allow them better to prioritize resources and start asking more questions.

Figure 7-11 shows Minitab's ANOVA output for the datacenter event data. In the session window, the ANOVA test can be seen to have produced a p-value of 0.009, which is less than the 0.05 threshold necessary to reject the null hypothesis. The project team did reject the null and accepted the alternative hypothesis that the average number of events occurring across the data centers was different. The output also included a boxplot of the four datacenters, which provides a visual analysis of the event means for the data.

As a result of these metrics, the project team found that the security environments at the four datacenters were different and recommended to the CISO that these differences be considered when allocating security resources and budget. The project team

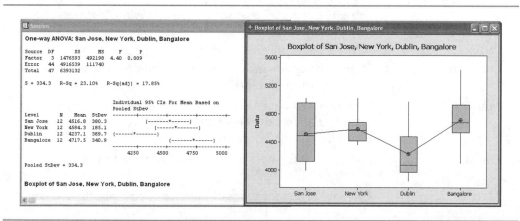

Figure 7-11. Results of one-way ANOVA test for datacenter perimeter security events

also recommended further SMPs to determine why the differences might exist and to look at ways to understand more thoroughly the threats and behaviors that were present at each datacenter.

Chi-Square Test for Data Loss Prevention Initiative

The next SMP is similar to the datacenter security event analysis, with one important difference. This project involved a company that was conducting an initiative to prevent data loss by means of the corporate e-mail system. The company was responsible for adhering to several regulations that mandated the protection of sensitive personal data, and the company had internal data that it wanted to protect as well. After experiencing several incidents in which sensitive data was mistakenly included in e-mails leaving the company, the Director of Information Security set up a data loss prevention (DLP) program and began working on ways to improve the situation. One of the areas of concern was the type and source of data that was being included in e-mail traffic. The Director knew that he was going to meet political resistance from various business functions within the company to a blanket system of controls, so he wanted as much information as possible on where the problems existed. A SMP was set up, and the GQM template is listed in Table 7-10.

The company's information security group was already working with a commercial DLP product vendor to pilot an e-mail–based DLP solution, and the vendor allowed

Goal Components	*Outcomes* – Improve, assess *Element* – Data loss prevention initiative *Element* – Incidents of data loss by e-mail *Element* – Corporate divisions *Perspective* – Security and compliance owners
Goal Statement	*The goal of this project is to improve the corporate data loss prevention initiative by assessing the incidents of data loss incurred by several corporate divisions from the perspective of security and compliance owners.*
Question	How often does sensitive or controlled data leave the company through e-mail?
Metrics	E-mail–based data loss events, overall and by data type; ratio of data loss events of all types between corporate divisions
Question	Are there differences in the type of data lost by corporate divisions?
Metrics	Chi-square test for types of data loss by corporate division

Table 7-10. GQM Template for Data Loss Prevention Improvement Project

Division	PII	CCI	CPI
HR	80	62	60
Finance	36	60	40
Sales	27	35	39
Engineering	11	10	18
Marketing	40	43	55

Table 7-11.   Data Loss Events by Data Type and Corporate Division

the company to use the pilot devices to collect data regarding the type and amount of information that was leaving the company. Working with the vendor, the company had developed three categories of data that were of concern: personally identifiable information (PII) that was covered by privacy regulations, corporate confidential information (CCI) that was internally sensitive to the firm, and contractually protected information (CPI) that was protected by customer and partner agreements. The pilot project was set up to monitor e-mail from five divisions within the company. After eight weeks of data collection, the company had the DLP metrics data shown in Table 7-11. The numbers indicate unique incidents of specific types of information contained in outgoing e-mails from employees in each division.

In many ways, this looks like the same analytical challenge posed by the security events for the datacenters in the preceding project, but there is a key difference. The DLP-related data is categorical, with the number of e-mails divided between different buckets for the type of information and the corporate division from which the messages originated. Unlike the datacenters, the divisions were not necessarily similar in makeup, and comparing the means between them for each type of protected information would not have been appropriate. But the director of information security still wanted to know if there were differences between how the various divisions were sending out inappropriate e-mails, or if everyone in the divisions under scrutiny was treating (or mistreating) all types of protected data in the same way.

The chi-square test is a statistical test that can determine whether a relationship exists between categorical data variables, and this statistical test was chosen for the DLP project. Like the one-way ANOVA test in the preceding project, the chi-square test required that the project team set up null and alternative hypotheses to test, and that they would choose a level of significance necessary to reject the null hypothesis. In this case, the null hypothesis was that there was no relationship between the business divisions and the types of data that were being lost. If the null hypothesis held true, it would make more sense to institute blanket DLP policies and solutions across the organization, since it didn't matter which division or which type of information was being considered.

The alternative hypothesis was that there was a relationship between the divisions and the types of information being lost. While the test could not tell the project team why certain divisions were more likely to mishandle certain information, rejecting the null hypothesis would indicate that certain divisions handled certain protected information differently, and this would provide the director of information security with insights he could take to the rest of the company as he expanded the DLP initiative. Like the datacenter project team, the DLP project team selected a p-value of 0.05 as the level of significance necessary to reject the null hypothesis.

Figure 7-12 shows the Minitab session output for the chi-square test. Much of the information contained in the session window describes the specifics of the statistical test and, despite the appearance of some of the chapters in the book, explaining the math of these tests is beyond the scope of what I am trying to do (not to mention that others have already done a far better job). Most security metrics professionals (me included) will rely on tools similar to Minitab or other stats packages to do the mathematical heavy lifting and will jump right to the most important part of the output, the p-value at the bottom of the session window. This value is less than the 0.05 necessary to reject the null hypothesis. Accordingly, the project team rejected the explanation that all divisions were treating different types of information in the same way. Instead, the

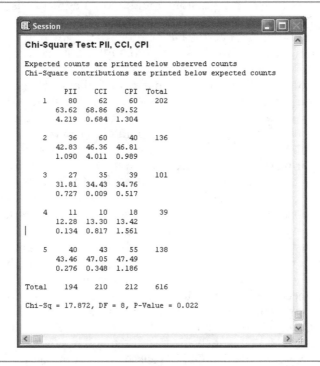

Figure 7-12. Results of chi-square test for DLP initiative

team accepted the alternative explanation that there was a relationship between the business divisions and the types of data most likely to be lost. This finding provided the director of information security with more insight into the nature of the DLP challenge at the company, and gave him important discussion points to take back to the heads of the various divisions as well as company senior management.

Summary

The purpose of this chapter has been to show some of the security metrics techniques discussed so far in the book in the context of practical examples of SMPs. The collection and analysis of data makes any security metrics program effective, and that collection and analysis should be done as part of a defined measurement project with well-understood goals, data sources, and analytical techniques.

Measuring security operations does not have to be limited to automated data and descriptive analysis. As shown in the risk assessment project, there are innovative ways to revisit even generalized and subjective measurements using experts and elicited opinions. Descriptive statistics can be very valuable as part of a project, but you should consider adding more advanced descriptive techniques such as measures of central tendency (such as mean and median) and measures of dispersion (such as standard deviation) to your metrics program if you do not already do so. Inferential statistical tools can also be quite useful when used properly, and tools such as ANOVA and chi-square tests can identify relationships between variables and data that may not be immediately obvious from your descriptive statistics.

No matter which statistics and tools you decide to use for your measurement projects, you should always be aware of the limitations and caveats that are involved with your choices. There is no requirement to be able to do the calculations necessary for an ANOVA or chi-square test by hand (that's what software is for), but you should always be concerned that you understand what you are trying to accomplish and why a particular statistic or test will get you the correct results.

Further Reading

Galway, L. *Subjective Probability Distribution Elicitation in Cost Risk Analysis: A Review.* RAND Corporation, 2007.

Goodwin, P. *Decision Analysis for Management Judgment.* Wiley, 2004.

O'Hagan, A., et al. *Uncertain Judgements: Eliciting Experts' Probabilities.* Wiley, 2006.

Several of the books recommended at the end of Chapter 5 will also be useful for exploring the techniques outlined in this chapter.

CHAPTER 8 | Measuring Compliance and Conformance

C hapter 7 described metrics and sample security measurement projects that could be applied to specific (and often technical) security operations. This chapter shifts a bit to talk about measuring compliance with and conformance to mandated ways for conducting those security operations.

These required approaches can be found in the laws, regulations, standards, contracts, service level agreements, and general best practice frameworks that are quickly crowding the security industry landscape. Some apply to specific industries or types of information, while others apply to everyone doing business in a certain way (such as publicly traded companies). And as most security managers increasingly tasked with answering regulator and auditor questions can tell you, their systems do not come with buttons you can push or command-line arguments you can enter that tell the system to "measure my compliance" (despite an increasing number of vendors that claim to be peddling just that function). Instead, CISOs and security directors face complexities that can often leave them scratching their heads (and in extreme cases fearing for their jobs).

The Challenges of Measuring Compliance

One very important reason why compliance is so challenging to measure is because compliance is not one single thing and this frustrates our efforts to simplify and bound the problem space. Compliance today is a fuzzy and subjective concept that involves a dynamic mix of new and changing regulations and rules, the personal interactions of organizations with auditors and regulatory agents, and the problems that accompany our lack of insight into the nature of our security operations themselves.

In most of the treatments of compliance-related security metrics I have reviewed, the metrics promoted appear to be similar to what you would expect for IT systems. They tend to be quantitative and narrowly focused on the specific controls required by particular compliance frameworks. The risk, however, is that this approach can create a "checkbox" mentality that favors simplistic but easily validated data points over exploring the actual complexities of IT security. In some cases, a myopic focus on controls causes metrics proponents to miss the real purpose of a particular compliance framework. ISO/IEC 27001 and 27002, two international standards for IT security, are good examples of this effect.

Confusion Among Related Standards

ISO/IEC 27001 and ISO/IEC 27002 are part of a family of international standards developed by the International Standards Organization (ISO) that address the security of information systems. These two standards have a long history of changes and development, with different names and designations used over the years, and finally stabilizing as the 27001 and 27002 designations around 2005. The standards themselves are closely related, with ISO/IEC 27001 acting as a standard for IT security—a defined set of requirements for an information security management system against which an organization can formally certify itself. ISO/IEC 27002 is a framework of best practices and guidance in the form of control objectives and controls that can be used to build robust security architectures within an organization, even if that organization does not choose to become certified.

And here is where the confusion begins. In addition to the 27001 and 27002 standards, the ISO/IEC 27000 family includes a number of other standards that have been released or are being developed. Other 27000 family standards available from ISO include ISO/IEC 27004 (information security management measurements), ISO/IEC 27005 (guidelines for information security risk management), and ISO/IEC 27006 (guidance for certifying to the ISO/IEC 27001 standard). All ISO standards are available directly from ISO or other standards organizations such as the American National Standards Institute (ANSI). The standards are not free, however, as these organizations charge for licenses to use the documents.

ISO/IEC 27001 overlaps with ISO/IEC 27002 in that the control objectives and specific controls recommended in ISO/IEC 27002 are included in ISO/IEC 27001 as an annex to the standard. Because of this, many readers of the ISO/IEC 27001 (including many security and compliance professionals) assume that 27001 is just a certifiable version of 27002 and that what is being certified are the presence of those controls. But the controls are written in a somewhat ambiguous way that leaves them open to the interpretation of both the organization implementing them and the auditors assessing them. Some security metrics experts have used this ambiguity to make the case that ISO/IEC 27002 is a poor choice for measuring security. This argument asserts that the standard is written mainly from the perspective of the certification auditor and is too subjective to use in building metrics. Over-focused on audit and under-focused on measurements, the standard provides no way of measuring objective success.

I disagree with this reading of ISO/IEC 27002, however, for two reasons having to do with the question of whether and how we can measure compliance and conformance. First, the ISO/IEC 27002 standard that is critiqued as too audit-focused is not a certifiable standard. This means that you cannot audit against it or become ISO/IEC 27002 certified because the standard is not prescriptive, mandating no particular controls, and instead acts as a guidance document for information security. ISO/IEC 27001 is the auditable security standard in the 27000 family. What makes ISO/IEC 27001 auditable is not the set of controls from ISO/IEC 27002 that are included as an appendix. ISO/IEC 27001 is a standard for implementing a security management process, centrally focused on requirements for developing, implementing, reviewing, and improving an organization's security management process. While the specific controls that are used to enforce that process are important, they are supplementary to the standard's requirements. The requirements in ISO/IEC 27001 can be quite specific, although they may not always be expressed in numbers and they require that the organization implementing the standard perform some of the intellectual heavy lifting necessary to determine the best way to measure performance. ISO/IEC 27001 requirements include such things as documented risk assessment results, formal statements of selected controls and the justifications for those choices, and the implementation of defined written policies and procedures. You can quantify these things to an extent, but they do not always lend themselves to numerical baselines.

Auditing or Measuring?

This brings me to the second mistaken belief of quantitatively-biased metrics experts. Some complain that ISO/IEC 27002 talks a lot about audit and very little about measurement. By focusing on audit, the standard places an emphasis on choosing and assessing and not on monitoring and measuring. This argument echoes Lord Kelvin and his assertion of quantitative bias (my paraphrase): "If I can't easily turn what I am looking at into a number, then it has no real meaning." I simply disagree with this narrow philosophical position, as you may have already assumed, having read this far. The definition of *audit* is "a systematic or methodical examination or review of something," and this is awfully close to many definitions of measurement. Of course, if your definition of measurement is so narrow as to include only data or analysis that directly involves a quantity of something, you will disagree with me.

But my point here is not to rehash the numbers argument or even to debate the merits of the ISO/IEC 27000 standards or compliance auditing in general. My concern actually echoes that of others, in that if compliance can be this ambiguous, how are we supposed to measure (or audit) it at all? Some might say this is impossible, and that you should toss out compliance frameworks in favor of easily derived, quantitative performance indicators that can be retrofitted into what the auditors want to see in the results. I think this a recipe for bad compliance and bad security, however, because it ignores the spirit of many of the frameworks in favor of low-level, "objective" metrics.

Such granular data does not tell a story and does not provide context on its own. Such data still requires interpretation and "spin" to explain the meanings it represents. I believe that if you have to explain and interpret the data, you might as well give some thought to context and meaning as part of your measurement. Interpretation and context are how we make sense of the individual observations with which we are bombarded every day, and interpretation and context allow us to apply those objective data to a variety of situations.

By downplaying people's role in measurement in favor of "just the facts," you risk stifling intuition and creativity and turning your security metrics program into an uninteresting collection of statistics that are unlikely to move anyone to action. The same holds true for audit environments that have been reduced to nothing but present/not present control checklists. A real audit is like a detective story—the auditor attempts to understand and interpret the complexity of compliance, not just the trappings of controls. Real measurement is like science, with a researcher looking at ideas and theories beyond just what the data can immediately tell her. In both cases, we are searching for truth, which is not always reflected in the facts.

If this seems like I am getting romantic about something as boring as measuring and auditing IT security, then so be it! If your security metrics program doesn't impart at least a little curiosity and wonder in addition to your successful audits and visibility into technical operations, then, frankly, you are not doing it right.

Confusion Across Multiple Frameworks

If it is so difficult to understand how an organization stacks up against two standards that are in the same family, such as ISO/IEC 27001 and 27002, consider the problems associated with organizations that are required to adhere to multiple compliance frameworks (that may also be changing over time as the framework is revised). Theoretically, you can have every control included in ISO/IEC 27002 in place and functioning and still not be compliant with ISO/IEC 27001, because ISO/IEC 27001 compliance measures something other than the effectiveness of technical controls (it measures the comprehensiveness and maturity of the security management program, including people, process, and technology). To attain compliance to any standard or compliance framework, you must first understand what the framework actually requires—and this can differ in both direct and subtle ways across compliance regimes.

In my day job, I work with many clients regarding issues of IT Governance, Risk, and Compliance (IT GRC). *IT GRC* is a catch-all term that describes several areas of IT, risk, and security management and includes everything from regulatory compliance to assessing business risks associated with human and organizational information behaviors. Much of what IT GRC deals with is unclear and would drive a pure-quant metrics professional up the wall. But you cannot ignore the demands and drivers of IT GRC simply because you don't think it lends itself to the kind of measurements you prefer.

Today's security environment is increasingly subject to the influence and interference of many different stakeholders, including state and local governments (laws and regulations), industry associations (best practices and formal requirements), international bodies (standards), and even our partners and customers (contracts and satisfaction or retention). Like it or not, you need to figure out how to assess and measure these many aspects of your security and automated, quantitative analyses of your log files, or your vulnerability scanner report charts will simply not suffice in every case.

When working with my clients to help them achieve IT GRC goals, I focus on determining how to tie together the various compliance requirements they are facing into something approaching a cohesive set of needs. Today, many organizations handle compliance requirements with little or no coordination between the individual efforts to meet specific needs. The HR team may be running a Health Insurance Portability and Accountability Act (HIPAA) compliance program, for instance, while the security team is dealing with preparing for a Payment Card Industry Data Security Standard (PCI DSS) audit. These two teams may not communicate at all, and neither may be aware that the office of the CFO is busily engaged in Sarbanes-Oxley (SOX) requirements in preparation for an annual report to the board. As these projects grow and develop methods and metrics for their individual goals, they become silos within the enterprise; it becomes less and less likely that anyone involved in any particular initiative will be looking to collaborate with anyone outside his own team. Yet, in many cases, the controls and objectives of the frameworks they are separately implementing share a great deal of overlap and redundancy. One result of this fragmentation is the tangible duplication of effort and wasted resources that could be more effectively utilized elsewhere. Another result is the increased risk that the different compliance initiatives end up creating risks to the company, because compliance is not standardized across the entire organization.

Even if you wanted to apply straightforward, easy-to-collect metrics to your compliance problem space, you will have a hard time doing so if you don't understand the actual boundaries and specific components that make up your compliance posture. To make matters even more complex, not all the compliance obligations that impact security are actually security-specific. So to measure your compliance from a security perspective, you might not even have the luxury of keeping your efforts localized to the security group, and you'll need to engage finance, legal, and risk management organizations within the enterprise to address the actual compliance requirements. As with many problems that appear difficult to solve, your first step in measuring compliance and conformance is to measure (or assess) what compliance and conformance really *means* for your environment. After that, you can get more specific about the kinds of compliance metrics you want to explore.

Vendors offer products in the IT GRC space that try to help automate the IT GRC process. These vendors' solutions can be complex, providing enterprise-wide management of governance activities, risk-management efforts, and compliance efforts. But understanding which vendor or solution is right for your environment can be a challenge, because there is no universal agreement on exactly what constitutes a full IT GRC software solution, and some vendors focus on one area of IT GRC more than others.

The bottom line is that even expensive, well-designed software cannot provide you with a solution to a problem that you do not fully understand. And implementing large-scale automation to solve business problems carries its own risks, to which many with experience implementing enterprise resource planning (ERP) and customer relationship management (CRM) solutions over the years can attest.

Sample Measurement Projects for Compliance and Conformance

The following security measurement project (SMP) examples are an attempt to determine how to combine, or rationalize, several different compliance frameworks to reduce redundancies and duplication of effort. Later examples include projects to measure specific aspects of a few sample compliance concerns.

Creating a Rationalized Common Control Framework

Controls rationalization is a process by which multiple compliance frameworks are analyzed and equivalencies are mapped between the specific control requirements of one framework against another. The goal of the mapping process is to identify requirements that are the same for both frameworks, and to then document these relationships so that a single control may be leveraged to support multiple compliance initiatives. The control may exist in the security domain, within general IT management, or elsewhere within the organizational management structure. The point is to ensure coordination so that different groups are not implementing different controls that essentially overlap but are administered separately for each framework or compliance program.

The end result of this process is usually some form of common controls frame-work (CCF). A CCF is a documented conceptual map of the control requirements of an organization that identifies the equivalencies between different control frameworks. The CCF can be used as the basis for a unified enterprise compliance initiative that will meet the needs of the entire organization and eliminate the waste of silos and unco-ordinated compliance activities. From a security metrics perspective, a CCF can then be used to develop the requirements-driven measurement projects for any particular control or control objective. But even before the development of the CCF, compliance-related metrics are available that can help define the success of the controls rationaliza-tion project.

For this project, the entity conducting the study was a publicly traded hospital system. The hospital system's risk management team was asked to review and streamline IT compliance costs, particularly from a security perspective, in the face of the current economic downturn. The general feeling was that compliance efforts were mushroom-ing, creating not only increased costs, but uncertainty regarding how well the hospital security program was meeting regulatory mandates. Table 8-1 shows a basic Goal-Question-Metric (GQM) template for the project.

Goal Components	*Outcome* – Reduce, analyze, create
	Element – Costs
	Element – Control rationalization
	Element – Common control framework
	Perspective – Corporate risk managers
Goal Statement	*The goal of this project is to reduce overall costs for meeting multiple compliance requirements across the company by analyzing the rationalization strategies for required compliance frameworks and identifying the most appropriate CCF model for the company from the perspective of the corporate risk management team.*
Question	What are our current compliance management costs?
Metrics	Costs (people, time, money) of meeting multiple compliance frameworks for the company
Question	What is the most effective way of rationalizing our controls to reduce the overlap between compliance framework requirements?
Metrics	Equivalencies between controls across frameworks, documented in a CCF

Table 8-1.   GQM Template for Rationalized CCF Project

Metrics for Compliance Costs

The first data that needed to be collected for this project involved the current costs of the compliance program. These metrics then provided a baseline against which to measure any increases or decreases in costs that may have resulted from the adoption of a particular CCF. Table 8-2 lists a selection of the metrics used to develop this data. Note that these metrics have nothing to do with how well the compliance initiatives are performing, their effects on audits, or other compliance performance criteria. These are simply current state costs for the compliance efforts undertaken.

Metric	Notes
Total number of compliance initiatives or projects currently ongoing (including compliance with regulations, industry standards, contractual requirements, and internal policies)	Collecting this data often involves high-level project support, detective work to identify projects across the company, or both. This is particularly true for organizations with many silos, but the data is necessary for understanding the distribution and complexity of the current compliance environment. Without this data, it is difficult to assign more granular metrics at all. If too complex, compliance initiatives may be limited to a smaller set of known frameworks (as in the case of our example hospital) or to a particular functional area (e.g., the protection of personally identifiable information). In either case, this limitation must be made explicit. You must also understand which groups and compliance frameworks are associated with each initiative.
Total number of compliance projects completed in previous (1, 2, etc.) years	This data provides historical perspective and allows the organization to situate current state in context (i.e., are compliance costs increasing?). You might document which groups and compliance frameworks are associated with each project.
Number of full-time equivalent employees per compliance project	This data begins to explain how large each compliance project is and should use actual numbers where possible for each project, although means may be used with less precision. This metric may also include roles, groups, and ratios of consultants or contractors to internal employees.

Table 8-2.   Sample Metrics for Compliance Costs

Metric	Notes
Mean duration of compliance projects	By identifying the duration of a typical compliance project, the organization gets closer to understanding true compliance costs over time.
Mean or median salary per compliance project resource	This data allows the organization to assign actual financial costs to the overall compliance initiatives in place. Similar metrics could be established for the costs of space, IT systems, and other factors that involve resources supporting the compliance initiatives. This metric may also include costs and fees for consultants or contractors.

Table 8-2.   Sample Metrics for Compliance Costs (*Continued*)

Rationalizing Control Frameworks

Strategies for rationalizing control frameworks and creating a CCF vary, and not every strategy would be equally effective in meeting the hospital's goal of reducing costs. So the next phase of the measurement project was the exploration of equivalencies between three compliance frameworks of most concern to the risk management team:

- **HIPAA**   Healthcare regulation covers patient data
- **PCI DSS**   The hospital accepts point-of-sale credit card transactions
- **Sarbanes-Oxley Act**   The hospital system is publicly traded

The actual frameworks are of less importance to this example project, but I will use them to illustrate the CCF strategies considered by the company. The hospital system reviewed three control mapping strategies as part of the project: normative, transitive, and granular. Each of the rationalization strategies had associated benefits and limitations that impacted the risk assessment team's decision.

Normative Control Mapping   In a normative mapping, all the control frameworks under consideration are analyzed and equivalencies are developed that map into a new "meta" framework that becomes the central set of controls for compliance. The goal is to develop a smaller, more streamlined controls catalog that still covers all the necessary requirements but with a standardized set of controls that apply to everyone, regardless of their specific areas of concern or focus. Figure 8-1 shows an example of the concept for a small subset of the hospital system's control requirements.

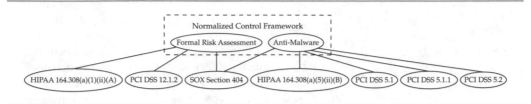

Figure 8-1. Normative control mapping of HIPAA, PCI DSS, and SOX controls

The normative mapping arrangement would assign equivalence to controls by assigning them to new controls within the normalized framework. The new framework would represent the unified set of controls that everyone in the company had to meet, and it no longer required the various compliance projects to concentrate on the specifics of HIPAA or of PCI DSS. Another advantage of this approach included a greater flexibility in treating more ambiguous controls, such as those required under SOX, in a way that best met the goals of the organization.

The limitations of the normative mapping strategy included a need for standard, sometimes more generalized language to be used to address the controls of multiple frameworks. This raised concerns that in an audit situation the auditors would be looking for very precise terminology specific to the compliance requirements they were assessing. This would require careful scrutiny by the hospital's corporate counsel and thorough documentation of the new controls framework so that mapping these controls back to the original framework requirements would be straightforward.

Transitive Control Mapping   The transitive mapping strategy did not involve creating an entirely new controls framework, but instead took the approach of prioritizing one of the existing frameworks into a "key" compliance requirement against which the others were mapped. It was decided that HIPAA was the priority framework and therefore should be the central control set. Figure 8-2 shows the same sample set of previously examined controls reconfigured into a transitive control map. The risk managers thought this strategy benefited from the need for fewer resources on the front end to map between the

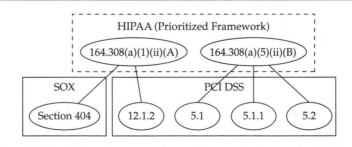

Figure 8-2. Transitive control mapping of HIPAA, PCI DSS, and SOX controls

various controls. Since no new framework was needed, the majority of the effort could be focused on identifying specific equivalencies between the HIPAA controls and the other frameworks. If controls did not overlap, they would remain as they were and be handled by the specific teams responsible for that area of compliance. It was assumed in this scenario that the main goal would be a CCF of only those controls that overlapped, which would then be assigned and coordinated among the various teams.

The risk managers also identified several limiting factors of the transitive mapping strategy. The first limitation involved the assumptions when mapping the frameworks together. When a PCI DSS control was mapped to a HIPAA control, an equivalent relationship was established. The same thing occurred when a SOX control was mapped to the same HIPAA control. By mapping these two controls to the same HIPAA control, however, there was also an implied equivalence between the PCI DSS and the SOX control, although these controls were not explicitly mapped to one another. The risk management team saw in these implied relationships the potential for audit risks if controls that had not been mapped were implemented as though they were the same control, even if they met the primary control requirement.

The second limitation identified was the inverse of the first. By choosing to map only through HIPAA, equivalent controls in other frameworks might not be identified, because they had no equivalent in the primary framework. This would mean that redundancies and duplicated efforts would continue among the compliance teams. The false positive and false negative equivalents that were possible under this system were viewed as the primary limiting factors of the strategy.

Granular Control Mapping   Granular control mapping attempts a one-to-one cross-referencing of every control in every framework against every other control in every framework. All equivalencies are identified and documented. Figure 8-3 shows the sample of controls mapped under a granular strategy. In a granular map, nothing is left to chance, and every relationship between every control is identified and documented.

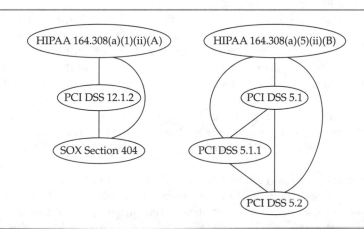

Figure 8-3.   Granular control mapping of HIPAA, PCI DSS, and SOX controls

This type of CCF can be deployed to analyze the efforts and overlap involved with every aspect of the various compliance frameworks undertaken by the enterprise and to determine exactly where equivalence occurs. But when dealing with more than two or three frameworks, the amount of analysis begins to increase exponentially as each new framework control added must be cross-referenced with every other framework control across the entire set. While the benefits of this strategy were apparent to the risk management team in that all the relationships between the controls would be formally established, the project team quickly discounted this mapping strategy as a viable approach because the resources required to accomplish the mapping were seen as prohibitive.

Choosing CCF Mapping Strategies

The results of the mapping exercises allowed the hospital risk managers to make a more informed decision about which rationalization strategy to choose. Given the three approaches available, one (the granular mapping) could be rejected immediately as too costly on its face. A careful analysis of the other two options aided the project team in deciding on the likely best approach for streamlining the company's control requirements and reducing the cost of compliance efforts. At the conclusion of the project, the risk management team decided that a transitive mapping strategy that prioritized the HIPAA security regulations would be the optimal approach. This decision was made, in part, because of the limited number of frameworks chosen for the compliance initiative. The main job would be to map HIPAA requirements with PCI DSS requirements and to include SOX control requirements as necessary. The logic of the project team was that the HIPAA and PCI DSS frameworks were similar enough that equivalence false positives and false negatives would remain at an acceptable level, while the cost savings from streamlining the controls would allow for the elimination of several initiative silos. Should new compliance frameworks or requirements be added at a later date, it was agreed that the measurement project and the mapping strategies would need to be revisited.

This type of security analysis will not meet a strictly quantitative definition of measurement and metrics. But if this is the case, it must be said that most scientific or research endeavors are not about measurement either. One of my main complaints about an overly simplistic definition of security metrics is that it makes gathering "facts" more important than trying to understand what it is those facts are supposed to explain. No scientist describes to people our need to explore space, to cure disease, or to create better computing technologies by spouting numbers and equations. They start with a context in which those numbers begin to make sense, usually in the form of a problem statement, an expression of curiosity, or even in the relatively simple telling of a story.

IT security metrics can and should be treated no differently. You cannot separate the "metrics" from the larger context of measurement in which they exist without losing your purpose—or worse, never understanding that purpose in the first place. In fact, even IT security metrics proponents recognize this fact, whether they admit it or not. You will not find discussions of security metrics that promote facts, figures, and data on their own merits. Instead, books and articles situate and explain the importance of metrics in terms of the problem space of poorly understood security and stories of better articulating the business value of security. Stories matter and facts don't make stories any more than the entries in a dictionary make a novel. I don't believe artificially parsing the stories from the facts helps the process of security measurement.

Applying Cost Metrics to the CCF Mapping

The measurements and analyses undertaken during this project let the hospital's risk management staff derive a baseline for one indicator of compliance performance, develop the cost of compliance initiatives for the company, and explore alternative compliance strategies that might reduce those costs. Table 8-3 lists the data collected for the compliance cost assessment.

After establishing some basic cost measurements around compliance as well as a reasonable strategy for CCF creation, the hospital's risk assessment team was positioned to begin developing a quasi-experimental set of follow-on measurement projects that would compare the costs of compliance before and after the adoption of the new CCF. This outcome was not part of the immediate project, which was bounded at measuring just the baseline costs and assessing a strategy that the project team felt was most likely to reduce those costs. The measurement project did not assess how well the compliance initiatives performed or whether the controls in place were effective. The project did not look at comparisons between the resources spent on compliance and the results of formal regulatory or industry audits.

Metric	Data
Total number of compliance initiatives or projects currently ongoing	3 HIPAA related 2 PCI DSS related 2 SOX related
Total number of compliance projects completed in previous (1, 2, etc.) years	2008 – 4 2007 – 3 2006 – 3 2005 – 1
Number of full-time equivalent employees per compliance project	Mean = 7 FT employees per project Median = 4 FT employees per project
Mean duration of compliance projects	Mean duration = 12 weeks Median duration = 6 weeks
Mean or median salary per compliance project resource	Mean salary per resource = $52,000 Median salary per resource = $50,000

Table 8-3.   Compliance Cost Data for CCF Project

   Although all of these are appropriate considerations around which to build metrics and measurement projects, remember that the goals of a security improvement program (and of the security process management framework in general) involve incremental and ongoing measurement and analysis. The hospital system could have chosen to conduct a much more extensive measurement project that attempted to define some of the listed compliance performance indicators, but the larger and more comprehensive the project becomes, the more difficult it is to manage. And there is no need for massive, comprehensive projects when you recognize your security metrics efforts as an incremental and ongoing process that never stops.

Mapping Assessments to Compliance Frameworks

   Continuing to use the example of the hospital system, the next two example projects focus on specific aspects of compliance that the organization sought to measure and assess. In the first project, the risk management project team developed a high-level compliance map that would show how well or how poorly the company was managing the overall compliance posture for the three previously identified frameworks (HIPAA, PCI DSS, and SOX). In this project, the data results from two assessments—one of policy and another of security vulnerabilities—were used to provide a compliance scorecard to aid management decisions about where to focus compliance remediation efforts. The GQM template for this project is shown in Table 8-4.

Goal Components	*Outcome* – Understand, map *Element* – Compliance posture *Element* – Policy and vulnerability assessments *Element* – Priority control frameworks *Perspective* – Corporate risk managers
Goal Statement	*The goal of this project is to understand at a high level the overall compliance posture of the company by mapping the results of policy and vulnerability assessments against three identified priority compliance frameworks (HIPAA Security Rule, PCI DSS, and SOX Section 404) from the perspective of the corporate risk management team.*
Question	Which compliance requirements are not being met by policy and vulnerability controls?
Metrics	Cross-reference of policy and vulnerability data with control objectives required by compliance frameworks

Table 8-4. GQM Template for Assessment to Control Framework Mapping

The methodology used to complete this assessment was a detailed comparison and analysis of each required control framework with the results of previously conducted policy and vulnerability assessments. The policy assessment had resulted in data and findings regarding the structure and effectiveness of the company's security policies, but most applicable to this measurement project was a detailed policy catalog that was developed during the review. The catalog included all security-related policy documents in place within the company, annotated with notes on the purpose and applicability of each policy document (based on interviews with security program personnel). The policy catalog provided a ready set of data that could be compared with the major requirements of each compliance framework identified by the company.

The vulnerability assessment provided similar data based on a vendor's assessment of physical and logical security within the company. The findings of the vulnerability assessment were analyzed against specific control requirements found in each compliance framework. In both cases, the primary analytical work was the measurement of relationships between the findings of the assessments and the control objectives of the required frameworks. Where necessary, the project team referred questions to corporate and outside counsel to ensure that the associations made were reasonable from a legal and regulatory perspective. Following is a sampling of specific findings that were used in the analysis:

Policy Assessment Findings

- No policy document formally specifying responsibility for compliance requirements
- No process for measuring contract performance regarding security of partners
- Poorly documented and unenforceable standards for router configurations

Vulnerability Assessment Findings

- Personal health data discovered on unprotected systems
- Physical media containing personally identifiable information found unsecured
- Multiple shared user IDs identified, including system administrator IDs

The cross-referenced assessment and compliance data were used to construct several tree maps that provided an intuitive visualization of the hospital system's compliance posture. In each tree map, compliance with a given required control objective for one of the regulatory frameworks was indicated in green, compliance failures were in red, and requirements that were partially met or required revisiting were in gray. The tree maps for the policy mapping and for the vulnerability assessment mapping are shown (in grayscale) in Figures 8-4 and 8-5, respectively.

The results of this measurement project provided high-level, intuitive results that the risk assessment team intended to use with senior management to demonstrate the strengths and weaknesses of the company's compliance posture. The project team was careful to explain the limitations of the project findings: it was based on two specific

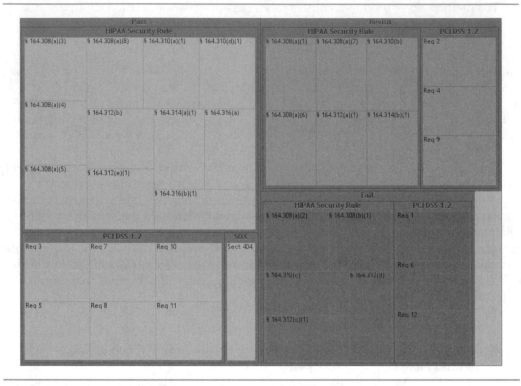

Figure 8-4. Tree map for cross-referenced policy assessment findings and compliance requirements

sets of assessment data and did not reflect a complete review of all compliance requirements for which the company was responsible. But the project team did use the resulting information to stimulate ideas for other, similar assessments that could produce complementary results. The project team also made recommendations based on the findings for several follow-on measurement projects that would be designed to explore more fully and at greater depth the relationships among policy architectures, vulnerabilities, and compliance obligations that the company was failing to meet.

Analyzing the Readability of Security Policy Documents

The final security measurement project discussed in this chapter reinforces my position that not all IT security metrics are about the output of IT systems, how many of something exists, or how often an event occurs. IT security metrics can and should be as varied and creative as the elements and concepts we find across the field of information security. Sometimes vulnerabilities are subtle, and it takes an eye for new and innovative measurement ideas to get at them. This is particularly true in the case of compliance and conformance challenges, where the very nature of the security problem space is a mash-up of people, processes, and technologies.

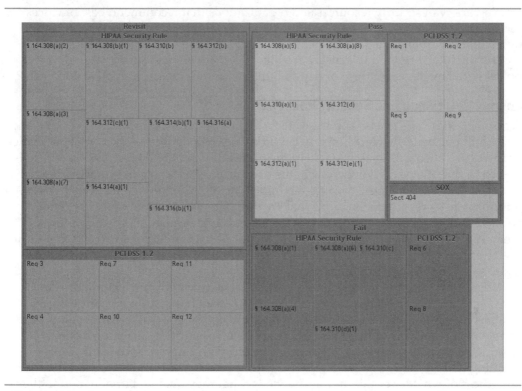

Figure 8-5.   Tree map for cross-referenced vulnerability assessment findings and compliance requirements

As part of my professional work, I provide clients with security policy assessments. Security policies are the bedrock of any effective IT security program, absolutely essential to success. Without an effective and well-written security policy architecture, any process or technical controls that you implement will have no guiding principles, no expectation of enforcement, and no baseline against which to measure success. Or at least this is the standard party line that everyone quotes while installing policy architectures that often prove fundamentally worthless.

If we all really believed that security policies were so important, why wouldn't everyone put as much effort into constructing them, verifying them, and measuring their success as we put in to our technical infrastructures? Most security policies I see seem to be written almost as afterthoughts, or they are copied whole cloth from freely available templates that are never customized to the unique environment and culture of the organization that adopts them. They are the epitome of checkbox compliance, designed primarily to be able to say "we have a security policy."

We assess our security policies in much the same cavalier way. The typical security policy assessment involves finding someone who a) can read, and b) knows something about security, and turning them loose. They can, of course, refer to many guidelines from a variety of security resources and organizations that recommend best practices for security policies—but in the end, security policy development and assessment comes down to individual opinion more than just about any other element of the enterprise security architecture. And this means it is likely you are not measuring your security policy with any degree of rigor or depth. But how do you measure a policy document?

Johnny Can't Read (the Security Policy)

A number of metrics can be applied to security policies, but this project focuses on one that I find particularly interesting: readability. One of the policy measurement activities I provide for clients is an assessment of the readability of the policies they have developed and that they expect everyone in the organization to follow to protect IT security. I like readability as a metric because it reminds me of usability in other IT systems. We intuitively understand that systems that are difficult or impossible to use tend not to be used. But many of my clients don't understand why so many of their employees seem to disregard the organization's security policies. They don't think of their security policy as something that has a usability factor. But most of my clients do understand when something is difficult to read.

Whether we are trying to read an updated privacy policy from a credit card company, a click-through license agreement when we install new software, or the latest Thomas Pynchon novel, we all know what a difficult text looks like. This is why most people never read any of these things. When system security policies are difficult or impossible to read, many users of the policy simply give up on reading and understanding it. And if users make this choice with regard to the company's security policy, regardless of whether or not they acknowledge that they read and understood it, they put the company at risk. It is cold comfort to fire someone for a policy violation after the damage has already been done. If the violation occurred because the policy was incomprehensible in the first place, then the punishment is unfair as well as untimely.

As with other metrics and data analysis methods that could benefit our field, readability is only innovative in that it hasn't been widely implemented in IT security. But it is used in many other environments, from measuring the usability of military manuals (you need to make sure that 18-year-olds understand how to operate that tank) to healthcare (you need to make sure that 80-year-olds understand how to take their medicine). Studies have shown that the average reader in the United States reads and comprehends at a tenth-grade level or lower. As a result, many documents are written so that your reading skills need be no greater than that to comprehend the text. In some cases, the market takes care of it (most popular novels are written at about an eighth-grade level), while in other cases, readability must be mandated (many organizations require that manuals and other procedural instructions be written at a level no higher than high school to ensure that everyone can follow them). My experience with security policies is that they are almost never written with the average reader in mind. More often, they require higher levels of comprehension skills, often at the graduate or postgraduate levels, to understand them fully. Methods and tools are available for assessing readability of documents, including many freely available web tools, as well as basic features built into word processors such as Microsoft Word.

Measuring Readability as Part of Compliance

While there are no formal requirements for the readability of security policies in typical compliance frameworks, it can be assumed that any framework mandating that a policy be in place also mandates that the policy be easily understood and followed by every member of the organization to which it applies. This usually means that the more general the security policy, the easier it must be to read, since it affects a wide variety of people across the organization. Specialized policies that impact smaller audiences, including those that are assumed to be more educated (coders, IT specialists, or managers), may not be compromised by higher readability levels. But without a good understanding of policy audiences and users, an enterprise may put itself at risk of a policy failure or, worse, legal claims in the event that problems occur because of an inappropriately written policy document.

For continuity, I have kept this example project in the context of the hypothetical hospital system's risk measurement activities. The project developed out of findings from the policy assessment described in the previous example project. During the policy assessment it was noted that no standard style guide or manual existed for writing security policies and one of the project staff proposed that the project team adopt the hospital's style guide for writing medical procedures. Part of that style guide mandated ceilings on the reading comprehension levels necessary to follow the procedures. The project team was then motivated to determine the usability levels of the security policies. The GQM template for the project can be found in Table 8-5.

Goal Components	*Outcome* – Improve, assess *Element* – Compliance rates *Element* – Readability and difficulty *Element* – Security policy documents *Perspective* – Security policy user
Goal Statement	*The goal of this project is to improve security policy compliance rates for the company by assessing the readability and difficulty levels of different policy documents from the perspective of the general security policy user.*
Question	How difficult is it to read and understand company security policy documents?
Metrics	Readability test scores (Flesch Reading Ease)
Question	Are the readability levels for the security policy documents appropriate for the specific policy document audience?
Metrics	Estimated reading levels for policy document users (based on known education levels)

Table 8-5.   GQM Template for Policy Readability Assessment Project

Statistic	Data
Number of sentences	103
Number of difficult sentences (> 20 words)	47 (45.6%)
Average sentence length	21.6 words
Minimum grade level (for which the document is suitable)	16.8 (graduate level education)

Table 8-6.   Sample Results for Readability Test of General Security Policy

The reading difficulty tests for the security policies were conducted using Readability Studio, a commercial product used for analyzing the readability of texts. Table 8-6 shows a selection of the resulting readability metrics data for the hospital system's general information security policy. This policy outlined the overall security program and all employees of the company were required to read and acknowledge that they understood this policy. Figure 8-6 provides a more detailed breakdown of the security policy, detailing the number of difficult words as compared with the total word count of the policy.

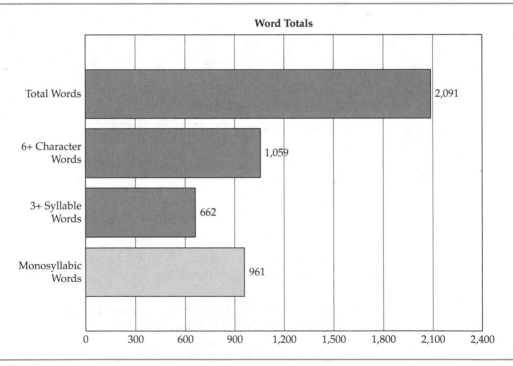

Figure 8-6.   Word breakdown for general information security policy document

Score	Description
90–100	Very Easy
80–89	Easy
70–79	Fairly Easy
60–69	Standard
50–59	Fairly Difficult
30–49	Difficult
0–29	Very Confusing

Table 8-7. Flesch Readability Ease Scores

In addition to the basic statistical analyses of the lexical and grammatical structures of the security policy documents, the project team conducted a Flesch Reading Ease test for the security policies under review. The Flesch Reading Ease score is often used by government agencies, where it has become a standard test of the readability of technical manuals and other procedural documentation. The test calculates a readability score based on the sentence length and number of syllables contained in a text. Table 8-7 lists the score levels for the Flesch test. Higher Flesch scores indicate easier reading levels, while lower scores mean a text is increasingly difficult to understand.

The Flesch test for the hospital's security policy indicated that the document was very difficult to read and confusing, as shown in the Flesch score chart in Figure 8-7. This readability score, combined with the results of other tests that placed minimum suitable education levels necessary to read the document effectively at the graduate school level, indicated serious flaws in a security policy that was intended to be used by everyone in the company. If the hospital system was on par with the national average, and the typical reading skill level was at the high school level, it was considered very likely that most employees would simply be unable to use the policy effectively, even though they acknowledged that they had read and understood the content of the policy.

Readability Project Findings

The results of the readability metrics convinced the project team that they were dealing with a potentially serious, but quite unconventional, security problem. For most of the security and risk managers working on the project, security policies had been traditionally viewed as the responsibility of the employee who was required to read and acknowledge his or her understanding of the policy. The way the policies were written could even be interpreted as a sort of contract, as they specified sanctions up to and including termination for anyone who violated those policies.

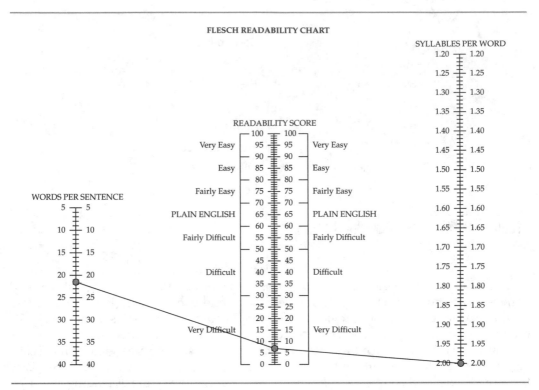

Figure 8-7. Flesch readability chart for the general information security policy

The project team concluded that the role of the company in creating usable and appropriate policies had been neglected, and that two immediate risks resulted from this oversight. First there was the real risk of security breaches that might be caused by employees who did not understand their responsibilities under the security policies. The risk management team felt that the presence of the policy had provided a false sense of security, as the company assumed any violations were deliberate or the result of gross neglect rather than lack of comprehension. Second, the project team believed that the problems with the readability of the policies could potentially open the company to lawsuits if employees were fired for policy violations. In both cases, the readability study had measured elements of security risk that had previously been completely unidentified.

As a result of the readability tests, the project team recommended a complete review and overhaul of the company's policy documents. As part of this review, they reached out to both corporate counsel and technical documentation experts who designed policies and procedures where readability was considered an important component of the documentation. As part of the ongoing security improvement program, the project team also recommended follow-on security measurement projects be conducted after the redesign of the security policy to measure whether the new, more easily understood, policies could be correlated with declines in security incidents and events across the company.

Summary

IT Governance, Risk, and Compliance (IT GRC) is a complex challenge and encompasses how you manage your security as a process, the controls that you choose to protect specific resources, and the many requirements that are imposed on you by laws, regulations, industry standards, and business contracts. Measuring compliance becomes a particularly challenging activity because of so much variation and uncertainty between compliance frameworks and the organizational and human interpretations of those frameworks. Even frameworks such as ISO/IEC 27001 and 27002, which are closely aligned, often cause confusion among security managers. Whether you call your activities an audit, measurement, or something entirely different, your goal is to understand fully the requirements you are obligated to meet and then to meet those requirements effectively and efficiently.

One exercise that is increasingly common in security is the use of rationalized common control frameworks (CCFs) that align multiple compliance requirements into more easily managed or aligned control systems. There are several ways to rationalize control frameworks, including normalized, transitive, and granular strategies. Each strategy has strengths and limitations. A CCF can be used to break down silos in the organization's compliance program and help the organization better coordinate and actively measure compliance efforts.

In addition to CCF mapping, specific measurement projects may be undertaken regarding compliance requirements that are limited only by the imagination and creativity of the organization. Two projects examined in this chapter dealt with the alignment of the results of policy and technical assessments to the compliance requirements for an example hospital environment and with the assessment of readability metrics of the hospital's security policies. By taking a broad approach to security metrics in the context of regulatory compliance or conformance to other control structures, your organization can develop innovative measurement efforts that cover a wide variety of situations and security performance indicators.

Further Reading

Flesch, R. *How to Write Plain English: A Book for Lawyers and Consumers*. Barnes & Noble, 1981.

Hayden, L. Designing Common Control Frameworks: A Model for Evaluating Information Technology Governance, Risk, and Compliance Control Rationalization Strategies. *Information Security Journal: A Global Perspective*, 18(6), p. 297-305, 2009.

National Assessment of Adult Literacy (NAAL). http://nces.ed.gov/naal/

CHAPTER 9 | Measuring Security Cost and Value

One of the most promising aspects of using more sophisticated IT security metrics is the possibility of developing more sophisticated assessments of how much security costs and how much value security activities bring to an organization. At the end of the day, if a CISO cannot articulate what security means in tangible terms (such as money), his value will be limited in the eyes of other business leaders who think in these terms.

This does not mean that all security metrics should have a monetary goal, any more than all metrics should have a quantitative result. But techniques that can measure these values become important components of the security metrics toolbox. Measuring cost and value is an activity that remains tightly coupled with measuring risk, as fluctuations in cost and value can negatively impact everything from the company bottom line to the ability of the security team to resource their operations adequately.

Understanding how much security actually costs an enterprise is the first step toward understanding how to reduce those costs and what that money is actually buying. How to show the value of security is one of the most common questions I am asked by clients engaging in security work, but often security value remains tied to the concept of preventing attacks and losses. Other cost and value metrics, such as total cost of ownership and return on investment in security technologies, often are left to vendors and analysts and do not enter into the everyday analyses of the security team.

Sample Measurement Projects for Compliance and Conformance

This chapter will explain, using simple examples, several interesting methods for measuring cost and value that are used widely in other industries and could benefit IT security programs. These methods are not the only such measurement and modeling techniques available, but they do illustrate some metrics practices that you may not have considered. I will describe three methods for measuring the cost and value of security:

- The Poisson distribution
- Monte Carlo simulation
- Security process cost analysis

Measuring the Likelihood of Reported Personally Identifiable Information (PII) Disclosures

The first security measurement project I describe uses a technique known as the Poisson distribution, which was developed by Siméon Poisson, a nineteenth-century French mathematician. The Poisson distribution provides insight into how many events occur within a given time period, region of space, or particular process or product.

One characteristic of the Poisson distribution is that the events under consideration are rare, and that they are assumed to be random and to occur independently of one another.

History and Applications of the Poisson Distribution

The most famous application of the Poisson distribution, which is often used to explain it, is an 1898 study of fatal horse kicks in the Prussian cavalry. A goal of the study was to determine whether these deaths were randomly occurring. The data used in the study tracked the number of cavalry soldiers kicked to death by horses every year during a 20-year period, which was found to follow a Poisson distribution. The distribution applies to more than just horse kicks, and allows us to quantify the probability that an event will occur based on previous occurrences.

Modern applications of Poisson include understanding how many people or vehicles will arrive at a given location in a certain time period, or the number of defective rivets in an airplane fuselage. By incorporating existing data regarding occurrences or events, the Poisson distribution can be used to predict the probability of future events of the same type. The distribution has been used for everything from optimizing schedules based on likely customer traffic, to designing more efficient parking lots, to identifying how many injuries are likely during sporting activities. The Poisson distribution's emphasis on the occurrence of random, rare events makes it quite applicable to measuring certain problems in IT security.

Using the Poisson Distribution to Predict Reported PII Disclosures

In this example, the company that conducted the measurement project, for regulatory purposes, tracked all reported disclosures of personally identifiable information (PII) by the enterprise from any source. PII breach disclosure was a company-wide endeavor, with stakeholders coming together from Finance, Legal, IT, and the business units involved to form a quick response team to investigate the breach, track causes, and send appropriate notifications to affected individuals. An analyst from the security group represented the CISO on the quick response team, and this individual was chosen on an ad hoc basis depending on who was available at the time. The company had collected data on these reported breaches since the beginning of 2006 on a quarterly basis, as shown in Table 9-1. Based on historical data, the security team determined that the average resource cost for participating in the tiger team was 40 full-time equivalent (FTE) hours per reported incident and included meetings, investigations, and reporting requirements.

Given the increasing regulatory scrutiny of PII disclosure and breach notification at the state and federal levels, the board had grown concerned about delays in the breach notification process. The CISO decided after a senior management offsite that she wanted to assign a dedicated analyst to PII disclosure efforts to ensure that the security group was not the cause of any delays by a breach quick response team, and she requested input from her staff. About half the CISO's team recommended that she assign a full-time resource to PII disclosure response team duties. The logic behind the recommendation was that as many as 14 breaches had occurred in a quarter, which

Quarter	Reported PII Disclosures
Q106	7
Q206	10
Q306	13
Q406	5
Q107	7
Q207	2
Q307	14
Q407	4
Q108	3
Q208	11
Q308	3
Q408	6
Q109	12
Q209	9
Q309	10
Q409	8
Minimum Reported Disclosures	2
Maximum Reported Disclosures	14
Mean Reported Disclosures	7.75

Table 9-1.   Example Data on Reported PII Disclosures by Quarter

resulted in an average of 560 hours of effort representing the response teams—more than justifying a full-time resource. A significant minority of the staff recommended a 50 percent assignment to a single analyst, basing their recommendation on the average number of breaches per quarter (7.75). The logic of this recommendation was very few breaches occurred during a quarter and a full-time resource would be underutilized.

The CISO wanted to make sure that she was appropriately addressing an issue with board-level visibility, but she did not want to waste her people's time unnecessarily. One member of the CISO staff suggested setting up a security measurement project to determine the probability that the company would experience 14 reported disclosures in a single quarter and to identify the likely number of reported disclosures against which the CISO should budget the team's time. The GQM Template for this measurement project is shown in Table 9-2.

Goal Components	*Outcome* – Allocate, analyze, calculate *Element* – PII disclosures *Element* – Historical disclosure data *Element* – Probability of PII disclosures *Perspective* – CISO staff
Goal Statement	*The goal of this project is to allocate resources effectively for future reported disclosures of PII by analyzing historical disclosure data and calculating the probabilities of reported PII disclosures on a quarterly basis from the perspective of the CISO staff.*
Question	What is the likelihood of 14 reported disclosures of PII in a single quarter?
Metrics	Analysis of historical PII disclosures using Poisson distribution
Question	What is the average upper limit of reported disclosures of PII in a single quarter?
Metrics	Analysis of historical PII disclosures using Poisson distribution
Question	What is the most effective resource level based on the likely risk of reported PII disclosures?
Metrics	Probable upper bound of reported PII disclosures combined with average hours necessary for response team support

Table 9-2.   GQM Template for PII Disclosure Measurement Project

A formula can be used for calculating the probability of a certain number of events occurring, using the Poisson distribution:

$$P(x; \mu) = (e^{-\mu}) (\mu^x) / x!$$

where

- $P(x; \mu)$ is the probability that x events occur if the mean number of events in the sample is μ

- $e \approx 2.7183$ (the base of the natural logarithm)

So to answer one of the project questions, the probability that 14 reported PII disclosures will occur in a single quarter, the project team could have used the formula:

$$P(14; 7.75) = (2.7183^{-7.75}) (7.75^{14}) / 14! = 0.01393 = 1.39 \text{ percent}$$

The calculation shows that the probability of getting 14 reported PII disclosures in a quarter, when the mean number of reported disclosures per quarter is 7.75, is pretty low.

I like the Poisson formula because it is not that difficult to understand, as intimidating as it may look at first. But being a security professional and not a mathematician by trade, I don't like doing calculations by hand. And besides, the formula did not intuitively help the project team answer its second question about the likely high point of reported disclosures. This is where software comes to the rescue.

Minitab software provides several tests for Poisson probabilities, including calculating the likelihood of getting a particular number of events such as those described. Minitab's Poisson tests can also be used to construct confidence intervals and bounds for the true mean of the population being sampled.

Applied to this PII disclosure project, Minitab was used to calculate the likelihood of getting 14 reported PII disclosures within a single quarter (as was calculated manually) as well as to identify the average upper limit of disclosures. Looking at the second question first, Minitab was used to calculate the average upper limit (or "bound") of the quarterly reported PII disclosures with 95 percent confidence.

Figure 9-1 shows the Minitab interface as a Poisson test is conducted. In the session window, Minitab has calculated the various descriptive statistics for the quarterly

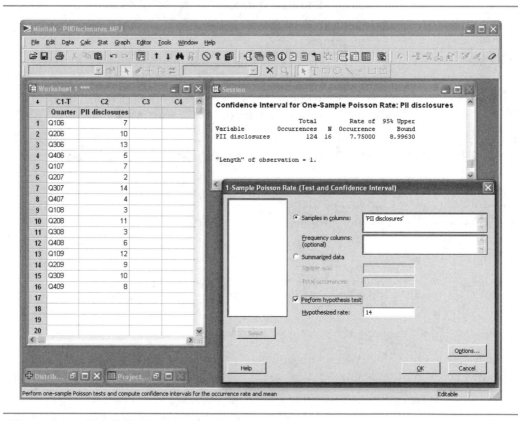

Figure 9-1.   Minitab Poisson results for 95 percent upper bound of mean PII disclosures

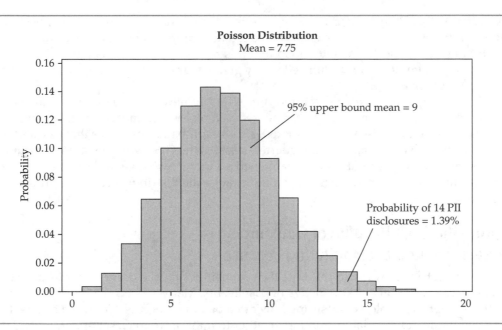

Figure 9-2. Poisson distribution histogram for reported PII disclosures per quarter

disclosures and computed the 95 percent upper bound at approximately nine disclosures per quarter. This figure may be interpreted as meaning that the project team could say with 95 percent certainty that the true mean number of the disclosures was no more than nine per quarter.

Going back to the first question of the probability of getting 14 reported PII disclosures in a given quarter, Minitab can also provide this information and can even construct a histogram to display the probabilities for all the possible values, as shown in Figure 9-2. A review of the chart shows the 1.39 percent probability for getting 14 reported PII disclosures during the quarter, and that the highest probability for quarterly disclosures is 7 (14.4 percent likelihood). Other interesting insights available from this chart for the purposes of the CISO's staffing decisions include the following:

- The likelihood of getting 14 or more reported disclosures in a quarter was less than 3 percent.

- The likelihood of getting less than 5 reported disclosures in a quarter was only about 10 percent.

Supporting Decision-Making with the PII Disclosure Project Results

Using the Poisson distribution to calculate the likely number of reported disclosures allowed the CISO to reduce the level of uncertainty she faced in terms of how to staff the quick response teams. Given the 95 percent upper bound of nine reported disclosures per quarter, the CISO decided to dedicate 0.75 FTE analysts to PII disclosure projects and thus be reasonably sure that she was adequately protecting the security group from becoming a bottleneck. The likelihood that this resource would be completely over- whelmed or completely underutilized in any given quarter was sufficiently low as to be an acceptable risk.

This example has been deliberately simplified somewhat, and other dynamics would be at work that need to be considered in a real-world measurement project. Similarly, since the Poisson distribution deals with probabilities rather than certainties and is subject to new data, as more quarters passed, the CISO would want to repeat the tests to ensure that her assumptions remained accurate. A change in the mean reported disclosures per quarter, for example, would change the distribution and the probabili- ties associated with it.

Measuring the Cost Benefits of Outsourcing a Security Incident Monitoring Process

The Poisson test allows us to calculate the probabilities for the occurrence of future dis- crete events based on our knowledge of past events. Many aspects of security cost and value are not as simple as measuring how often one thing occurs. Costs can be a factor of several uncertain variables coming together to make a complex set of parameters that are beyond the predictive capabilities of the Poisson distribution. Monte Carlo simulations allow us to model these complex uncertainties by repeating variations of specific scenarios thousands of times using random variable inputs.

History and Applications of Monte Carlo Simulations

Like the story of the Poisson test and the Prussian cavalry, Monte Carlo simulations gained fame through their military applications. The Manhattan Project, which devel- oped the first atomic bomb, developed the Monte Carlo simulation technique to model the complex activities that occurred during nuclear reactions. The simulation involves heavy application of random chance, and the scientists who invented it named it after the city of Monte Carlo, which is famous for its casino. Monte Carlo simulations have a history that can be traced back before the Manhattan Project, but it was only after the invention of computers that the techniques involved for these simulations began to be studied in earnest. Since then, Monte Carlo simulations have been widely adopted across many fields as a tool for modeling uncertainty and risk.

Among the many applications of Monte Carlo simulations, they are used to make decisions regarding financial investments, to optimize production capacity for manu- facturing, and to estimate product-related costs and risks. When applied to problems involving large measures of complexity and uncertainty, a Monte Carlo simulation does a good job of predicting outcomes for decision-making purposes, which makes it a good candidate for inclusion in a security metrics toolbox.

Using Monte Carlo Simulations to Evaluate Outsourcing Returns

This measurement project concerns a company that was considering outsourcing its security incident monitoring and response to a managed security services firm. The CISO knew his team spent quite a bit of time chasing down security incidents each month, a process that involved investigating the source and cause of the incident, undertaking necessary remediation work, and creating reports for senior management review and compliance requirements. For the 12 months before the project began, the security team had been tracking and collecting data regarding the resources required for security incident management and was now ready to consider a managed services vendor that would take over this function. Table 9-3 shows the collected historical data regarding IT security incidents at the company, which accompanying descriptive statistical analysis.

Using this data, the CISO wanted to understand how outsourcing his incident management process would affect his bottom line. The problem involved several "moving parts," as all four aspects of incident management are variable. Although fewer incidents may occur in a month, they could all be severe and require more investigation

Metric	Data
Security incidents (per month)	Min: 1 Max: 30 Mean (μ, or mu): 16.25 Standard Deviation (σ, or sigma): 8.27
Investigation effort (FTE hours per incident)	Min: 4 Max: 24 Mean (μ): 14.25 Standard Deviation (σ): 5.67
Remediation effort (FTE hours per incident)	Min: 2 Max: 16 Mean (μ): 10.72 Standard Deviation (σ): 4.88
Reporting effort (FTE hours per incident)	Min: 1 Max: 8 Mean (μ): 4.64 Standard Deviation (σ): 2.02
Average hourly wage of security analysts (in-house resources)	$32.00

Table 9-3.   Historical Data for Monthly Security Incident Resource Efforts

and remediation. On the other hand, in some months, the security team felt as though they were dying by a thousand cuts, as many minor incidents distracted team members constantly, but no single incident required a great deal of effort. One way of estimating the monthly costs of the security incident management process would be to simply play the averages:

(Mean Investigation + Mean Remediation + Mean Reporting) × Mean Incident Rate

or

(14.25 hours + 10.72 hours + 4.64 hours) × $32.00 × 16.25 incidents = $15,397.20

By this calculation, the average cost of the security incident management efforts of the team totals more than $184,000 annually. Senior security staff believed that outsourcing this particular function would free up resources and save the CISO (and by extension, the company) money. After evaluating several vendors, the team received a bid for an annual managed security services fee of $180,000 to take over incident management and response, including investigation, remediation, and reporting functions. The annual fee was slightly less than the estimated average cost of incidents overall and less than the average cost of two full-time analysts. The general sense among the staff was that the internal incident response process was unnecessarily tying up three or four analysts under the current status quo and that even in a break-even outsourcing scenario, productivity would increase.

How could the CISO be sure that he was making a good investment? One area that concerned him is the fact that, overworked or not, his staff was motivated and did a good job of managing the incidents that arose. Bringing in the security management vendor was an unknown, and any savings or increases in productivity had to be weighed against the risk that the vendor would not take the same care with the company's security posture as his own team or might not be as effective for other reasons. The CISO wanted to know that the likely cost savings would be significant enough that it justified taking these risks. To assess the likely cost savings, he set up a security management project to evaluate the current and future security incident data. The GQM template for this project is shown in Table 9-4.

Setting Up a Monte Carlo Simulation

Monte Carlo simulations use randomly generated numbers to create scenarios based on a particular set of parameters, such as the variable costs of the company's incident management efforts. By randomly generating values for the investigation, remediation, and reporting of a number of security incidents during the course of a month, the simulation creates a scenario similar to the preceding estimation, in which all the averages were used to create an overall average cost for monthly incident management. But instead of averages, a Monte Carlo simulation chooses values from the entire range of probabilities for that parameter. This is possible because both the mean and the standard deviation are known. With the mean and the standard deviation, we can construct a normal distribution of probable values that will define both the ranges of values and

Goal Components	*Outcome* – Evaluate, analyze, compare *Element* – Cost benefit *Element* – Outsourced security incident management *Element* – Probable monthly savings *Element* – Fee for outsourced services *Perspective* – CISO
Goal Statement	*The goal of this project is to evaluate the cost benefit of outsourcing the security incident management process for the company by analyzing the probable monthly savings on incident management and comparing them with the fee for outsourced services, from the perspective of the CISO.*
Question	What are the probable savings for monthly incident response efforts through outsourcing?
Metrics	Monte Carlo simulation of cost savings (investigation, remediation, reporting) when outsourced
Question	Is it better to outsource the incident management activities or keep them in-house?
Metrics	Cost-benefit analysis of probable savings against monthly fees for outsourced incident management service

Table 9-4.   GQM Template for Security Incident Management Monte Carlo Simulation Project

the likelihood that any particular value will be observed as part of the scenario. Each scenario then models a particular probable outcome produced by a random combination of the variables involved.

Before I completely slide down the statistical rabbit hole, let me stop and remind you that Monte Carlo simulations didn't catch on until the invention of computers, and with good reason. Not even the nuclear physicists that built the first nuclear weapons could or wanted to do this stuff by hand. And neither do IT security pros. We need computers not only because constructing each scenario with random numbers is tedious, but because a Monte Carlo simulation does not include a single scenario. Conducting a Monte Carlo simulation involves creating thousands or tens of thousands of these scenarios and then building probability models based on the results. It is like flipping a coin or rolling a die 100 times to model how the results are distributed, but with many parameters included. As more and more scenarios are included, the overall model's predictive capacity increases.

Monte Carlo simulations can be built using spreadsheets. Not all spreadsheets contain the functions necessary for these simulations, but Microsoft Excel and the open source spreadsheet Gnumeric both have features for building and running simulations.

Many commercial tools are available for conducting Monte Carlo simulations as part of more sophisticated risk analyses, but most of these are quite expensive and many are add-ins for Excel. If you are just beginning with Monte Carlo simulations, spreadsheets are the way to go; you can find many resources in print and online that can help you figure out how to construct them.

Let's get back to the security measurement project. To run the simulation, an analyst on the project team created a spreadsheet-based Monte Carlo model that included all the parameters for scenario creation and produced a result for each scenario. In Excel, the formula NORMINV allowed the analyst to create a random result from a normal distribution based on the mean and standard deviation for each parameter. The assumption was that outsourcing would save the company the effort of managing security incidents; therefore, each parameter was constructed as a cost savings based on the number of hours spent investigating, remediating, or reporting the results of the incident, combined with the number of incidents in a given month. Table 9-5 illustrates the result for a single scenario.

After a spreadsheet row was constructed to produce the randomly generated scenario, the project analyst copied the row 9999 times to create a simulation with 10,000 randomly generated scenarios, as shown in Table 9-6.

The project team now had 10,000 cost-savings scenarios that were directly drawn from the statistical characteristics of the data collected during the previous year. In terms of likely incident management costs, the scenarios would reflect average months, extreme months, and every kind of month in between, over and over again as patterns in the data emerged. Looking at Table 9-6, you can see that savings scenarios vary widely and include both very low months (scenario 7, in which less than $500 is saved) and very high months (scenario 2, with more than $28,000 saved).

Using the mass of randomly generated scenarios, the project team could analyze the results of the simulation. Recall that the managed services quote was $180,000 per year, or $15,000 per month for outsourcing the company's incident management and response processes. The company had to save $15,000 or more each month to break even on the outsourcing. The project analyst used the spreadsheet functions to calculate the

Investigation Savings	Remediation Savings	Reporting Savings	Security Incidents	Savings by Outsourcing
NORMINV generated hours × $32.00	NORMINV generated hours × $32.00	NORMINV generated hours × $32.00	NORMINV generated incidents (single month)	Sum of Savings × Security Incidents
9.57 × $32 = $306.24	17.25 × $32 = $552.01	5.18 × $32 = $165.77	19.36	$19,825.02

Table 9-5.   Example Scenario for Outsourced Incident Management Savings

Simulation Scenario	Investigation Savings	Remediation Savings	Reporting Savings	Security Incidents	Savings by Outsourcing
1	$306.24	$552.01	$165.77	19.36	$19,825.02
2	$543.11	$448.74	$219.57	23.61	$28,599.61
3	$51.31	$320.08	$256.16	7.55	$4741.08
4	$550.12	$502.42	$163.44	9.77	$11,877.81
5	$324.34	$563.68	$111.23	9.51	$9501.36
6	$376.50	$226.12	$136.91	15.03	$11,116.11
7	$389.77	$357.07	$165.06	0.51	$466.81
8	$577.74	$106.08	$21.63	12.92	$9117.28
9	$355.61	$151.03	$75.14	3.56	$2068.62
10	$400.71	$407.87	$97.10	20.95	$18,970.70
...	...	...	...	...	...
10,000	$267.78	$410.70	$166.42	16.08	$13,589.73

Table 9-6.   10,000 Random Scenarios for Outsourced Incident Management Savings

probabilities that the company would save more or less than $15,000 per month, as well as to calculate the likelihood of specific savings, as shown in Table 9-7.

A more visual illustration was provided by constructing a histogram of the observed scenario breakdowns, shown in Figure 9-3. The chart shows all the statistically derived possibilities in the simulation model, with the number of observed scenarios for that savings range.

Savings	Probability of Savings
Save less than $15,000 per month	5091 observed scenarios / 10,000 = 50.91 percent
Save more than $15,000 per month	4909 observed scenarios / 10,000 = 49.09 percent
Save less than $5,000 per month	1113 observed scenarios / 10,000 = 11.13 percent
Save more than $30,000 per month	670 observed scenarios / 10,000 = 6.7 percent

Table 9-7.   Savings Probabilities Based on Observed Simulation Scenarios

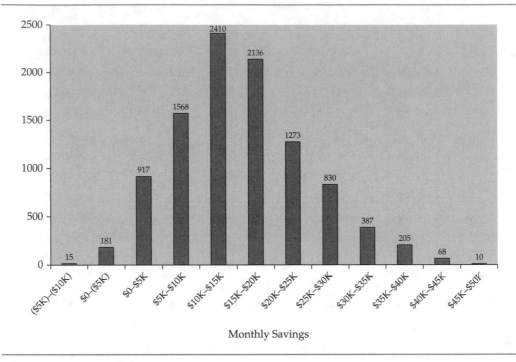

Figure 9-3. Histogram of observed savings scenarios

Supporting Decision-Making with the Outsourced Savings Simulation Project Results

The Monte Carlo simulations constructed during the security measurement project provided the CISO with interesting results to help him decide whether outsourcing his security incident management was a good investment or a good idea. The likelihood that the company would break even on the outsourcing contract was about 50/50. For every month that the company lost money on the contract, they would likely make money another month. But there was about a 58 percent chance that the company's savings on the outsourcing contract would fall between $10,000 and $25,000 per month. The CISO could now better gauge the financial risk of the outsourcing contract, as well as balance his concerns about the quality of his own team's work with the likely savings he would see if he hired the vendor to take over operations.

The CISO might have decided that the risk of significant losses some months were low enough that improved morale and productivity on the part of his staff was worth the downside. He might have decided to attempt to renegotiate the bid in order to give himself a bit more favorable odds on his break-even point. As with the PII Disclosure project, this simulation should be run regularly with new data being input into the model as it becomes available for continued accuracy. In the case of the managed service project, a good time to reconstruct the model would be prior to renewing or renegotiating the annual service fee.

Measuring the Cost of Security Processes

The last measurement project example of the chapter is concerned less with building cost probability models based on mathematical functions than with mapping cost on to existing activities to improve them. The techniques for accomplishing this are known by various names, including *business process improvement, statistical process control, detailed process charting*, and other similar terms. At its most basic, the technique involves creating flowcharts, visual representations of activities and processes that break down the process into component steps and allow the reader of the flowchart quickly to become familiar with each detailed component of the activities involved.

Flowcharts are everywhere in industry, including IT and IT security. I see many process flowcharts created by clients to map out the activities of the security group. But most IT security groups using process charting only scratch the surface of the security measurement opportunities that these charts and diagrams provide. I illustrated a generic process in Chapter 5. Figure 9-4 shows a slightly more specific process diagram with an oversimplified process for requesting and approving system changes.

I have found that security teams often diagram their processes, usually for the purposes of training or compliance with company documentation requirements. But the visual representation of business processes was only a part of the reason that these techniques were first developed. The more important benefit of business process mapping is to figure out ways that the process can be made more effective and cost-efficient.

History and Applications of Business Process Analysis

The main purpose for the creation of business process charts was to dissect, measure, and analyze human industrial activities scientifically to make factories more efficient. In Chapter 4, I briefly reviewed the history of scientific management, Taylorism, and business process reengineering. The theories and techniques for measuring industrial processes have developed and matured over the century-plus since they were first introduced, but the general principle is the same. You analyze a process by breaking down that process into as many detailed components as possible (or as is appropriate for the task at hand), assigning values to those detailed components (time, money, effort, and so on), and using that data to analyze problems, shortcomings, and ways that the improvement of individual components might improve the overall functioning of the process as a whole. Business process analysis has become a complex industry unto itself these days, but at its core it is about simple observation, visibility, and the analysis of data that are produced by those efforts.

Business process analysis found its widest application in manufacturing, beginning with the factories of the industrial revolution and moving forward to much more recent quality techniques such as Six Sigma, Total Quality Management, and ISO 9000. But as the techniques have been perceived as successful, business process analysis has been applied to everything from software development to service industries. My purpose here

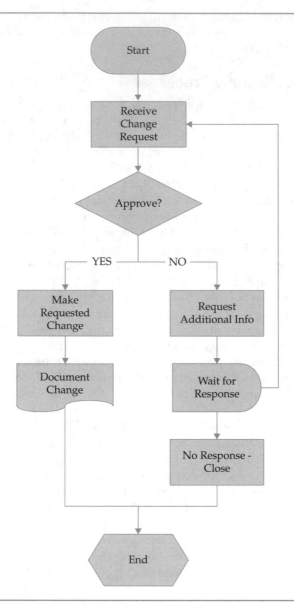

Figure 9-4. Simplified change request process diagram

is not to explore these techniques in detail (as with other analytical techniques I discuss in this book, other resources are available if you want more details). Instead, I want to situate business process mapping in the context of IT security metrics and provide an introduction to how you might consider using them in your own measurement program.

Business Process Analysis of Patch Management Activities

This example security measurement project concerns a security organization that was attempting to streamline operations in the face of economic downturn. The IT organization as a whole was facing budget cuts, and the CIO had warned his senior staff that additional resources and new hires would be scarce until the economic situation improved. The director of IT security had experienced difficulty articulating the financial value of security operations within the company and knew that some other members of the senior staff had openly questioned the efficiency of his group. Without justification, however, the director could not hope to get needed resources to improve his operational effectiveness. He decided to get proactive. One of the areas of greatest complaint, including among the security team members, was the system patching process, with a rollout that consistently took days or weeks. The patching process was informally documented, and patching was a shared responsibility among several members of the security staff as an additional duty. As a pilot project, the director decided to try to improve the efficiency of system patching and set up a measurement project to accomplish this goal. The GQM template for the measurement project is shown in Table 9-8.

Mapping Process Activities and Assigning Values

Business process mapping involves several steps and data sources. The first step, as in the patching process measurement project, is to identify the process to be mapped and develop the objectives for mapping. In this case, the director was interested in improving efficiency, so this project examined costs and duration for the process, two metrics that can be used objectively to assess improvement over time. From there, several aspects of the process may be identified:

- Who owns the process?
- Who completes each process activity?
- What systems are involved with each activity?
- How much does each activity cost?
- How long does each activity take?

Assigning values to these activities can involve a combination of interviewing techniques, actual observation of process activities, and gathering data from other sources to support the analysis. In many cases when flowcharts are constructed based on a process, the development of the chart is undertaken by a single individual (usually an owner or someone close to the process) and perhaps (but not always) submitted for review by other stakeholders. Formal business process mapping is a project-based activity that involves empirical data collection and formal analysis techniques.

The patch management project team gathered data regarding the patch management process by first identifying that there was no single owner for security patches. Instead, an informal team of five analysts and engineers shared part-time responsibility for identifying and obtaining necessary patches, testing the patches, and rolling them out to production systems. The team interviewed these individuals about the time they devoted to patch management, the tasks involved, and the results of the process.

Goal Components	*Outcome* – Improve, map, analyze, understand
	Element – Efficiency
	Element – System patching process
	Element – Process activities
	Element – Opportunities to improve effectiveness
	Perspective – Director of IT security
Goal Statement	*The goal of this process is to improve the efficiency of the system patching process by mapping and analyzing the business process activities for system patching and understanding any opportunities for improving the effectiveness of the process from the perspective of the director of IT security.*
Questions	What are the detailed component activities of the security patching process?
	What relationships exist between process owners and contributors within each process as well as between connected processes?
	How much does each system patching process activity or component cost in terms of money, people, and time?
Metrics	Process map of system patching activities
	Description of processes, owners, and relationships between process components
	General cost data for each process component activity
Question	Can gaps, bottlenecks, or other problem areas be identified and improved?
Metrics	Detailed costs per activity (financial, FTE effort, and calendar time delays)

Table 9-8. GQM Template for Process Cost Analysis of Patching Process

The team members also observed specific activities to understand better how the process flowed. Once they had collected this data, the project team created a process map that showed each activity, decision, delay, or the production or storage of documentation. At this point, the map looked like most of the process flowcharts that exist in IT shops.

A crucial step for the project team involved revisiting each of the process stakeholders interviewed during the map building, showing them the evolving process flows, and asking for input and corrections to the map. The goal was to ensure that all stakeholders accepted that the final map accurately represented the actual process flow.

Too often, process mapping exercises involve outsiders interpreting a process from stakeholder inputs but never gaining consensus that the final interpretation actually looks like what those stakeholders thought they were describing. When conflicts arose during this project's reviews, the project team discussed them with various stakeholders and escalated unresolved conflicts as necessary to define responsibilities appropriately and match the "official" way that the process was supposed to function.

The power of business process mapping was apparent when the project team began to assign values to the chart. Based on the interviews with the process stakeholders, the project team assigned basic resource commitments to each activity in the process chart. The project team also used existing data sources for the patch management process, such as system logs and time reporting systems, to determine how long each activity took and the calendar duration until an activity was completed. This data was then added to the process map to begin identifying how each activity in the process functioned from a resource and cost perspective.

Many tools are available for business process mapping. Flowcharts can be created in a variety of readily available software packages including Microsoft Office and OpenOffice, as well as specialized drawing and diagramming products such as Microsoft Visio or SmartDraw on Windows machines and OmniGraffle on the Mac. These products allow you to create process maps that you can then annotate to include the results of other data collection efforts regarding costs and resources.

Another option for process mapping, which was used in this project, is a program from the makers of the Minitab statistical program. Quality Companion by Minitab® can be used to manage quality control projects and is designed primarily to support Six Sigma projects, for which Minitab is a widely adopted tool. But Quality Companion does not have to be used exclusively for Six Sigma and is widely customizable. For the purposes of the patch management measurement project, Quality Companion provides features for building process maps and embedding metrics data into the map itself, as well as for managing other aspects of the project.

Figure 9-5 shows the Quality Companion user interface, including customized fields used by the project team to enter specific cost and duration data for each process activity. Other products are specifically focused on the business process management market, and they provide similar mapping features as well as complex and sophisticated process modeling and management functions, but these tools are often enterprise suites that actually integrate with systems and process flows. If you are just starting out with mapping and analyzing your security business processes, you don't need (and likely are not ready for) these larger solutions.

Using Quality Companion, the project team was able to map the specific activities of the project and assign data to each activity, including resources committed to the activity (based on interviews with the staff), the average duration of each activity in terms of FTE hours spent, and the calendar duration of each activity. The complete chart is shown in Figure 9-6.

This application of Quality Companion was fairly basic, but for the purposes of the director of IT security's measurement pilot, it provided interesting insights into how the process functioned. This tool can also help you develop variables for process

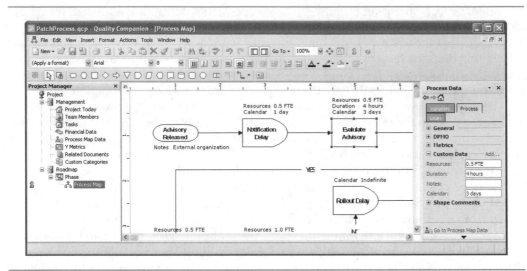

Figure 9-5. Quality Companion process mapping interface

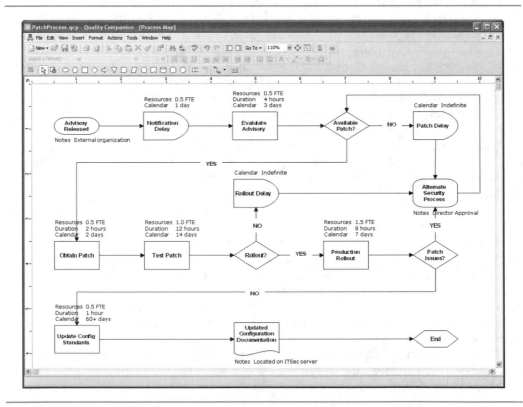

Figure 9-6. Quality Companion process chart for patch management process activities

activities and integrate them with Minitab statistical software so that a metrics team can conduct exploratory, analytical, or experimental projects to help improve their operational activities. At this point, the director was content with the simple reduction of some of the uncertainties regarding the company's patch-management process.

Supporting Decision-Making with the Business Process Mapping Results

Beyond the immediate finding by the project team that the patch management process had no single owner, the data that emerged from the mapping exercise was instructive in helping the director understand why the process was inefficient. With duties split among several people, none of whom were assigned patching as a primary job responsibility, the coordination that took place among them was not enough to overcome the fact that patching was understaffed. The patching virtual team shared monitoring and evaluation duties, communicating primarily via e-mail. Security advisories were picked up pretty quickly, but evaluation of the advisories and their impact on the company could take days as the team researched and communicated back and forth. In some cases, no patch was available and alternative processes for ensuring security were kicked off until a patch was released.

Once a patch was obtained, it required testing before rollout, and at this stage of the process, the most significant delays were introduced. Patch testing required dedicated lab time and the virtual team members were often too busy with other activities or projects to begin the tests immediately. Altogether, the amount of time dedicated by the company to this task was one full-time equivalent employee across the five members of the virtual team. The resulting delays as the team members found time to test the patches in queue could result in delays of two weeks or more before a decision could be made on rolling out the patch to production systems. When a patch failed testing, this delay could increase even more as the team had to research alternatives and look for other mechanisms of securing affected systems. Once testing was complete, the delays diminished as the members of the team were able to work with system owners to implement the patches as part of their normal duties. Rollout was usually completed within a week, giving system owners sufficient time to identify any issues resulting from the patch.

One major discrepancy identified by the mapping exercise concerned the documentation of the patching efforts and the updating of appropriate configuration standards. This activity was required by the company's security policy, but the project team found that in most cases the required updates to the standards were not completed within months of the rollout, and in some cases they had never been documented. This oversight could be attributed to the staff members involved in patching quickly moving back to their normal duties after patching was complete—every patching team member described feeling that patching was about getting the critical tasks "off the plate" and moving on quickly to other priorities.

Using the insights from the business process analysis pilot, the director began making more informed decisions about how to improve the process. He changed the job descriptions within the security team to assign one individual full-time patching responsibilities and put that person in charge of coordinating the virtual team.

He also used the project data as a justification for more headcount, showing the CIO that the inefficiencies in the security processes were not the result of poor operations but of a lack of sufficient resources that was putting the company at risk of a major virus outbreak or an attack on vulnerable systems. Most certainly, the measurements conducted during this project led into subsequent measurement projects.

One follow-on project was to design an experiment around the assignment of the single point of responsibility for the patching process. After implementing the change, process data was be reevaluated periodically to determine whether reductions resulted in the calendar durations of any activities. Should such reductions be achieved, analysis could be conducted to determine whether those reductions were the result of the changes to the process or of random chance. This is another area where the features of Quality Companion and similar process analysis tools can be put to use.

The Importance of Data to Measuring Cost and Value

A central theme that runs through all three sample measurement projects in this chapter, and through the techniques used to accomplish them, is the need for the collection of appropriate data as an input into the measurement activities. Each of the techniques discussed involve more or less sophisticated ways of modeling the current and future state of certain aspects of security. The accuracy and reliability of your model improves as you incorporate more information into your assumptions, but you also must understand the basis of those assumptions before you can select the appropriate data. For these reasons, the security measurement project construct and the GQM basis for selecting and bounding the measurements you will analyze provide a good way of articulating and understanding the assumptions you are making and the data you will need.

Models often fail when we try to cram too much into them and lose sight of the fact that they simulate rather than reflect real conditions. I've made the case several times that understanding the limits of data and analysis is perhaps the most important (and most often neglected) aspect of measurement. If your assumptions are flawed, then so, too, will be your data, your model, and any decisions that you base upon it. And the hard truth is that all your assumptions will be flawed. The goal of measurement is to introduce no more error and uncertainty into your metrics analysis than you can understand and reasonably accept, and to recognize and make explicit those assumptions and flaws humbly and self-consciously when making decisions or presenting your results.

Summary

Measuring the costs and value associated with IT security can be daunting and requires a combination of appropriate data, creative analytical techniques, and defined objectives. This chapter explored three specific techniques that can be used to analyze the cost and value of security and to predict how cost and value might occur over time.

The Poisson distribution is a statistical construct that can be used to determine the probability of discrete events occurring based upon past rates of occurrence. It has been used to measure probabilities as diverse as the likelihood of getting a fatal kick from a horse to how many cars or customers will enter a place of business on a given day. From an IT security metrics perspective, the Poisson distribution can be used to calculate the probabilities that an event such as a reported disclosure of personally identifiable information will occur in a given time period based upon historical data. When combined with other information, such as financial impact of events, Poisson tests can help answer questions of risk analysis and risk-based allocation of resources.

Monte Carlo simulations are another statistical modeling technique that can be used in situations more complex than the Poisson distribution. They allow you to model the probabilities of events and outcomes that involve several variables. Monte Carlo simulations were developed to help physicists model the complexities of nuclear chain reactions and have since been applied to everything from project management to financial risk management scenarios. Applied to IT security, Monte Carlo simulations provide powerful tools for exploring the outcomes associated with security decisions such as evaluating the potential returns from outsourcing a security function such as incident management, as well as others.

Business process analysis is a modeling technique that takes well-known principles of flowcharting and process diagrams to a more sophisticated level, where they can be used to analyze the costs and constraints of individual process activities statistically and to identify areas for improvement and increased efficiency. Many security organizations use flowcharts for training and documentation purposes, but few have explored the possibilities for statistical process control and improvement using variations of those charts. Specialized tools and the association of data to process diagram components, such as in the case of analyzing a company's patch management process, allow you to achieve greater visibility into security operations and to begin developing metrics data and measurement projects and experiments that can significantly improve your efficiency and effectiveness.

Further Reading

Hubbard, D. *How to Measure Anything: Finding the Value of "Intangibles" in Business*. Wiley, 2007.

Jacka, J. Mike, and P. Keller. *Business Process Mapping: Improving Customer Satisfaction*. Wiley, 2002.

Minitab, Inc. "Quality Companion 3 – Getting Started." 2009. www.minitab.com/en-US/products/quality-companion/documentation.aspx

Winston, W. *Excel 2007: Data Analysis and Business Modeling*. Microsoft Press, 2007.

CHAPTER 10 | Measuring People, Organizations, and Culture

Y ou'll find the measurement and analysis explored in the project examples of this chapter somewhat unconventional in their approach, especially if you are accustomed to thinking about security and its measurement primarily in terms of technology or the quantifiable, easily obtained metrics data with which many security professionals are most comfortable. Given that you have read this far, you already understand that I am no enemy of quantitative analysis, although I do think that qualitative techniques are neglected and underutilized in the security industry. This neglect is ironic, since the majority of our measurements are qualitative in nature—it's just that the qualitative inquiry we undertake is typically haphazard and not very rigorous. (Which, in turn, is often justified by the misinformed and self-serving argument that there is no way to be rigorous since our methods are so qualitative!) The idea that we have to choose between (supposedly) vague and subjective measures of security or else we must completely embrace numbers as the only true security metric sets up a false dichotomy that hinders our ability to accomplish our mission: to protect the information assets of our respective organizations and, increasingly, our information and IT-dependent society.

Let's look at another type of security as an example. Suppose you were asked to measure the national security of the United States. How would you respond? You could certainly cite the size and budget of our military, the number of nuclear and conventional weapons we possess, or the response time involved with focusing satellites or other intelligence-gathering capabilities on a new trouble spot. You could even compare those figures with those of our rivals and competitors. But would those facts accurately measure national security? Of course not—although the data would provide certain insights into the concept of national security, the reality is too complex and broad to be defined by any single set of metrics. You would also have to consider qualitative measures of security, such as the political stability of our society or our ability to create and maintain alliances with other nations. These metrics are also central to the picture, but they are not easily quantified, and you can find similar measures in economic security, transportation security, or (drum roll, please…) IT security. In fact, most recently as a result of high-profile attacks such as those conducted against Google in early 2010, IT security has begun to be defined in terms of national security, so our knowledge of the former influences our analysis of the latter.

To measure one of these macro-level concepts completely, you would have to be able to measure every aspect that creates or informs that concept. In the case of IT security, this includes not only IT systems, but also the organizational structures, people, and even the social and cultural norms that impact and are impacted by the effort to protect information assets and information capital. And many of those elements of security are conceptual; therefore, they are measurable only in conceptual terms. There is no "culture" command in your security management system that will tell you everything about the shared practices and beliefs of your enterprise. But this does not mean you have to give up on understanding such things as culture or organizational (meaning human rather than technological) behavior. The opposite is, in fact, true: you must understand these aspects if you are to understand and effectively manage your security and risk management operations. Security infrastructures are not made up of machines, but of people. Machines are simply the tools people use. The same holds true for threats and attackers. People are central to IT security—from the attackers who imagine and design sophisticated technical exploits, to the marketing people who try to convince us that technology can solve our problems by automating people out of the equation, to the user who clicks his way into a botnet because he lacks the awareness to distinguish an advertisement from a trap.

The two example projects in this chapter are designed to stimulate your thoughts and further discussion on ways that we can measure things that we often consider "immeasurable" in our security programs. These projects make use of data, techniques, and tools that have long and productive histories in the social sciences and in industries outside information security. They are often messy, time-consuming, and dependent upon interpretation and consensus. But, when used properly, they work exceptionally well at providing important social and cultural insights into your security operations that all the numbers and security event correlation tools in the world will never provide. So, by all means, be skeptical. (After all, skepticism and self-reflection on the part of the researcher are two of the hallmarks of rigorous qualitative research design.) And while you are at it, take some of that healthy skepticism and apply it to the question of whether the metrics data (quantitative or otherwise) that you collect today allows you to answer any of the questions that are posed in the pages to come.

Sample Measurement Projects for People, Organizations, and Culture

Both of the security measurement projects (SMPs) that follow used novel measurement techniques to arrive at findings and conclusions about very traditional security challenges, such as how to promote the value of the CISO to other business units and functions and how to drive better security practices down into the organizational culture and fabric. The project teams involved relied on analytical constructions such as stories and metaphors to explain their security operations. At first glance, these targets of analysis may appear to be very unscientific indicators of the tangible and factual elements of a security program; however, they are at the basis of how all of us, including scientists, understand the world. Equations are great, but they rarely explain why you should care about them. When applied to security, conceptual communication vehicles can provide context and strategic insight into which more targeted and specific metrics can be utilized.

Measuring the Security Orientation of Company Stakeholders

This example measurement project was conducted by a medical technology company with a progressive security team. The CISO had been brought in with the full support of the CIO after the company had experienced several security incidents in previous years, including one that had resulted in the loss of valuable intellectual property that had negatively impacted annual revenues. As a result, the security operations group was heavily involved throughout the company, setting standards, developing security policies, and conducting audits and assessments. The downside of the situation was an increasing resentment of the security group's activities as overly meddlesome and an attempt by the CISO at "empire building." Complaints had been increasing about security charge-backs for required projects, and the CISO was told by his boss that some business units were telling him that "the security bureaucracy" was impacting the company's ability to stay competitive.

Building a Security Outreach Program

The CISO took these concerns and complaints seriously, because he realized that the CIO's support was the main factor that enabled him to accomplish many of the security initiatives he had rolled out. The CISO, while sympathetic to the impact of security on other business activities, also believed that many people in the company resented having any security requirements at all and wanted to return to the more relaxed attitude toward security that previously made the company vulnerable to attacks and security-related losses. This obviously was not an option, but the CISO understood that his team needed to do a better job of selling themselves and showing others in the company the importance of protecting their information assets.

To accomplish this goal, the CISO set up what he called a "security outreach" program for the company. With the direct support of the CIO, the security team developed a program that was designed to move the security group from the role of cop or watchdog to that of valued partner to the various departments in the company. Changing the perceptions of the security operations group would require two strategies: The CISO needed to educate critics and convince them that security was enabling rather than limiting their operations. But in defining the strategies, the security team realized that they didn't know very much about the security needs and concerns of the rest of the company. Security direction and requirements were set within the CISO's team and then communicated outward, and that direction was of a one-size-fits-all variety, with set standards and requirements to which everyone was required to adhere. As a result, the CISO realized that he first needed to educate himself and his team as to whether their claims that security was enabling other company stakeholders were true. If security was indeed limiting productivity and efficiency, then the CISO needed to know that before he could hope to make improvements. To get the buy-in that he needed to be successful, the CISO realized that his team needed to do much more listening.

Conducting an Information Audit

To assess the unique information security needs of the other stakeholders throughout the organization, the CISO set up a measurement project to conduct an information audit. Unlike an IT audit that focuses on systems or a security audit that explores weaknesses and gaps in the overall security posture, an information audit is a specialized assessment that comes from the fields of information management and information policy development. Information audits aim to understand what information assets are in place within an organization as well as how information flows and is used by the organization's members.

Working with a consultant who specialized in information auditing, the security measurement project team wanted to adapt the information audit methodology to try to understand the information priorities of other stakeholders within the company. The audit would not be directly related to security, but was aimed at learning about which information assets and information behaviors existed within various groups. Armed with this data, the project team could begin making recommendations about how to improve the partnership between the security team and organizational stakeholders based not only on the priorities of the CISO, but also on those of other groups. The Goal-Question-Metric (GQM) template for the information audit project is shown in Table 10-1.

Goal Components	*Outcome* – Understand, identify, develop *Element* – Information assets and uses *Element* – Unique stakeholder requirements *Element* – Improved security practices *Perspective* – CISO, company stakeholders
Goal Statement	*The goal of this project is to understand the information assets and uses in place among company stakeholders and to identify unique requirements and priorities across different stakeholders to develop more appropriate and effective security practices for departments within the company, from the perspective of both the CISO and other stakeholders.*
Question	What are the information assets and flows in place within different departments?
Metrics	Information audit results including survey, interview, and focus group data
Question	What are the most important information processes, assets, and flows in place within the company?
Metrics	Information audit results including survey, interview, and focus group data
Question	What are the security-related concerns and priorities of the various departments?
Metrics	Information audit results including survey, interview, and focus group data
Question	How can the security group build more customized support to engage departments as partners?
Metrics	Comparison of department priorities to identify security outreach opportunities

Table 10-1.   GQM Template for Information Audit Project

The information audit was conducted via a series of focus groups with various company departments, followed up by individual interviews with specific stakeholders and information users. The goal of the group and individual data gathering was twofold: to identify specific types and values (subjective or objective, as available) of information assets and to identify the informational activities that were most directly (usually negatively) impacted by the security requirements imposed by the CISO's operations. The questions and conversations were not security-specific but instead asked the participants to talk about how information enabled their activities and what information problems would disrupt their business processes.

The result of the information audit was a great deal of data about how information was created, used, transferred, and shared within the organization. Since the questions were not framed in terms of security, and the presence of the consultant added an element of neutrality to the interactions, many of the participants felt encouraged to share broadly about the importance of information to their groups and individual jobs.

With the consultant's help, the security team began to analyze the data and responses of the other stakeholder groups to identify patterns and opportunities for outreach. This was not always easy, because several measurement project members expressed frustration that the information had little to do with security and that the security team was about protecting IT systems and not analyzing other groups' business operations. The CISO and the consultant attempted to use these observations as teachable moments, drawing comparisons between the project team's frustration and the frustration experienced elsewhere in the company when people were told they had to do things that seemed to be the responsibility of the security team. The point was for each set of stakeholders to try to help the other understand more about concerns and priorities they may not have considered.

Assessing the Security Orientation of Participating Groups

One exercise conducted using the information audit data attempted to measure and map the company's security orientations, defined as the priorities and concerns of other groups within the company, based on what those groups had said about information assets and behaviors in general. Group and individual participants were asked questions that did not specifically reference security, but were meant to identify issues that were security-related. These questions included the following:

- How bad would it be if a competitor was to get access to "X" information asset?

- What is more important: being able to customize information quickly or being sure that all information comes from a trusted source?

- How negatively would your operations be affected if an application such as e-mail or Internet access went down for four hours?

Participant responses to these questions were analyzed using a commercial qualitative data analysis tool to identify themes and patterns in the data. Categories were created based on the responses that framed general information responses into themes that the CISO's team could begin to relate to security-specific functions and responsibilities. Two sets of categories were created:

■ **Information asset concerns**   These responses reflected concerns about the risks and requirements associated with types of information assets.

■ **Information behavior concerns**   These responses reflected concerns about the way information was used and how the participants needed to deal with information assets.

For each category, several themes were developed from the response data. Table 10-2 shows a selection of these categorical subthemes.

To analyze the security orientation of the groups participating in the information audit, the focus group and interview data was assessed to determine how often particular categories and subconcerns appeared in people's discussions of their information environments and their responses to the questions about their information priorities. The metric used was a simple percentage of the number of participants who expressed

Information Asset Concerns	Information Behavior Concerns
Compliance Concerns about regulatory, industry, or contractual requirements for the handling or protection of specific information assets	**Confidentiality** Concerns about the need to protect data from unauthorized access
Data loss Concerns about the effects of the loss of control or disclosure of specific information assets	**Integrity** Concerns about the need to protect information from unauthorized alteration
Uptime Concerns about the impact of interruption to specific information assets	**Availability** Concerns about the need to ensure access to information
Malware Concerns about the impact of viruses, spyware, and other endpoint threats	**Flexibility** Concerns about the ability to customize systems to meet business and stakeholder needs
Development Concerns about the need to balance secure coding practices with the need to build new tools and applications	**Agility** Concerns about the need to change or update systems quickly or react to problems
	Autonomy Concerns about the need to set policy and manage systems without interference

Table 10-2.   Security-Related Categories and Themes from Information Audit

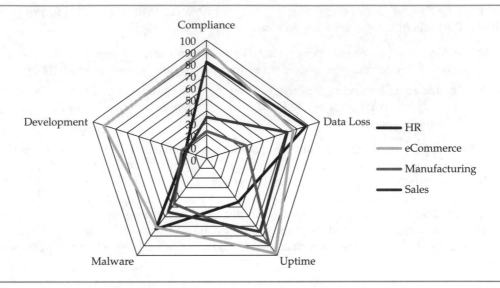

Figure 10-1. Security orientation shape for information assets

a particular concern in either category. The results were used to construct security orientation "shapes" using radar charts for both categories. The orientation shapes for four of the groups participating in the project is shown in Figure 10-1, and the orientation shape for information behavior is shown in Figure 10-2.

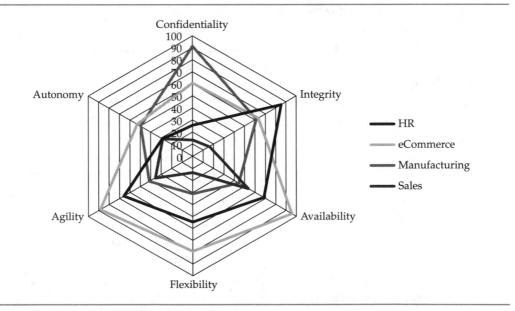

Figure 10-2. Security orientation shape for information behaviors

Interpreting the Results and Developing Outreach Strategies

Analysis of the orientation charts visually showed differences between the orientations of the four groups, reflecting differences in priorities and concerns across the company. To be successful in partnering with other groups, the CISO would need to develop a greater understanding of these differences and adapt security operations accordingly.

Several immediate findings by the project team concerned how the CISO might make a better internal partner for the various departments:

■   The eCommerce department expressed the broadest set of concerns, indicating that security played a role in their operations in many areas, from Payment Card Industry Data Security Standard (PCI DSS) compliance requirements, to the desire for flexibility and agility in their operations. In fact, it was the perceived lack of flexibility and agility that caused most of the complaints on the part of the department, as the security team was viewed as too inflexible regarding standards and policies around security.

■   The Manufacturing department had relatively few concerns regarding security. This group was content to let the security team drive policy and standards, so long as the manufacturing production systems experienced no downtime. One complaint indicated that manufacturing workers were asked to participate too much in security operations and would prefer to give up control and management of systems so long as they could count on the uptime of the systems they cared about.

■   Opportunities existed for broad efforts in those areas where most or all of the groups participating identified similar concerns, such as data loss and integrity. In these cases, generally applicable standards and technologies could be pitched across groups. Conversely, the CISO could consider special approaches unique to the concerns of the eCommerce department concerning development standards and more focused coordination around exceptions and flexible configurations specific to that group.

So what did this project measure? The data that was analyzed as part of the measurement project were the responses to the focus groups and interviews. These responses were real and observed things, empirical data, even if they could not be quantified directly. The categories and themes developed through analyzing the data were inductive and interpretive, based on the reasoning and judgments of the measurement project team with the help of the consultant. The combination of empirical data and interpretive analysis provided measurement insight into the attitudes and opinions of stakeholders that the CISO needed as partners in order to be successful and to make the company successful. The results of the project also helped the security operations group identify opportunities for further measurement projects, including more traditional security metrics that would be made more realistic as other departments bought into security as a company-wide priority.

As a final deliverable of the project, the CISO decided that the results needed to be shared outside the security team. He created a marketing strategy as part of his outreach program that made a point of showing other departments and stakeholders the different ways that security was viewed within the company and the conflicts that often resulted. Rather than keeping his new knowledge in a silo, where only the security team could benefit from the insights, the CISO took a "customer service" approach that encouraged people outside the security department to share their concerns and unique challenges with the security team and allowed the security team to respond in a more flexible and sensitive manner to competing ideas about what made for "good" security.

An Ethnography of Physical Security Practices

Physical security, even more than IT security, is a matter of intimate concern in today's post-9/11 world. While we may talk about the threat of a "digital Pearl Harbor" or cyberwarfare as a new battleground, the loss of information does not compare with the visceral impact of a physical threat. And it is far more difficult in cases of physical security to discount the human aspect of the threat by throwing up new technologies (not that this works very well even in the case of information security, even though your security vendor will tell you otherwise). Physical security reminds us that protection exists in the context of a messy mix of physical space and human interactions that can affect everything from traditional IT security concerns to basic human feelings of fear, safety, and trust.

The following measurement project describes a joint attempt by an IT security group and a facilities security group to measure and understand their physical security challenges in the wake of an IT security incident. The incident involved an attack on the IT infrastructure of the company that was traced back to a rogue device that had been physically connected to the company's internal network. The origin of the rogue device was never discovered, but in the course of the investigation it became apparent that the company suffered from physical security challenges that could have easily led to an external attacker being able to install the attack box in question. Most frustrating to both the facilities and the IT security groups was that the company had invested significant resources in a physical security awareness campaign, in response to several compliance requirements around securing facilities and physical assets. There were reviews undertaken as part of the joint security improvement effort, but the interest relevant to this chapter involved an experimental project that attempted to approach the problem from a different direction by conducting an ethnographic review of the organization's physical security behaviors.

Ethnography in Practice

Ethnography is a qualitative research technique typically associated with anthropologists and sociologists that involves the detailed, immersive observations of a particular group or society and the interpretation of the behaviors and values of that are observed. The end goal is the development of both descriptions and explanations for the shared social practices of the group or society that can begin to describe the culture of the society. Culture may include rituals, religious beliefs, formalized social relationships, and many other aspects of how people come together to form complex and dynamic communities of practice. Ethnography is not just for academics. Industry has increasingly adopted ethnographic techniques to help companies understand how their customers use their products in daily settings or how they might react to new designs and features.

Ethnography can be painstaking work, requiring trained observers and enough time to develop familiarity with the environment being observed. Ethnography also has ethical dimensions, as the conduct of ethnographic field work often requires that observers build trust and be accepted to at least some degree into the group or society that they are observing. But from the perspective of empirical inquiry, ethnography is one of the foundations of qualitative research.

The goals of ethnographic studies are far different from the statistics and key performance indicators that provide diagnostic insight into an operational process. Ethnographers seek to understand how the entire complex system works, with human beings at the center of focus. Some practitioners of ethnography would take offense at the notion that they were measuring something, agreeing with those in the quantitative camp that what they are observing is not something that can be measured. But an ethnographer would not equate measurement with understanding, and would instead say that she were seeking a richer and more nuanced understanding of what she observed than any statistical assessment is capable of providing.

Observing Physical Security

Using outside expertise, a local professor who was a practicing ethnographic researcher, the company set up a security measurement project that would take a close look at the way physical security functioned within the company—closer than any previous study had attempted. The ethnographer would be partnered with several members of the facilities and IT security teams during a three-month period. (The company employees were assigned to the project part-time so as not to impact their daily jobs too much.) The ethnographer was given temporary employee status, assigned to the Director of Corporate Security, with full access to the company campus and resources. She would coordinate her activities with whichever member of the project team was "on duty" at the time.

The ethnographer's task was to be a part of the company for the period of the assessment, but with a very specific role: She was to observe and explore how company employees engaged in physical security practices. Her participation in the company was open and announced, and employees were encouraged to approach her if they chose to do so. She was assigned a cubicle and was for all intents and purposes another employee. At the end of the project, she prepared a report of her analysis and findings. Table 10-3 shows the GQM template for the project.

Example Finding: The Competing Narratives of Tailgating

Ethnographic studies produce a great deal of data that can be used to reconstruct social and organizational practices as well as explore ways in which members of a group view and understand those practices and their particular activities. To demonstrate the findings that can emerge from an ethnographic study, I will focus on a single outcome of the physical security measurement project: the narratives, or stories, that emerged around "tailgating" practices.

All building entrances were controlled by electronic locks and badge readers that were centrally managed by the facilities security team, but tailgating was an acknowledged problem within the company. Tailgating occurred when an authorized employee

Goal Components	*Outcome* – Understand, observe, elicit, improve *Element* – Physical security practices and behaviors *Element* – Employee explanations and opinions *Element* – Physical and IT security posture *Perspective* – Physical and IT security teams
Goal Statement	*The goal of this project is to understand the physical security practices and behaviors taking place throughout the company by closely observing physical activities and eliciting employee explanations and opinions regarding these activities in order to improve the company's physical and IT security posture from the perspective of the physical and IT security teams.*
Question	What are the physical security practices and behaviors taking place throughout the company?
Metrics	Ethnographic observation of company facilities and employee activities
Question	Why are the physical security practices and behaviors undertaken?
Metrics	Observations, interviews, and discussions with employees and other stakeholders within the company
Question	How is physical security perceived and enacted by the members of the company?
Metrics	Qualitative analysis of ethnographic data to identify categories, patterns, and themes regarding the practice of physical security within the company

Table 10-3. GQM Template for Physical Security Ethnographic Project

badged into an entrance and then allowed others to enter without using an access badge. The rogue device had been installed under a vacant cubicle within 30 feet of an exterior door at the side of one building. When the original physical breach occurred, it was strongly suspected that the individual who had planted the attack box inside the corporate network perimeter had gained access to the facilities by tailgating into the building. Despite warning signs at every entrance warning against allowing people to enter without "badging in," and training and awareness programs emphasizing that tailgating was dangerous and prohibited under the company's security policy, tailgating was understood by the security teams to be a common practice.

During the project, the ethnographer had many opportunities to tailgate into one of the five campus buildings, both alone and with her points of contact from the security teams. In addition to observing the process of tailgating by participating in it, the ethnographer would attempt to engage others in talking about tailgating, both at the time of a tailgating incident or in other social settings such as the cafeteria. She would explain her job at the company and, in a non-threatening and friendly manner, ask for permission to talk with the other individual about life at the company. While many employees chose not to respond (some even reported the incident to ensure that she was a legitimate employee), the ethnographer was able to collect interview data from nearly 30 employees over the duration of the project. When added to interviews with managers and security staff participating in the project, this data was then qualitatively analyzed using Computer Assisted Qualitative Data Analysis Software (CAQDAS).

The tailgating interviews generated many stories from interview participants regarding why tailgating happens, why the person did or did not tailgate or allow others to do so, and why it was a dangerous practice. These stories had plots, characters, and events that formed a coherent personal explanation for some aspect of tailgating, and the storytellers used them to understand and rationalize their own behavior as well as to explain that behavior to others. Given the story nature of these explanations, the ethnographer recommended that the project team use narrative analysis to try to understand more about how tailgating functioned at the company. These stories, or narratives, could then be used to construct less soft, more formalized use cases and threat vectors about tailgating that could be better addressed by security operations.

Narrative analysis is a formal method used by researchers in the fields of public policy, organizational communications, and even more traditionally "hard" scientific disciplines such as medicine. Like other qualitative measurement techniques, narrative analysis tries to get at the nuanced and interpretive aspects of an issue that targeted statistical hypothesis testing cannot uncover. Narrative analysis is particularly useful when more than one narrative or story exists and the stories compete with one another. This happens a lot in public policy, when both sides of an issue can have different stories about what that issue represents. These stories serve to organize both facts and beliefs into an argument that can then compete with the facts and beliefs of the stories of others. Competing narratives also exist in business and industry, where facts exist in the context of organizational politics and competitive drivers. Narrative analysis does not reveal the "true" story of an issue, but it can help an organization gain visibility into competing stories and assess them rationally with the goal of overcoming conflicts.

The analysis of project interview data revealed a number of stories that explained how tailgating functioned within the organization. These stories were constructed from the direct responses provided during interviews and discussions, categorized to identify common themes and patterns across the responses. Table 10-4 describes the nine major narratives that were identified.

Examination of the narratives immediately revealed several different concerns and priorities among those providing responses. To further identify relationships between the narratives, the project team analyzed the data to show which narratives were

Narrative	Description
"Culture of Trust"	The company fosters an environment of community and trust that would be at odds with guards, barriers, and surveillance cameras.
"Avoiding Confrontation"	People at the company do not want to be seen as rude or aggressive by demanding to see one another's badges.
"Matter of Convenience"	It is often more time consuming and inefficient not to tailgate.
"Theft and Loss"	Tailgating opens the company to the risk of loss for both personal and company property.
"Keeping People Safe"	Making sure a violent criminal or terrorist does not access the building is everyone's responsibility in today's environment.
"Hackers"	Physical access allows a computer criminal to bypass most of the technical controls protecting the company's IT perimeter.
"Prohibitive Costs"	Upgrading the badge reader system or installing more cameras and guards is too expensive in the current economic environment.
"Lack of Compatibility"	Different doors and badge readers exist, making it difficult to manage physical access between the buildings on campus.
"Location and Geography"	Some places physically encourage tailgating.

Table 10-4.   Tailgating Narratives Identified During the Project

common among interviews. In other words, narratives were connected when they would appear in the same interviews. As these connections were made, the narratives were then grouped into "metanarratives" that defined an overall rationalization around tailgating practices. These metanarratives included the following:

- Tailgating Is Understandable
- Tailgating Must be Prevented
- Tailgating Is Hard to Prevent

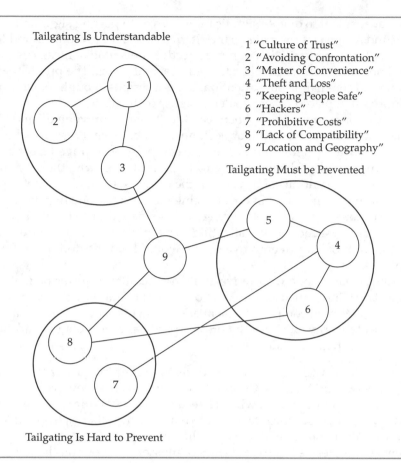

Figure 10-3.   Narrative network analysis of tailgating practices

Finally, the relationships among the stories, the metanarratives, and the interview data were rendered visually through a network analysis map, as shown in Figure 10-3. The larger circles represent metanarratives, the smaller circles are the specific narratives identified in the data, and the connecting lines represent the relationships between the narratives as described by the participants in the data collection.

Project Conclusions Regarding Tailgating Practices

The narrative networks in place within the organization showed three distinctive storylines about tailgating that were more or less at odds with one another. While the security teams strongly believed that tailgating had to be prevented, a storyline that compelled management to devote significant resources to posting signs and conducting training and awareness campaigns, the alternative story of resources and limited budgets preventing the installation of more effective preventative measures directly contradicted how important a problem tailgating actually was. The problem was serious enough to command some attention, but not serious enough to overcome the budget priorities that placed other problems higher on the list.

While many connections existed between the "must be prevented" and "hard to prevent" narratives, there was little or no connection between these and the stories of why tailgating was a common practice. The company encouraged trust and community but struggled with the negative effects of employees who therefore did not naturally suspect ill intentions of anyone on the campus. Even the physical geography of the campus played a role in encouraging tailgating in one instance, in which the cafeteria entrance directly faced an unguarded side entrance to another campus building. The result was pervasive tailgating as people carrying lunch trays found assistance in the form of helpful employees who would hold the door open for multiple people at a time.

To reiterate an earlier point, narrative and other qualitative forms of analysis do not offer statistical certainty, much less truth, about an issue. But they can help you reduce the uncertainty present in complex problem environments. Key findings that emerged from the physical security ethnography project, partly as a result of the narrative analysis of tailgating practices, included these:

- Physical security often meant very different things in practice to the members of the two security teams. Corporate security practices revolved around protecting lives and property, while IT security practices prioritized information assets. In both cases, each team tended to view the other as the simpler and more easily accomplished responsibility. Exposure to one another's practices showed both teams the complexities of their operations and the impacts that their respective domains had upon each group's mission.

- Security managers on both sides (facilities and IT) expressed significant frustration at why problems such as tailgating continued despite the perception of significant efforts being undertaken to address the challenges. The project shed light not only on how the priorities and practices of everyday employees were the result of larger environmental issues, but also on the ways that the security teams' practices and priorities were heavily influenced by complex organizational dynamics such as budgets and regulatory compliance.

- As with other such efforts to ask broad questions about an environment, the physical security ethnography project led to a number of ideas regarding other projects and measurement efforts. Many of these proposed follow-on projects were more targeted and quantitative in nature, designed to test and assess the general findings and insights that emerged from the qualitative measurement work.

Summary

Measuring people, organizations, and culture in the context of IT security cannot be accomplished solely through the use of statistical methods or quantitative data, yet these aspects of our security operations must be explored and understood in order to make our security programs as effective as possible. The mantra of "people, process, and technology" is becoming more prevalent throughout the security industry as this realization sinks in, but measurement remains a challenge. A good example is the idea of risk tolerance, which is a function of organizational culture and individual personality that goes hand-in-hand with quantitative measures of financial or organizational risk based on empirical data.

This chapter reviewed two examples of security projects that relied heavily on formal qualitative approaches to conducting a security measurement project. Unlike the commonly accepted definition of qualitative security or risk assessment, which is often used as a catch-all phrase to describe projects that gauge opinion without rigorous standards of data collection or analysis, qualitative data analysis can be highly empirical and rigorously conducted, and it can require specialized training and expertise to perform. In both cases discussed here, outside consulting experience was engaged to complete the projects.

Information auditing is an organizational research technique from the fields of information management and information policy development. Traditionally used to help businesses and other organizations evaluate the uses and flows of their information assets, information auditing techniques were applied to security as part of an IT security outreach program in which a CISO was attempting to gather better data on stakeholder perceptions and practices around information use and the security of that information. By measuring the perceptions of other stakeholders within his company, the CISO was able to develop more effective strategies for promoting IT security as an enabler, with the IT security group as a partner rather than as an antagonistic and bureaucratic obstacle to the business.

Ethnography and narrative analysis are both qualitative approaches that are also used in many industries to assess organizational and social practices and relationships that can affect aspects of a business. Often used to evaluate product uses by consumers or to assess the effects of new product designs or features, ethnography involves the close observation of a group, organization, or society by researchers who are also participating in the group being observed. Ethnography was applied to a project seeking insight into the physical security practices of a company, including both facilities and IT security elements. One of the analyses conducted during the project involved gathering narratives, or stories, about how tailgating was practiced at the company. The narrative analysis provided evidence that competing priorities and environmental factors, and the stories with which these priorities and factors were associated, set up trade-offs and compromises that made it very difficult to prevent tailgating within the company. The resulting findings allowed the project team members to understand where their efforts could be impactful and where they were likely to be less effective.

Further Reading

Boje, D. *Narrative Methods for Organizational & Communication Research*. SAGE Publications, 2001.

Creswell, J. *Qualitative Inquiry & Research Design: Choosing Among Five Approaches*. SAGE Publications, 2006.

Henczel, S. *The Information Audit: A Practical Guide*. K.G. Saur, 2001.

McBeth, M., et al. "The Science of Storytelling: Measuring Policy Beliefs in Greater Yellowstone." *Society and Natural Resources*, 2005.

Merholz, P., et al. *Subject to Change: Creating Great Products and Services for an Uncertain World*. O'Reilly, 2008.

Orna, E. *Information Strategy in Practice*. Gower, 2004.

Case Study 3 | Web Application Vulnerabilities

Caroline Wong's discussion of a software vulnerability measurement project adds to the examples I've provided throughout this section. Her case study shows that there is no single, dogmatic way to approach IT security metrics. Caroline is an established metrics expert in our field, and her work measuring software risk carries its own unique challenges.

This book offers a framework and examples for security measurement, but you should look at these only as a starting point. You can incorporate these ideas as you study your own organization and your own security efforts. Caroline's case study leverages some of the techniques I have described, but the accomplishment of the project's goals is uniquely situated within the context of her own professional experience and environment. There is no other way to do it.

Undertaking IT security metrics at the project level is an experience that cannot be scripted. You can read books and study methods but the authors and architects of those resources cannot perform the project for you. In the end you must take the knowledge and skills that you come by and make them your own. This means adding new insights and techniques that may not have been covered in your lessons and throwing out those "rules and tools" that do not make sense for what you are trying to accomplish. Caroline's chapter enhances the book by describing a project that is both similar and very different from my own examples. Her contribution can help you think about how best to incorporate the lessons of this book into your own specialized practices.

Case Study 3: Web Application Vulnerabilities
by Carolyn Wong

In this example, the CTO was an executive at the company responsible for overseeing web site development of several distinct business units. The CISO was responsible for security of each of these business units. The CTO and the CISO already had a good working relationship. Although the CTO was not an expert in security, the CTO trusted the CISO for his security recommendations in this area.

The CTO approached the CISO asking for information about the security status of each of the web sites. Specifically, the CTO was interested in using a security metric to improve the security posture of each of the web sites, something that could be tracked month after month to improve the sites' security posture.

The Goal-Question-Metric (GQM) methodology was the perfect place to start as this security organization began to define the objectives for this metrics project:

- **Goal**   The goal of this project is to understand and gain visibility into the security status of the web sites of several distinct business units. This will be reported to the CTO on a monthly basis for the purpose of improving the security posture of each of the web sites.

- **Questions**   How vulnerable is each of the functions on the primary customer facing web site? How vulnerable are each of the smaller business unit web sites?

- **Metric**   Number of web application vulnerabilities

Source Data and Normalization

The complexity and size of the web sites differed greatly. One business unit's web site was much more complex and had many more lines of code than most of the smaller business units' sites. Several teams of developers wrote the code for the primary site, whereas some of the smallest business unit sites had only a few individual developers. Because the primary site was constantly changing, the number of lines of code also changed over time.

To normalize the identified metric—the number of web application vulnerabilities— across the different business units, the security organization decided to normalize the number of web application vulnerabilities by dividing by the number of millions of lines of code for each web site. This made it much easier to compare the numbers against each other and better understand the relative security of each site. Figure 1 shows the results of this normalization.

Outcomes, Timelines, Resources

The next step our security organization took to achieve the goal outlined in the GQM methodology was to define the desired change to the metric to reflect improvement in the security posture of the web sites. The goal for this project was straightforward: more vulnerabilities indicated a less secure web site and less vulnerabilities indicated a more secure web site. Once the number of security vulnerabilities was identified, the level of improvement required for a desired outcome needed to be defined.

NOTE Severity vulnerabilities were not addressed during this particular metrics project. Severity and count are completely different metrics. A follow-on analysis or security metrics project in addition to the project described here might address severity of vulnerabilities.

We needed to consider a few factors, including the rate of fixing vulnerabilities in the past and the amount of work that could be reasonably expected from the development teams toward remediation efforts. The metrics project lead met with development managers to discuss how quickly vulnerabilities had been remediated in the past to get a sense of what was likely to occur in the future. Having this conversation at the beginning of the metrics project ensured that the specified outcome was also achievable. We chose to specify an outcome of a 20 percent reduction in web application vulnerabilities.

	BU 1	BU 2	BU 3	BU 4	BU 5
# Web Application Vulnerabilities	500	100	90	50	300
# Million Lines of Code	20 M	5 M	3 M	1 M	15 M
# WAV / # MLOC	25	20	30	50	20

Figure 1. Normalized data

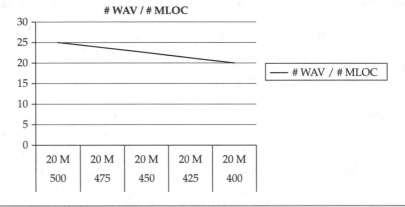

	Baseline	5% reduction	10% reduction	15% reduction	20% reduction
# Web App Vulnerabilities	500	475	450	425	400
# Million Lines of Code	20 M	20 M	20 M	20 M	20 M
# WAV / # MLOC	25	23.75	22.5	21.25	20

Figure 2.   Outcome and timeline

Accomplishing this outcome required time and resources, and these were also specified up front. Our security organization identified the development managers responsible for coding various functions on the web sites and talked with these metrics stakeholders to ensure that resources would be appropriately allocated to perform this work. A timeline was decided and an initial baseline measured. We decided that the 20 percent reduction in web application vulnerabilities should take place during the course of one year.

Figure 2 shows the mapping of the outcome of this security metrics project to the specified timeline.

Initial Reporting with "Dirty Data"

We identified teams of people who were responsible for owning the remediation of the vulnerabilities and worked with these owners to identify resources to do the work. We discovered that a development manager existed for each major function on the primary web site, and that one development manager existed for each small business unit web site. Therefore, we were aiming to obtain the following security organization data:

- The current number of security vulnerabilities per million lines of code for each of the primary web site's functions

- The current number of security vulnerabilities per million lines of code for each of the smaller business unit's web sites

After desired outcomes, resources, and timelines were identified, our next step was to begin gathering and cleansing the data. Many issues arose during the data gathering and cleansing phase. Following are a few of the challenges we encountered.

Ambiguous Data

Sometimes data will be categorized in a manner that is too general to be useful. For this project, we were looking for the names of functions on the largest business unit web site, such as Search, Upload, Update Profile, and Perform Transaction. However, we initially found all these categories bucketed into a single category called "Site-wide." This was a lot less useful because there was no way to assign a specific development manager to remediate the vulnerabilities on any given function.

Once ambiguous data was identified, we needed to clean it up and categorize it correctly for proper assignment to owners. Our team needed to go through each and every remediation ticket and reassign the tickets with ambiguous owners to a more specific category. This took a lot of time, but we looked at it as a beneficial side-effect of the measurement project. The messy reporting highlighted a defect in our process and gave us the opportunity to fix it. Without clear ownership, it would have been impossible to get the vulnerabilities remediated.

Figures 3 and 4 show dirty data and clean data, respectively. They can also be viewed as before and after views into the data.

Determining Which Source to Use

We encountered multiple options while trying to choose a source from which to pull metrics data for this project. To choose the correct source(s), we decided to take a close look at the different steps involved in the vulnerability management process. Our process was as follows:

1. Discover vulnerabilities via an application vulnerability scanning system, penetration test, or other manual discovery method.

2. Either automatically or manually enter the vulnerability information into an Information Security–managed vulnerability tracking system.

Site Wide

Figure 3.   Ambiguous data example

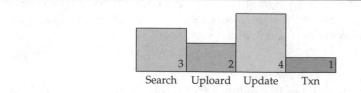

Figure 4.   More useful buckets for remediation

3. Either automatically or manually identify owners for remediating the vulner-abilities and communicate the remediation activities each owner must under-take. Ensure that this data is documented in both the Information Security–managed vulnerability tracking system and the developer bug tracking system.

4. Track the remediation of vulnerabilities as they occur and close out tickets in the Information Security–managed vulnerability tracking system and the de-veloper bug tracking system.

We realized that we had three choices for source systems from which to pull metrics reporting data: the vulnerability scanning system, the Information Security–managed vulnerability tracking system, and the developer bug tracking system. Each of these systems, as well as the part that they played in the multi-step process, is displayed in Figure 5.

The specific process required to discover, track, communicate, and remediate vulnerabilities will be unique to each security organization. In this example, we found that although a process was in place, it was not consistent or well documented. This is not uncommon for security organizations, especially prior to starting a security met-rics or security process optimization program. Often there are small differences in the

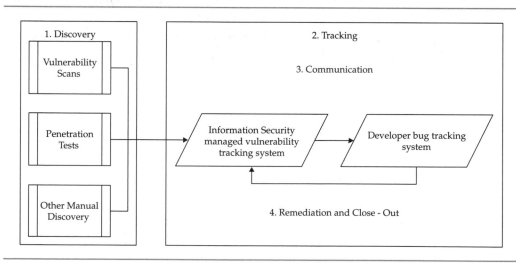

Figure 5.   Process overview

way that the team members execute the process, depending on which team member is involved and how that person has been trained.

In this example, the security metrics project lead started to gather and analyze data from each of these source systems. We discovered that a number of discrepancies existed in the way that the vulnerability data was captured, tracked, and managed:

- Vulnerabilities that were discovered automatically through scanning were automatically entered into the developer bug tracking system; however, they were manually entered into the Information Security–managed vulnerability tracking system.

- Vulnerabilities that were discovered through penetration testing were manually entered into the Information Security–managed vulnerability tracking system.

- Vulnerabilities that were discovered through other manual methods were manually entered into the Information Security–managed vulnerability tracking system.

- The data entry form used in the Information Security–managed vulnerability tracking system had several different fields that might refer to ownership of a vulnerability. This is shown in Figure 6. The Information Security team was leveraging a ticket type used by many different groups in the company, and as this ticket had evolved over time, it had accumulated data fields that were somewhat redundant.

Information Security Vulnerability Management Ticket #12345	
Requestor: Caroline Wong	
Date: 12/19/2009	
Discovery Method: Penetration Test	
Business Unit: Primary	
Site:	
Domain:	
Vulnerability Information: Cross Site Scripting Vulnerability located at http://BU1website.abcd.html	
Criticality: High	
Check this box to automatically create a remediation ticket in the developer bug track system	☐

Figure 6.   Data entry form

■ Checking an option box in the Information Security vulnerability tracking ticket automatically created a ticket in the developer bug tracking system. This option was not consistently used by various team members who went through the process.

These discrepancies were identified when the project lead responsible for this metrics project attempted to pull data from each of the possible fields in the ticket to obtain baseline data and categorize the vulnerabilities by web site. Upon gathering and reviewing the data, the project lead found that the data did not make sense. It became clear that the data gathering and tracking processes had not been consistent.

The next step was to meet with the team responsible for executing the process, present the metrics project findings, and work with the responsible team to clean up the process and the data.

Working with Stakeholders to Perform Data Cleansing

The metrics project lead found discrepancies in analysis of the source data that indicated discrepancies in the process. The process turned out to be inconsistent or undocumented at this point. Although these challenges resulted in delays that were not originally anticipated and incorporated into the project plan, we did not view them as failures in the metrics project. In fact, we identified this broken process as a huge side benefit of the project. We not only did the work to obtain the right data, but we also discussed, clarified, documented, and fixed the process. This resulted in better security overall.

It was a challenge at first to bring up a broken process when the process owner was under the impression that nothing was wrong. However, we found this effort to be very worthwhile as the process owner was then more confident regarding the consistency and effectiveness of the process after it was fixed.

We performed a series of interviews with stakeholders responsible for executing different steps in the process and carefully documented inconsistencies. Then we brought the group together to discuss the discrepancies, which led to healthy debates on the best way to perform the process. I recommend a team member with strong communication, documentation, and project management skills to take on this type of documentation and discussion facilitation work.

Once the process was defined, documented, and approved by the process owners, rework was required to clean up the data remaining from the broken process. We made a note for the team's project managers to include this step and the time required to perform the work in future project plans so that these costs and the time can be accounted and planned for. We also set aside time for training on the new version of the process.

We decided to use the Business Unit field to capture which small business unit web site and which large web site functions were affected by the web application vulnerabilities. The Site and Domain fields in Figure 6 were eliminated as redundant and no longer used for data capture.

We found that going through the backlog of existing tickets that were entered inconsistently was a worthwhile effort and enabled us to obtain more accurate metrics and

	Baseline	5% reduction	10% reduction	15% reduction	20% reduction
# Web App Vulnerabilities	500	475	450	425	400
# Million Lines of Code	20 M	20 M	20 M	20 M	20 M
# WAV / # MLOC	25	23.75	22.5	21.25	20

Figure 7.   Baselines identified

reporting data. An additional advantage of going through the historical data was that the tickets that originally lacked clear ownership now had clearly defined owners. Ownership was key to the vulnerabilities getting remediated, and the clean data allowed us to collect more accurate baselines. These new baselines are shown in Figure 7.

Follow-up with Reports and Discussions with Stakeholders

The last step in the process was to report the baseline data, goals, and timelines and discuss these with key stakeholders. The key stakeholders included the development managers ultimately responsible for remediating the vulnerabilities and the sponsors, including the CTO and the CISO.

After the baseline data was obtained, cleansed, and determined to be accurate, the CISO met with the CTO to communicate the number of web application vulnerabilities that existed in the business unit web sites. The Information Security managers responsible for the vulnerability remediation process met with the development managers to communicate specifics regarding the vulnerabilities in their areas. Because the development managers heard a consistent message both from the Information Security team as well as the CTO, everyone involved was on the same page, and we were set up for a successful decrease in the number of vulnerabilities on the web sites (and a successful increase in the security posture of the web sites).

The CISO met with the CTO and the Information Security managers with the development managers on a monthly basis to report the status of improvement in reducing the number of vulnerabilities. One nice advantage to having the data normalized (displaying the number of vulnerabilities as a number divided by the number of millions of lines of code) was that it was immediately clear to the Information Security team, the CTO, and the development managers which web sites were most vulnerable. When the development managers were not remediating as quickly as the goal had specified (a 20 percent reduction by the end of the year), these metrics reports enabled open discussions with the CTO and the development managers regarding allocation of more resources and higher prioritization of security remediation projects.

Lesson Learned: Fix the Process, and Then Automate

Security organizations that are anxious to get started with a new metrics program or technology deployment sometimes make the mistake of automating too quickly. They believe that an automated process will save time and create efficiencies, and that there is always a future opportunity to fix a broken process once it has been automated. Following are the steps that are typically involved in a rushed approach to automate before a broken process has been fixed:

1. Initially, the Information Security team manages a process that is performed manually and is broken. A manual process typically involves hands-on involvement from a member of the Information Security team and may require data gathering and input into a system for managing, tracking, and reporting. Manual processes often involve data being collected in many different places and stored in many different formats. A broken process may not have roles and responsibilities clearly defined, may not be executed consistently, or may be missing steps or include steps that are not correctly executed.

2. The Information Security team is interested in automating and improving the process. Automation may reduce the amount of hands-on involvement required from a member of the Information Security team, making more time available to focus on other high-priority work. Reducing the amount of human involvement can also reduce errors. Additional advantages of automating a manual process may include the ability to keep all the data in a single, organized, repository with consistent formatting and the ability to search and manage data quickly.

3. Development work is required and occurs to transform the manual process to an automated process. Now the team has the advantages of an automated process over a manual process, but the process is still broken.

4. The broken process continues to have negative impacts even after automation. Once these negative impacts have reached a certain threshold, which may come to light as a result of a risk assessment or an audit finding, they are prioritized for fixing.

5. The process must be reviewed to identify issues, and these issues must be discussed. Roles and responsibilities as well as the steps required in the process must be discussed with process stakeholders who are responsible for executing the steps in the process. Everything should be documented to ensure that as team members change in the organization, the process is still being performed consistently and correctly. Documentation also ensures consistent and correct process execution in the case of outsourcing or off-shoring the process work.

6. After the process is fixed, additional development work must take place to translate the process fixes into the existing automated (broken) process.

There is a better way to fix and automate a broken manual process, however. The following steps are involved in the recommended approach:

1. Start with the same initial set-up: The Information Security team is managing a process that is broken and manual.

2. The broken process negatively impacts the Information Security program. After these negative impacts have reached a certain threshold, which may come to light as a result of a risk assessment or an audit finding, they are prioritized for fixing.

3. Fix the process first. Continue to perform the process manually. Even when the process is freshly fixed, perform the process manually to ensure that no additional changes must be made.

4. Once the process is fixed, documented, approved by key stakeholders, and manually operational, perform the work to automate the process.

A visual comparison of these two methods is shown in Figure 8.

The second, recommended approach achieves the same result in only three steps rather than five. Two key advantages to fixing a process before automating has two key advantages: less work and better security.

Security organizations usually have more work to do than resources to do it. This recommended approach saves time, resources, and money because development work is done only once, instead of twice. The advantage of less work is depicted in Figure 9.

In the first approach, time passes while the process is still broken. During this time, steps may not be executed consistently or correctly, roles and responsibilities may not

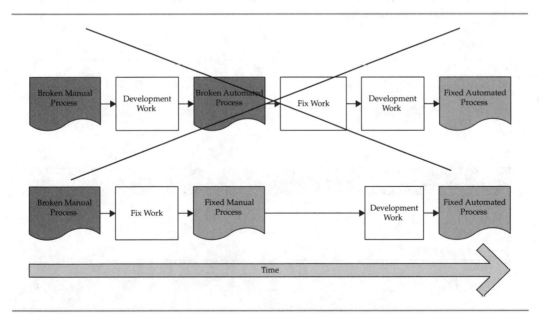

Figure 8.   Comparison of two methods for fixing and automating a broken process

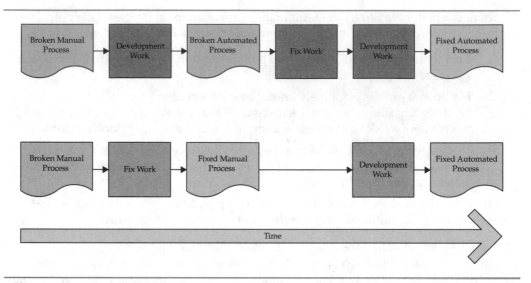

Figure 9.   Advantage #1

be clear, and the security work intended to occur may not be happening at the level desired by the Information Security team. The process remains broken for longer in the first approach, while in the second the process is improved more quickly. Even if the process is manual for some period of time, better security is being achieved for a longer period of time using the second, recommended approach. The better security advantage is depicted in Figure 10.

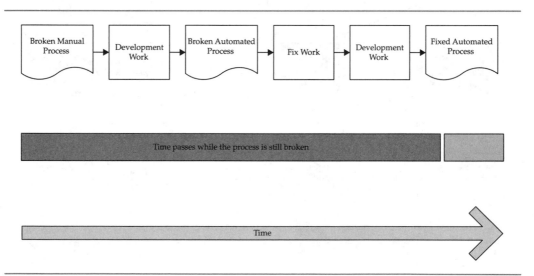

Figure 10.   Better security

Lesson Learned: Don't Wait
for Perfect Data Before Reporting

Many organizations try to get the most accurate data possible before beginning to report to anyone, even internally within the Information Security team. The benefits of this approach are clear: stakeholders will respond better to more accurate data, and having the most accurate data paints the clearest picture of the security situation. However, one major downfall can be that the work effort put toward getting better data can be never-ending, as data sources are constantly changing and updated. If a team is waiting for perfect data before beginning to report, perfect data may never be achieved and reporting the data (which is often good enough) never begins, as depicted in Figure 11.

The recommended approach with regards to data quality is to begin reporting right away. I recommend thinking carefully about the audience for reporting. It is wise to begin sharing the reporting data sooner than later (even if the data quality is poor at first) with the security team members responsible for owning the process and obtaining the data. This will often lead to the security team members responsible for cleaning the data to move more quickly in their attempts to increase the data quality, because they want to ensure that the data quality is good before the reporting reaches a larger audience.

Generally speaking, I recommend that the security metrics lead share the initial reporting containing lower quality data with the team responsible for executing the process immediately. Once clean-up is underway, these reports can also be shared with the CISO to help escalate the data cleaning process. Another approach is to discuss with the responsible team a specific date for presenting the data reports to the CISO so that he or she is aware of the timeline and will still have the opportunity to obtain better and more accurate data prior to it being presented to management.

This model of showing the reporting (or scheduling a time to show the reporting) to a team's management can be extended beyond the Information Security team if the team depends on another group for obtaining quality data. For example, in this case, if the development managers are not consistently closing out the tickets when vulnerabilities are remediated, this will show up as more vulnerabilities on the web sites and the reports will display a poorer security posture than actually exists. The metrics project lead will likely get a positive response from the development managers if the initial inaccurate data is displayed to his or her group or management.

Get
Perfect Data
This never ends!

Begin
Reporting
This never happens.

Figure 11.   Waiting for perfect data never ends

Continuous reporting generates better data.
Start reporting right away.

Figure 12.   Continuous reporting

In summary, reporting often drives up data quality. This can be a continuous cycle that constantly drives better data, because the appropriate audiences are being exposed to the latest information. This continuous cycle is shown in Figure 12.

Summary

This chapter presented a case study of a metrics project regarding web application vulnerabilities. Here is a list of the consecutive steps that were taken from beginning to end of the project:

1. We defined the scope of the project. The scope covered the web sites of several different business units under the governance of a single CTO.

2. We defined objectives using the GQM methodology.

   a. **Goal:** *The goal of this project is to understand and gain visibility into the security status of the primary customer-facing web site as well as the security status of each of the smaller business unit customer-facing web sites. This will be reported to the CTO on a monthly basis for the purpose of improving the security posture of the web sites.*

   b. **Questions:** How vulnerable is each of the functions on the primary customer facing web site? How vulnerable are each of the smaller business unit web sites?

   c. **Metric:** Number of web application vulnerabilities

3. We decided how to normalize the data across business units. We divided the number of web application security vulnerabilities for each site by the number of millions of lines of code for each site.

4. We defined a specific outcome. The goal was to achieve a 20 percent reduction in the number of web application vulnerabilities on each web site.

5. We defined a specific timeline. The 20 percent reduction in the number of web application vulnerabilities was to be completed in one year.

6. We identified ambiguous data to be an issue and cleaned up the data for proper assignment to owners.

7. We determined the best source to use for data gathering. To do this, we identified each of the steps in the process for managing web application security vulnerabilities.

   a. Discover vulnerabilities via an application vulnerability scanning system, penetration test, or other manual discovery method.

   b. Either automatically or manually enter the vulnerability information into an Information Security–managed vulnerability tracking system.

   c. Either automatically or manually identify owners for remediating the vulnerabilities and communicate what needs to be done to the owners. Ensure that this data is documented in both the Information Security–managed vulnerability tracking system and the developer bug tracking system.

   d. Track the remediation of vulnerabilities as they occur and close out tickets in the Information Security–managed vulnerability tracking system and the developer bug tracking system.

   e. Next, identify discrepancies in the process for presentation to the team responsible for managing the process.

8. We interviewed team members and other stakeholders to identify and highlight other issues in the existing process so that these could be discussed and fixed.

9. We defined and documented the process going forward and obtained buy-in from process owners and other key stakeholders involved in the process.

10. We worked with key stakeholders to perform data cleansing. This involved going through historical existing data to clean it up and following the new process moving forward to ensure that the data was entered consistently.

11. We obtained an accurate baseline count for each web site.

12. We began reporting baseline data, goals, and timelines with key stakeholders.

13. We followed up on a monthly basis with key stakeholders.

I also presented a couple lessons related to the case study material:

- Fix the process first, and then automate. This results in less work and better security.

- Do not wait for perfect data to begin reporting. Continuous reporting drives continuous improvement of the data.

PART IV | Beyond Security Metrics

CHAPTER 11 | The Security Improvement Program

Chapters 7–10 described a variety of security measurement projects, each developed using goals, questions, and metrics, and each designed to provide data and insights into the operational security of the organizations undertaking the projects. This project-centric approach to security is probably not that different from what you may be used to seeing in your own security operations—other than the specific goals for these projects, which all explicitly include measuring aspects and characteristics of IT security, and some of the methods used (not many in the security industry today are using qualitative narrative analysis as a means of understanding their security posture).

In most of the companies I visit during consulting engagements, security is managed on a project basis, whether the purpose of those projects are assessment, development, or implementation. We all understand security projects, but many of my clients complain that the project approach to security meets only some of their needs. Even organizations with strong capabilities around security and numerous projects in place for protecting systems and information find themselves in positions where risks and security incidents occur almost in spite of the organization's efforts to understand and improve its posture. This only reinforces the fact that it is impossible to eliminate risk. Instead, we must learn to manage risk and to do that we need to measure it, and we must decide how much we are willing to accept and how much we can afford to mitigate.

Moving from Projects to Programs

Projects are bounded, focused, and finite efforts that have a defined beginning and end and a relatively unambiguous set of criteria for completion and success. When you set up a project, you know what you are trying to accomplish. Maybe it is an upgrade to the latest version of a particular operating system or software application. Or it's the measurement of a particular aspect of your company's security operations, as I've been writing about. Regardless of the purpose, the nature of projects is that they start, they progress, and they end as they have throughout the history of human activity. The central characteristic of project-centric approaches to problems is that projects (and the people that run them) are not as concerned with long-term memory or a sense of context. Project thinking is about the internal management of the project, about risks of staying on time and on budget, and about controlling the scope and resources involved in completing the project and moving on to other priorities.

Programs, on the other hand, are all about memory and context and include missions, charters, visions, and strategies. Programs are broad initiatives with the goal of coordinating a variety of often independent and distinct activities (such as separate projects) and allowing these different efforts and activities to contribute to larger goals that are greater than the results of any single project. Program-centric approaches to problems are not as tactical and do not have the same granular level of visibility into daily activities. Instead, program management concentrates on managing the overall direction of an enterprise, for which each individual project may be just a single step along the path.

If that path is to maintain some semblance of forward motion, rather than just meandering in circles, you must pay attention to how each project fits into a grand scheme. One easy example comes from the military: a single squad or platoon may be trained for a very specific purpose or mission, with minimal concern for and visibility into the campaign strategy, or the larger interoperation of the military forces. But ensuring that the unit gets where it needs to be to maximize its value will require the broad coordination of many other individual units just like it. I have seen a more security-specific example in recent years around the Payment Card Industry Data Security Standard (PCI DSS), which has given many companies a program-level strategic goal (pass the next audit) that drives them to view their security projects (network segmentation, encryption strategy, policy development, and so on) in a more contextualized way.

Empirical research into the effects of IT governance and compliance programs shows that companies that have deliberately and formally instituted these programs have enjoyed increased bottom-line benefits such as increased revenue, increased customer satisfaction and retention, and improved cost and delivery of products and services. If you think about it, this makes intuitive sense. If you take the time and effort to figure out exactly what you are doing and why, chances are you will see where you can improve, and then you'll begin to do those things better. As IT security grows into a mature industry function, more emphasis will be placed on how security management also drives profit, productivity, and operational effectiveness even in those areas that are not directly security related.

Managing Security Measurement with a Security Improvement Program

I began discussing the Security Improvement Program (SIP) in the context of Security Process Management (SPM) in Chapter 4. The SIP is designed to contextualize and guide security measurement so that the metrics and data that result from particular efforts at measuring security operations are used strategically as well as tactically. In Figure 4-3 of that chapter, the SIP is shown as a string of security measurement projects that are connected over time. In this model, each project is part of a knowledge loop in which the efforts and results of the previous project are explicitly used to inform and guide the next project. Like many of the ideas in this book, this is by no means a revolutionary concept and is a central tenet of organizational knowledge management. But after years of managing and consulting on security, I've found that capturing and reusing this knowledge is not typically prioritized in security organizations. I've seen repeated security engagements that stretch over years in which the connections between the engagements, even those that are similar or repeated efforts, are never explored. Instead, these projects are just one more box on a checklist of annual activities that need to be completed, an attitude that speaks as much to problems with security vendors as it does to the companies engaging them.

The Chapter 4 image of the SIP is overly simple in itself, focusing on the connections between repeated projects over time. A more accurate, but still very simple, expansion of this concept can be found in Figure 11-1, which shows the relationships among multiple projects during several years. In this visualization, a single security measurement project (SMP) conducted in 2007 leads to a repeat of the project in subsequent years, but it also spawns related projects that are specifically driven by the findings of the first. As more projects are added, the information flows between the projects increase, and the result begins to show the real complexity of holistic security practices. The most important aspects of the SIP concept are the arrows in the diagram, representing the knowledge relationships between individual projects. Projects are the way that things get done in an enterprise, but programs are the way that these efforts are made to represent something larger than the sum of the parts. In IT security measurement, SMPs can provide data and insights, but it is only through the programmatic approach of the SIP that these individual measurement efforts can be used to measure and manage security as a real business process.

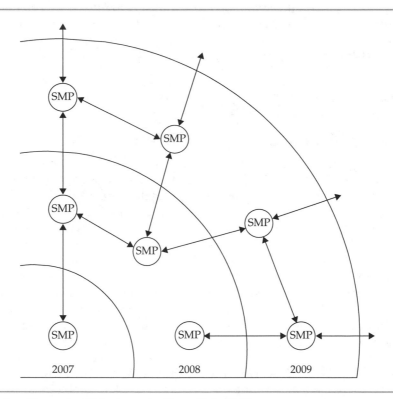

Figure 11-1.   Expanded SIP concept with multiple SMPs over several years

Governance of Security Measurement

What I am proposing in the SIP is a method of governance over your security metrics activities. Defining, managing, and improving the collaborations and connections between SMPs is different from operating those projects. Governance is about big picture management, and at an even larger level it is currently a hot-button topic in industry, as companies are increasingly being asked to be more accountable for the ways that they run their businesses by everyone from governments, to industry groups, to shareholders and customers. Governance is often associated with regulatory compliance and the management of public institutions or publicly traded corporations, but governance has a broader definition with regard to effective strategy development and execution. Nevertheless, as I noted earlier in this chapter, evidence shows that effective governance at a high level can have definite bottom-line impact on organizational effectiveness at all levels.

If you consider an individual SMP, such as those that I have described in the preceding chapters, you will find the goals, questions, and metrics that you use to define, limit, and bound the project. A main purpose of the GQM model is to create smaller, more manageable projects to avoid scope creep and to make the measurements and data involved in each project as meaningful and as specific as possible. In an SMP, you drill deep, but you do not focus broadly, which has advantages when you are exploring a security question in detail. But if you are trying to improve security across the complex and interrelated elements of enterprise-wide security, this focus on the specific can become a disadvantage if you have not thought about how you will pull all those results together. You will end up with a lot of interesting specialist data and information, but not much knowledge about what it means for managing organizational risks as a whole. The resulting uncertainties that exist between projects and measurement can produce significant risks. Identifying a lot of dots is not the same thing as connecting those dots to create a meaningful picture. Worse, if all you know are your own dots, you may make the mistake of assuming that you have the complete picture when you really are taking a parochial view. Governance is about getting high enough above the details to see the patterns, risks, and opportunities that are not visible at the lower levels of detail.

Governance, at heart, is about strategy and does not apply to any single thing. As you implement your security metrics program, you need to assess not only how you are measuring those aspects of security that you feel are important, but also how you decided what was important and how those decisions fit into your overall security strategy. I can't tell you how to prioritize your particular challenges or how to decide what is important to your organization beyond the most basic common sense advice. What I can tell you is that governance is about defining and documenting those decisions so that if anyone does ask, you aren't left looking like a deer in the headlights.

Defining what constitutes risk and security within an organization is one of those things that often may seem so basic that many people do not even bother to do it. Many security managers have been unable to give me a specific answer to the question, What is your risk? Of course, they have a lot of ideas about problems or challenges that they face, but not enough formal definition or analysis of those problems and challenges to begin to measure them to any degree of precision. The purpose of implementing a formal SIP in support of your security metrics program is to provide the necessary governance structures to help guarantee that the SMPs you undertake will support more than just the tactical goals and questions that make up the projects.

The SIP: It's Still about the Data

If your SMPs were about collecting and analyzing data in support of the goals and questions that you established for each project, then the SIP is about making that data more useful to more people in more contexts. IT security metrics have at least two values: The first value is to the immediate measurement project that needs the data to meet a project goal. The second value is to the project teams, managers, and others who will benefit from the metrics data later when they replicate the project, conduct a related project, or seek to understand broader security issues by examining case studies and historical evidence.

Replicated or Repeated Projects

In many cases, SMPs are not one-time projects, but are repeated on a regular basis, such as in the case of vulnerability or risk assessments, monthly or quarterly reviews, or decision support projects around budget or staffing. You would think that, of all the examples here, these types of repeated projects would benefit from governance structures of the sort proposed by the SIP. After all, these projects are expected and scheduled and often are conducted by the same people over some time period.

Unfortunately, even these projects are all too often treated as stand-alone efforts, more or less disconnected from what went before or what may come in the future. Part of the problem can be a checklist approach to security, in which a list of annual activities exists, based either on a formal compliance requirement or on various definitions of best practice that mandate certain activities will be completed regularly. When projects are conducted for these reasons, the motivation to understand what the project actually accomplished (knowing what tasks have been completed and the resulting changes, as opposed to completing a task and checking off the box) is far less than if the project were part of a security improvement strategy. I've seen many examples of repeated security assessments in which the final deliverable each time is virtually the same as the previous versions, indicating that the real security benefit was the ability to say an assessment had been completed.

A SIP approach, on the other hand, would focus not on the immediate findings of any single project, but on the attempt to determine whether or not security was changing as a result of all SMP efforts. By measuring the lack of progress in correcting or improving security problems among projects, the SIP can provide valuable insight into the real functions of your security operations.

Follow-on or Related Projects

An SMP, particularly one that is bounded and specific, will often lead to questions that are obvious, but that are not addressed directly by the metrics and data that emerge from that particular SMP effort. Several examples of this sort of follow-on project opportunity existed in the projects discussed in earlier chapters. In these situations, two capabilities need to be in place if the opportunity is to be effectively addressed:

- A capability for driving the questions and requirements from the first SMP into a new, separate SMP

- A capability for aligning and mapping the results of the related SMP among projects

The need for effective measurement governance in these situations is particularly important, because the projects in question may cross functional or organizational boundaries. If a penetration test, for instance, discovered widespread availability of intellectual property on user laptops or workstations, then an obvious follow-on question might be this: What process deficiencies were contributing to this lack of protection of sensitive information? The network security team, however, might have no authority or ability to drive a security measurement project through other business units to determine why this information was so prevalent. In these types of situations, a dedicated SIP capability with appropriate management support could step in to ensure that the appropriate actions were taken.

Historical or Exploratory Projects

It has been said that history does not repeat itself, but it rhymes. In the companies with which I have worked for more than two decades, new initiatives are always being designed to improve this or that element of operations. If you stay with one organization long enough, you will invariably begin to come across initiatives that make you ask, "Didn't we do this five years ago, when it was called Project X?" The same holds true for security. As technologies change and evolve, it is as if we come back around full-circle to challenges and solutions that are eerily reminiscent of things we have seen before. Sometimes the repetition is direct as staff turns over and old ideas are introduced as new initiatives by people who don't realize that their ideas have already been proposed and implemented. Or the goals and ideas are new, but past activities can offer instruction on risks and benefits that can make an impact on the new efforts. In both cases, without easy access to the data and results of previous attempts, progress can move very slowly.

A deliberate application of SIP principles can provide institutional memory and a repository of data that can help security grow more agile by reusing and recycling knowledge across projects and over time. From general reviews of past efforts prior to beginning any new project, to exploring untapped areas of security improvement, a well-documented and deployed SIP can offer benefits in this regard. At a more general level, the SIP can also help to break down silos between security functions and project teams and encourage more active collaboration and experience-sharing both within the security group and across the entire organization. Developing such institutional knowledge and awareness is at the core of corporate improvement research and many initiatives around quality and sustainable growth across many industries. I cover some of this research in Chapter 12.

Requirements for a SIP

By following several key principles when setting up an effective SIP to govern and support security measurement activities, you'll help ensure that the efforts you make will actually improve your organization's security rather than simply collect data about it. Many of these principles are common sense necessities for any organized effort, but with careful thought, you can make them specific to the needs and challenges of your metrics program.

The SIP concept operates on three core principles:

- Documentation of security measurement projects and activities
- Sharing of security measurement results
- Collaboration between projects and over time

Before You Begin

As with other components of the SPM framework, you should explore several specific considerations prior to beginning the work. Your SIP activities will benefit from your understanding of how these considerations affect your initiatives and program before you start implementing them.

Management Support and Sponsorship

As with just about any security initiative—in reality or on paper—management support is a key issue. If management does not directly support your efforts, your prospects for long-term success are limited. Every high-level framework you might consider applying to your security program—from ISO 27000, to Control Objectives for Information and Related Technology (COBIT), to Information Technology Infrastructure Library (ITIL)—emphasizes management support and commitment as a core component of success. Yet such commitment can be hard to come by, and it can be just as easily lost to other priorities.

My general advice on management support is to trade ambition for stability. I would rather have director or senior-manager support of a security initiative, based on regular conversations and involvement, than a memo from the CIO I have met once promising that the company will make security a top-five priority (after which I hear nothing until the next annual memo). Even if the support of middle management limits the scope of what I may accomplish immediately, it makes it far more likely that I will be able to show the continuous improvement and sometimes exploratory leaps in insight that can eventually demonstrate value to that CIO in the financial and business terms that will get his or her attention. I recommend that you find a sponsor at the highest level possible who will actively and regularly support the SIP. This will often be the CISO, but it can be a lower level manager or even a project lead. Many improvement programs start with the efforts of a single individual.

The great thing about an effective SIP is that it can function as narrowly or as broadly as is necessary so long as the three core principles are met. As the SIP grows, the ability to adhere to these principles can grow quite complex, of course, but for most security metrics programs, implementing a SIP can be quite manageable for a security operations group. Setting up documentation, sharing, and collaboration practices does require a commitment to the sort of program-level thinking and activities that the SIP represents.

Staffing and Resources to Support the SIP

Making the SIP effective will require that it be appropriately supported in terms of staff and resources, although the requirements for such support do not need to be onerous. Much of what is accomplished in the SIP is about making sure that information is made available to a larger audience. This takes organization, documentation, and a focus on actually doing the sharing rather than simply talking about it. Today's corporate environments are embracing collaboration and information sharing to an unprecedented degree, making these goals in the development of the program easier to accomplish.

Staffing and resource allocation for the SIP is very much dependent on the structure of the organization, the size and makeup of the security group, and the skills available among existing staff. It is unlikely, at least in the beginning, that a dedicated employee will be available for managing SIP-related activities. But at least one individual should be responsible for ensuring that the results of specific measurement projects are properly documented and stored. Just as the assignment of project leads ensures central responsibility for the activities around completing a project, the security improvement program lead will be responsible for ensuring that individual projects are coordinated, that the appropriate documentation is generated and stored for future use, and that reporting on the results of the program is accomplished at regular intervals.

One strategy for developing SIP staffing is to approach your company's existing knowledge management (KM) team, if one is available. These groups already understand the importance of information sharing as well as techniques and tools that may be in place to facilitate such sharing. If your organization does not have a formal KM function, you should explore how company information is disseminated in other ways, such as via content management systems or the corporate intranet. The groups that manage these infrastructures can also be important sources of advice on how to create, store, and manage your SIP elements.

Definitions of SIP Elements and Objectives

Just as the security measurement projects you create depend on definitions and objectives to be tactically successful, the SIP requires that you make some formal efforts to understand what it is you are trying to accomplish strategically. These definitions will provide the frame story and the context within which your measurement project activities will align and contribute toward the larger goals of the program. In some ways, SIP-level definitions parallel the GQM model used to set up an SMP. But instead of answering specific questions about security by collecting and analyzing data, the SIP will attempt to determine how well those answers are supporting the larger security strategy across projects.

Defining Security   If we parse out the term *security improvement program*, we must formally define several elements if we are to understand what we are trying to accomplish. I've already defined *program*: a systematic approach to managing multiple projects and initiatives so that the results of these activities are documented, shared, and successfully leveraged across different teams and efforts over time. But what about the other two elements? Let's begin with security. How is it defined? When you talk about security, what do you mean? Security is one of those terms that is used so often and in so many contexts that it has begun to lose any specific meaning. Security is simply what we do. If you are responsible for a DMZ, security is your assurance that no one can penetrate that perimeter. If you are the HR specialist writing the company's acceptable use policy for the network, security may be the assurance that your employees will not use the network for prohibited activities and, if they do, it can entail your ability to take action and protect the company from liability.

Local definitions are just a fact of life in the security world, which can become highly specialized, but it makes it difficult to measure security outside of one's own area. As you set up a SIP to manage and coordinate projects that may originate in a variety of functional areas, you'll find it increasingly necessary to define precisely what you mean by *security*. In the insider threat case study described later in the chapter, *security* is formally defined as the likelihood that a company employee will be the root cause of a security incident, whether intentional or otherwise. This definition of security allows a SIP to be put into place that will coordinate and manage the efforts of multiple SMPs that focus on preventing internal security incidents. Whether the measurement project involves people, processes, or technologies becomes secondary to the question of whether the project measures the capability of someone inside the company to become a security problem.

Defining Improvement   You also need to define the concept of *improvement*. Security managers often talk of security as more of a zero-sum game, in which either there is a security incident (failure) or there is not (success). This binary view of security has done a lot of damage to security programs by discouraging more nuanced approaches to protection.

By way of example, I have been involved in many vulnerability assessments. One frequent argument during these assessments arises when the team is able to use a vulnerability to gain root access to a system, completely compromising it. A common temptation is to play up the fact that the security on that system allowed complete compromise, regardless of whether or not the system actually had any important information on it or was in a position to damage the organization conducting the assessment. In many cases, the nature of vulnerability testing is such that the testers have no way of knowing the actual impact of a particular vulnerability, as they function at a definitional level of security that deals only with whether or not the configuration of the system allows it to be compromised. As a result, improvement can be measured only at the level of technical vulnerabilities on individual systems, rather than regarding actual business impact. This tends to create a myopic and incomplete perception of security. Using this criteria, security remains reactive and backward-looking and the organization has little opportunity to get ahead of the problem.

Definitions of improvement must be considered in a wider context when constructing your SIP objectives. Improvement is not just about correcting existing problems, but identifying the root causes of those problems so that you can reduce the chance that they will be repeated in different forms. Improvement is also about establishing the baselines and SIP-level metrics that allow you to determine whether you are making improvement process and by what degree. In the case study that follows later in the chapter, security improvements regarding insider threats were defined using several different baselines that allowed the organization to determine whether or not progress was being made.

Documenting Your Security Measurement Projects

The first core principle of building an effective SIP revolves around the need to have reliable, documented information available on all the security measurement activities that you conduct. This is a challenge, particularly since most security programs do not have formal documentation for many basic operational activities, much less for the various projects and implementations that are done in support of those operations. The reasons for this lack of documentation can range from simple lack of time to the perception that documentation is nothing but a bureaucratic waste of time. But whatever the excuse, a lack of sufficient documentation regarding your security program and activities indicates a lack of maturity in those activities.

Supporting Capability Maturity

Capability maturity as a concept has developed primarily out of defense research initiatives. Capability maturity has been applied both to military operations as well as to the development of systems and software, and many models and frameworks exist for discussing capabilities maturity. The concept is to move from ad hoc, unmanaged, and conflicting processes and activities, which are characterized as immature, to increasingly mature processes and activities that are standardized, formally managed and measured, and synchronized through collaboration and coordination. The level of maturity exhibited by an organization or function defines how well it can learn from its own efforts and how effectively it can apply those lessons to continuous improvement and progress.

The most well-known example from an IT perspective is probably the Capability Maturity Model and its subsequent versions developed at the Software Engineering Institute, a U.S. Department of Defense funded institution run by Carnegie Mellon University. The Software Engineering Institute's Capability Maturity Model has also been adapted by others, including as a component of the Control Objectives for Information and related Technology (COBIT) framework developed by Information Systems Audit and Control Association (ISACA) for IT governance. Defense institutions have also applied capability maturity concepts to the operation of command and control systems for military and intelligence activities.

But capabilities maturity is not just about coordinating projects or military campaigns. The organization of knowledge and scientific progress is also a measure of capabilities maturity and has been a foundation of scientific progress for centuries.

The field of library and information science (LIS), for example, has a primary mission of organizing and disseminating information to ensure that entire communities and societies can increase their effectiveness and growth.

The Basics of SMP Documentation

Most security projects are documented to some degree, although measurement projects will perhaps demand more contextualized information than security upgrades or the implementation of a new system. Fortunately, if you are building GQM templates for your measurement projects, you will already have a basic documentation component completed. GQM forces you to define your scope and purpose and to develop formal mechanisms for gathering and analyzing data. At the very least, the GQM template will represent a record of a project's purpose and criteria for success.

As an SMP progresses, more opportunities for documenting the progress of the project can come from many different sources:

- Project team e-mails and meeting notes
- Documents, memos, and project presentations
- Analysis and project findings
- Feedback from stakeholders and project team members

You should consider up front how the project team will manage and collect the data necessary to document the SMP sufficiently, as this will help prevent your having to reconstruct that documentation after the fact from people's memories and other less-reliable sources. Basic documentation components of the SIP might include the following:

- A SIP *overview template* to identify, describe, and define the objectives of the improvement program
- A *project catalog* to track the goals, questions, and metrics associated with individual SMPs
- A *metrics catalog* to document the kinds and types of measurement activities you have undertaken
- An *analysis catalog* that contains findings, lessons learned, and opportunities and challenges that might prove useful to other measurement project teams
- *Project journals* and other knowledge-capture tools to facilitate the collection of project-specific information not contained in catalogs or final project reports

Sharing Your Security Measurement Results

After projects have been documented, information collected during and as a result of the project must be made available to appropriate audiences. Given the sensitivity of specific security-related data, it may not be appropriate simply to throw the results of the vulnerability assessment on to the company intranet. But there is also no value in hiding or compartmentalizing project information that could actually support other security measurement activities.

Considerations for Sharing Measurement Data

At minimum, general information about projects, metrics, analyses, and lessons learned should be made widely available as part of the SIP. I would even recommend sharing this information beyond the security team. Visibility into security operations can help non-security–related stakeholders better understand how they can benefit from as well as support the organization's information protection strategies. By creating general catalog data of the type of security work being done, you can ensure that participation in the security process can be achieved without exposing details that might pose an additional threat to IT systems. Increased transparency can also help other stakeholders with responsibilities for compliance and corporate risk management to engage with the security team more easily. The bottom line is that sharing security measurement results does not mean sharing them only with the security function of the organization.

No matter how you choose to share your metrics results, some considerations will usually apply:

- Where will the documents be stored?
- How will documents be organized? Will they be indexed and searchable?
- What access controls will be placed on the documents? What approval process for access will need to be developed?
- How long will documents be stored and maintained? Will they fall under the corporate records retention schedule and will they be archived?
- How will documents be traced and their authenticity established?

Tools for Document and Information Sharing

Document storage and management falls under the larger topic of enterprise content management, which is outside the scope of this book. Most companies today employ enterprise-content management systems of varying levels of sophistication, ranging from static web pages and file shares up through full-blown enterprise content-management suites that also include functionality for collaboration and workflow management. The tools you choose for managing documents are less important than your commitment to manage them. Simple solutions using a dedicated e-mail alias combined with file sharing can serve to provide an adequate platform for sharing and disseminating SMP content so long as that content is there.

Collaborating Across Projects and Over Time

Like document management, collaboration has become an industry unto itself, with a variety of techniques and tools that are themselves the subjects of implementation frameworks and trade books. A lot of research in recent years has focused on how to foster and encourage more collaboration in the workplace, and while technology can play an important role in encouraging collaborative behavior, most agree that technology cannot create a collaborative environment. Collaboration is, at heart, a social function and requires that users be encouraged to share and explore with one another (and trained on how to do so effectively and appropriately) to be effective. The point is less about whether you choose to collaborate on security projects by e-mail, wiki, or collaborative working environment systems that incorporate all of these and more into one software solution. Instead, you should be focusing on getting your organization to embrace the value of creating, disseminating, and exchanging information and content.

Fostering a Collaborative Security Measurement Environment

Before technology even comes into the picture, you can encourage more collaboration within your SIP in several ways. Remember that the point of the SIP is to increase the awareness of specific measurement projects and activities, to include project teams that may be conducting similar projects over time and to make new projects more meaningful and more effective. In academic and industry research environments, where the goal is to increase and improve knowledge about specific issues or questions, these principles are deeply ingrained. I've suggested earlier in the book that the research program metaphor can add benefit to a security metrics program. In the SIP, the primary task is to synthesize and share the knowledge from a variety of individual measurement efforts, and a research approach can prove doubly valuable.

Collaboration can be encouraged in several ways:

- **Management support**   Management should visibly and explicitly support collaboration and provide encouragement not only in words, but also by providing collaboration tools and training employees in how to share information more effectively.

- **Open documentation**   The document repositories and catalogs I mentioned have a much greater chance of being used by others when they are easy to access. Working with your company's content management team can help identify ways that you can safely post and advertise your security metrics data.

- **"Silo busting"**   Taking a proactive stance on reaching out to other individuals and teams, both within IT security and elsewhere in the organization, can make a big impact on removing barriers to collaboration.

- **Making collaboration natural**   Adding collaboration to everyday activities such as meeting agendas and project plans can be useful for keeping the need to create and share content at the forefront during everyday activities.

Tools for Collaboration

We are fortunate in that we live and work in an environment that sees new collaboration tools appear every day. A great selection of open source and freeware tools are also available, and they can be used to build or supplement your SIP collaboration needs. A full list of available tools is not possible here, but you likely already have the following basics available within your environment that can be used to increase your collaboration capabilities:

- **Instant communications**   E-mail and instant messaging (IM) have become ubiquitous in most corporate environments (and if you have an IT security program, you probably have corporate e-mail and IM). If you use these tools as a primary means of collaboration, be sure to consider how you will archive and share the content that you create so that it remains available.

- **Web logs and video sharing**   Some enterprises have begun to encourage employees to use web logs, or blogs, and even shared video to communicate, create content, and share experiences through collaboration. If your organization has an internal capability for blogging, consider setting up a security metrics blog for one or more audiences to share your metrics results.

- **Brainstorming and mind mapping**   Software for documenting the relationships between concepts and organizing projects and concepts has become increasingly sophisticated and robust, allowing you to explore central concepts through a hierarchy of related ideas.

- **Wikis and peer review systems**   These tools allow people to collaborate by making it much easier for individuals to create, edit, and review the work of others while ensuring version control and the ability to track changes and progress over time.

Measuring the SIP

The SIP is subject to measurement and evaluation just like any other aspect of your security, and you should be considering ways to assess the effectiveness of your SIP-related actions. You can view SIP performance in two ways: how well those activities related to the improvement program are functioning, and the resulting effects on your security as a whole.

Security Improvement Is Habit Forming

Security will not magically improve on its own, even if you have an arsenal of techniques and tools available and at your disposal. Like losing weight, quitting smoking, or any other fundamental behavioral change, improvement is achieved only by replacing old habits with new ones. Security improvement is about building new organizational habits on a day-to-day basis. The best places to start, then, are those day-to-day activities that make up our security programs. If the SIP is a "big picture" process that is considered only at the end of projects, it will be less effective than if it is embedded in daily activities such as staff meetings, project plans, and performance reviews. The more people are responsible for contributing to the SIP by incorporating documentation and collaboration into their individual security activities and projects, the more successful you will be in improving security from the ground up over time.

Is the SIP Working?

Measuring the effectiveness of the SIP involves more specific and program-oriented metrics. The object of measurement here is how often the SIP is used and in what capacity. The point of improvement program metrics is to ascertain whether or not the daily activities and habits that contribute to long-term security improvement are being accomplished. Examples of these metrics include the following:

- How many SMPs (ratio) include a formal review of previous, related measurement projects?

- How many SMPs (number or ratio) have been documented and made available as content to other groups?

- How often are SIP-related activities or metrics included in meeting agendas? In project plans? In management briefings?

- How many employees have security improvement objectives formally included in their job descriptions or performance plans?

Is Security Improving?

Of course, the main purpose for implementing the SIP is to improve security by coordinating the efforts of multiple projects and initiatives over time. To do this, metrics must be in place that can be used to judge whether or not the SIP is having the intended and desired effect. If the SIP is properly designed and the concepts of both security and improvement appropriately defined, then the baselines needed to determine whether security is indeed improving security should already be in place.

Security improvement can be measured only over time. This emphasizes the importance of making sure that SIP activities are consistent and conducted regularly so that a store of longitudinal data can be built and correlations made between projects. If previous project results are not revisited and reviewed, and then measured against the established baseline to determine whether they had an effect, then only static, single-point inferences will ever be achievable. Ongoing comparative program review requires commitment and repeated effort; this is not easy to accomplish in any organization, but it is at the heart of true, continuous improvement of security.

While specific metrics are more difficult to illustrate, given the fact that baselines depend on the needs and measurements of your unique program, you should be looking for the following types of evidence that the SIP (and by extension your SMPs) are having an effect:

- Is the baseline changing over time? Is the quality, quantity, or character of your measured security activities different after each successive project? Is the difference significant (not just a product of random chance or noise)?

- Are more projects being added, reviewed, and incorporated into the SIP? Are the measurement activities in which you are engaging leading to repeated activities as well as inspiring new activities that take your security measurement farther and provide more insights?

- Is security becoming more visible within your organization? Are silos being overcome and security value being better articulated to other business stakeholders?

- Do your security measurement activities reduce your uncertainty, and by extension your risk? Are the results of your security metrics and your SIP allowing you to make more informed decisions (including decisions in which security traditionally did not participate)?

Case Study: A SIP for Insider Threat Measurement

To demonstrate how a SIP may be constructed, consider the case of ACME Inc., a company that became concerned with its insider threat posture after experiencing a potentially damaging security incident. Following the termination of an employee with the IT department, the company received reports that the individual was approaching the firm's competitors with proprietary information and intellectual property. The individual was hoping to sell the information or use it to find a new job.

An investigation into the incident revealed that the former employee was offering very sensitive information that had not been part of his job, and some of the information dated from after his termination. It turned out that the employee still had access to the company's network and was using that access to break into company systems and steal data. While the employee's official access had been discontinued upon termination, he had used guest accounts to access the network and had been able to find vulnerable internal systems that he compromised and used to steal company data. The investigation also revealed that the employee had been motivated in part because of financial debts incurred through an addiction to gambling. This gambling problem had also been a root cause of the performance issues that had resulted in the employee being fired, which had motivated the individual to "get some payback" from the company.

The investigation of the security incident caused the company to revisit its security operations on a number of levels, and several security measurement projects were developed and proposed:

- Identifying internal network vulnerabilities that could allow access to the network and the theft of proprietary data or other problems

- Revisiting the security policy architecture and compliance requirements for protecting the organization's data

- Assessing security awareness and the internal protective culture of the company to build better training programs

- Proposing projects to assess other vectors of data loss, such as e-mail, and to measure the effectiveness and use of the company's employee assistance program, which might have helped mitigate the employee's gambling problem before it became acute

Given the interrelated nature of these SMP activities, the company also developed a SIP to coordinate the results and to ensure that a holistic and comprehensive approach was taken to combating future insider threats. The SIP was assigned sponsors and an owner and was used strategically to manage the various insider threat projects involved. The objective of the SIP was to ensure that the component initiatives and projects maintained their context and could be used to build organizational knowledge and experience. A SIP overview document was developed and a storage repository set up through a protected wiki so that various project teams could share ideas and post their results. The SIP overview document for the program is shown in Table 11-1.

SIP Document Number	SIP2008.03-01
SIP Description	This SIP covers security measurement projects related to insider threat management for ACME Corporation.
SIP Executive Sponsor(s)	John A. – CISO Lisa B. – VP, Corporate Risk Management Henry C. – VP, Human Resources
SIP Owner	Susan D. – Data Protection Analyst
SIP Objective	Identify most likely risks and highest impact threat vectors for insider security compromise <u>Baseline</u>: number and type of identified insider threat risks <u>Baseline</u>: business impacts for threat vectors
SIP Objective	Assess current level of insider threat activity <u>Baseline</u>: number of insider-originated security incidents <u>Baseline</u>: ratio of intentional to unintentional incidents
SIP Objective	Identify root causes of insider security risks and potential mitigation strategies <u>Baseline</u>: number and type of identified root causes of insider risks <u>Baseline</u>: effectiveness of insider threat mitigation
Review Schedule	Quarterly
Review Process	Progress report at CISO quarterly review

Table 11-1.   SIP Overview Document for ACME Corporation Insider Threat Improvement Program

In addition to the overview document, the SIP provided catalogs of various projects, metrics, and findings that were also communicated over the wiki. Updates on the individual SMPs were provided through normal project management and reporting channels, and the SIP owner communicated the program-level results and findings to the CISO during quarterly reviews. The relationship between projects was captured in a detailed project catalog document, shown in part in Table 11-2.

SIP Document Number	SIP2008.03-03
General Project Data	Completed Projects: 3 Active Projects: 1 Proposed Projects: 2
Security Measurement Project A	
Project Name / Number	Internal Network Vulnerability Assessment SMP2007.05
Project Sponsor / Lead	Sponsor: John A. – CISO Lead: Susan D. – Data Protection Analyst
Project Begin / End	Begin: 04.09.2007 End: 04.27.2007
SMP GQM Goal(s)	Identify and understand security vulnerabilities existing on internally networked systems, including severity of vulnerabilities and risk of compromise, from the perspective of ACME InfoSec operations.
SMP GQM Questions / Metrics	Question: How many internal ACME systems are vulnerable to attack from the network? Metric: number of systems with existing security vulnerabilities, based on automated vendor scans Question: How severe are internal system vulnerabilities? Metric: mean CVSS scores and CVSS standard deviation by system Question: What are the business risks involved with compromise of internal networked systems? Metric: expert confidence intervals for system vulnerability business impacts

Table 11-2.   SIP Project Catalog for ACME Corporation Insider Threat Improvement Program

SMP Findings	Numerous, and in some cases systemic, vulnerabilities were identified on internal systems. Severity levels were established and mean CVSS scores were relatively high. Business risks and impacts were considered high. For complete report details contact SMP lead Susan D.
Lessons Learned and Proposed Follow-on SMPs	This was an initial project to begin formally conducting vulnerability tests on the internal systems. Follow-on SMPs were proposed to repeat the vulnerability tests annually and measure improvement against the identified vulnerability findings.
Security Measurement Project B	
Project Name / Number	Security Policy Architecture and Compliance Assessment SMP2008.03
Security Measurement Project C	
Project Name / Number	Security Awareness and Culture Survey SMP2008.09
Security Measurement Project ...	

Table 11-2.   SIP Project Catalog for ACME Corporation Insider Threat Improvement Program (*Continued*)

The SIP owner also found it useful to maintain a visual map of the relationships and connections among projects. Using an open source mind-mapping application, FreeMind, she was able to build graphical diagrams of the various projects and their status, components, sponsors, and interconnections. An example of such a diagram in FreeMind is shown in Figure 11-2.

The goal of the SIP, both in the case of ACME and in general, is to create and guide the organizational habits that keep an objective present and visible in the face of complex activity. The concept is not new or particularly revolutionary, but developing a coordination program to help manage projects and encourage cross-functional documentation and collaboration is absolutely necessary in order to transform your security into an effective business process.

Of course, there is always a level of coordination in any security organization, and no project is ever conducted completely in a vacuum. But in nearly every security environment I have experienced, the level of cross-project collaboration and documentation is less than optimal. In most cases, companies struggle with effectively documenting

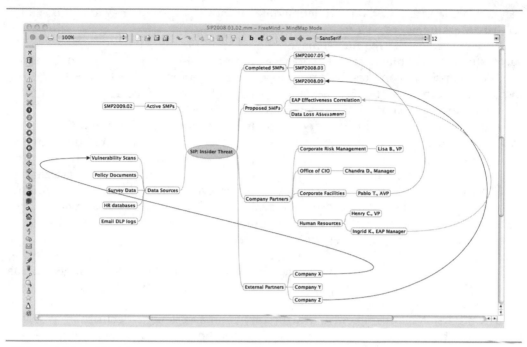

Figure 11-2.   Mind map of Insider Threat SIP developed in FreeMind

and managing single projects and initiatives, let alone understanding and identifying the ways that these projects interrelate and draw upon one another at a strategic level.

The SIP phase of the SPM Framework is an attempt to add a level of strategic thinking to an otherwise highly tactical and dynamic set of activities. Your SIP efforts do not need to be incredibly complex or sophisticated to be successful. Much more important is that they be conscious, consistent, and continuous over time in managing the increasing and varied levels of information and data that emerge from your security metrics projects.

Summary

The SIP component of the SPM Framework is meant to guide you from the tactical management of individual security measurement projects to the strategic management of groups of SMPs devoted toward a unified objective or initiative. The SIP approach still places primary importance on the metrics and data collected during the SMP process, but it seeks to contextualize the results of multiple measurement efforts and to extract insights not only from the individual results of these efforts but also from the relationships and interactions among them. These insights can include higher level security knowledge based on correlating data, or they can result in new directions for security measurement goals and activities.

Implementing a SIP requires some forethought and planning if the program is to be successful. Issues of management support and appropriate staff and resource allocation should be considered and resolved prior to starting the effort. Similarly, the SIP requires that you give careful thought to the definitions and objectives of security necessary to define the strategy that the SIP is being used to coordinate.

Primary SIP activities include documentation, information storage and sharing, and collaboration over time. In many ways, the SIP applies principles of knowledge management to the security metrics program, and you can enhance your efforts by engaging existing content and knowledge management teams within your organization to help you set up and drive your improvement program. By establishing appropriate documentation, making that information available to the organization, and encouraging its use and reuse, the SIP can become a powerful tool of organizational learning and capability maturity. A variety of tools, both commercial and open source, can be used to help you manage SIP activities, ranging from traditional communication techniques such as e-mail and instant messaging, to new information sharing tools such as blogs, wikis, and groupware applications that are available to encourage and enable collaboration.

The SIP itself is also subject to measurement and assessment. Security process management and improvement is less about revolutionary leaps and much more about the changing of daily organizational habits and the creation of ongoing action that is regular and stable, keeping security improvement as a constant top-of-mind concern. Metrics can be developed as a part of the SIP that not only track the effectiveness of the program, but also use baseline data from repeated SMPs to establish whether or not your organization's security is improving over time compared with the definitions and goals that you have established.

Further Reading

Archibald, R. *Managing High-Technology Programs and Projects*, 3rd Ed. Wiley, 2003.

Rosen, E. *The Culture of Collaboration*. Red Ape Publishing, 2007.

CHAPTER 12

Learning Security: Different Contexts for Security Process Management

I have come a long way from my initial descriptions of how we measure IT security today and why we should try to do it better. The Security Process Management (SPM) Framework is one way of structuring your security metrics efforts, and, if implemented correctly and conscientiously, the framework can seriously improve your ability to understand and protect information assets. But this can also be said of many other frameworks and models for security. The secret is not in the strategy, but in the correct and conscientious implementation of that strategy and then living and tweaking the strategy day in and day out over time. The SPM Framework is my take on how to measure IT security effectively, based on my years of experience, research, and interpretation.

Even if you accept some or all of what I've proposed and you decide to employ those elements of IT security metrics within your own organization and environment, your experiences, knowledge, and interpretation will be unique. Your organization will be unique, as will the culture in which you measure security and the resources that you have available to institute a metrics program.

Since the SPM framework requires that you not only embrace metrics and data, but that your organization embraces learning from those metrics and data, you will need to decide how best to adapt measurement and metrics to your unique challenges. Everyone has his or her own way of learning. To make your security metrics powerful and successful, you must determine how to articulate the true value of your data and your findings. It is not enough to describe your security—you have to convince others in the organization to make decisions based on those descriptions and analyses and to incorporate your insights into their own operations.

Organizational Learning

Much academic and industry research has examined the ways that organizations learn and adapt to their changing environments. Some of this research has been conducted in the fields of knowledge management and enterprise collaboration, areas I discussed in the preceding chapter in the context of the Security Improvement Program (SIP). But sometimes research takes these ideas a bit further and looks at how organizations create, share, and use knowledge in novel or innovative ways.

I am always interested in research that moves from mechanics and technologies into the ways that organizations function as systems and even begin to look less like *organizations* and more like *organisms* in the way they operate. When you dissect something, you lose some perspectives in order to gain others. If you ever dissected a frog in biology class, you know that identifying internal organs is very different from experiencing the hopping, swimming, croaking animal in a pond. But which is the real frog? A similar question can be asked of an e-mail or of an organization: Is an e-mail just the bits and packets involved, or does it include the words, meaning, and intent? Is the company the collection of machines, people, and buildings that make up the individual parts, or is it the entity that grows, competes, and succeeds? When a security incident occurs, is it just a machine that was compromised or an individual who was responsible, or did the company itself get hacked?

Attempts to build a learning organization are often concerned with moving knowledge and awareness from the individual to the group and back, and using the results to support better decisions. When a disconnect occurs between individual and group understanding, all sorts of problems can crop up. We are all aware of situations in which common sense for the company is completely at odds with the common sense of individual employees. (These are the sorts of conflicts that have made Scott Adams, the creator of the "Dilbert" comic strip, a wealthy man.) Overcoming these tensions and building an adaptable balance between listening to the individual and dictating to the individual is an important characteristic of a true learning organization, however, it may be accomplished. Organizational learning can be viewed along this continuum, moving from a focus on how people gain new knowledge and putting it to use as individuals doing a job, up through the ways that an enterprise gains and uses knowledge and makes itself into more than just a collection of individual skills and experiences.

There is no one sure way that an enterprise can make itself into a learning organization. This chapter offers a few different perspectives on how companies learn and make sense of the world and how this can apply to IT security measurement and managing the security process for continuous improvement. As I said earlier, we all learn differently. Organizations do, too, and each organization faces its own internal and external contexts in which it must make sense of security-related information. Thinking about how your organization learns and adapts, and implementing the SPM Framework within an appropriate context, can mean the difference between successful measurement and failed metrics.

Three Learning Styles for IT Security Metrics

The following examples offer three views of organizational learning, built around existing tools and concepts that can support IT security. These examples are deliberately general, and most organizations would be able to use a combination of styles and approaches to meet their needs. But they do serve to illustrate how differences in a company culture might need to be considered to achieve the sort of continuous process improvement of the SPM Framework.

As the framework is implemented, security measurement projects (SMPs) conducted, and the results analyzed and interpreted, you will need to understand how those results will be put to work in the larger context of enterprise-wide security. Will it be more important to assign and tightly control the metrics, perhaps because your company is heavily regulated or exists within a very conservative or competitive environment? Or does your business operate in a world that values rapid adaptability and pushes more authority and autonomy down the organizational chart to ensure maximum agility? These, too, are important metrics to explore and questions to answer as you decide how you plan to measure and improve your security.

Standardized Testing: Measurement in ISO/IEC 27004

In late 2009, the International Standards Organization and the International Electro-technical Commission (IEC) published a new international standard for building a security metrics program. ISO/IEC 27004, "Information technology—Security techniques—Information security management—Measurement," is designed to complement ISO/IEC 27001, the standard for setting up an information security management system (ISMS) within an organization. ISO/IEC 27004 describes a set of best practices for measuring the results of the ISMS, a requirement under ISO/IEC 27001. Since 27001 is the only certifiable standard in the family, meaning the only one that you can actually audit against, the rest of the 27000 standards are closely integrated into the certification requirements, although they can also be used for general best-practices guidance.

The thing about standards is that, by definition, they have to apply in the same way to everyone. So they tend to be very structured approaches to achieving outcomes. In a standards-based learning organization, progress is defined by measuring the same things over and over again and seeing if they improve. You might call it "no company left behind," and it inherits all the benefits and the baggage of standardized testing in public schools. On the positive side, results of standardized testing (audits, in the case of industry standards) provide a set of reliable, repeatable data against a clearly defined baseline of performance. You either pass or you don't. Success is meant to be unambiguous. Of course, on the negative side, you have all the problems that come with the pressure to conform to something that may be seen as a least common denominator or that may poorly reflect reality. You also encounter the business equivalent of "teaching to the test" as organizations worry more about passing the audit and less about actual quality or improvement.

In the case of the ISO/IEC 27000 standards, the standards bodies recognized that every organization was unique and that the standard could not dictate every detail of IT security to those adopting ISO/IEC 27001. So the 27000 standards don't tell you how to do everything, but what they do tell you to do must be done in a very specific way. Certain activities are required, such as conducting risk assessments and periodic formal management reviews of the security program, as are certain key documents regarding the ISMS. The standard also requires that a compliant organization formally define metrics and a measurement process for the ISMS, although 27001 does not specify how to do this.

ISO 27004 does specify how to set up a measurement program for the ISMS, including the objectives, models, and criteria for success that such a program should contain. The standard defines how measurements should be constructed, how data should be collected and analyzed, and how the measurement program should be documented and integrated into the ISMS. The standard is very structured and quantitatively focused, and the measurement criteria that it recommends is designed to keep metrics and measurement results simple, easy to obtain, and easy to understand. This diagnostic approach to security is good at answering the daily questions of who, what, when, and where, but it is unlikely to provide much insight into the how's and why's of your security program.

ISO/IEC 27004 typifies an organizational learning style that prioritizes data over knowledge and defined, repeatable metrics over innovation or exploration. This does not mean that 27004 reflects a poor learning style. Standards are used to put structure around a set of operations such as security or quality, and they accomplish this by normalizing those operational processes against predefined criteria. In this context, measurement is about reinforcing the baseline. Improvement is part of the process, but improvements under these standards tend to be conservative and incremental.

ISO/IEC 27000 encourages control above everything else. An organizational environment in which a 27004-based metrics program is likely to be the most valuable will often be one that realizes the need for strong centralized control and authority. Companies looking to establish structured security operations to improve existing ad hoc or chaotic operations, or companies that function in highly regulated or low-margin industries where a security incident can mean the real difference between success and failure, will care more about making sure things work than experimenting with new ideas.

Perhaps because they reflect the current state of many security organizations today, these types of metrics programs are currently top of mind in industry. Security is viewed as an increasing problem, and the general perception is that security isn't done very well, even in large and sophisticated enterprise environments where protecting information assets should be a critical operation. Even if their recommendations are not as structured and mechanical as ISO/IEC 27004, most security metrics experts today recommend implementing measurements that deliver easy, repeatable data rather than answer deeper security questions or create theories about why security is the way it is.

Implementing standardized measurement requires top-down management commitment and the ability to implement and maintain controls and processes across the entire corporate structure. For a company that has little or no security measurement capability, simply employing a sustainable metrics program can be innovative and revolutionary in itself.

Finally, there is nothing wrong with taking metrics a step at a time. Too often, when an organization tries to bite off more than it can chew with any project or initiative, it turns out in hindsight that a more modest and achievable approach would not only have been easier but also more productive and valuable.

The School of Life: Basili's Experience Factory

You might recall that Victor Basili was the creator of the Goal-Question-Metric (GQM) methodology that I adapted to IT security as part of the SPM Framework. While GQM was designed for use in creating more effective metrics, Basili also developed a model for organizational learning called the *experience factory*. Like GQM, the experience factory concept was first developed to support software quality engineering, but Basili and his research colleagues expanded the concept to apply to a variety of institutional settings.

The purpose of an experience factory is to collect, store, and disseminate all of an organization's experience, usually regarding a particular topic or activity, as a formal and structured operation. An experience factory exists as a dedicated organization within a larger organization, comprising specialists whose task is to provide a learning infrastructure for everyone else. The experience factory metaphor comes from the idea that the factory takes inputs from all areas of the organization, including the results of measurement projects, information about the company or industry environment, and data from a variety of company performance indicators, as raw materials. These materials are then processed, value is added to them, and they are used to create experience products that can be disseminated and reused throughout the rest of the organization to support strategy. The result is the creation of an enterprise-wide feedback loop that facilitates the development of data that may be specific to an individual or specialized function into knowledge that is usable and provides value to all decision-makers. Experience factory products may include regular reports, information-on-demand capabilities, and internal consulting services to help business units and departments meet their needs.

The experience factory concept is about building capabilities within an organization that are similar to what you might find in vendors such as Forrester, Gartner, or IDC that provide industry analysis and market intelligence. Less security-specific than ISO/IEC 27004 and certainly less prescriptive, the experience factory concept does not rely on a highly structured metrics baseline that is pushed out to the company and audited. The experience factory is about collecting metrics data and insights from many different sources and many different perspectives, including audits against standards, to support decisions and strategies. Measurement in this environment is less about top-down control than it is cross-functional collaboration. That being said, the experience factory is also an actual infrastructure that requires resources and commitment from the organization. There will still be a need to mandate the creation and management of the factory and to ensure that others use it. But a successful experience factory will, through the products and feedback that it provides to the organization, require less and less direct intervention by the powers that be. As internal stakeholders make use (and reuse) of collective organizational experience, they will begin to depend on the products of the factory and find their decision-making abilities hindered without these products. This self-perpetuation is quite different from the concept of a standard that must be continually reinforced by the organization, because the perceived value of the standard itself is known only to a few stakeholders while the rest of the organization perceives value primarily from passing the audit.

The experience factory reflects an organizational learning style that puts more emphasis on building connections between existing baselines than on building the baselines themselves. To extend the factory metaphor a bit, if the organization has no ready source of the raw materials it needs to operate (data and experiences), then it has nothing to which it can add value and cannot produce anything, just as a manufacturer cannot produce widgets without raw physical materials. Organizations building an experience factory must produce a chain of suppliers for their data first. In the case of IT security, the components of the SPM Framework can provide such materials. In fact, the experience factory builds upon the concept of the SIP, creating a formal capability for taking metrics data and forming it into security experience products for the entire organization.

Mindfulness: Karl Weick and the High-Reliability Organization

This last example of organizational learning styles is perhaps the most unconventional for security professionals who may be accustomed to and comfortable with technology, defined baselines, and quantitative metrics. But those same professionals may be surprised at how applicable this style of learning is to the situations and environments that CISOs and security managers must deal with every day. This example is drawn from the work of Karl Weick, a scholar and organizational theorist at the University of Michigan. Weick has spent decades researching how organizations use and share information in order to function, learn, and grow as systems and social entities, and how they make sense of their environments and business processes. His book *The Social Psychology of Organizing* has been selected as one of the top ten business books ever written. One of the most interesting ideas Weick developed, and one very suited to IT security, is the concept of *mindfulness* and its role in *high-reliability organizations*, or HROs.

Weick and his colleagues studied organizations such as aircraft carriers, nuclear power plants, and firefighting crews, all of which operate in complex and extremely dynamic environments where unexpected events and opportunities for failure are high. When failure does occur in these environments, it can result in exceptional risk and disastrous consequences for the organization, including loss of life and physical destruction. Simple math would seem to indicate that if an organization's chances for failure were greater than average and the potential damage from those failures was also greater than average, the organization would experience more than its share of failure-related loss. But counterintuitively, Weick found that such organizations actually experienced failure less often than other enterprises and were more reliable than the average, leading them to be designated as an HROs. Weick wanted to know why HROs failed less often in environments where opportunities for failure were much greater, and the results of his research reveals a lot about organizational learning styles.

Put simply, HROs fail less often than other organizations because when they do fail, the results are often catastrophic. Failure for these organizations might very well mean that some or all of the organization ceases to exist physically. Weick's research proposed that HROs were forced to operate differently as a result, with different processes and business structures that increased their reliability and performance. Weick found that HROs were structurally different from other organizations in some ways, but that the real reason they were more successful had less to do with operational processes and more to do with how the organization viewed itself and the world, and how it made decisions based on this different model of thought. At the core of this difference was a learning style that Weick calls "mindfulness," in which the organization is constantly and continuously maintaining awareness of what is happening. Of particular interest to mindful organizations is the near real-time awareness of small events that, over time, can cascade and grow into a serious crisis.

Weick identified several central traits that could be observed in a mindful organization:

■ HROs thrive on failure, seeing mistakes not as something that should not be allowed to happen but as things that are bound to happen and should be identified and corrected while they are still small.

■ HROs accept complexity and are much less likely than other organizations to oversimplify their activities or their environments.

■ HROs focus on operational resiliency, meaning that they take a detailed interest in the daily, mundane activities that keep the organization functional, and they are good at brainstorming how things can go wrong with those activities.

■ HROs allow authority and decisions to flow up and down the organizational chart as they follow experience and expertise, meaning that hierarchy and position are less important than who has the best answer to the question at hand.

Weick's research is very applicable to IT security, where many security groups seem to be the opposite of an HRO. I often find that security managers will stress over the threat of super-hackers and zero-day attacks, while neglecting to understand mundane operational issues such as passwords and principles of least privilege that are far more likely to result in failure. Problems are simplified (users, compliance, technology) as are solutions (policies, checklists, more technology). And when failure does occur, it is often followed closely by blame and recrimination about who is at fault. Security can often look less like an aircraft carrier and more like a dysfunctional family.

Weick's prescription for success is for organizations to study the operations of HROs and model themselves after them. The result is less about changing enterprise structure or mandating certain controls and much more about changing the psychology and culture of the organization, which is much more difficult. Adopting a mindfulness style of organizational learning in the context of IT security metrics is probably best suited to companies that already have established metrics programs and the means to share experience. In these cases, the SPM Framework can provide defined measurements and operational baselines to address the empirical assessment of security that would need to accompany the transition into a high-reliability organization for IT security.

Final Thoughts

Thinking about your organization's learning style and psychology may seem a bit beyond your goal of setting up an IT security metrics program, but that is simply not the case. Everything in this book is about organizational learning in one way or another. I am a firm believer that measuring security activities is one of the single most important efforts that an organization can undertake as we move into the twenty-first century's digital infrastructure. But simply handing a student a ruler doesn't guarantee that he will become a successful scientist and not just someone who can tell you how long things are but not give you any other answers. I began this book by discussing

Lord Kelvin and the belief that things that cannot be expressed in numbers cannot be understood, as well as the play that this idea has received in the security metrics field. I'll tell you now that I think things that can be completely explained just using numbers are not really worth understanding and require so little information to be associated with them that they are unlikely to improve anything.

Measurement is about learning and understanding, and metrics are the building blocks of measurement, but they are not the totality of it. Measurement is about priorities and consensus, symbolism, and meaning. I have tried to build a metrics framework in these chapters that remains practical and grounded but never loses sight of the fact that human collaboration and interpretation must be included in any measurement attempt that you undertake. Indeed, they will be there lurking beneath your numbers and graphs even if you choose to pretend they are not.

Summary

Security metrics should be considered in the context of organizational learning and the capabilities of your enterprise to use, reuse, and benefit from the information that is generated by your measurement efforts. Organizational styles of learning can be estimated and applied to security metrics to try to match your organization's culture and environment to how you measure security and share results. Three styles of organizational learning were discussed here, including standards such as ISO/IEC 27004, which is part of the ISO/IEC 27000 family of international security standards; the experience factory developed by Basili, who also created the GQM methodology; and the concept of mindfulness in high-reliability organizations, developed by organizational theorist Karl Weick. Each style has its own characteristics, and a successful security metrics program will consider how metrics data and findings can be best applied to organizational strategy and decision support based on the learning style of your particular company or enterprise.

Further Reading

Basili, V., et al. *Implementing the Experience Factory Concepts as a Set of Experience Bases.* www.cs.umd.edu/~basili/publications/proceedings/P90.pdf

Basili, V., et al. *The Experience Factory.* www.cs.umd.edu/projects/SoftEng/ESEG/papers/fact.pdf

Weick, K. *The Social Psychology of Organizing.* Addison-Wesley, 1979.

Weick, K., and K. Sutcliffe. *Managing the Unexpected: Assuring High Performance in an Age of Complexity.* Jossey-Bass, 2001.

Senge, P. *The Fifth Discipline: The Art & Practice of the Learning Organization.* Broadway Business, 2006.

Case Study 4 | Getting Management Buy-in for the Security Metrics Program

Craig Blaha has been a friend and colleague for several years in my university life. The fact that he's also a security professional allows us to talk about our day jobs in the light of the social science research that we were and are engaged in as academics. Research in the corporate IT security world can mean a very different thing from research in academia, and it is great to have a colleague with whom I can talk (and complain) about things such as the neglect of qualitative methods, validity and reliability in industry research, and the need for a more rigorous approach to measuring security. Craig and I also share another understanding that is central to his case study: the fact that the political environment of universities can make the corporate world look like a hippie commune. In academia, where common goals such as revenue growth or shareholder value are alien concepts, outreach, consensus, and buy-in can be hard to come by. In academic environments you may find that working together can actually be viewed as detrimental to one's long-term interests and success is considered by many to be a zero-sum game.

Craig's case study concerns a research project that was designed to measure and improve buy-in in a university IT environment; it's a lesson from the trenches. We all face competition for resources and status in our IT security activities, and Craig's point that becoming what I like to term "a security diplomat" is necessary for success is well taken. As any good politician knows, the best way to advance your goals is to understand the goals of others and show them that their goals *are* your goals.

Craig's case study is a good closer for the book, because his points are central to Security Process Management (SPM). IT security is rapidly losing its ability to function in a relative vacuum with little visibility or accountability. No matter your organizational psychology or your approaches to solving your security challenges, you will need help from other stakeholders. Craig's insights into getting buy-in from those stakeholders can help you better understand how to get buy-in from your own.

Case Study 4: Getting Management Buy-in for the Security Metrics Program

by Craig Blaha

Information technology, in both the private sector and higher education, has one thing in common: technology is the easy part. My job at various institutions during the past 15 years has been to convince stakeholders that the chosen direction, whether it be the implementation of a new software package, major changes to existing software, or process change, is the right one. Not only have I had to convince people that we were moving in the right direction for the organization, but I had to prove that this move was in the best interest of both their particular unit and their individual career. I've worked in both corporate America and higher education, with the bulk of my years spent in higher education. I've had a range of responsibilities, from standing up an information security organization where none had existed before, to implementing an incident response team, to developing an IT policy division.

I have also been in the position of acting as the point person on some major projects, where I spent the majority of my time providing evidence, building relationships, and giving presentations to convince people that the IT unit knew what it was doing. I am currently pursuing a Ph.D. in Federal Information Policy, focusing on information security, privacy, and the preservation of records. This diverse background puts me in a unique position to discuss not only the implementation of a metrics program, but how to make that program "stick" over time.

Through all of this experience, I have found that one of the most difficult aspects of working in the field of IT is getting people to agree that the work you are doing is worthwhile, to trust you and your team, and to communicate effectively the things you think are important for them to know related to security and technology. To illustrate my insights, this case study will describe an experience in which I was part of a team of researchers that set out to determine what IT metrics matter to different groups of stakeholders. The answers we found may surprise you, but first I want to offer an example of a security leader successfully navigating these human, political, and social waters.

The CISO Hacked My Computer

I heard the following anecdote while attending a SANS leadership course. Will Peregrin, the director of New York's Office of Cyber Security and Critical Infrastructure Coordination, worked with the SANS Institute and AT&T to develop a phishing awareness program. This program had two alternating parts: an awareness program and what they referred to as "inoculation." The initial awareness phase consisted of a phishing awareness raising e-mail that was sent to 10,000 employees. About a month after that initial e-mail, the inoculation phase began. A phishing e-mail was sent to those same employees, asking each for his or her username and password. Seventeen percent of the targeted employees typed in their username and password, which triggered a message that let them know they had failed the test.

Failing the test meant that you were required to sit through a training video and answer some questions about phishing. After this second training session, the phishing test was tried again. This time, only 8 percent of those tested responded with their username and password.

It is easy to see how 17 percent and 8 percent are useful metrics. These numbers help to tell the story of a security awareness program that is working, at least to an extent. Getting the last 8 percent of employees to avoid giving away their username and password may be a case of diminishing returns, but the metrics help tell the story. Now imagine if Peregrin tried this inoculation without first making sure his colleagues at the senior management level were not only aware of the program, but had given explicit permission to use their personnel time in this way, or if SANS and AT&T had independently conducted the inoculation test without Peregrin's awareness. Regardless of the numbers generated by such a test, the business leaders of that organization would be up in arms! Getting buy-in from senior management and important stakeholders is critical not only for career longevity, but for the long-term success of your SIP.

What Is Buy-in?

Buy-in is *not* approval. A manager or colleague can approve an action without having any "skin in the game." In fact, in some highly political situations, you will find leaders who will approve of a tactic or program, even though they completely expect it to fail. Sometimes the failure of a program will help them achieve some other long-term strategic goal, often at the expense of the current security team.

Buy-in is more than just approval, it is both agreement that you are doing the right thing and an investment in the success of that action or strategy. Buy-in is most likely to be achieved when other leaders in your organization trust you to use institutional or corporate resources in a responsible manner that supports the goals and mission of the organization.

Buy-in matters for a number of important reasons. Even during positive economic times, financial resources within an organization are limited. These resources inevitably are divided up among competing priorities. As financial times become more challenging, as they are now, this competition heats up even more. If you happen to be a leader who has demonstrated appropriate use of organizational resources in the past, the chances of your securing those resources in a competitive environment are greater. If you can convince a critical mass of your colleagues to support your initiative, you are effectively gaining their buy-in when they publically support your project, especially if by supporting you they are reducing the funds available for their own projects and initiatives. This sets up a feedback loop in which successful competitors for resources have a leg up the next time a competition comes around, allowing them an opportunity to garner more resources. This cycle lasts only if you have the continued support of your colleagues and senior management.

Getting buy-in prior to making changes that require significant financial or political support from your organization makes continued support possible. Part of maintaining buy-in and support is letting your stakeholders know when there is a problem. This allows them to be "in the know," rather than learning of the problem in a surprise hallway conversation with the CIO that puts them in an awkward political position. By making key people aware of a problem as soon as you become aware of it, they have an opportunity to advocate on your behalf in those hallway conversations.

Building these relationships over time, developing trust, and aligning your goals in support of both the mission of the institution and the goals of other senior leaders and key players helps you make the case to continue your program during tough economic times. If key decision-makers aren't convinced of the value your program is bringing to the organization because you haven't developed these relationships, you may be doing your organization a disservice. When the senior leadership of your organization is faced with tough economic choices, they won't be well informed enough about the security needs of the organization to make decisions that are grounded in a foundation of fact.

Corporations vs. Higher Ed: Who's Crazier?

Higher education is the "big leagues" of organizational politics. The wide variety of funding, missions, politics, and regulations leads to a plethora of different stakeholders that you need to consider when undertaking a measurement project in the university environment. Any one of these stakeholders can bring your project to a halt, even if your project has little to do with their operation. The political reality of this environment forces you either to complete projects before anyone notices the project is underway or manage the risks by getting buy-in up front.

Corporations have a significant advantage over higher education: a shared goal. Each employee of a corporation can point back to profit as a significant driving factor. Higher education can't even conduct an ROI calculation! The investment can be measured, but what would the return be? Enrolling more students? Improving the ranking of the school? Hiring more hotshot professors? These goals can be at odds with one another, and there is no accepted quantitative way to measure return. The culture supports individual contributions and contributors, granting individuals the opportunity to command significant resources, even if by doing so they damage the overall health of the organization.

This hyper-politicization of higher education is what makes this case study so valuable. You may not need to address all the findings from this study in your project or program, but your chances of being blindsided by a political football are reduced by being aware of them.

Higher Education Case Study

We have talked about what buy-in is and why it is important, and how we can use the supercharged political environment of higher education to bring some lessons back to the real world. With that said, determining what to measure, how to measure it, and to whom to report the results can be more of an art than a science. All of the factors discussed so far were derived from a research/business study conducted at four major research universities during the course of a year. This study was both an academic study meant to look at the organizational, social, and political issues related to security and IT, and a business study geared toward the ongoing measurement of management buy-in for the implementation of an IT metrics program.

The original study was designed to accomplish three different goals. The first goal was to account for all IT spending at each university and to look for trends and opportunities for cost savings. The second was to identify key metrics related to the IT services provided by the central IT organizations at each university. The third was to identify key services the central IT unit provided.

The interviews began with a broad focus on quantitatively measuring the IT services, but the scope of the project changed considerably as we progressed through the interviews with the different stakeholders. It became clear that buy-in couldn't be measured quantitatively. Interviewing individual stakeholders about their concerns, sometimes in an unstructured interview format, produced some very clear narrative themes that helped us figure out what steps needed to be taken to make our continuing metrics program successful.

Project Overview

The original project had some ambitious goals: to account for all IT spending at each university, to develop service catalogs related to the services provided by the central IT departments at each university, and to identify key metrics that would represent the services covered in the service catalog in a way that was meaningful both to the service provider and the customer. One of the overarching questions of this research was how to use metrics to communicate the importance of IT and security to the various stakeholders of the university. While the overall scope of the project was general IT, my own background and experience made me particularly interested in how the findings of the study could be specifically tied back to buy-in for security metrics programs. The metrics we hoped to develop based on the research were measurements of IT effectiveness from the customer perspective, a goal that is easily applied both to security and non-security–related aspects of IT.

The approach of the research team was to interview key stakeholders outside of the central IT administration. The following questions were asked of each interviewee:

- From your perspective, what are the goals, strategies, or objectives you are striving to achieve to make the university a better learning and working environment (what matters)?
- What measurements are you using to gauge the progress toward achieving these goals (how do you know you are succeeding)?
- From your perspective, how does IT help you make your work successful (role of IT)?
- What do you think IT should measure and why?

Themes

We noticed three themes in the responses from our subjects:

- Operational goals (what we are trying to do)
- Barriers to those goals (what is keeping us from doing it)
- The role of IT in supporting those goals (what we think you can do to help)

Not surprisingly, each interview the team conducted resulted in the identification of the operational goals of the interview subject and his or her department. In addition, respondents were quick to identify the barriers that they believed were inhibiting their ability to achieve these goals. Lastly, the respondents were usually pretty clear on what role they believed IT could play to remove barriers or help them achieve their goals. Importantly for our purposes, the idea of data security was surrounded by fear and confusion.

Operational Goals

The operational goals of each area varied widely, as shown in Table 1. In the teaching and learning group, goals predictably surrounded the development of professionals and leaders as part of the educational experience. There was an emphasis on developing the skills of reasoning and moral and ethical thinking in students, as well as computer competency broadly defined. In addition to these foundational skills, leaders from the teaching and learning areas emphasized the development of problem-solving skills, teamwork, and communication as important to the long-term success of the students.

The representatives of the outreach function identified two broad goals: support the combined university goals of research, teaching, and service, and leverage the talents in the university to help industry partners with research and development and to raise the profile, and hopefully increase the endowment, of the university.

The outreach group wanted to continue the educational community and culture created at the university. This seems contrary to what we usually hear about alumni and development just trying to squeeze as much money out of the alumni as possible, but I have worked closely with leaders in a variety of alumni and development departments in the past, and the most dedicated ones say fundraising is a side-effect of doing their job well. A university tends to develop a certain worldview in its students, often as a consequence of the academic culture created by the faculty and the social culture created by the students. If that experience is valuable to a student, she tends to want to offer support to ensure the part of the culture she enjoyed or found valuable will continue. Whether it was studying abroad, using the computer lab, or learning from a favorite professor in economics, donating money allows former students to be part of a continuing conversation about how the world should be. The best alumni and development officers engage alumnus in that conversation.

Operational Unit	Operational Goals
Teaching and Learning	Reasoning, moral and ethical thinking Computer competency Problem solving Teamwork and communication
Outreach	Research, teaching, service Leverage talents of university
Research	Research grants and contracts, published works Positive educational and economic impact Collaboration
Administration	Efficiency, transparency, integrity Collaboration and communication Savings

Table 1.   Operational Goals

The research group identified three major goals: The first was to increase the volume and quality of research grants and contracts, and published work. Second, the research group wanted to contribute to the university's ability to create a positive educational and economic impact. Lastly, increasing collaboration was one of the most difficult goals the research group had set for itself. With hundreds or thousands of researchers all working on their own particular set of interests and problems, some jealously guarding their discoveries, increasing collaboration was a difficult social and technical problem.

The various individuals representing the administration group communicated goals that were distinctly different and more operationally focused than the other groups. Efficiency, transparency, and integrity were at the top of the list. The goals of collaboration and communication were also mentioned, as were cost effectiveness and reduction.

Regardless of the industry, it is important that you understand the goals of the operational units you are trying to protect through your SIP. To convince these units to comply with your efforts and to educate them to understand the overall program you are trying to implement, you will need to speak their language and understand what exactly they are trying to accomplish.

Barriers

Each group also mentioned barriers that kept them from achieving the goals they had set, limited their success, or frustrated their efforts in some way, as shown in Table 2. The most common barrier mentioned by everyone was funding— a situation that will also be familiar to anyone chasing resources in the for-profit world.

Operational Unit	Operational Barriers
Teaching and Learning	Many faculty married to old learning models High student-to-faculty ratios Funding
Outreach	Funding Resistance to change External forces Politics and minority stakeholders
Research	Funding Improving access to resources Available infrastructure Highly competitive environment
Administration	Funding Marketing/perception Geography Little involvement locally

Table 2. Operational Barriers

Funding is a barrier in just about any organization, but major research universities often have a more complex challenge. Some of this complexity comes from the multiple funding sources that institutions of higher education depend on. Some people assume that tuition is the primary source of funding, but a variety of different sources actually make it possible for a university to keep its doors open and its lights on. State funding is one source, particularly for public education institutions, but this source has been dwindling to the extent that higher education leaders no longer refer to their institutions as state-sponsored but state-molested! For many institutions, state funding has decreased, but the state's rules, requirements, and mandates have not.

In addition to the complexity of funding, universities have to deal with state and federal regulations, just as any corporation must. Most states have sunshine laws or open records acts that allow citizens to request certain records from public institutions. A variety of statutes are related to data breaches, and some states require reporting of data breaches based on the state of the data subject—in other words, if a university in Montana hosts data about a student from California and experiences a data breach, the Montana university has to report the breach, at least to that one California resident. Finally, universities manage everything from student records to health records to financial records, and are covered by an alphabet soup of statutes: the Family Educational Rights and Privacy Act (FERPA), the Health Insurance Portability and Accountability Act (HIPAA), Gramm-Leech-Bliley (GLB), and Sarbanes-Oxley (SOX).

For the teaching and learning group, one significant cultural barrier was the perception that many faculty are married to old learning models. Persuading tenured faculty members to make a change to teaching styles they have developed during the past 20 or more years was a significant barrier. Another barrier was the fact that an individualized, flexible learning model is difficult to achieve with one teacher and many students—sometimes up to 1000 students in one class.

For the administration group, resistance to change was also an important barrier—not only technological change and the operational and business process adjustments that such change requires, but organizational change such as reducing administrative overhead and collaboration across administrative groups. External forces were also cited as a critical barrier to success in the administrative group. Financial challenge is the most salient recent example, but over the course of the last ten years, the move to outsource or automate more administrative tasks has also been a challenge. I briefly discussed the complexity of politics in higher education, and the amount of overhead that this complexity adds to any significant change effort was held out by the administrative group as one of the major barriers to success. In addition to the political issues discussed earlier, respondents focused on minority stakeholders—those individuals who have a strong influence on the outcome of an effort without having a strong vested interest in the ongoing results.

The respondents from the research group put funding for research at the top of the list. Acquiring adequate funding to support research is a continuous competitive process, and the grants that are secured to provide financial support require a significant effort to manage once they have been acquired. Corollary to research funding is access to resources. This category covers a wide range of details, including office space and supplies, qualified and committed research and administrative assistants, and technological resources such as infrastructure, network, and security support.

Research grants account for a significant source of funds at research universities. At most top-level research universities, the institution takes 50 percent of the grant funds brought in by researchers or research teams, right off the top. This means a $1 million grant brings $500,000 to the institution and $500,000 to the researchers, and some of this is used to pay someone else to teach the courses the faculty are required to teach so they can spend time doing the research for the grant.

Related to research is the commercialization of intellectual property. Researchers can earn income from their discoveries in a variety of ways, but many of them include not only the granting agency, but also the institution and often the commercial entity that will make products based on the discovery.

Outreach respondents identified a set of barriers that were qualitatively different from those of the other groups. At the top of the outreach list of barriers was the funding issue that had been highlighted by others, but marketing and the perception of the university were a close second. The combination of these two elements played a major role in the success or failure of the outreach representative's efforts. Geography was also cited as a barrier; making connections with alumni or potential partners is easier when you are in close geographic proximity, but it is much more difficult if the university is located in rural Pennsylvania, for example.

The Role of IT

The role of IT in supporting the goals and daily operations of these groups is the last theme and is shown in Table 3.

Operational Unit	Role of IT
Teaching and Learning	Accessibility
	Resource-saving
	Interaction and collaboration
	On-the-spot information
	Student perceptions
Outreach	Not technology, but what we do with it
	IT helps us provide services
	High stakes: IT failure is organization failure
Research	Enabler and enhancer
	IT as a common good or a utility for all
Administration	Research grants depend on IT infrastructure
	Sharing IT resources promotes big science

Table 3.   The Role of IT

The teaching and learning group put accessibility at the top of their list, which is reasonable since accessibility is mandated by Section 508 regulations, which require institutions to make learning and administrative material available in an accessible manner or to provide an accessible alternative to those materials. IT often provides a solution to this problem. Technology plays a more and more significant role in teaching and learning, although the role technology plays can be overstated. For example, when I worked as the webmaster at The College of New Jersey, we experienced a prolonged power outage that sent home all administrative staff with a recommendation that faculty leave as well. It was a beautiful spring afternoon, and as I walked past the philosophy building I noticed a professor had convened his class on the lawn. This emphasized for me the support role IT plays in the classroom: it is important, but often it is by no means essential.

Resource saving, interaction, and collaboration are all roles that IT can play, according to the teaching and learning group. With incredibly large classrooms and few instructors, technology makes it possible to make the student-to-teacher ratio seem lower than it actually is. This can be achieved through recorded podcasts of a lecture, online discussions of the readings or homework assignments, and other methods. Instructors, administrators, and students all expect on-the-spot information. Instructors expect to be able to determine who has actually attended their large lecture sections or how many students are eligible to take the next test. Administrators want to be able to forecast classroom utilization, and students want up-to-the-minute information about availability of their favorite class.

IT was also seen as either an opportunity or a liability when it comes to student perceptions. Educause, a higher education IT practitioners' group, even publishes a pamphlet to grade higher education institutions based on the technology the institution provides to students. More than ever, students see themselves as consumers of higher education, looking critically at each institution and shopping for the best deal.

For respondents in the administration group, the consistent message about the role of IT was it is not the technology, it's what we do with it that matters. IT was seen as essential to the administrative group's ability to provide services. The success of the administrative organization was tied closely to the success of the IT department, and vice versa.

The outreach group characterized the role of IT as an enabler and enhancer to their ability to achieve their mission and goals. IT was seen as fundamental to some core initiatives as well as supporting the overall functionality of the group. IT was described as a utility and the sentiment was expressed that much of it should be considered a common good, and priced accordingly.

The research division respondents depended heavily on technology infrastructure and emphasized that sharing IT resources from around the world promotes big science.

Findings

The research team noticed some very interesting threads when we compared notes from our various interviews. One of our most important takeaways was the fact that people had not had a conversation like this with a representative from the central IT unit ever! Another very interesting trend that was consistent throughout almost every interview was the clear sentiment that metrics don't matter! Without prompting, a large number of respondents stated that they were particularly not interested in metrics or a metrics program. The most important takeaways were these:

- Communication
- Metrics don't matter
- Alignment

Communication: Two Ears, One Mouth; Do the Math

The communication theme included some of the most common refrains we have heard time and again when it comes to communication. The fact that these same familiar warnings have come up again means I should share them one more time.

"No news is good news" was the most common refrain, indicating that customers and stakeholders believed that if they didn't hear anything from the IT group, things must be as they should be. The flipside is that when they did hear from IT, they expected bad news. This preconception of bad news bred mistrust, since the first exchange in any communication was the customer trying to figure out what exactly the IT person was saying is broken. At the same time, this sentiment was backed up by the request for better communication from the IT group, in both good times and bad. A communication plan that focuses both on communicating positive change before it happens and a consistent approach to communication when things do go wrong will go a long way.

One of the most common questions we heard was "What's going on?" It is common for an IT organization to spend the time to troubleshoot a problem, with technicians believing that their time is far better spent figuring out and fixing whatever is wrong than communicating to the community when they really don't have any information to share. The customer does not support this sentiment, however.

Consistently, respondents requested to be informed of the state of affairs, especially during an outage, even if there is no change in status. And these communications better be in plain English, not techno-babble. Consistently throughout our interviews we were warned that IT people had no idea how to communicate with normal humans; our use of tla's (three letter acronyms) and dependence on deep technical details to explain an issue made us impossible to communicate with.

We also heard that IT had a real marketing problem. We lacked the ability to listen to the customer and try to understand what the real issue was, or what the customer was trying to request. Our customers didn't believe we understood their real mission, that we didn't really know what they were trying to accomplish and how, through our expertise in IT, we could help. To establish trust and build a relationship, our respondents recommended that we work harder at establishing relationships with our constituents, focusing on working toward shared goals, metrics, and alignment.

To this end, some of the recommendations that appeared consistently in our conversations were that we ask some essential questions. What is the value derived from IT by the customer? What are the IT-driven results that matter to the customer? This question allows for measuring performance against desired outcomes, but it requires IT staff to convert customer expectations to service standards. How are these results measured?

There are many different types of performance measures: reliability measures, responsiveness measures, project measures, utilization and adoption rate measures, and client satisfaction measures.

Many Metrics Don't Matter

When these groups were asked about metrics, their responses indicated that they were not in the least bit interested in metrics, because too often the metrics become the goal. Only metrics that support a goal should be considered. Two statements really stood out among the others: it doesn't matter unless you measure it; and if it doesn't matter, *don't* measure it!

The respondents that we spoke to all agreed that behavior beats metrics; if the security staff or IT staff have taken the time to build a relationship and understand the mission and challenges of the operational unit, the words and deeds of the security folks will be judged based on these prior efforts. Overall, operational leadership is tired of metrics that don't matter. These are measurements that are held up as examples of success, which are meaningless to the operational units. "Defensive metrics" is a term we encountered as well. This term was used to indicate CYA (cover your ass) metrics that may not mean anything significant to the people trying to support the mission of the operational unit, but that make it difficult to discuss areas for improvement in the IT or security staff. Much of this was perceived as fear of accountability—metrics that are created for the sake of protection, not for the cold, hard, objective feedback that such measurement could offer.

Align the Business with the Needs of Security

The third finding, collaborative metrics, highlighted the customer sentiment that leadership from the IT department was required for such a thing as collaborative metrics to be possible. It was up to the IT leadership to start the conversation about metrics with the various departments they served.

The process proposed by the individuals we interviewed maps exactly to the assertions in the SIP model. The first step, according to the customer, is for the IT department to present a metric. This metric should be based on repeated conversations with the customer that have led the IT or security department to understand the mission and goals of the customer—conversations that should build trust. The IT department should discuss the proposed metric(s) regularly, especially if the measurements indicate progress or problems. The customer and the security or IT department should together determine whether the metric ends up being useful, and this process should be repeated on an ongoing basis, since both business requirements and the capabilities of the IT service provider will change.

The process of finding alignment between the security staff and the operational unit is a continual one. One of the first and most important steps is to identify the stakeholders that will be affected by your Security Improvement Program. These individuals or groups are not necessarily the people that will consume the metrics that you create—but I'll talk more about stakeholders a bit later, when I discuss tools that can influence the direction of other operational units.

After stakeholders are identified, you must engage them during key parts of the planning process. One of the common complaints we heard was about planning that leaves out the middle. Although you may engage the leadership of an important stakeholder group, for particularly important projects you should keep in mind that communication is a difficult task in any organization. If having your message heard at all levels of the organization is important to the success of the project, you may need to make the extra effort to determine on your own whether the message is getting out, and then take steps to improve communication within other groups, at least for the short term or during critical periods of your project.

A great way to get to know the culture, values, and communication style of an organization is to ask people what metrics and measures they already have in place that are valuable, and ask which of these they find less valuable or redundant. This will give you a sense of how the organizations measure themselves and how they map either the services they provide or the services they consume from other providers to measurements, to determine the success, failure, or general status of the services in question. In addition, this will give you a sense of how much work you will need to do to integrate the metrics that your security improvement plan creates into the planning and processes of the operational unit.

Key Points

Key points we took from the series of interviews performed at the four major research universities included first and foremost, *focus on the mission*. Not our mission—theirs! The operational units that you are working with and trying to convince to change or to get on board with your Security Improvement Program are all working hard to accomplish some very specific goals. In a well-managed department, everyone in that operational unit is aware of that goal or set of goals and is working hard to limit anything that will keep them from achieving those goals.

One of the more difficult things to keep in mind and to adjust to is the fact that these goals may be different for each unit, depending on the size of the organization. In a large organization, the Security Improvement Program will span multiple units, some of which may not have heard of each other or worked together in the past. Understanding customer needs in any environment is important, but in a complex environment with multiple, conflicting priorities, understanding the varied needs of the customer is sometimes the only way to resolve conflict or negotiate buy-in.

We also learned that *metrics need to be collaborative*. Working with the customer to determine what they find valuable and how they are perceiving your efforts and the metrics that you are sharing with them, and then adjusting to that feedback, are important for the long-term success of your Security Improvement Program. An important point to underscore here is that *active listening is communication*. As technologists, we can sometimes forget to listen and switch quickly into problem-solving mode, sometimes before the problem has even been thoroughly defined.

Lastly, strategic and operational planning done in conjunction with an operational department can have a fatal flaw: the quality of communication within the operational unit.

Depending on the importance of the particular piece of your Security Improvement Program in which you are engaged, you may want to "supplement" communication on the other side of the fence to make sure that the right messages are getting to the right people.

Influence and Organizational Change

Inherent in this discussion is the need to persuade others of the importance, relevance, and value of the SIP you are undertaking. Our study showed how a variety of stakeholders wanted to be communicated with, but the underlying assumption is that you and your stakeholders have a shared goal. We know this is not always the case, especially with security. Business schools refer to this type of influence as a non-market strategy because it does not focus on supply and demand, as a market strategy would, but on four factors:

- Issues
- Stakeholders
- Power
- Information

The combination of these four factors offers important tools that will improve your ability to influence individuals and groups.

Issues

Issues are basic topics of interest or areas of concern that are important to the business. Issues include policy, technology, and events and activism. Policy issues include regulations imposed by agencies that cover the industry in question including federal, state, or local agencies. Issues include industry standards such as those imposed or recommended by NIST, IEEE, and other industry-level professional organizations. Federal and state laws are also considered part of the policy arena, since laws often drive policy at the organizational level. Many of these factors end up being implemented, especially at large organizations, as regulations, standards, and processes that are imposed internally. Smaller organizations tend to have a reduced policy overhead, but they are still held to the same standards and laws—they just aren't always mirrored within the organization as local policy or process. Change or a new proposed policy at any one of these levels can be considered an issue if it changes the non-market environment of the business.

Technology changes can also be considered issues. New technologies that stand to revolutionize the business usually require significant adjustment and can sometimes even lead to business failure. Changes in existing technologies that aren't necessarily revolutionary can increase or decrease competitive advantage—either your advantage or that of your competitor—leading to a new set of opportunities and challenges that the business had not faced in the past.

Events and activism are a separate category, because they are both difficult to predict and control. These can include societal events such as the September 11 bombings or the fallout from the discussion of global warming. The category of events also includes natural events such as natural disasters and their societal and social impacts. The devastating earthquakes in Haiti are a clear example of the level of influence a natural disaster can have on public discourse. A significant natural disaster almost always has an economic impact (as well as many societal ones). Water, fuel, and other resources can be cut off when a natural disaster occurs in the supply country.

Political events can have a similar effect on the supply of raw or finished materials essential to the business in question. Regime changes or coups are clear examples that have been historically significant, but subtler and sometimes more difficult to deal with (from a business relationship perspective) are political shifts within stable governments. New politicians or parties have their own set of preferred vendors or suppliers that a business will have to learn to maneuver around and deal with.

Stakeholders

Clearly determining the issue that you are trying to address is a critical first step in being able to persuade an individual or group to follow the path you have outlined. The next step is determining the stakeholders. The term "stakeholder" used to mean literally the holder of the stake—the third party who holds the money in a bet. It has come to mean something different in business and project management and these days refers to a person or group that has an interest in the outcome of a project or process. As mentioned, accurate determination of stakeholders is important, since these are the people you will be attempting to influence regarding the issue.

Power

Influence is also dependent on power and is most clearly seen in the fierce competition for scarce resources. In this setting, power comes from two sources: positional and personal.

Positional power comes from a person's title and position in the organization chart. It is this type of power that can compel compliance, if not enthusiastic participation. The president, provost, deans, and vice presidents all have the ability to snap their fingers and get things done, just by the weight of their title.

Ignoring the org chart, we find another source of power that is relative to the individual. We can call this "personal power," and it comes from both recognition of accomplishments and building relationships over time. Personal power that originates from recognition often occurs because some people are considered excellent, or at least well recognized, in their field.

Another source of this type of power is the ability to bring in high-dollar amounts of funding. Relationships are another source of personal power. Some individuals have been around for a long time and "know where the bodies are buried." These people maintain the institutional knowledge and culture of the organization, and their opinions are respected and often sought out, regardless of their position in the org chart. Others have taken the time and made the effort to build relationships with other groups around campus, and their opinions and decisions are respected because of the trust and political capital they have built up over time.

This doesn't mean that every step of every project or initiative needs to include all of the people in your stakeholder list, but it is a career-enhancing move to think through the list as you undertake a significant initiative and see if you should communicate with one of these groups.

Information

Information, in this context, refers to what the stakeholders know or believe about the factors affecting the issue. If we consider security, for example, news coverage of a particular event can raise fear, whether rational or irrational. As the chief security officer, you may have received a phone call or a question one Monday morning such as "How does the Chinese Google hack effect us?" and this may not have been such an irrational question. I worked at one institution where the head of finance for our department would regularly show up to meetings with one question: How come computers cost so much? She would bring in a newspaper clipping with an ad for a $349 special on home computers, asking why we weren't purchasing these and saving significant amounts of money. Explaining why *may*—not always, but it can—limit the amount of time you spend on this type of question. Other times it is more effective simply to explain it to the other people at the table, with the hope that they don't maintain the same expectation.

Conclusion

This empirical study has direct relevance for the implementation of security programs in corporations. Politics, power, and influence are significant factors in any environment, but in higher education, these issues are brought to the fore. The lack of a shared goal such as profit, the provision of service, or the production of a product makes higher education a highly charged political environment and the perfect place to study the influence these factors have on the implementation and maintenance of a metrics program.

You don't have to have buy-in before the Security Improvement Program is implemented. In fact, it is advisable to start with the small but important aspects of security over which you have complete control. This will allow your team to demonstrate success in ways that are not threatening to other departments and their budgets, so that you can create a solid foundation on which to build.

Index

References to figures are in italics.